The U.S. Motor Vehicle Reference Book

2010 Edition

The National Guide to State Driver and Vehicle Licensing Services and Regulations

©2010 By BRB Publications, Inc.
PO Box 27869
Tempe, AZ 85285
800-929-3811
Fax 800-929-4981
www.brbpub.com
www.mvrdecoder.com

BRB Publications, Inc.

The U.S. Motor Vehicle Reference Book

©2010 By BRB Publications, Inc.
PO Box 27869
Tempe, AZ 85285-7869
800 929-3811 • Fax 800 929-4981

Editor: Michael L. Sankey
Cover Design: Robin Fox & Associates

Cataloging-in-Publication Data
   (Provided by Quality Books, Inc.)

   The U.S. motor vehicle reference book : the national guide
   to state driver and vehicle licensing services and
   regulations / [editor, Michael L. Sankey]. -- 2010 ed.
      p. cm. -- (MVR book series)
      Rev. ed. of: The MVR book.
      ISBN-13: 978-1-879792-95-1
      ISBN-10: 1-879792-95-8

      1. Automobile drivers' records--United States--States
--Information services--Directories. 2. Drivers'
licenses--United States--States--Information services--
Directories. 3. Traffic violations--United States--
States--Information services--Directories. I. Sankey,
Michael L., 1949- II. BRB Publications. III. Title:
MVR book. IV. Series: MVR book series.

HE5614.2.M87 2010   364.1'47
                              QBI09-3791

All rights reserved. Printed in the United States of America. No part of this book may be used or reproduced in any form or by any means, or stored in a database or retrieval system without the prior written permission of the publisher, except in the case of brief quotations embodied in critical articles or reviews. Making copies of any part of this book for any purpose other than your own personal use is a violation of United States copyright laws. Entering any of the contents into a computer for mailing list or database purposes is strictly prohibited unless written authorization is obtained from BRB Publications, Inc.

This directory is sold as is, without warranty of any kind, either expressed or implied, respecting the contents of this directory, including but not limited to implied warranties for the directory's quality, performance, merchantability, or fitness for any particular purpose. Neither the publisher nor its dealers or distributors shall be liable to the purchaser or any other person or entity with respect to any liability, loss, or damage caused or alleged to be caused directly or indirectly by this directory.

The 2010 U.S. Motor Vehicle Reference Book

Table of Contents

A Special Thank You   4

Introduction   5

About Motor Vehicle Records   6

State Profiles   11
51 Individual State Chapters with Subsections—
Each chapter contains the following sections:
- Driver Licensing Facts
- Safety and Enforcement Facts
- License Plate Facts
- Overview of Record Access

Appendix (4 Sections)
1. Glossary of Key Organizations, Programs, and Laws   **259**
2. Tables of Federally Mandated CDL Disqualifications   **265**
3. Federally mandated Data Retention for Commercial Drivers   **268**
4. Table of State Driver License Formats and Driving Record Fees   **269**

Thank You

The objective of this publication is to provide a practical, essential guide to each state's policies and procedures regarding driver licensing issuance, suspensions and revocations, and financial responsibility issues. Keeping this content accurate and up-to-date involves many, many hours of research and fact-checking.

With this in mind ... I wish to acknowledge and sincerely thank certain people who continually play a major role in the publication of this book—

State Motor Vehicle Agency Administrators and their staffs
Every year certain individual state administrators assist with the compilation and verification of the detailed facts within this book that pertain to their state. They insure the information is accurate and timely. I wish to sincerely thank each of you for not only your time, but also because you genuinely care. It is indeed a pleasure to work with you. This publication would not exist without your help and ongoing support over the years.

The American Association of Motor Vehicle Administrators
The AAMVA plays an important role in helping the states implement the changes demanded by Congressional legislation that affect the motor vehicle industry. Many of the programs and agreements profiled in this book are administered to a large degree by AAMVA. I sincerely wish to thank the AAMVA for the ongoing guidance they have provided over the past two decades.

Sincerely,

Michael Sankey
January 2010

Introduction

How to Use This Book

The U.S. Motor Vehicle Reference Book contains a plethora of information about each state's policies and procedures regarding driver licensing issuance, suspensions and revocations, financial responsibility issues, and record access. The state chapters section is the portion of the book most readers will use, but please do not overlook the important information that is present in the record of the book.

About Motor Vehicle Records

The *About Motor Vehicle Records* section is a primer. This text provides insight on how the states' driving record practices and access procedures work.

State Chapters

All 50 states and the District of Columbia are examined. Following a list of general help telephone numbers and web addresses, each state chapter has four sub-chapters. Below is a summary list showing how the sub-chapters are organized and where to look for specific data. We suggest you take a few minutes and review a state chapter so you become familiar with the format. Later, this will help you quickly find the information you need.

Driver License Facts—
- Format
- Appearance
- Issuance and Renewal Requirements
- License Classes
- HAZMAT Endorsement Procedure

Safety and Enforcement—
- Insurance and Financial Responsibility
- Chemical and Alcoholic Content
- Accident Reporting
- Suspensions and Revocations
- Reinstatement Requirements
- About the Point System

License Plate Facts—
- Registration
- Renewal
- New Residents
- Inspections and Emissions Testing
- Plate Descriptions

Overview of Record Access—
- Driving Records
- Accident Records
- Vehicle Records
- Watercraft Records

Note: Each records section presents you need to know about fees, access methods, and special programs.

The Appendix

The Appendix has extensive coverage of the federal regulations and of the agencies, agreements and programs that affect the access of motor vehicle records. The knowledge of how these agencies and agreements affect the states is very useful for the understanding of the states' driving and vehicle record practices and procedures. We strongly urge readers to review these pages.

Yes – We Modified the Books this Year

Those of you who have used *The MVR Book* or the *MVR Decoder Digest* in the past will readily see that we have replaced these books with new titles for 2010. Also, we updated and reformatted the layout of the text to make the content easier to find and read.

The bottom line is that the same content is printed although distributed differently and the price for purchase of both books decreased by $1.00. We feel these changes will be beneficial to all users and welcome your feedback. Please send any comments you have to msankey@brbpub.com.

About Motor Vehicle Records

What Does the Term MVR Mean?

The acronym MVR actually comes from the phrase Motor Vehicle Record or Moving Violation Record. When the term MVR is used, the majority of the time people are referring to a driving record. But the term can also refer to a vehicle registration or vehicle title record. When communicating with someone at a state motor vehicle department (DMV) about records, be sure you are clear on exactly what record you have in mind. For example, a state motor vehicle official could hear the words motor vehicle record or MVR and may think you are referring to a vehicle title or registration record or a status record, yet you may be referring to a driving record.

The Inconsistencies and Idiosyncrasies of Records

Who is legally permitted to access driving or vehicle records? What degree of authority is needed to obtain a full history record? What data is found on a record? What information is masked from the public's view?

Answers to these questions are all subject to individual state statutes, state administrative rules and regulations, and compliance with federal laws. The manner in which states communicate internally or externally, and their policies of reciprocity reflect the diversity that contributes to making each state unique.

Three Critical Factors about Motor Vehicle Records

There are three important rules to consider when accessing motor vehicle record data—

1. Each state maintains its own separate, unique database(s) of licensed drivers, vehicle registrations, vehicle ownership, accident reports, and other associated records. There is NO national, all-inclusive database of motor vehicle records.
2. There is no firm consistency among the states on data reporting.
3. The federal Driver's Privacy Protection Act (DPPA) sets specific standards when personal information can be included on a record, dependent upon the purpose of the request. All states comply with DPPA and some states are more restrictive.

The Affect of DPPA on Record Access

The Driver's Privacy Protection Act has had an important influence on motor vehicle records because DPPA mandates that states differentiate between permissible use and non-permissible use of personal information found on records. DPPA designates fourteen permissible uses. The reason for the record request determines who may receive a record with personal information. Personal Information means "...information that identifies an individual, including an individual's photograph, social security number, driver identification number, name, address (but not the 5-digit zip code), telephone number, and medical or disability information." Records with personal information are only given to those with a listed permissible use OR with the written consent of the driver.

All states are in compliance with the DPPA standards. Note that these standards are only minimal and states can be more restrictive. Nearly half of the states sell sanitized records (with personal information redacted) to casual requesters (requesters without a permissible use). In some states, sanitized records can be viewed or purchased online. On the other hand, a number of states refuse to disclose the personal information contained on the records to anyone from the public, even with consent of the subject.

A copy of DPPA including the permissible uses can be found in the Appendix. A copy of DPPA is online at www.mvrdecoder.com and at http://uscode.house.gov/download/pls/18C123.txt.

Driving Records

The business of accessing driving records is big. An estimated 700,000+ driving record requests are processed daily in the U.S, generating over $4,000,000 a day in state revenues.

Key Data Found on Driving Records

A driving record is a historical index of a driver's moving violation convictions, accidents, and license sanctions. Depending on the state's record reporting procedure, the record will show activity anywhere from three years to a lifetime. Nationally, the information found on each state's record is standardized to a point, but not all states provide the same information, and certainly not in the same format.

Traffic Violations and Accidents

At the core of the driving record is a list of traffic tickets resulting in a conviction. The only time a pending conviction will appear on a record is if the incident involves a situation that triggers an immediate suspension — such as if alcohol-related — or if an alleged violator fails to appear in court.

Typical information on a driving record includes date of violation, date of conviction, location of incident, points assessed, and description or descriptive code of the violation. Other possible pieces of information include the state statute related to the violation, the type of court, and court location. Accident involvement is also reported, but reporting who is at fault is spotty, at best. Generally, the driver at fault will have a citation on the same date appearing on the record.

Withdrawals and Administrative Actions

Motor vehicle officials often use the term withdrawal actions when referring to restrictive action taken against an individual's privilege to drive. The most common actions are suspensions, revocations, disqualifications, and denials. Sometimes a withdrawal may be triggered by a specific violation or series of violations. At other times the withdrawal may be administered by a judge or DMV official.

The information listed on a driving record typically includes the history of withdrawals with effective dates or when the driver is eligible to be reinstated. Some states cloak information of prior withdrawals, depending on the requester.

Record Content and Record Types

The data found on a driving record often varies by the record type. Depending on the state, driving records sometimes can often be requested by a category type. For example, the state of Washington offers eight different types of driving records. Typical record types include—

- Employment (as a commercially-licensed driver)
- Non-Employment
- Insurance
- Certified

What is reported can also vary widely. Some states do not report certain low-level moving violations, especially to insurance companies. Accident reporting is not consistent, neither is the length of time shown for previous suspensions or major convictions such as alcohol-related incidents. How far back records reports go and what is actually reported are other common, non-consistent variables for state to state. The exception is record reporting on commercially licensed drivers, which is more precise.

In most states, the standard reporting period generally coincides with insurance purpose requests. This standard is at least three years of moving violations and five to ten years of administrative actions. However, a number of states provide a longer time period on a standard record, and many states offer options for more in-depth records. For example, besides the standard three-year record Georgia also provides a seven-year record, Vermont an eight-year record, and Pennsylvania a complete (lifetime) record. Extra fees are often involved.

An employment record usually will only report actions occurring when an individual with a commercial driver's license (CDL) is driving a commercial motor vehicle (CMV). A non-employment record usually excludes CMV-related incidents. An insurance record may be filtered so not include certain low-impact moving violations (such as a speeding ticket less than 10 mph over the limit) or even accident involvement. Certified records are paper records with a state seal affixed. Sometimes records can be a combination of insurance and employment, or for a specific type employment.

Data Retention

How long the states keep record data varies also. But, there are federally mandated data retention and reporting standards for commercial drivers per Federal regulations, most recently updated by provision in the Motor Carrier Safety Improvement Act (MCSIA). This Act and the mandated standards are examined in the Appendix.

Record Access Methods

Typically, a request for an individual's driving record must include the full name with middle initial, driver license number, and/or date of birth. Similarly, vehicle record requests require the name and plate number and/or VIN. States do not perform a *name only* search for the public.

Access methods fall into two overall categories: manual and electronic.

Manual Access

Manual access request methods include by mail, in person, fax, and telephone. Every state does not offer every access method. Most do not offer access records by telephone or fax, but some do for approved, ongoing accounts (MO, NV, and OR for example). There are at least four states that do NOT provide a centralized counter service to the general public (CA, ID, MI, and WI). In a number of states, the county or local licensing agencies provide record access services, but sometimes this service is only available to the record holders.

Electronic Access

All states offer electronic access. The methods can vary by the way orders are grouped or submitted, and by the media type. In general, there are two types of electronic access: batch and interactive.

Batch processing is when a large group of record requests — including the specific names and necessary identifiers — are submitted at once. Results are "picked up" hours later. Interactive processing occurs when requests are sent individually and results are returned immediately, sometimes this can be done in rapid succession. This method is popular when a quick decision needs to be made about hiring or about the issuance of a new insurance policy.

There are special programs that some state offer on an electronic basis.

Driver Monitoring: A monitoring service is provided by some states to employers or insurance companies. The participating company provides a list of driver names to the state agency, then the agency will inform the requester when there is activity on a submitted person's record. Descriptions of these programs are found in the state chapters.

Records Viewed by License Holder: Another progressive trend is allowing license holders to view their records online, with a PIN or coded password.

The License Status Check: Another useful record is the license status report. Taken from the top portion of a driving record, the license status indicates the type or class of license issued, any special conditions placed on the license holder, and if the license is valid or under suspension or revocation.

As you will find in this book, a number of states offer status checks online and the list is growing. Some checks are accessible for free and some for a fee, as indicated within the state chapters.

Driving Record Fees

The fees that states charge to access their motor vehicle records vary widely. There is no consistency. The state fee for a driving record ranges from pennies in Missouri to $19.25 (electronic access) in Rhode Island or $20.00 (manual access) in Connecticut. Overall in the U.S., the average fee for electronic access is just over $7.00.

A state's fee structure can vary by the type of access method. At least seventeen states charge more per record for electronic access than for manual, and six states charge more for manual processing than electronic. For example, Louisiana charges $15.00 for a manual record and $6.00 for an electronic record, while Montana charges $4.00 for a manual record, $10.00 if certified, and $7.25 if the record is secured electronically.

If access is online, states may also charge set-up fees or annual fees to be an online subscriber. Generally, these fees are under $100 per year. Also, some states require extensive deposits or even performance bonds to be placed as collateral. See California.

About Commercial Drivers

Since April 1, 1992, drivers are required to have a commercial driver's license (CDL) in order to legally drive a commercial motor vehicle (CMV) involving interstate, intrastate, or foreign commerce. Derek Hinton, President of DOTJOBHistory.com, estimates there are over 3.5 million licensed commercial drivers operating in the U.S.

The Federal Highway Administration (FHWA) has developed and issued standards for testing and licensing CMV drivers. As part of these standards, states are required to issue CDLs to CMV drivers only after the drivers have passed knowledge and skills tests administered by the state, related to the type of vehicle to be operated. Federal standards also designate specific CDL license classifications depending upon the type of commercial vehicle operated:

Class A Any combination of vehicles with a GVWR

of 26,001 or more pounds provided the GVWR of the vehicle(s) being towed is in excess of 10,000 pounds.

Class B Any single vehicle with a GVWR of 26,001 or more pounds, or any such vehicle towing a vehicle not in excess of 10,000 pounds GVWR.

Class C Any single vehicle, or combination of vehicles, that does not meet the definition of Class A or Class B, but is either designed to transport 16 or more passengers, including the driver, or is placarded for hazardous materials.

CDL drivers must pass additional tests to obtain an endorsement from a state in order to operate specialty vehicles such as tankers, double or triple trailers, or to operate vehicles that haul hazardous materials. Each state chapter provides a complete list of commercial (and non-commercial) license classes, endorsements, and other state-imposed license restrictions.

CDL Regulations and Driving Records

The Code of Federal Regulations 49 CFR § 383.51 provides standards for maintaining and checking conviction records of commercial drivers, and provides penalties for traffic convictions by commercial drivers.

The Motor Carrier Safety Improvement Act of 1999 (MCSIA) amended the Code of Federal Regulations by establishing the Federal Motor Carrier Safety Administration (www.fmcsa.dot.gov). MCSIA also provided for additional standards and enhanced penalties which recently took affect. More information about these regulations and the specific penalties and recordkeeping is found in the Appendix.

The ACD Codes — A Key Component to State Reciprocity

Each state has unique conviction reporting language and codes inherent to their motor vehicle statutes and specific violation language. As function of the programs and compacts described in the Appendix, each state must communicate with one another or with a centralized index regarding commercial drivers, problem drivers, out-of state actions, and license disqualifications. The question then is—*How do states know what the conviction codes from other states mean and how do they translate this information into their own language and code set?*

The answer is the states utilize the AAMVA Code Dictionary (ACD) as a translation table. The primary function of the ACD Codes is to enable the Commercial Driver's License Information System (CDLIS) to exchange convictions and withdrawals. Other applications use the codes, such as the Problem Driver Pointer System (PDPS), knowing that the ACD Codes are defined for CDLIS. CDLIS and PDPS are reviewed in depth in the Appendix

So in practice, the ACD Code System is used to exchange conviction and withdrawal information between the states' driver licensing authorities. A number of states have incorporated the ACD Codes within their own conviction and action tables. For example, Alaska, has converted their conviction table to the ACD Code system as their primary conviction code table. Many states use the ACD to indicate out-of-state convictions.

Therefore, the knowledge of what a specific ACD Code means can be a helpful indication when deciphering the meaning of a conviction or withdrawal action.The ACD Code Table is presented in the *MVR Access and Decoder Digest*.

Accident Reports

Many states (Texas and Missouri, for example) prefer to use the term *crash reports* rather than *accident reports*. An accident report is created when a either there is an injury or death, or a threshold of property damage is reached. There are two different accident records created; 1) from reports filed by the citizens involved and 2) from reports prepared by the investigating officers. For the purposes of this publication, we will designate accident or crash records as reports prepared by the investigating officer. Copies of citizens' accident reports are not usually available to the public and are not reviewed herein.

There is no overall national database of historical accident information maintained by either a government agency or by private enterprise. A good rule of thumb is that accident records must be obtained from the agency that investigated the incident. When accident records are maintained by the same agency that holds driving records, the DPPA guidelines are followed with regards to honoring record requests.

Typical information found on a state accident report includes drivers' addresses and license numbers as well as a description of the incident. Only a handful of states offer online access to accident reports.

Vehicle Records

Typical vehicle records include detailed information about ownership, titles, liens, and registration data. Generally, vehicle ownership and title records can be ordered as a record of current ownership, or as a historical record showing all previous owners. Title data can also indicate if a vehicle was at one time a junk vehicle or if the vehicle was once a subject of title washing (previously branded as a salvage or flood-damaged vehicle), or perhaps previously a government vehicle. Information found on records can include vehicle identification numbers (VINs), license plate or tag numbers, and address information of owners and lienholders.

Usually the same state agency that administers driving records also administers vehicle records, such as in Arizona or Florida. In other states vehicle records are controlled by an entirely different state government department or division, including Montana and Oklahoma. Also, liens on vehicles may be recorded at the county level in some states or at the Secretary of State's Office where UCCs are filed in others.

If vehicle records are administered by the same agency that handles driver records, then there will be similarities between accessing driving records and vehicle records, especially in regard to fees and forms. Regardless of which state agency oversees the record-keeping, the data found on records is regulated by the federal DPPA.

Vehicle record data that includes personal identifiers is never sold for marketing purposes, per DPPA.

About the VIN

VIN stands for *Vehicle identification Number*. This number is internationally recognized as the way to identify an individual vehicle. When buying a used vehicle, many consumers and dealers check the history of a VIN with a private vendor to help make an informed decision about the quality and value of the vehicle. Vehicles have a metal plate stamped with unique VIN located somewhere on the dashboard or door. The VIN may also be found attached to other locations on the vehicle.

A VIN consists of 17 characters (vehicles manufactured before 1981 may have fewer characters) in a highly coded but strict format structure based on the manufacturers and vehicle models. A code table showing all the possible meanings for each position is a very extensive document, and this list is added to frequently. Several excellent Web resources to decode a VIN include—

www.autocheck.com
www.cardetective.com
www.carfax.com
www.decodethis.com

Watercraft Records

Often the state agency that administers vehicle records also administers vessel records. But in some states vessel records are controlled by an entirely different state government department or division. Examples include the Department of Wildlife and Parks in Kansas or the Natural Resources in Minnesota.

Not all states title watercraft. Those that do generally only require titles if the vessel is over a certain length or if motorized. Requirements similar to motor vehicles maybe imposed on vessels when registration is mandatory.

When watercraft and watercraft records are governed by a different government agency, the agency's access policies are usually not governed by DPPA. In these states, access is governed by administrative rules or by statute and the policy can be stricter or less restrictive than DPPA.

Similar to liens on vehicles, liens on watercraft can be recorded locally or at the Secretary of State's Office. The state chapters provide details about each state's access procedures to watercraft records.

About Large Commercial Vessels

Vessels weighing more than five tons are registered with the U.S. Coast Guard, www.st.nmfs.noaa.gov/st1/CoastGuard/. Another handy resource to search for larger vessels, or to search by lien or title, is the Coast Guard's National Vessel Documentation Center found at www.uscg.mil/hq/cg5/nvdc/.

Alabama

Administration	Important Telephone and Web Contacts

Major Charles Andrews, Division Chief
Driver License Division
301 S Ripley St, Montgomery 36104
334-353-1470
http://dps.alabama.gov/DriverLicense/
 	
G Thomas Surtees
Department of Revenue, Motor Vehicle Division
50 N Ripley St, 1202 Gordon Persons Bldg
Montgomery 36104
334-242-9000
www.revenue.alabama.gov/motorvehicle/index.html
	Driver Licensing......................................334-242-4400
	Financial Responsibility..........................334-242-4222
	Commercial Driver License 334-242-3427
	General Registration............... 334-242-9006 or 9007
	IRP 334-242-2999
	State Dept of Insurance 334-269-3550
	Highway Patrol, DPS 334-242-4393
	
	State statutes look-up at:
	   www.legislature.state.al.us
	Motor Vehicle Rulebook is found at:
	   www.revenue.alabama.gov/motorvehicle/mvrules/
	   mvrulebook.html

Driver License Facts

License Format
Seven numbers; there is no code or sequential arrangement which determines the characters making the license number.

Document Appearance
In late 2005, the plastic license was replaced with a new digitized license. Both documents are described below.

Newer Documents
Security Characteristics — The new cards have a laminate coating. Features include a 2-D barcode, magnetic stripe, digitized portrait image, signature and various security features including a optically variable image of the state outline text that changes color as license is tilted. The new card design includes the state capital and state seal.

Position of Photo — Bottom left, for under 18/21 bottom middle.

Minor Age Driver Locator — The "Under 18/21" driver licenses and identification cards are issued in a vertical format. Cards display the words "UNDER 18 UNTIL" or "UNDER 21 UNTIL" followed by the date the cardholder will turn 18 or 21 in bold red text. This text is positioned vertically next to the portrait.

CDL Indicator — The words "Commercial Driver License" appear on the card.

Older Documents
Security Characteristics — A red state seal appears.

Position of Photo — Bottom left.

Minor Age Driver Locator — A heat embossed star.

CDL Indicator — "CDL" is bordered with broken lines and is to right of DOB.

Issue and Renewal

Age Requirements
A Learner's License is required at age fifteen and valid for four years or until driving test is passed. The minimum age for an operator's permit is sixteen; eighteen for intra-state CDL; twenty-one for CDL; fourteen for motor driven cycle; and twelve for a vessel.

Renewal
Four years from date of issue, driver keeps same number when renewing. Military personnel, their dependents, students or other licensed drivers who are temporarily out-of-state due to job requirements may be eligible to apply if they have obtained an AL driver license with photo and signature within past 4 years. The license must be renewed every four years. An Alabama driver license may be renewed without examination within a three-year period after it has expired.

Elderly-Related Restrictions
None are indicated by the DPS.

Residency
New residents must apply within thirty days of establishing residency.

License Classes
Commercial Classifications
- Class A   This classification applies only to "combination" vehicles with a Gross Combination Weight Rating (GCWR) exceeding 26,000 pounds, provided the Gross Vehicle Weight Rating (GVWR) of the vehicle being towed exceeds 10,000 pounds. The holder of a Class A license, which includes any appropriate endorsements, may operate all vehicles included in Class B, C, and D.
- Class B   This class includes single or combination vehicles where the GVWR of the single vehicle exceeds 26,000 pounds. The vehicle in tow must not exceed 10,000 pounds. Class B licensees, with appropriate endorsements, may drive all vehicles in Class C or D.
- Class C   Vehicles designed to transport 16 or more passengers, including the driver, and vehicles placarded for hazardous materials, that do not meet the criteria for Class A or B above fall under this classification and may drive all vehicles in Class D.

Non-Commercial Classifications
- Class D   Operator (if Learner's License, then must have Y restriction)
- Class M   Motorcycle (motor driven cycle only with B restriction)
- Class V   Vessel (4-year license for all boat operators)

HAZMAT Endorsement Procedure
The state is in compliance with the Patriot Act. All applicants applying for a new or renewal or transfer HAZMAT Endorsement (HME) must first obtain the application from https://hazprints.tsa.dhs.gov/Public/ or by calling 877-429-7746. The driver must also be fingerprinted. EMSI is the state-designated entity to process fingerprints. There are four locations in the state that perform this service. Visit the web page listed above to find the address locations. The cost of the fingerprint process is $89.25. The fingerprints and application information is sent to the Federal Transportation Security Administration (TSA). TSA performs the background checks and notifies the DMV whether the application is approved or denied. When completed and approved, the HME is valid for the term of the CDL.

Safety and Enforcement Facts

Insurance and Financial Responsibility
Self-propelled vehicles registered in Alabama are required to have liability insurance coverage and proof of coverage must be carried in the vehicle. The mandatory insurance provisions are in the amounts of $25,000/$50,000/$25,000, or must be covered by a motor vehicle liability bond or cash deposit of $50,000. Proof of coverage must be presented at all traffic stops and accidents or the vehicle's tag registration will be suspended. Proof is required with an SR-22 if convicted of having no insurance, if judgment is rendered following an accident and for revocation actions. Violations of the state's mandatory insurance laws are punishable with a fine of up to $500 for the first conviction and $1,000 and/or suspension of the driver's license for up to 6 months for each subsequent conviction.

Alcohol and Chemical Testing
Alabama has provisions for urine, blood, and breath testing. The intoxication limit level is .08 BAC, .04 for drivers of a CMV, .02 for school bus and day care drivers, and .02 for persons under 21 years of age. The state also has an implied-consent violation. Riding a horse or bicycle under the influence is also considered illegal.

Accident Reporting
Accidents resulting in injury, death, or damage in excess of $250.00 must be reported immediately to the local or state police, and a written report (Form SR-13) must be filed within 30 days with the Safety Responsibility Unit, PO Box 1471, Montgomery 36102. This form can be filled out real time on a computer, or downloaded from http://dps.alabama.gov/public/driverlicense/forms/sr-13.pdf. For questions, call 334-242-4222.

Suspensions and Revocations
The state is in compliance with the mandatory CDL disqualifications, see the Appendix.

Driving Under the Influence
No Previous Convictions	Ninety-days minimum suspension.
One Previous Conviction within 5 years	One-year revocation.
Two Previous Convictions within 5 years	Three-year revocation.
More Than Three Previous Convictions (Class C felony)	Five-year revocation.

CDL - No Previous Convictions not Carrying Hazardous Material ..... One-year disqualification.
CDL - No Previous Convictions Carrying Hazardous Material .... Three-year disqualification.
CDL - Previous Convictions not Carrying Hazardous Material .... Lifetime disqualification.
CDL - Previous Convictions Carrying Hazardous Material .... Lifetime disqualification.

Other Violations Which May Result in Suspension
- DUI-Drugs
- Altering or Mutilating License
- Attempting to Elude a Peace Officer
- Racing on Highway
- Failure to Appear or Pay
- Failure to Pay Child Support Payments
- Points Accumulation
- DUI-Combined Alcohol and Other Controlled Substances
- DUI-Under Influence of any Substance Which Impairs Mental or Physical Faculties
- Refusal to Submit to Chemical Test
- 2 Convictions of License Restriction Violation
- Minor in Possession of Alcohol Beverage

Other Violations Which May Result in Mandatory Revocation
- Hit-and-Run/Leaving the Scene
- Manslaughter; Second-Degree Murder with Vehicle
- Commission of Felony Involving Operation of Vehicle
- Homicide by Vehicle
- Unauthorized use of Motor Vehicle Belonging to Another
- Perjury/False Statement Relating to Ownership or DL Laws
- Three Reckless-Driving Convictions in Twelve Months
- Two Convictions for Driving While License Suspended, Revoked, or Cancelled

Violations Which May Result in CDL Disqualification
- Accident Resulting in a Fatality in a CMV
- CDL Used in Commission of a Felony
- Two or More Serious Violations in a CMV (3 yr period)
- Railroad Violations in a CMV DUI .04 or More in CMV
- DUI Any Substance in CMV
- Refusing the Chemical Test in a CMV
- Admin Per Se .04 or More in CMV

Reinstatement Requirements

Suspension $100 reinstatement fee and time lapse.
Revocations $175 reinstatement fee; time lapse; proof of financial responsibility; and re-examination.
Extra Fee is $275 if alcohol involved. There is a $25 additional fee if drug-related; $50.00 additional fee on all non-payment of child support; $50 additional fee if fail to surrender license within thirty days. Vessel reinstatements are $50.00.

Point System Overview

Points are assigned and retain their value for a period of two years from the conviction date. Points will range from 2 to 6. The schedule for suspension for an accumulation points is as follows:

12-14 points in 2 years .... 60-day suspension
15-17 points in 2 years .... 90-day suspension
18-20 points in 2 years .... 120-day suspension
21-23 points in 2 years .... 180-day suspension
24 or more points in 2 years ... 365-day suspension

Serious violations occurring within three year time frame in a CDL will result in a disqualification as follows:
2 serious violations .... 60-day disqualification
3 or more serious violations ..... 120-day disqualification

License Plate Facts

Registration

Motor vehicles are registered through the offices of county license plate issuing officials. Trucks and truck tractors operating to points outside the State of Alabama are registered through the Department of Revenue, Motor Vehicle Division, Motor Carrier Services Unit. Motor vehicles owned by the State, county, municipality, public utility departments, or volunteer fire departments are registered through the Department of Revenue, Motor Vehicle Division, Registration Section.

Alabama law does not require registrants to show proof of insurance prior to registering a vehicle. Registrants are required, however, to maintain liability insurance by a company licensed to conduct business in Alabama. Registrants affirm, by signing the registration receipt, that the vehicle being registered is insured.

Renewal

Alabama registers vehicles under a staggered registration system, January through November, based on the first letter of the owner's last name. For example, someone whose last name begins with the letters F, G, or N is required to re-register his/her vehicle in the month of **April**, with the previous registration expiring on **April 30**. Leased vehicles, commercial, and fleet vehicles are subject to renewal in the months of October and November.

As of January 1, 2005, the expiration date for motor vehicle is the last day of the renewal month. Prior to that date, Alabama law provided that registrations expire on the last day of the month prior to the renewal month.

Thirty-three of the sixty-seven Alabama counties offer online vehicle registration.

New Residents

Section 40-12-262, Code of Alabama provides that the owner of a non-commercial vehicle with a **valid registration** from another jurisdiction has thirty days from the date entered the state to register the vehicle. Also, the vehicle owner has twenty calendar days from the date of vehicle purchase or acquisition to register the vehicle without penalty.

Inspections and Emissions Testing

Alabama has no state-required annual inspection or emissions test; however, a prerequisite to titling is a mandatory Identification Inspection. Also, cities have the right to impose either type of test.

Plate Descriptions

Typical Plate Patterns	Passenger plates and light trucks through 12,000 pounds are NLNNLNN or NNLNNLN. Commercial Vehicles are NNLNNNNN or NLNNNNNN; NNNNNN for interstate commercial.
County/City Codes	The first number(s) of the plate designate the county. The coding runs as follows: 1 is Jefferson, 2 is Mobile, 3 is Montgomery; numbers 4 through 67 correspond to an alphabetical listing of the remaining counties, thus 4 is Autauga and 67 is Winston. There is no city code.
Plates & Stickers in Force	One plate, two decals (MO) (YR).
Plate Remains with Car if Sold?	Since 01/01/98, tags follow the owner on self-propelled vehicles.

Overview of Record Access

About Driving Records

Driver Record Request, Driver License Division, PO Box 1471, Montgomery AL 36102-1471, 334-242-4400 or 4241. http://dps.alabama.gov/DriverLicense/ Email for driver-related questions is DriverLicenseInfo@dps.alabama.gov. The current fee is $5.75, $7.00 if accessed online, and no increases are planned. No personal checks are accepted.

Request Methods – Mail, Walk-in, Online.

What You Should Know – Alabama reports all convictions going back the past three years, regardless of type of conviction or status. Accident involvement is reported, but fault is not shown.

Alabama.gov is the state's designated online agent. Both Alabama.gov and the DPS must pre-approve all subscribers. See www.alabama.gov/portal/index.jsp.

About Accident Reports

Crash reports may be obtained from the Alabama Department of Public Safety, Accident Reports, P.O. Box 1471, Montgomery 36102-1471, 334-242-4241. Also, walk-in requests can be processed at Driver License District Offices in Birmingham, Dothan, Foley, Huntsville, Jacksonville, Mobile, Opelika, Sheffield, and Tuscaloosa. The cost is $15.00 per report. Only certified funds are accepted; no personal checks. Please include the names, license number (if possible), date, and county. A self-addressed stamped envelope is strongly suggested. Turnaround time is normally 10 to 12 days. SSNs are not released. There is no searching by telephone, but one may call to see if a report is ready. Records are available for past 10 years. A specific form is suggested, download from www.dps.alabama.gov/driverlicense/forms/DLCrashReportRequest.pdf.

About Vehicle Records

Dept. of Revenue, Motor Vehicle Division, Records Unit, 50 North Ripley Street, Ste 1222, Montgomery 36140, 334-242-9056 and 334-242-9006 or 9007, www.revenue.alabama.gov/motorvehicle/index.html Certificates of title are not issued by the Department of Revenue for ATVs, snowmobiles, and travel trailers, mobile homes and utility trailers that are designated as 1989 or older. A printout of the current title record including owner and lien holder information is $15.00 per vehicle. A three-year limited title history is $15.00. A complete title history is $15.00, however title records are not available pre-1975 vehicles. A year must be included as part of the request or a printout of the registration record for each year to be searched is $3.00 per year. Personal checks are not accepted. Registration records are retained for 10 years maximum. Email vehicle-related questions to mvrecords@revenue.alabama.gov, email title-related questions to titles@revenue.alabama.gov.

Request Methods – Mail, Walk-in, Online, Bulk.

What You Should Know – Certificates of title are not issued by the Department of Revenue for ATVs, snowmobiles, and travel trailers, mobile homes and utility trailers that are designated as 1989 or older.

About Watercraft Records

Department of Conservation and Natural Resources, PO Box 301451, Montgomery 36130, 334-242-3673, www.outdooralabama.com/boating/, email questions to dcnr.boatreg@dcnr.alabama.gov. Operators must be licensed and at least 14 years of age to operate a boat alone, or 12 years old with an adult present. A written examination is required for applicants, except those who have successfully completed boating courses given by the U.S. Coast Guard Auxiliary, the U.S. Power Squadron or the Alabama Marine Police "Boating Basics" course, or have an age exemption. The vessel class "V" must be added to your license if you intend to operate a motorized vessel.

All mechanically propelled, sail or rental boats must be registered. Vessels that have been commercially documented by the Coast Guard are not required to register in Alabama. Boat trailers do not need to be licensed and vessels do not need to be titled. The owner's name, boat hull number (decal) or registration number is required to do a search. There is no fee unless large lists are presented, then the fee is $1.00 per search. Requests can be faxed to 334-242-0366. Requests can be emailed (call first). Turnaround time is usually 1-2 days, but can be longer in the summer. It takes 2 months before new records are available for inquiry. Liens are not recorded here, but at the central state location for UCC filings, call 334-242-5231.

Alaska

Administration	Important Telephone and Web Contacts

Whitney Brewster, Director
Carl Springer, Register
Division of Motor Vehicles
3300 B Fairbanks St, Anchorage, AK 99503
907-269-5559
 	
Research and Correspondence
1300 W Benson Boulevard, Ste 200
Anchorage, AK 99503-3600
 	
http://doa.alaska.gov/dmv/
	Driving and Vehicle Record Information 907-269-5551
	Financial Responsibility and SR-22 907-465-4361
	State Division of Insurance 907-465-2515
	State Trooper Headquarters............................907-269-5511
	
	Email dmv_webmaster@alaska.gov
	           MIL@alaska.gov
	An excellent topic index is found at:
	         http://doa.alaska.gov/dmv/general/index.htm
	Statutes www.legis.state.ak.us/basis/folio.asp
	(Rules)

Driver License Facts

License Format
Seven numbers. Normally, low numbered licenses are started with zeros, i.e. 0000001, 0000002, etc. There is no code for license format; numbers are assigned by computer in a numerical order.

Document Appearance
The appropriate section of the application card is photographed with the driver. Since 2004, Alaska has issued a digitized license document. The replacement of older documents will take at least six years.

Newer Format
- **Security Characteristics**: License is a plastic card, laminated on both sides, 2D bar code on back. Also, includes ghost image, optical outline of ALASKA followed by outline of state flag alternates in two horizontal rows on front. ALASKA is printed on left and right edges and is visible under UV light.
- **Position of Photo**: Top left corner.
- **Minor Age Driver**: Card in vertical format, photo at lower left. "Under 21" in white in red on right bar above photo.
- **CDL Indicator**: "COMMERCIAL DRIVER LICENSE" on blue print in yellow bar.

Older Format
- **Security Characteristics**: Location number and state seal overlap the photo and licensing information. Licenses issued prior to August 2000 may include hologram on license pouch. Since 2001, the state name is center of license in optical reflective lettering that changes color when license is tilted.
- **Position of Photo**: Top left corner.
- **Minor Age Driver**: "Under 21" is printed in red on right side and left of license. All print is in red (not blue).
- **CDL Indicator**: None, other than classification..

Issue and Renewal

Age Requirements
An applicant must be at least 16 and have held a valid driving permit for at least six months. A 14 year old may apply for an Instructional Permit. Applicants under 18 with parental consent may apply for a Provisional License. New drivers under 18 must have had an Instruction Permit for 6 months before the driver is issued a license. During the first year after a license is issued to a person under 18, the license is considered a Provisional License. There are stringent guidelines regarding such items as who can be in the vehicle and time of day driven. For more information, visit the web page.

Renewal
Birth day and month of fifth year, driver keeps same number when renewing. An active duty military personnel non-

commercial license expires 90 days after discharge from military or 90 days after return to the state of Alaska, whichever comes first. If an Alaska resident is temporarily out of state and discovers that the license is expired, an extension letter can be mailed or faxed to extend the expiration date. CDL extensions are limited to 30 days.

Elderly-Related Restrictions
None indicated.

Residency
New residents must obtain license within ninety days, if CDL then within thirty days.

License Classes
Commercial Classifications

Class A	Any combination of vehicles (excluding motorcycles) with a GCWR of 26,001 or more pounds, provided the GVWR of the vehicle(s) being towed is in excess of 10,000 pounds (e.g., eighteen-wheelers, log trucks, etc.).
Class B	Any single vehicle (excluding motorcycles) with a GVWR of 26,001 or more pounds, or any such vehicle towing a vehicle not in excess of 10,000 pounds GVWR (e.g., dump trucks, cement-mixer trucks, box trucks, motor coaches).
Class C	A motor vehicle or a combination of a motor vehicle and one or more vehicles (except motorcycles) in which:

1. The GCWR is greater than 26,000 pounds while the GVWR of the towing vehicle is 26,000 pounds or less, and the combined GVWR of the vehicle or vehicles being towed is 10,000 or less; or
2. Does not meet the definition of Class A/CDL or Class B/CDL and
    A. is designed to transport more than sixteen passengers (including the driver); or
    B. is used in the transportation of materials which require the motor vehicle to be placarded under the Federal Hazardous Materials Regulations. Holders of a Class C/CDL may also operate a Class D vehicle.

Instruction Permits Commercial Drivers
Alaska recently began issuing new instruction permits for commercial drivers. The permits are IA for Class A, IB for Class B, and IC for Class C. These permits allow a beginning driver to practice driving skills to qualify for the road test in the respective commercial vehicle. The permits are not intended to legalize the operation of a commercial vehicle by underage persons during the period when they are waiting to become old enough for the issuance of a commercial license.

Non-Commercial Classifications

Class D	Single vehicle less than 26,001 pounds or combination of towed vehicle which is less than 10,000 pounds (except motorcycle).
Class M1	Motorcycle.
Class M2	Motorscooter (under sixteen years of age).
Class IP	Instruction Permit.
Class IE	Driver Training Permit (good for 6 months while under supervision).

Off-System License
To serve Alaska residents in rural communities, the DMV issues an "Off-Systems" license that allows an individual to drive in specific Alaskan communities. An Off-Systems license allows an individual to drive on roads that are not connected to the State highway system and on roads that are not connected to a highway or vehicular way with an average daily traffic volume greater than 499. To obtain an "Off-Systems" license, the applicant must complete all licensing requirements except for the skills (road) test and photograph.

HAZMAT Endorsement Procedure
The state is in compliance with the Patriot Act. All applicants applying for a new or renewal or transfer HAZMAT Endorsement (HME) must first obtain the application from https://hazprints.tsa.dhs.gov/Public/ or by calling 877-429-7746. The driver must also be fingerprinted. EMSI and COMNETIX are the state-designated entities to process fingerprints. There are five locations in the state that perform this service. Visit the web page listed above to find the address locations. The cost of the application and fingerprint process is $89.25. A press release about this program is found at http://doa.alaska.gov/dmv/akol/hme.htm. The fingerprints and application information is sent to the federal Transportation Security Administration (TSA). TSA performs the background checks and notifies the DMV whether the application is approved or denied. When completed and approved, the HME is valid for five years.

Safety and Enforcement Facts

Insurance and Financial Responsibility
Alaska has both Financial Responsibility and Mandatory Insurance laws. Proof must be shown after any reportable accident. Minimum financial responsibility limits are $50,000/100,000/25,000.

However, insurance is not required in areas where registration is not required, with the exception of a driver who has received a ticket for a violation of 6 points or more within the last 5 years and must have liability insurance. A list of these locations is shown at http://doa.alaska.gov/dmv/akol/hme.htm.

Alcohol and Chemical Testing
Alaska's under-the-influence laws and the administrative license revocation law take effect at a .08 percent level and .04 level for those operating a commercial vehicle. The state has an implied-consent law. There is a zero (.00) tolerance for those under 21 years of age. Breath, blood, or urine testing may be used.

Accident Reporting
A driver who has been involved in a collision, regardless of fault, is required to show proof of motor vehicle liability insurance if the collision resulted in personal injury or death, or damage to property exceeding $501. Accidents involving property damage in excess of $501, injury, or death must be reported to the local police or state troopers. An Accident (Crash) Report form is required when there is a crash resulting in either an injury or total property damage of $2,000 or more. This report is not required if the crash was investigated by a peace officer. This report must be filed within ten days with the Department of Administration, Division of Motor Vehicles, PO Box 110221, Juneau, AK 99811-0221. The report can be made directly via the Web; go to https://myalaska.state.ak.us/home/app. There are no special reporting requirements for commercial drivers.

Suspensions and Revocations
The state is in compliance with the **federally mandated disqualifications for offenses occurring in a CMV per MCSIA**. See the Appendix for a list of these disqualifications.

Note: A revocation may result for refusal to submit to a breath, blood, or urine test for the purpose of determining alcohol content or the presence of controlled substances.

Defaulting on Promissory Note	Indefinite suspension.
Driving Under the Influence	
No Previous Convictions	Ninety-days minimum revocation.
One Previous Conviction	One-year revocation.
Two Previous Convictions	Three-year revocation.
More Than Two Previous Convictions	Five-year revocation.
Driving Under the Influence, Minor	
No Previous Convictions	Thirty-days minimum revocation.
One Previous Conviction	Sixty-days revocation.
Two Previous Convictions	Ninety-days revocation.
Three or More Previous Convictions	One-year revocation.
Failure to Appear for Driver Improvement Interview	Waives the right to hearing, action becomes final.
Failure to Pay Child Support	Indefinite Suspension.
Failure to Show Proof of Insurance	Ninety-days to one-year suspension.
Fraudulent Use of License Document -	
Under 21, 1st Offense	Sixty-day suspension.
2nd or Subsequent Offense	One-year suspension.
Non-Compliance with Recommendations	
of DI Specialist	Suspension of one year or until compliance, whichever comes first.

Point Accumulation
Twelve or more points in twelve months	One-month suspension.
Eighteen or more points in twenty-four months	One-month suspension.
Second point suspension in twenty-four months	Three-month suspension.
Third point suspension in twenty-four months	One-year revocation.

Note: Drivers receiving traffic citations which total 6 or more points in a 12 month period or 9 or more points in a 24-month period, must take a nationally certified defensive driving course. Otherwise, the DMV may suspend the privilege to drive.

Reinstatement Requirements
Suspension 100 reinstatement fee if only one license action is in effect within the past 10 years; $250 if more than one action in past ten years; SR-22.

Revocation 200 reinstatement fee if only one license action is in effect within the past 10 years; $500 if more than one action in past ten years; SR-22; knowledge test. Road test may be required. Alcohol treatment verification is required following a conviction of DWI or Refusal or for an administrative revocation for "Minor in Possession." 1st offenders must submit proof of compliance with an alcohol education or rehabilitation program, 2nd or more offenders must submit proof of completion and payment for said program.

Point System Overview
Alaska employs a point system with points ranging from 2 to 10 points. A driver can be suspended with 12 or more points in a 12 month period or 18 points in 24 months.

License Plate Facts

Registration Renewal
Registration is biennial. Online registration for all vehicles (car, truck, motor home, trailer, boat, snowmachine, ATV) is found at www.alaska.gov/dmv/faq/renewal.htm. Address changes may also be done online.

New Residents
Non-residents must register vehicles after sixty days or within ten days of accepting employment or intention of establishing residency.

Inspections and Emissions Testing
Although there is no annual required safety inspection, Alaska State troopers may inspect—at their discretion—when it is believed a vehicle is unsafe.

There is no provision for emissions testing statewide. However, the Municipality of Anchorage requires an emission test on gasoline-powered vehicles that have a net vehicle weight of 12,000 pounds or less for 1968 or newer models. The program is run by the local government - the Division of Motor Vehicles has no responsibility for administering or conducting the inspections. The Division is responsible for enforcing the program to the extent of assuring the vehicle is in compliance with the program prior to issuing a title or registration for the vehicle. As of January 2010, vehicles 2006 and newer are exempt for the first six years. Previously, vehicles were exempt for the first four years.

Plate Descriptions
Typical Plate Pattern	The typical patterns for all plates are; LLL222, 222LLL, NNNN22, 22NNN, or personalized.
County Code	None reported.
Plates and Stickers in Force	Two plates, one decal (MO/YR) on rear plate.
Plates Remain with Car when Sold?	Yes, with the exception of specialized plates.

Overview of Record Access

About Driving Records
Division of Motor Vehicles, Attn: Research, 1300 W Benson Blvd. Ste 200, Anchorage, AK 99503, 907-269-5551. The fee for a driving record is $10.00 per request for all access methods, but some data vendors can obtain for less if online. The last fee increase was July 2006. Alaska gives a credit for "no record found" reports. As mentioned above, the DMV requires a release form signed by the licensee to access a driving record. Volume requesters can maintain the signed release forms on file, rather than forward with requests

Request Methods – Mail, Walk-in, Fax, Online.

What You Should Know – Generally, the first four letters of the driver's last name, the license number, and date of birth are required to receive a record.

About Accident Reports
Copies of accident reports are considered private and confidential—only legal representatives and insurance agents of participants or the participant him/herself may obtain copies. A lawyer or legal representative must have a signed and notarized release from the participant. An insurance agent can only obtain a copy of the accident report of his/her insured, not the other participants. The request does not need to be notarized, but must be in writing with a proper explanation.

New records are available for inquiry in 30 days or less. The cost of obtaining an accident report is $10.00 per record, credit cards are accepted. Written requests should be submitted to: Division of Motor Vehicles, Driver Services, PO Box 110221, Juneau, AK 99811-0221.

About Vehicle Records

Division of Motor Vehicles, Attention: Research, 1300 W Benson Boulevard #200, Anchorage 99503-3600, 907-269-5551. The Division of Motor titles motor vehicles including trailers and mobile homes, and registers motor vehicles including trailers, snow vehicles, powered and non-powered boats, and all terrain vehicles. The Division is prohibited from issuing titles to snow vehicles and ATVs.

Personal information is integrated into the vehicle record so the record cannot be released unless the person, business, or organization requesting the record qualifies under one of the authorized exceptions shown on Form 851-Request

What You Should Know —For purposes of the law "personal information" includes name and both mailing and residence addresses of any individual on the record. The definition of "individual" includes a person, an organization, or an entity. This is broad enough to include people, businesses, trusts, organizations, and lienholder, if the lienholder is an individual. If the lienholder is a business or institution, the release is not required. There is a $10.00 fee for all vehicle records. Personal checks are accepted if in-state. The search includes a computer printout and any copies of documents retained in the microfilm files, if requested. "Motorized snow machines" are not titled and are not required to be registered if only ridden on private property. Mobile homes may be titled at the DMV, but are not required. Procedures for records and liens are same as for vehicles.

Request Methods – Mail, Walk-in.

About Watercraft Records

Alaska is not a "title" state. As of January 1st, 2001, the Division of Motor Vehicles assumed the boat registration program from the U.S. Coast Guard. Prior to January 1st, 2001, the Coast Guard registered powered boats that are used on navigable waterways of the state. Now, only large commercial vessels are registered with the US Coast Guard (call 800-799-8362). Boats are registered by hull number, AK number and by name. There is a $10.00 fee per search. As of June 4, 2004, non-powered boats are not required to be registered. State law requires the following to be registered:

- All powered boats used on any water in the state. (This includes all rivers, streams, and lakes, regardless of size, and all salt water within 3 miles of land.)
- All boats used by registered Sport Fishing Guides (including non-powered boats).

What You Should Know – Liens are filed with the Department of Natural Resources, Recorder's Office 907-762-2104.

Arizona

Administration	Important Telephone and Web Contacts
Stacey K Stanton, Division Director Motor Vehicle Division Department of Transportation P.O. Box 2100, Mail Drop 500M Phoenix 85001-2100, 602-712-8152 General Email: mvdinfo@azdot.gov www.azdot.gov/mvd/index.asp	Driver Licensing and Vehicle Information ....602-255-0072 *This general number provides access to different areas depending upon caller's need.* Financial Responsibility & SR-22 ....602-255-0072 Commercial Driver License..............................623-932-7731 State Department of Insurance.........................602-364-3100 Department of Public Safety.............................602-223-2000 Statutes and Rules www.azdot.gov/mvd/mvdrules/index.asp

Driver License Facts

License Format
Licenses are issued as one letter plus eight numbers. However, in the past some licenses were issued using the Social Security Number as the DL# and some of these licenses are still active. Current military licenses remain valid until out of service, some duplicates are issued without photo.

Document Appearance
The license is printed on standard plastic credit card stock.

    Security Characteristics   Hologram overlay, bar code, magnetic strip, secondary "ghost" signature and digital signature.
    Position of Photo   Lower right.
    Minor Age Driver Locator   "UNDER 21 UNTIL..." is printed in red.
    CDL Indicator   "COMMERCIAL DRIVER'S LICENSE" is printed on heading.

As of February 7, 2001, the Motor Vehicle Division modified the document with these additional security enhancements:
- Background image of the Grand Canyon
- Horizontally printed license for drivers age 21 and over.
- Vertically printed license for drivers under age 21. Displays date when licensee will be age 21.
- Magnetic "MAG" stripe contains license information, including endorsements and restrictions.
- Barcode moved to back of license. Secures credential information.
- Optically Variable Ink (OVI) technology used to provide security and reduce fraud.

Issue and Renewal
Age Requirements
The minimum age for an operator's permit is 18. Effective July 1, 2008, a new Graduated Licensing Program was put into force. A Graduated Instruction Permit is issued to an applicant who is at least 15 years and 6 months old. The teen must have a licensed driver at least 21 years of age seated in front seat at all times. The Graduated Driver License is issuable to those at least 16 years of age. For at least 6 months a variety of requirements are in place, including supervised driving practice and requirements on whom can be in the car. A driver can apply for the Class D driver license at age 18. Exact requirements are indicated on the web.

Renewal
Extended licenses expire at age 65 with mandatory photo update every twelve years. Limited licenses expire on the birth date of the fifth year. The driver keeps same number when renewing. Driver's license reinstatement and address changes can be done online at servicearizona.com, but not renewal.

Elderly-Related Restrictions
When driver is over 65, renewal licenses are issued every 5 years.

Residency
Non-residents must obtain license upon establishing residency, accepting employment, enrolling children in public school, or remaining in the state for seven months or more.

License Classes
Commercial Classifications
Class A   Any combination of vehicles with a GVWR of 26,001 or more pounds—provided the GVWR of the vehicle(s) being towed is in excess of 10,000 pounds (holders of A, B, C, and D license categories).

Class B   Any single vehicle with a GVWR of 26,001 or more pounds, or any such vehicle towing a vehicle not in excess of 10,000 pounds GVWR (holders of a B license may also operate all vehicles within the C and D license categories).

Class C   Any single vehicle less than 26,001 pounds GVWR; or any such vehicle towing a vehicle not in excess of 10,000 pounds GVWR; or any such vehicle towing a vehicle which is in excess of 10,000 pounds GVWR—provided the GCWR is less than 26,000 pounds, or is: placarded for hazardous materials; designed to transport sixteen or more persons (including the operator); and to operate a school bus with at least ten passengers (including the operator). Holders of a C license may also operate all vehicles within the D license category.

Non-Commercial Classifications
Class D   Any single vehicle less than 26,001 pounds GVWR, and such vehicle towing a vehicle not in excess of 10,000 pounds GVWR, and any such vehicle towing a vehicle which is in excess of 10,000 pounds GVWR—provided the GCWR does not exceed 26,000 pounds.

Class M   A motorcycle or motor-driven cycle.

Class G   Graduated driver license, between the ages of 16 to 18. Effective 07/18/00, an instructional permit must be held for 5 months or until age 18. The applicant is not required to hold the instruction permit past his/her 18th birthday. However, this does not preclude the applicant from obtaining a permit for 4 months or less.

Note: A restricted driving permit can be issued in certain situations or if directed by the court. Examples include when a breath, blood or urine test has been submitted to MVD indicating a blood alcohol level of .08 or more and it is the first DUI within 5 years and the DUI did not result in serious physical injury, or if found guilty of driving without insurance.

HAZMAT Endorsement Procedure
All applicants applying for a new or renewal or transfer HAZMAT Endorsement (HME) upon having successfully completing all state required CDL and HME written tests must first obtain the application from https://hazprints.tsa.dhs.gov/Public/ or by calling 877-429-7746. The driver must also be fingerprinted. EMSI, the only state-designated entity to process fingerprints, has four locations, contact EMSI at 602-252-0077. The cost of the fingerprint process is $89.25. The fingerprints and application information is sent to the Federal Transportation Security Administration (TSA). TSA performs the background checks and notifies the MVD whether the application is approved or denied. When completed and approved, the HME is valid for five years. An excellent Q&A about the HME is at www.azdot.gov/mvd/faqs/scripts/faqs.asp?section=hmbc. Enter "HME" to view.

Safety and Enforcement Facts

Insurance and Financial Responsibility
Arizona minimum limits are $15,000/30,000/10,000. Proof is not required at the time of annual vehicle renewal or registration. Law enforcement officers will ask for proof of insurance at the time of traffic stops or accidents. Insurance companies notify the MVD of all policy cancellations, non-renewals, and new policies. SR-22 forms are used in this state. **De-insurance** is a method of temporarily not maintaining the required insurance on a vehicle until it is ready to be driven or placed on the road again. A de-insured vehicle will not be suspended due to lack of insurance unless driven on the roadways of this state.

Alcohol and Chemical Testing
Arizona's illegal intoxication level is .08 % and above for ages 21 and older; 0 % for ages 16 to 21; and .04 % for commercial vehicle drivers. Urine, blood, and breath testing are authorized. Extreme DCCI is .15 and above. Arizona has both an implied-consent violation and a provision for an administrative suspension. Operating a bicycle under the influence is also considered illegal.

Accident Reporting
Reports must be filed immediately with the local police within the municipality for accidents involving injury, death or damage over $1,000; accidents outside the municipality should be reported to the county sheriff or the nearest state police patrol. Accident reports completed by law enforcement must be filed in the same way. Commercial drivers must report convictions to employers within ten days of conviction and must report to their home state within thirty days of conviction. No special form is required; a letter with information is sufficient.

Suspensions and Revocations
The state is in compliance with the **federally mandated disqualifications on CDLs**. See the Appendix for details.
The State Shall Revoke the License of a Driver for Any of the Following Offenses—
- Any Felony Committed While Using a Motor Vehicle
- Any Homicide Resulting From the Operation of a Motor Vehicle
- Conviction or Forfeiture of Bail Not Vacated, Upon Second or Subsequent Charge of Reckless Driving, Racing or Any of the Above in Combination With DUI Driving
- Driving Under the Influence of Drugs or Alcohol-Multiple Offenses Within 60 Months
- Failure to Stop and Give Aid When Involved in an Accident Resulting in Personal Injury or Death
- Perjury or Making a False Affidavit Under Oath to the Department
- Second or Subsequent Conviction for DUI Within Sixty Months
- Violation of Railroad Crossing Law or Regulation

The State May Suspend the License of a Driver for Any of the Following Offenses—
- Committing or Permitting Unlawful or Fraudulent Use of a License
- Conviction of Driving or Being in Actual Physical Control of a Motor Vehicle, While Under the Influence of Liquor or Drugs
- Failure to Pay Child Support
- Failure to Complete Traffic Survival School (TSS)
- Habitual Offender, Disrespect for Traffic Laws and the Safety of Others
- Incompetence
- Involvement in an Accident Resulting in Death, Personal Injury or Serious Property Damage
- Providing or purchasing spirituous liquor for an individual under 21
- Reckless Driving Conviction or Being Habitually Reckless or Negligent

The Following Suspensions are Mandated—
Drag Racing .... One year revocation
DUI for Minors Under 21 years of age .... Two-year suspension
Failure to Complete TSS for a Red Light Violation .... Indefinite suspension
Failure to Stop and Give Aid When Involved in an Accident Resulting in Personal Injury or Death:
    Revoked for 5 years if involving death or serious physical injury
    Revoked for 3 years if involving injury other than death or serious physical injury
    Suspended for 1 year if involving only damage to a vehicle
Moving Violations for Minors under 18 years of age (first violation not cited if subject attends driving school):
    3rd Violation (2nd conviction) .... Three-month suspension
    4th Violation (3rd conviction) .... Six-month suspension
    Refusal to Submit to a Chemical Test .... One-year suspension.

Reinstatement Requirements
Suspension $10.00 fee, plus re-application fee according to age; SR-22 required in some cases. $50.00 fee for DUI or "Admin Per Se."
Revocation $20.00 fee, plus re-application fee according to age; SR-22 may be required for three years; time lapse of at least one year.
Note: Disqualification for a BAC .04 in Commercial Motor Vehicle requires a $10.00 fee, plus re-application fee according to age; no SR-22 required.

Point System Overview
The Arizona point system ranges from 2 to 8 points. 8 to 12 points attained in one year will result in either a suspension or assignment to Traffic Survival School. 13 points or more in a one-year period will result in suspension.

License Plate Facts

Registration Renewal
Renewal is annual or biennial and is not systemically tied to last names or location. The MVD offers renewal of vehicle registration and address changes online at servicearizona.com.

New Residents
A new resident is required to immediately obtain AZ plates for his/her vehicle. A resident is generally defined as someone employed or with children in school.

Arizona

Inspections and Emissions Testing
Arizona has no provisions for statewide emission testing or annual safety inspections. However, Maricopa, Pima and portions of Yavapai and Pinal counties require an annual emissions test for vehicles manufactured in 1967 or later, but exempt most vehicles of the newest five years.

Plate Descriptions
Typical Plate Patterns .... Older issued passenger and light truck plates are 3 alpha and 3 numeric. Older issued commercial vehicles have 6 characters, typically 1 numeric, 2 alpha, and 3 numeric. Recently, the license plate field was expanded to 8 digits; personalized, alternate fuel, handicap, commercial and apportioned plates were expanded to 7 digits. New plates ranges include: handicap WC-AAANN; commercial C-ANNNNN: apportioned AANNNNN. Interstate trucks have an "X" as a first character.
County/City Codes...................... Arizona does not use a code on a plate designating the county of issuance.
Plates & Stickers in Force .... One plate, one tab. The tab displays the licensed number of the vehicle and the month and year of expiration.
Plate Remains with Car if Sold? . No. Effective January 1, 2002, the plates belong to the original owner.
Notes: Under the Title and Registration program, approved third parties can provide the following service: issue plates, tabs and titles; issue and renew registrations; and issue various temporary permits. Typical third parties are title service companies, dealer associations and companies with large fleets of vehicles, including car rental agencies.
About trailers weighing 6,000-10,000 lbs - A trailer will be permanently (PERM) registered with a one-time fee if it has a gross vehicle weight (GVW) of 10,000 lbs or less and is used for noncommercial purposes. Travel trailers and tent trailers are not eligible for the PERM designation. Trailers 10,000 lbs or less and classified as commercial must continue to be registered annually or biennially. If the trailer has a specialty and/or personalized plate, a renewal notice will be sent for the plate fee only.

Overview of Record Access

About Driving Records
Record Services Section, PO Box 2100, Mail Drop 504M, Phoenix 85001-2100, 602-255-0072. Arizona provides both a thirty-nine-month (insurance) record and a five-year record. Employers and individuals may request a five-year record. Fees vary by request method. For paper records, the fee for an uncertified 39-month record is $3.00 if accessed immediately (limit of 4 only) or $2.00 if picked up the next day. The fee is $5.00 for a certified 5-year record. For electronic records, the fee for an interactive record is $3.00 (39-month) and $5.00 (5-year) plus a $1.25 portal fee per record. An NRF is $3.00. The fee for batch records is $2.00 (39-month) and $3.00 (5-year) plus the portal fee of $1.25 per record. A NRF is $2.00. It takes a minimum of two weeks before new records are available for inquiry.
Request Methods – Mail, Walk-in, Online (call for details).
What You Should Know – A citation for "Speed Greater Than Reasonable and Prudent" allows the police officer to cite for speed due to conditions rather than specific miles per hour over limit. This cite is frequently used with accidents.
Special Access Programs Available – Arizona will sell driver history or status in bulk if the purpose is DPPA related. Reportedly, at least one vendor is using the courts to monitor drivers, and not the DMV.

About Vehicle Records
Record Services Section, PO Box 2100, Mail Drop 504M (Note - driving records is 539M, vehicles is 504M), Phoenix 85001, 602-712-8420. The Record Services Section handles search requests for vehicles and mobile homes, both attached and unattached. Fee is $3.00, but if dropped off and picked up overnight $2.00; and certified requests are $5.00. The $3.00 search fee is for a legal document which is defined as one page, both sides. Vehicle liens are filed with the MVD. A title history will show liens. A separate lienholder record may be purchased for $1.50.
Request Methods – Mail, Walk-in, Fax, Online, Bulk.

About Watercraft Records
Game & Fish Department, 5000 West Carefree Highway, Phoenix 85086, 602-942-3000, fax is 623-236-7919. www.azgfd.gov/outdoor_recreation/boating.shtml. All watercraft must be registered unless they are non-motorized. Titles are not required in this state. Records are available from 1977 to present but only indexed on computer the past 5 years. Anyone can search in-person or by mail but only if either the hull ID, owner's name, or registration # is presented. Otherwise, record release with personal information follows DPPA guidelines. Also, the department is selective as to who can receive record information by phone. These requesters are limited to law enforcement, private investigators and attorneys. Mail requests are returned within 30 days. There is no fee. Lien records are not maintained here and must be researched at the county recorder offices. Note that the agency no longer accepts watercraft renewals by telephone.

Arkansas

Administration	Important Telephone and Web Contacts	
Tonie Shields, Administrator Office of Driver Services PO Box 1272, Room 2067 Little Rock 72203 501-682-7060 www.accessarkansas.org/dfa/motor_vehicle/mv_index.html	Driver License Issuance	501-682-7059
	Driver Control	501-682-1631
	Driving Records	501-682-7207
	Financial/Safety Responsibility	501-682-7098 or 7100
	Insurance Verification	501-682-7930
	Commercial Driver License	501-682-1400
Office of Motor Vehicles PO Box 1272 Little Rock 72203 501-682-4661 www.dfa.arkansas.gov/offices/motorVehicle/Pages/default.aspx	Titles & Registration	501-682-3333 or 501-682-4702
	IRP	501-682-4651
	State Dept of Insurance	501-371-2600
	General Email (records)	anita.boatman@rev.state.ar.us
	State Statutes found at	www.arkleg.state.ar.us/

Driver License Facts

License Format
Until July 2003, the number consisted of either the Social Security Number (SSN) or nine numbers. Since 07/03, the SSN is no longer permitted to be used as the DL number. Prior to July 2003 and if the DL is not the Social Security Number, the first digit is "9," the next seven are sequential, and the last is a check digit.

Document Appearance
As of December 11, 2006, Arkansas began issuing new DLs and IDs using a vertical format for drivers under 21 and under 18. It will take at least until 2011 for all older formats to be replaced. Below are profiles of both styles.

Document if Over 21
Core is card stock laminated with Advantage laminate.

Security Characteristics	The state seal is over the bottom half of the license.
Position of Photo	Lower left.
CDL Indicator	COMMERCIAL DRIVERS LICENSE" is printed in heading.

Document if Under 21
The core card stock is the same. The biggest differences are in format and colors. Vertical cards are issued to drivers under 21.

Position of Photo	Photo on the middle left edge and a smaller portrait photo on the lower left edge.
Current Minor Age Locator	"UNDER 18 UNTIL..." if applicable printed in yellow bar under the photo. "UNDER 21 UNTIL..." printed in red bar under the age 18 yellow bar or under the photo.
Old Minor Age Locator	"UNDER 21 UNTIL..." or "UNDER 18 UNTIL..." is printed in red below portrait.
CDL Indicator	"COMMERCIAL DRIVERS LICENSE" is printed in heading above name, in red block. A state outline is on upper right side in blue.

Issue and Renewal

Age Requirements
The Arkansas graduated licensing law, which became effective July 1st, 2002, provides for a progressive driver licensing program for young drivers. The three levels of licensing are Learner's, Intermediate and Regular licenses. The minimum for a Learner's License is fourteen; age sixteen to eighteen get an Intermediate License. All new licensees under eighteen must be accompanied by licensed adult for at least 6 months. A regular license is issued to a person at age 18 when the Intermediate License expires. Holders of an Intermediate Drivers License issued on or after July 31, 2009 are 1) Prohibited from operating a motor vehicle with more than one unrelated minor passenger unless accompanied by a licensed driver 21 years of age or older; 2) prohibited from operating a motor vehicle between the hours of 11:00 PM and 4:00 AM unless the licensee is: accompanied by a person 21 years of age or older; driving to or from a school activity,

church-related activity, or job; or driving because of an emergency. Applicants for a Regular License must have a record without any serious accidents or serious traffic convictions within the most recent 12 months. If the applicant has such accident or conviction within the most recent 12 months, he/she must retain the Intermediate License until such time that the record is free of these accidents/convictions for a period of 12 months. The age restrictions in this program do not apply to a person 16 years of age or older if such person is (A) married, (B) possesses a high school diploma, (C) has successfully completed a General Education Development test, or (D) is enlisted in the United States Military.

Renewal
Renewal is on birth date of fourth year. Driver keeps same number when renewing. Renewal is not offered online. Military personnel may renew by mail, but they must pass a vision examination with the results and signature of the examiner on the application provided by state.

Elderly-Related Restrictions
None.

Residency
A person must obtain an AR Driver License within thirty days of establishing residency. If the out-of-state license is expired over 31 days but less than one year, the driver is be required to take the written and vision examination, but will not be required to take the road examination. If the out-of-state license is expired over one year, the driver is required to take the written, vision, and road examination.

License Classes
Commercial Classifications
Class A	Combination vehicle with a GVWR of 26,001 pounds or more, provided that the GVWR of the vehicle(s) being towed is in excess of 10,000 pounds. Minimum age is 18.
Class B	Any single vehicle with a GVWR of 26,001 pounds or more, and any such vehicle towing a vehicle less than 10,000 pounds. Minimum age is 18.
Class C	Any single vehicle with a GVWR of less than 26,001 pounds or any such vehicle towing a vehicle with a GVWR less than 26,001 pounds or any such vehicle towing a vehicle with a GVWR not in excess of 10,000 pounds, comprising: 1) vehicles designed to transport sixteen (16) or more passengers, including the driver; and 2) vehicles used in the transportation of hazardous materials which requires the vehicle to be placarded under 49 CFR, part 172, sub-part F. Minimum age is 18.

Restricted Commercial Classifications
Class B or C	Issued to seasonal drivers of farm retail outlets and suppliers, agri-chemical, custom harvesters and livestock feeders. Restricts operating Class B or C vehicles only during a season not to exceed 180 days in a 12-month period.

Non-Commercial Classifications
Class D	Any vehicle which is not a commercial vehicle as defined above. Minimum age 14 with licensed adult; age 14 to 16 must hold adult restriction a minimum of 6 months.
Class ID	Identification Card.
Class M	Motorcycle only (over 250cc) - Minimum age 16.
Class MD	Motor Driven Cycle (50cc through 250cc) - Minimum age 14, expires on 16th birth date.
Class X	Dummy License.

Note: Employers are required by Arkansas law to search the Arkansas Commercial Driver Alcohol and Drug Testing Database prior to hiring commercial drivers. Employers are also required by Arkansas law to report a positive alcohol test result to the database for commercial drivers. In addition, employers must report drivers to the database that refuse to submit to an alcohol test.

HAZmat Procedures
The state is in compliance with the Patriot Act. All applicants applying for a new or renewal or transfer HAZMAT Endorsement (HME) must first obtain the application from https://hazprints.tsa.dhs.gov/Public/ or by calling 877-429-7746. The driver must also be fingerprinted. EMSI is the state-designated entity to process fingerprints. There are two locations in the state that perform this service. Visit the web page listed above to find these address locations. The cost of the application and fingerprint process is $89.25. At present, there is no agency website that details the procedures. The fingerprints and application information is sent to the Federal Transportation Security Administration (TSA). TSA performs the background checks and notifies the DMV whether the application is approved or denied. When completed and approved, the HME is valid for five years.

Safety and Enforcement Facts

Insurance and Financial Responsibility
Proof of insurance (compulsory) is required at registration, after a reportable accident, and upon demand from police. Minimum financial responsibility limits are $25,000/50,000/25,000..

Alcohol and Chemical Testing
The legal limit of alcohol level is .08 % for non-commercial drivers, .04 % for commercial drivers, and .02 % for drivers under 21. Arkansas will conduct urine, blood, and breath tests. The Arkansas under-the-influence law contains a provision for implied consent.

Crash Reporting
A Safety Responsibility SR-1 accident report must be submitted within thirty days when damage to the property of any one person is in excess of $500 or results in the injury or death of any person regardless of who is at fault. The report is submitted to the police as well as the Safety Responsibility Section, Department of Revenue, PO Box 1272, Little Rock 72203 (501-682-7098). The report can be filed online at https://www.ark.org/dfa/sr1/index.html or downloaded from www.accessarkansas.org/dfa/motor_vehicle/pdf/sr1.pdf or by calling Safety Responsibility at 501-682-7098. Otherwise write to the State Police at #1 State Police Plaza, Little Rock AR 72209, 501-618-8130 or visit www.asp.state.ar.us/divisions/rs/rs_crash.html.

Suspensions and Revocations
The state is in compliance with the mandatory CDL disqualifications per federal regulations as shown in the Appendix. Other mandatory suspension and revocations are shown below.

Accumulation of Points
- Fourteen to Seventeen Points .... Possible three- to six-month suspension.
- Eighteen to Twenty-three Points .... Possible six- to twelve-month suspension.
- Twenty-four or More Points.............. Possible one-year suspension—may be subject to possible one-year revocation.

DWI Suspensions
- First Offense (if .08 to .14 BAC)........ Minimum 120 days.
- First Offense (if .15 BAC or higher) . Minimum 180 days.
- Second Offense .... Minimum 2 years.
- Third Offense .... Minimum 30 months.
- Fourth Offense .... Mandatory four-year revocation.

No Proof of Financial Responsibility..... Indefinite suspension.
Unsatisfied Judgment (accidents) .... Indefinite suspension.
Refused Chemical Test .... First offense - 180 day suspension.

Reinstatement Requirements
Suspension   Determined by point accumulation and reason for suspension. $100.00 fee; $150.00 if DWI.
Revocation   May reapply after one-year time-lapse, test required. $100.00 fee; $150.00 if DWI.
Note: If convicted of DUI, must also complete a rehabilitation program before reinstatement.

Point System Overview
Points are assigned for various traffic violations ranging from 0 to 14 points depending on the severity of the violation. Accumulation of 10 through 13 points will result in a computer-generated warning letter. Accumulation of 14 or more points may result in driving privilege suspension for up to one year.

License Plate Facts

Registration Renewal
Annual renewal of registration is online at www.arstar.com/. Operators can also make addresses changes online.

New Residents
Non-residents must register vehicles within thirty days of becoming a resident.

Inspections and Emissions Testing
At one time Arkansas had a required annual safety inspection, but this was no longer required as of 01/01/98. There are no statewide provisions for emissions inspections.

Plate Descriptions
Typical Plate Patterns   Passenger plates and light trucks are three alpha followed by three numbers or three numbers followed by three alpha. Commercial vehicles are one alpha followed by

Arkansas

County/City Codes	four to six numbers. The county of issuance is not coded or identified.
Plates and Stickers in Force	One plate, two decals (MO) (YR).
Plate Remains with Car if Sold?	Plate remains with seller on passenger cars and light truck. Plate may either remain with seller or transfers to buyer on large trucks.

Overview of Record Access

About Driving Records
Department of Driver Services, Driving Records Division, PO Box 1272, Room 1130, Little Rock AR 72203, 501-682-7207. www.accessarkansas.org/dfa/motor_vehicle/mv_index.html

The fees for manual records are $7.00 for an insurance type record (generally a three-year record) and $10.00 for employment and commercial driver records (may contain information longer than the three years). Fees for online access are higher at $8.50 for insurance record or $11.50 for commercial record, plus an annual subscription fee. The last fee increase was in January of 1990 and there are no increases planned for this year. There is a full charge for "no record found" reports.

Request Methods – Mail, Walk-in, Online.

What You Should Know – Violations on an interstate (not exceeding 75 mph) are not reported on an insurance record, but are listed if the record is requested for employment or law-enforcement purposes.

Special Access Programs Available – A monitoring and notification system for approved requesters to track incidents of drivers is available from Arkansas.gov (http://portal.arkansas.gov/services/Pages/servicesINA.aspx). The program, called Driver Watch, permits employers to receive notification on the change in the driver license status for registered employees. The fee is $11.50 per record; employers must be subscribers. Also, a weekly status check can be provided for an additional fee.

About Crash Reports
Copies of accident reports are sold by the Arkansas State Police, Crash Records Section, #1 State Police Plaza, Little Rock AR 72209, 501-618-8130. Requests must include the name of the driver, the location, and the date of the accident. Enclose $10.00 for each request and include a SASE. Access is also available online at www.asp.state.ar.us/divisions/rs/rs_crash.html. There is no fee to search, but a PDF copy of the report is $12.00. Use of a credit card is required, unless requester has an INA account. Records are available from 01/02/00 to present. Older records normally are not archived, but destroyed. Mail turnaround time is normally two to three weeks. It takes 1-2 weeks before new records are available for inquiry.

About Vehicle Records
Office of Motor Vehicles, MV Title Records, PO Box 1272, Room 1100, Little Rock 72203, (800) 662-8247, 501-682-4692, fax 501-682-4756. The Office of Motor Vehicles maintains title, registration, and lien records for vehicles and mobile homes. Also, this agency registers vessels; however, lien records on boats are found at the county level or at Secretary of State. Records are available from 1968 for plate information on microfiche. The agency films all records and does not hold paper copies. It takes 4 to 6 weeks before new records are available. Social Security Numbers are not released.

Request Methods – Mail, Walk-in, Telephone, Fax, Online, Bulk (limited)

What You Should Know – The current fee for VIN, registration checks, vehicle lien records, or boat registration records is $1.00 per search and $1.00 per copy of a record.

About Watercraft Records
All sail boats and all motorized boats must be registered with the Office of Motor Vehicles. Vessels are not titled by the state. The state has determined that boats do not fall under the rule of DPPA. Records are available from 1980. Search by name or registration number or hull number. Lien information is not shown since it is recorded at the Secretary of State office or at the local county level. The search fee is $1.00 per search and $1.00 per copy of a record. Account holders may order by phone or fax. Bulk purchase is available via FTP.

California

Administration	Important Telephone and Web Contacts
George Valverde, Director Jim Woodward, Chief of Information Services Department of Motor Vehicles, M/S F101 2415 First Ave, Sacramento 95818 Fax: 916-657-7393 www.dmv.ca.gov/ Note: The Department of Motor Vehicles is closed on the first three Fridays of each month through June 2010.	Mandatory Actions ....916-657 6525 Automated Service ....800-777-0133 Record Information ....916-657-8098 Commercial Requester Accounts ....916-657-5564 Financial Responsibility ....916-657-6677 Commercial Driver License.........................916-657-5771 State Department of Insurance ....213-897-8921 CA Only 800-927-4357 Highway Patrol Headquarters......................916-657-7261 Email Contacts www.dmv.ca.gov/contacts/contacts.htm CA Code Book www.dmv.ca.gov/pubs/vctop/vc/vc.htm

Driver License Facts

License Format
The driver license or identification card (DL/ID card) number has one letter followed by seven numbers which is computer generated but not in sequential order.

Document Appearance
Since July 1, 2001, the Department has distributed a distinctly secure, driver license with technologies to deter identity thieves and other criminals from duplicating or manufacturing fraudulent copies.

Security Characteristics   DL/ID number, expiration date, and birth date printed in red; a second, smaller picture of the holder; security features only seen under an ultraviolet light; fine line printing to deter scanning and photocopying; image of state flag across bottom; holograms of state seal and the DMV logo across the card; and a bar code and encoded magnetic stripe on back. **Older versions** many contain the following: DL number printed in green; micro-printing of California DMV; variations of print size on face of card; holograms of state seal and the DMV logo across the card; reflective laminate security with bar code and encoded magnetic stripe on the back.

Position of Photo   Adult is bottom left; minor bottom right.

Minor Age Driver Locator   Photo location and "AGE 21 in (year)" is in red bar, or "AGE 18 in (year)" is in blue bar.

CDL Indicator   Commercial Driver License is printed in red letters.

Issue and Renewal

Age Requirements
A Minor's Provisional Permit is issued to drivers at least 15 1/2 but under 18. A Minor's Provisional License is issued to drivers at least 16 until age 18. There are several requirements and restrictions that apply to the provisional permit and license holder, see the California Driver Handbook or visit www.dmv.ca.gov.

Renewal
The renewal license is valid for five birthdays from date of first application. The same DL/ID number is issued each time. Drivers may renew or make a change of address online at www.dmv.ca.gov/online/onlinesvcs.htm. See this site for eligibility information. Military personnel stationed outside of California may extend their licenses by mail (PO Box 942892, Sacramento 94290) or by telephone (916-657-7790). The license is considered valid beyond its normal expiration date while on active military duty in the U.S. Armed Forces.

Elderly-Related Restrictions
There are none, other than at age 70 a driver is not eligible for renewal by mail and the vision is checked once every renewal period or more often is required.

California

Residency
Non-residents must obtain California license with 10 days of establishing residency. Visitors between the ages of 16 and 18 may only drive for 10 days with a home state license or instruction permit. After 10 days, these drivers must obtain a Nonresident Minor's Certificate or a CA license.

License Classes
There are 10 classes of license.

- **Class A** — Allows any combination of vehicles, including Class B or a transit bus with a passenger transport endorsement and all vehicles listed under Class B and C. May tow any single vehicle with a GVWR of more than 10,000 lbs, more than one vehicle with endorsement, or a trailer bus with a passenger endorsement.
- **Class A Firefighter** — Operate Class A and B defined combination fire fighting vehicles and all vehicles listed under Class C. May tow a single fire fighting vehicle with GVWR of more than 10,000 lbs.
- **Class A Noncommercial** — Operate all vehicles listed under Class C. May tow a trailer coaches exceeding 10,000 pounds GVWR or any fifth-wheel travel trailer exceeding 15,000 pounds GVWR when not used in commerce or to transport passengers. With a vehicle weighing 4,000 lbs or more unladen, may tow a livestock trailer exceeding 10,000 lbs GVWR but not exceeding 15,000 GVWR if the vehicle is controlled and operated by a farmer, used to transport livestock to or from a farm, not used in commerce or contract carrier operations, and is used within 150 miles of the person's farm.
- **Class B** — Operate any single vehicle in excess of 26,000 GVWR, a three-axle vehicle over 6,000 lbs gross, any bus (except a trailer bus) with endorsement, any farm labor vehicle with endorsement, and all vehicles listed under Class C. May tow a single vehicle with GVWR of 10,000 lbs or less.
- **Class B Firefighter** — Operate only Class B defined single fire fighting vehicles and all vehicles listed under Class C. May tow a single vehicle with GVWR of 10,000 lbs or less or any vehicle under class.
- **Class B Noncommercial** — Operate a house car that is over 40 feet, but not over 45 feet on specified highway with endorsement. May tow any vehicle listed under Class C.
- **Class C Commercial** — Operate any Class C vehicle carrying hazardous materials or wastes which require placards. HAZMAT (hazardous materials) endorsement must be on license. Otherwise, may drive and tow the same vehicles listed in Class C.
- **Class C** — Operate any two-axle vehicle with GVWR of 26,000 lbs or less; a motorized scooter, any three-axle vehicle weighing 6,000 lbs or less gross; any house car 40 feet or less; a vanpool vehicle designed to carry more than 10 but not more than 15 persons including the driver. (See website for more information.) May tow a single vehicle with a GVWR of 10,000 lbs or less including a tow dolly, if used; a boat trailer under 26,000 lbs for recreational purposes or repair. With a vehicle weighing at least 4,000 pounds GVWR may tow (when not for compensation) any trailer coach not exceeding 9,000 lbs fully loaded or a fifth-wheel trailer over 10,000 lbs GVWR, but under 15,000 lbs GVWR with endorsement. May operate Class M1, M2 or both with endorsement.
- **Class M1** — May drive a two-wheel motorcycle or motor-driven cycle or motorized scooter.
- **Class M2** — May drive any motorized bicycle, moped or any bicycle with an attached motor or motorized scooter.

Note: With Class A, B, or C license may drive an ambulance used commercially in emergency service with an Ambulance Driver Certificate.

About Commercial Vehicles
A **"commercial vehicle"** means a motor vehicle or combination of vehicles used in commerce to transport passengers or property when any of the following conditions apply to the vehicle:

- A single vehicle with a GVWR of 26,001 pounds or more.
- A trailer with a GVWR of 10,001 pounds or more.
- Towing a set of double-trailers—regardless of weight.
- Towing a trailer-bus.
- Any vehicle which transports hazardous materials requiring placarding.
- A bus designed, used or maintained to transport more than ten passengers—including driver (except van-pools and vans designed to carry not more than fifteen persons while carrying only family members).

Note: The Commercial Vehicle Registration Act of 2001 (CVRA) requires most commercial vehicle registered owner(s)/lessee(s) to declare the operating weight of their commercial motor vehicle, or combination, and the heaviest load upon registration or renew whenever the operating weight changes.

About Implements of Husbandry
A driver license is not required when operating implements of husbandry incidentally operated or moved over a highway. A license of the appropriate class is required when operating other types of farm vehicles.

HAZMAT Endorsement Procedure
The state is in compliance with the Patriot Act. All applicants applying for a new or renewal or transfer HAZMAT Endorsement (HME) must first obtain the application from https://hazprints.tsa.dhs.gov/Public/ or by calling 877-429-7746. The driver must also be fingerprinted. EMSI and COMNETIX are the state-designated entities to process fingerprints. There are thirteen locations in the state that perform this service. Visit the web page listed above to find the address locations. An excellent web page that explains the program and fees is found at www.dmv.ca.gov/pubs/cdl_htm/sec9_a.htm. The fingerprints and application information is sent to the Federal Transportation Security Administration (TSA). TSA performs the background checks and notifies the DMV whether the application is approved or denied. When completed and approved, the HME is valid for five years.

Safety and Enforcement Facts

Insurance and Financial Responsibility
Minimum automobile liability insurance requirements are $15,000 for a single injury or death; $30,000 for injury to, or death of, more than one person; $5,000 for property damage caused by one accident. If a driver is under 18 years of age, the parents (or guardians) are responsible and liable for insurance and/or financial responsibility. A bond or cash deposit of $35,000 is acceptable alternatives (CVC §16434 and §16435). Liability insurance is required for drivers and vehicle owners.

Alcohol and Chemical Testing
For anyone who drives a commercial or non-commercial vehicle or vessel, aquaplane, water skis or similar devices, the limits for alcoholic consumption are .08 percent for adults and .01 percent for persons under 21. For a commercial driver (CDL) or for those who operate any vessel other than a recreational one, the limit is .04 or more percent. Driver license or permit holders have given their consent to take a blood or breath test (or urine under certain circumstances) if arrested or detained for driving under the influence. One can also be cited for driving under the influence if using any drug that impairs. The law does not distinguish between prescription, over-the-counter, or illegal drugs.

Ignition Interlock Devices (IIDs) must be installed on vehicles owned and operated by motorists convicted of driving on a suspended license due to a previous alcohol-related conviction. A 2009 law changed the administration of mandatory IID programs from the state courts to the Department of Motor Vehicles. This law also authorizes the DMV to require any driver convicted of driving with a suspended license due to a prior conviction for DUI to install an IID in any vehicle that the offender owns or operates.

Accident Reporting
Accidents resulting in bodily injury or death of any person involved in accident or damages in excess of $750.00 must be reported within ten days to the Department of Motor Vehicles, Financial Responsibility Office, P.O. Box 942884, Mail Station J-237, Sacramento, CA 94284-0884. This is regardless of fault and even if the accident occurred on private property. The form, Report of Traffic Accident Occurring California SR1 is available at www.dmv.ca.gov/forms/sr/sr1.pdf. Failure to submit the form will result in a suspension. This is in addition to any other report made to the police, California Highway Patrol or an insurance company. Accidents resulting in death or injury must be reported within twenty-four hours to the Highway Patrol or local police.

Commercial drivers are required to report to their employer *and* the Department—within thirty days of conviction—any out-of-state convictions received while driving. Under CVC Section 16002, commercial drivers must report accidents to their employers within five days, and the employer is required to file Form SR-1 (CA Traffic Accident Report) with the state within ten days. Commercial carriers must file a second report with the California Highway Patrol on or before the tenth day of the month that follows an accident which results in death or injury. Reports are to be sent to: California Highway Patrol, Data Processing Section, PO Box 942898, Sacramento, CA 94298-0001.

Suspensions and Revocations
The state is in compliance with the **federally mandated disqualifications on CDLs**. See the Appendix for details.

Failure to Appear The Failure to Appear (FTA) in traffic court (ignoring a traffic ticket) or Failure to Pay (FTP) a fine will appear on the driving record, and may cause the Department to suspend a license. A holder of Provisional License will be suspended for a FTP.

Negligent Operator
Class C or M
- Four or more points in twelve months
- Six or more points in twenty-four months
- Eight or more points in thirty-six months

Commercial Drivers and Fire-Fighters
- Six or more points in twelve months
- Eight or more points in twenty-four months
- Ten or more points in thirty-six months

In order for a commercial driver to be eligible for consideration under the higher point count, the commercial driver must request a hearing and appear. Additionally, the higher point count does not apply to certificate holders, drivers with hazardous materials endorsements or if the citations are attributable to the operation on a non-commercial vehicle.

Effective 2007, the state eliminated the issuance of a restricted commercial driver's license when privilege was suspended or because of serious family related health problem. The CDL holder may still operate a non-commercial vehicle if issued a restricted Class C or M license.

The department may suspend and place on probation or revoke the driving privilege of a negligent operator (as defined above). Although a Class A or B driver without a special certificate may be allowed two additional points, a violation received in a commercial vehicle carries one and one-half times the point-count normally assessed. A minor under eighteen may receive a thirty-day restriction for two points in twelve months or be suspended for three points in twelve months.

Conviction of Hit-and-Run or Reckless Driving Resulting in Injury .... License may be revoked.

Breaking Speed Laws (greater than 100 mph) or Reckless Driving
- First Conviction .... Up to thirty-day suspension, and up to $1000 fine.
- Subsequent Conviction Within Thirty-Six Months .... Six-month suspension, and up to $1000 fine.
- Subsequent Conviction Within Five Years .... One-year suspension, and up to $1000 fine.

Refusal to Submit to Chemical Test (Blood, Breath, Urine or PAS)
- First Offense .... One-year suspension.
- Second Offense (within ten years): .... Two-year revocation.
- Third Offense (within ten years): .... Three-year revocation.

Admin Per Se (APS) Actions
- .08 BAC or Higher, Over 21, Non-CDL, First Offense .... Four-month suspension.
- .01 BAC, Under 21, Non-CDL, First Offense .... One-year suspension.
- CDL Driver in Non-CDL Vehicle, First Offense .... Four-month suspension.
- CDL Driver in CDL Vehicle, First Offense .... Four-month suspension.
- Second Offense (within seven years), for All Above .... One-year suspension.

Note: Effective 01/01/2009, an APS Zero Tolerance Law took affect. If driver is on probation for a DUI offense and found operating a motor vehicle at any time with BAC of .0.01% or greater a one-year suspension is imposed. Refusal or failure to complete preliminary alcohol screening or chemical test while on probation will result in two-year revocation.

DUI Actions
Note: Effective 07/01/2009, if driver with prior DUI conviction is convicted of driving with a suspended license, the DMV will require installation and use of Ignition Interlock Device.

Non-Commercial Drivers over 21 with BAC of .08 or higher
- First Offense .... Six-month to one-year suspension.
- Second Offense (within ten years) .... 18-month to two-year suspension.
- Third Offense (within ten years) .... Three-year revocation.
- Fourth or Subsequent Offense (within ten years) .... Four-year revocation.

Non-Commercial Drivers over 21 with BAC of .20% or higher
Mandatory ten-month suspension and court ordered treatment program.

Commercial Driver in CDL Vehicle with BAC of .04% or higher
- First Offense .... Three-year commercial disqualification.
- Second Offense (within ten years) .... Lifetime disqualification.
- Third Offense (within ten years) .... Three-year revocation.
- Fourth or Subsequent Offense (within ten years) .... Four-year revocation.

Under 21 years of Age with BAC of .01 or higher

First Offense.. One-year disqualification.
Second Offense in Ten Years.................................. Revoked for two years.
Third and Subsequent Offense in Ten Years........... Revoked for three years.
Commercial Drivers, but if offense did not occur in a commercial vehicle:
First Offense.. One-year disqualification.
Second and Subsequent Offense .... Lifetime disqualification, but eligible for reinstatement in 10 years.

Habitual Truant-Minor
Persons aged 13 to 18 will lose license one year if convicted for being a habitual truant from school.

Possessing Firearms-Minor
Court will suspend or revoke driving privilege of any minor convicted of possessing a concealable weapon or live ammunition, or impose DL sanctions for minors convicted of misdemeanors involving firearms.

Road Rage
First Offense..Six-month suspension.
Second or Subsequent Offense...........One-year suspension.

Other Convictions Which May Result in a Suspension or Revocation of Driving Privileges
- Reckless Driving
- Recklessly Fleeing a Police Officer
- Vandalism
- Failure to Comply with Financial Responsibility Law
- Vehicle Theft
- Unlawful Use of Driver License
- Errant in Family Support Payments

Lack of Insurance
Since October 1, 2006, vehicle registrations are subject to suspension when:
- DMV is notified that a policy has been cancelled and a replacement policy has not been submitted within 45 days.
- Insurance information is not submitted to DMV within 30 days of the issuance of a registration card upon initial registration or transfer of ownership.
- The registration is obtained by providing false evidence of insurance..

Reinstatement Requirements
Suspension ....$$55 fee; SR1P/SR-22 required in some cases.
Revocations...$55 fee; SR-22 required in some cases.
If Admin Per Se Suspension or Revocation ....$125 fee ($100 if under 21); SR-22 required.
Excessive BAC ....$100 fee; SR-22 in all cases; Drinking Driver Program completion.
Note: There is an additional $120 fee if a departmental review of an Admin Per Se hearing decision is requested.

Point System Overview
Most moving violation driving offenses, such as hit and run or reckless driving are designated as 2 points and will remain on the record for 7 years from the violation date. If DUI-related then 10 years. Most other offenses are designated as 1 point and remain on the record for 3 years from the violation date. An "at fault" accident is normally counted as 1 point.

License Plate Facts

Registration & Renewal
Computer generated billing notices are mailed approximately 60 days prior to registration renewal date. If the notice includes a Registration Identification Number (RIN) the renewal may be processed online at www.dmv.ca.gov/online/onlinesvcs.htm.
Note about OHVs: Off-highway vehicles (OHV) must be operated exclusively off the highway on lands that are open and accessible to the public. The vehicle must display an identification plate issued by DMV. OHV vehicles include trail bikes, dune buggies, all-terrain vehicles, motorcycles, and snowmobiles.

New Residents
Owners must register vehicles within twenty days of establishing residency or upon accepting employment.

Inspections and Emissions Testing
A valid Smog Certificate is required for original/initial CA registration and for transfer of ownership. In addition, every two years (biennially) for renewal of registration for those vehicles registered in areas of the state subject to the Program. Check the Bureau of Automotive Repair website for the included areas at www.smogcheck.ca.gov. The following

vehicles are exempt from all smog requirements: diesel powered; electric; natural gas powered with a GV rating of 14,001 pounds or more; hybrid; 1975 or older model; motorcycle; and trailer. See the website for further explanation and exemptions.

The owner/seller must provide evidence of a current smog certification to the buyer except when a transfer occurs between a spouse, sibling, child, parent, grandparent, and grandchild. For vehicles sold or transferred, if the vehicle had a biennial inspection within 90 days of the transfer date, another smog certificate is not required.

Plate Descriptions

Typical Plate Patterns	Passenger plates are LLLNNN or NNNLLL or NLLLNNN. Commercial vehicle plates are NLNNNNN. Motorcycles plates are NNNNNN and NN LNNN.
County/City Codes	The county of issuance is not designated on the plate.
Plates and Stickers in Force	Plates are a variety of colors and designs; stickers change colors every year except boats and off-highway vehicles are every two years. Passenger and pickups are issued and must display two plates. The two stickers (mo) (yr) are on the back plate only.
	Commercial truck tractor trailers are issued one plate and two stickers (mo) (yr) and must be displayed on the front of the vehicle.
	Motorcycles are issued one plate, two decals (mo) (yr) and must be displayed on the back of the vehicle.
	Trailer coaches and park trailers are not part of the Permanent Trailer Identification (PTI) Program and will display a single trailer plate with two stickers (mo) (yr) on the back of the vehicle.
Plates Remain with Car when Sold?	Yes, except for special interest and personalized plates.

Overview of Record Access

About Driving Records

Department of Motor Vehicles, Information Services Branch, PO Box 944247, Mail Station G199, Sacramento 94244-2470. Information: 916-657-8098. **The DMV (and many other state offices) are closed the first three Fridays of each month.** Requests for forms (twenty-five or less) may be submitted in writing to the Department of Motor Vehicles, Public Contact Unit at the address listed above, or by telephone at 916-657-8098. Large requests for forms (over twenty-five) must be submitted in writing to: Department of Motor Vehicles, Forms and Accountable Items Unit, P.O. Box 932382, Sacramento, California 94232-3820 or fax your request on letterhead to 916-657-7243. Forms are provided at no fee to the requester. Visit the Department's website at www.dmv.ca.gov for information request forms, publications, Vehicle Code and related information. California has an extensive coding system for violations. Driving records are coded with very brief citation descriptions provided. *The MVR Access and Decoder Digest* provides a table with the codes and extensive descriptions for convictions found on driving records.

Note: The Department of Motor Vehicles is closed on the first three Fridays of each month through June 2010.

Requester Accounts

To establish a Requester Account, applicants must complete an application, pay the appropriate enrollment fee, sign a Requester Account Agreement, and receive approval from the Department. The enrollment fee is based on the type of record information requested ($50 or $250). Applicants who are statutorily authorized and are requesting confidential residence address information will be required to submit a $50,000 Surety Bond. For more information call 916-657-5564 or write to the following address: Department of Motor Vehicles, Account Processing Unit, Mail Station H221, PO Box 944231, Sacramento, California 94244-2310.

Non-Permissible Use Requesters

See detail description above. Non-permissible use requesters who want general information regarding forms, service fees, type of records available, record search criteria, etc., may telephone the Information Services Branch (ISB), Public Contact Unit, Monday through Friday, between the hours of 8:00am and 5:00pm at 916-657-8098, or write to: Department of Motor Vehicles, Public and Commercial Operations, Mail Station G199, PO Box 944247, Sacramento, California 94244-2470. General information is also available at www.dmv.ca.gov.

Prices of Driver License Record Requests

Note: Personal checks are accepted; credit cards are not accepted.

Current Driver Record (by Full Name and Birth Date or Name and DL Number) $5.00
Current Driver Record by Electronic Means $2.00
Copy of DL/ID application including Guarantor's Signature (each year) $20.00
DL/ID Photo (each year) $20.00

Online Access $2.00
Status Response (restricted online) through an approved vendor...$1.00

Request Methods – Mail, Walk-in, Telephone (by subject only), Online, FTP Batch, Bulk.

What You Should Know – Most convictions of traffic offenses, such as hit and run, and reckless driving will remain on the record for 7 years from the violation date. Effective 01/01/07, a DUI remains on the record for 10 years and this rule is retroactive. Most other convictions of traffic offenses will remain on the record for 3 years from the violation date. Accidents are reported for 3 years from the accident date. Actions taken against driving privilege, such as a suspension or revocation due to a DUI or a failure to provide proof of financial responsibility, will be reported for 3 years from the proof termination date or the reinstatement date, whichever is earlier. A Failure To Appear for DUI offenses will be reported for 10 years from the violation date. All other Failure To Appear and Failure to Pay Fine citations will be reported for 5 years from the violation date.

Special Access Programs Available: – The Department offers a Pull Notice Program to provide employers and regulatory agencies with an ongoing method to monitor driver records. The employer enrolls specified drivers in the program and is notified when the record has activity. For more information visit the website at www.dmv.ca.gov/vehindustry/epn/epnformlist.htm or write the DMV care of the Employer Pull Notice Unit - H265 or call 916-657-6346.

Vehicle Records

Department of Motor Vehicles, Office of Information Services, PO Box 944247, Mail Station G199, Sacramento 94244-2470. Information: 916-657-8098. **The DMV (and many other state offices) are closed the first and third Friday of each month.** Requests for forms (twenty-five or less) may be submitted in writing to the Public Contact Unit at the address listed above or by telephone at 916-657-8098. Requests for numerous forms (over twenty-five) must be submitted in writing to: Department of Motor Vehicles, Forms and Accountable Items Unit, PO Box 932382, Sacramento, California 94232-3820 or fax your request on letterhead to 916-657-7243. Forms are provided at no fee to the requester. Visit the Department's website at www.dmv.ca.gov for information request forms, publications, Vehicle Code and related information. See fee list below.

Note: The Department of Motor Vehicles is closed on the first three Fridays of each month through June 2010.

Request Methods – Mail, Walk-in, FTP Batch, Online, Bulk.

Prices of Vehicle or Vessel Registration Record Requests

Current Record or Automated History
    By license, vehicle identification number, or vessel CF Number........................$5.00
    By registered owner name and complete residence address..............................$5.00
Online Access $2.00
Batch record..$2.00
Photocopy of Vehicle/Vessel Record Document (each year)................................$20.00

What You Should Know – The Department no longer requires a subpoena to access hardcopy/microfilmed vehicle registration records. The Department began microfilming all vehicle and vessel documents in 1992. Liens are filed here. There are some records dating back to 1976 that may be accessed. Records with no activity, such as tickets, renewals, transfers etc., are usually purged from the database after 4 years. Records and/or information specified by statute as confidential or non-reportable will not be provided by the Department.

Special Access Programs Available: – The Department offers a Pull Notice Program to provide employers and regulatory agencies with an ongoing method to monitor driver records. The employer enrolls specified drivers in the program and is notified when the record has activity. For more information visit the website at www.dmv.ca.gov/vehindustry/epn/epnformlist.htm or write the DMV care of the Employer Pull Notice Unit - H265 or call 916-657-6346.

More About Watercraft Records

Vessel records may be obtained from the Department of Motor Vehicles. Liens are filed here. This is a title and registration state. All motorized and sail, and watercraft over 8 ft (except rowboats) must be registered. This includes boats used or moored on private lakes. Name searches are permitted, but you must use the state form. The vessel owner is notified and has 10 days to respond if the owner does not want information released. The state will not release bulk information for commercial purposes. Visit www.dmv.ca.gov/boatsinfo/boat.htm for more information.

Colorado

Administration	Important Telephone and Web Contacts

Joan Vecchi
Senior Director
Division of Motor Vehicles
Denver 80261-0016
303-205-5600
 	
www.colorado.gov/revenue/dmv
	General Driver Information 303-205-5613
	Titles...303-205-5608
	Registration..303-205-5607
	Enforcement 303-205-5609
	Division of Insurance...303-894-7499
	State PoliceHeadquarters 303-239-4500
	Administration 303-239-4400
	
	Motor Vehicle Industry Laws and Regulations:
	    www.colorado.gov/revenue/AID
	
	Motor Vehicle Rules
	    At home page, click on *Driver's License* and then on *Rules and Regulations*

Driver License Facts

License Format
Since January 30, 1994, a permanent nine-digit numeric number has been issued to each driver. The format of the number is the Julian Date and a four number sequence.

Document Appearance
Both current and previous documents have a photographic backdrop of the mountains. The current document has been in force since October 2003. All licenses and ID cards are laminated and tamper-proof. All previously issued documents are valid until expiration. The probationary driver's license is red in color.

Current Documents
- **Security Characteristics**....... A repeating, optically variable, UV-sensitive gold state seal is across the bottom of adult documents and down the left side of Under 21 documents. All documents contain guilloche security designs and micro printing. All documents have a magstrip and a 2D barcode on the back with the demographic information that appears on the front.
- **Position of Photo**................... Left side, above name and address of card bearer. There is a ghost image of card bearer located under the demographic data on the front of the card.
- **Minor Age Driver Locator** .. Under 21 documents are in a vertical format. *Under 21* is printed in red in the center.
- **CDL Indicator** .... The words *Commercial Driver License* appear underneath the header "Colorado," otherwise the CDL format is identical to basic license.

Older Documents
- **Security Characteristics**....... The repeating, optically variable gold state seal, UV-sensitive as of July 202, is across the bottom of adult documents and is down the left side of Under 21 documents. All documents have a magstripe and 2D barcode on the back with the demographic information that appears on the front.
- **Position of Photo**................... Left side, above name and address of card bearer. There is a ghost image of card bearer located under the demographic data on the front of the card.
- **Minor Age Driver Locator** .. Under 21 documents are in a vertical format. *Under 21* is printed in red in the center.
- **CDL Indicator** .... The words *Commercial Driver License* appear underneath the header "Colorado," otherwise the CDL format is identical to basic license.

Issue and Renewal
Age Requirements
The minimum age is 21 for a full Adult license. Minor licenses expire 20 days after the 21st birthday. For drivers under 18, there are specific permits available. The ages and available permits for these teen drivers are as follows:

Driver Education Permit .... 15 years to 15 years 6 months. Valid for 3 years.
Driver Awareness Permit .... 15 years 6 months to 16 years. Valid for 3 years.
Minor Instruction Permit............. 16 years to 21 years of age. Valid for 3 years.

All permits for anyone under 18 years must be held at least 12 months. Since July 1, 2005, regardless when license issued, age under 18 cannot drive a vehicle carrying a passenger under 21 unless the driver license has been held for at least 6 months, and cannot drive a vehicle carrying more than one passenger under 21 unless license held for at least one year. See the web page for exceptions.

Renewal
Drivers can renew a DL and make a change of address at the same time online at https://www.colorado.gov/vroom/renewlicense/index.jsf. One can renew an expired driver's license or State ID online if it has not been expired for more than one year. Drivers 60 years of age and older may not renew online. A credit card and an email address are required. This program is not available to drivers with a CDL. Renewal is organized as follows:

Licenses issued May 26, 2005 forward...........................Birth month of fifth year.
Licenses issued from July 2001 through May 26, 2005 ..Birth month of tenth year.
Licenses issued August 1989 through June 2001............Birth month of fifth year.
CDL License..Four years.
Under 21 licenses..Twenty days after the twenty-first birthday.

The driver keeps the same license number when renewing. Colorado drivers holding a regular license may request a Driver License Renew By Mail Application from the Colorado Department of Revenue's web page. Only Colorado drivers with clear driving records may renew their driver license by mail or online. When relocating, Colorado drivers have 30 days to change the address on their license.

An out-of-state extension is a sticker that is issued to extend the expiration date of a license if a person is out-of-state when the license expires. A civilian extension is for one year from the expiration date and can only be issued once, unless the person is out of the country then a second extension can be issued with a separate request done within 90 days of expiration of the first extension. Due to medical and testing requirements for CDL drivers, only a 30-day extension is available. A military extension is good for three years from the expiration date of the license and you may only be issued one military extension.

Elderly-Related Restrictions
None reported.

Residency
Colorado defines a resident as any person who: 1) owns or operates a business in Colorado, or 2) obtains gainful employed in Colorado, or 3) has resided in Colorado continuously for a period of 90 consecutive days. After becoming a Colorado resident, the driver has 30 days to obtain a Colorado driver license and register their vehicle.

License Classes
Commercial Classifications
Class A   Any vehicle combination 26,001 pounds or more GCWR which tows another vehicle 10,001 pounds or more GVWR; includes Class B and C.
Class B   Any single unit vehicle 26,001 pounds or more GVWR. May tow another vehicle—provided it weighs 10,000 pounds or less; includes Class C.
Class C   Any single unit vehicle 26,000 pounds or less. May tow another vehicle— provided it weighs 10,000 pounds or less. Includes vehicles designed to transport 16 or more persons (includes driver) or to transport hazardous material in the vehicle which is required to be placarded.

Non-Commercial Classifications
Class R   Regular operator
Class M   Motorcycle (Effective October 1, 1999, no new Class M licenses were issued. The "M" will only appear as an endorsement on a Class R or on a CDL.)

Note: A probationary driver's license (red) is a license to drive, for limited purposes, usually driving to and from the place of employment or to perform duties in the course of employment, during the term of a license suspension. A driving privilege for Commercial Vehicles is not granted.

HAZMAT Endorsement Procedure
The state is in compliance with the Patriot Act. All applicants applying for a new or renewal or transfer HAZMAT Endorsement (HME) must first obtain the application from https://hazprints.tsa.dhs.gov/Public/ or by calling 877-429-7746. The driver must also be fingerprinted. EMSI and COMNETIX are the state-designated entities to process fingerprints. There are three locations in the state that perform this service. Visit the web page listed above to find the address locations. The cost of the fingerprint process is $89.25. An informative web page is found at www.colorado.gov/cs/satellite/revenue_mv/1189759516698.

The fingerprints and application information is sent to the Federal Transportation Security Administration (TSA). TSA performs the background checks and notifies the DMV whether the application is approved or denied. When completed and approved, the HME is valid for five years.

Safety and Enforcement Facts

Insurance and Financial Responsibility
The state's minimum financial responsibility limits are $25,000/50,000/15,000. Proof of liability insurance must be shown when reinstating driving privileges upon conviction of being an owner/operator of vehicle and not having liability insurance. SR-22 forms are used and must be shown for any financial responsibility suspension, or most revocations, for cancel & deny for physical or mental disabilities, or for cancellation of a CDL/PDL.

Alcohol and Chemical Testing
Colorado has a "violation of driving under the influence," if alcohol content is .08 percent or greater, .02 or greater if the driver is under 21. If content is .05 percent to .079 percent, the violation is "driving while impaired." Colorado also has an "expressed consent" law, which allows the administration to revoke for failure to take a test for alcohol or drugs. Also allows for revocation if BAC is .08 or greater (.04 for commercial drivers and .02 for under 21). Only breath or blood tests are sanctioned for alcohol; urine and blood tests are sanctioned for drugs.

Accident Reporting
Accidents involving damage or any injury or death must be reported immediately to the local law enforcement agency. If no police officer was called to the scene of the accident, driver can obtain the form to file an accident report or can file online at https://crash.state.co.us/. If a police officer was called to the scene to obtain all the needed information, the person does not need to provide any forms unless he/she receives a letter from this department.

Suspensions and Revocations
The state is in compliance with the federally mandated disqualifications on CDLs. See the Appendix for these disqualifications.

Convictions as follows for alcohol or drug-related offenses or leaving the scene of an accident or a felony involving the use of a CMV:

First offense ....One-year revocation.
First offense while transporting hazardous materials requiring placarding................Three-year revocation.
Second offense..Lifetime revocation.
Conviction of the use of a CMV vehicle in the commission of a felony involving
    the manufacturing, distribution, or dispensing of a controlled substance............Lifetime revocation.

For Points
An up to one- year suspension is given for the following:
  Driver 16-17.... Six points in twelve months or seven points prior to turning 18.
  Driver 18-20... Nine points in twelve months or twelve points in twenty-four months or fourteen points for period of license.
  Over 21 .... Twelve points in twelve months or eighteen points in twenty-four months.

Ignition Interlock
Repeat alcohol offenders are required to have an ignition interlock device installed on their vehicle(s) before they can reinstate their driving privileges (Colorado Revised Statute 42-2-132.5). Reinstated licenses are restricted to the use of vehicles equipped with an approved ignition interlock device for a period of at least one year.

Other reasons the driving privilege may be suspended, revoked or canceled and denied:
- Accumulation of serious violations (speeding 15+ over, reckless,   fatal, etc.)
- Alter or deface driver's license
- Conviction of manslaughter as a result of motor vehicle accident
- Failure to report an accident or leaving scene of accident
- Failure to pay fine
- Failure to appear
- Failure to pay child support
- Failure to provide evidence of insurance when requested by law enforcement officer
- Failure to register all vehicles owned within 30 days of becoming a CO resident
- Give false information on driver license application
- Lend license to another or misuse it in any way
- Outstanding Judgment Warrant (OJW). If an OJW is incurred a fee is still owed to the court on a ticket (citation).

If an OJW is put on the record, it must be resolved or the license may be cancelled or denied.

Reinstatement Requirements
Suspension $95.00 fee; SR-22, or evidence of insurance.
FRA Suspension $95.00 fee; SR-22; also, release from liability or waiver of security.
Revocation $95.00 fee; SR-22. May also require a Alcohol Education Program and therapy and interlock device.

Point System Overview
Colorado utilizes a point system with points ranging from 1 to 12 points. Regular licensed adult drivers can be suspended for 12 or more points within a 12-month period.

License Plate Facts

Registration Renewal
Renewal is annual, there is no specific staggered system in place. Non-diesel vehicles registered in the following counties are eligible for online renewal: Adams, Arapahoe, Boulder, Broomfield, Chaffee, Delta, Denver, Douglas, Eagle, El Paso, Garfield, Gilpin, Grand, Jefferson, Larimer, Logan, Mesa, Morgan, Pueblo, Routt, San Miguel, Washington, Weld and Yuma. Diesel vehicles in non-emission counties are eligible to renew online.

New Residents
Vehicles must be registered within 90 days after establishing residency. Establishing residency is established when one of the following occurs: 1) own or operate a business in CO; 2) be gainfully employed in CO; 3) reside in CO for 90 consecutive days.

Inspections and Emissions Testing
Emission testing of gas powered vehicles is required when registering, re-registering or selling vehicles in the following Colorado counties known as the *Enhanced Area:* the full counties of Boulder, Broomfield, Denver, Douglas and Jefferson as well as parts of the counties of Adams and Arapahoe. The diesel emissions program area consists of the full counties of Boulder, Jefferson, Broomfield, Denver and Douglas, as well as parts of Adams, Arapahoe, Eagle, El Paso, Gilpin, Grand, Larimer, Logan, Mesa, Pueblo, Routt, and Weld counties.

Testing of gas powered vehicles is also required in parts of three counties (El Paso, Larimer, and Weld) known as the *Basic Area*. Contact the respective county clerk's office for assistance to determine if an address is in or out of the program area in the partial counties of Adams (303-654-6010), Arapahoe (303-795-4500), and in El Paso (719-520-6240), Larimer (970-498-7878) or Weld (970-353-3840). For emissions information call 303-205-5603.

Tests for 1982 and newer vehicles in the Enhanced Area are done by Envirotest Inc. Tests for 1981 and older vehicles are performed by Air Care Colorado or independent testing facilities within the Enhanced Area. Vehicles registering in the three Basic Area counties may be tested at Basic Area stations or Air Care stations.

Colorado has no statutes requiring a safety inspection. Contact the respective county clerk's office for assistance to determine if an address is in or out of the program area in the partial counties as listed above.

Plate Descriptions
Typical Plate Patterns ....Beginning January 1, 2000, all vehicle types are issued a pattern of NNN/LLL. For commercial vehicles, the typical pattern is NNNNLLN. Prior passenger plates and light trucks were LLLNNN or LLLNNNN.
County/City Codes............................Since January 1, 2000, re-issued license plates do not display county designations. Until that date, Colorado used extensive coding patterns, incorporating the county and the alpha characters on the plate, for all classes of vehicles.
Plates and Stickers in Force ....Two plates, two decals (MO) (YR) on rear plate.
Plates Remain with Car when Sold? .No, they remain with seller.

Overview of Record Access

About Driving Records
Division of Motor Vehicles. The mailing address is: *Driver Control, Denver 80261-0016*. The express mail or delivery address is *Driver Control Section, 1881 Pierce Street, Lakewood, CO 80214*. Phone: 303-205-5613. The record fee from Driver Control is $2.20, add $.50 for certification. Online access from the designated vendor is $2.00. See www.colorado.gov/registration. The last fee increase was July of 1991 and no increases are planned for the near future. Colorado charges for "no record found" reports.

Request Methods – Mail, Walk-in, Online.
What You Should Know – An entry on the record shown as OJW stands for Outstanding Judgment Warrant.

Convictions on the record indicate an accident occurred or not by a "Y/N." Thus, accidents are not reported on the vehicle record if the driver was not convicted of a violation.

Special Access Programs Available – Colorado Interactive www.colorado.gov/registration manages the Driver Monitoring service; requesters must be approved. Fees are based on number of individual monitored, starting at $.06 per record for 1 to 400,000 records monitored. Requesters submit names and indicate if monitoring to be for 1 month, 6 months or 1 year. Monitored is monthly, results are provided within 6 days. The service is open to insurers, trucking companies, employers, and third party providers.

About Accident Reports

Copies of accident reports may be obtained by written requests. If requester was not involved, permission must first be given by one of the involved drivers. Use Form DR 2559. These requests are subject to the same restrictions to access as driving records. Form 2489 Requestor Release and Information Request/Notice of Intended Use must also be submitted. Records are held for current year plus 6 years, records (except photographs and witness statements) are microfilmed for past 10 years. The request must include name, date of birth, date of the accident, and your mailing address. The fee is $2.20 for the report or $2.70 to have it certified. Giving the location is helpful. Requests should be sent to: *Motor Vehicle Division, Driver Services, Denver 80261-0016, 303-205-5613.*

About Vehicle Records

Division of Motor Vehicles, Title & Registration Sections, Denver 80261-0016, Titles at 303-205-5608, Registration at 303-205-5607, fax 303-205-5765. The search fee is $2.20 for vehicle, plate, lien and ownership records including mobile homes. Certification is an additional $.50 per record. Note that filing of liens on a motor vehicle is handled at the County Clerk and Recorder's office in the county where the vehicle is located. Using the proper forms, the search will provide the vehicle description, the name and address of the owner, and any lien information if there. Record requests are subject to review for DPPA. Additional documents may be required. Records are maintained for the current year plus 7 years past. Bulk delivery is available for commercial customers. The request must include the vehicle identification number (VIN), year and make of the vehicle. The Colorado title number is helpful.

Request Methods – Mail, Walk-in, Bulk.
What You Should Know – Note that filing of liens on a motor vehicle is handled at the County Clerk and Recorder's office in the county where the vehicle is located.

About Watercraft Records

Colorado State Parks, Registration, 13787 S Highway 85, Littleton 80160, 303-791-1920. This agency maintains records for boats, snowmobiles, and off-highway vehicles. Lien information is not recorded here and must be searched at the Department of Revenue. All sail and motorized vessels must be registered. A Release of Registration Records Form must be completed and signed by the requester. Records can be searched by registration number, last name and DOB, or serial number going back 5 years. After 5 years, records are put on microfilm and can only be accessed by registration number. The fee is $2.00 per search and $1.00 per copy per page. Records can be accessed by mail, or fax 303-470-0782. The owner's DOB is not released.

Connecticut

Administration	Important Telephone and Web Contacts

Driver Services Division
Department of Motor Vehicles
60 State Street, Wethersfield 06161-1896
860-263-5720
Branch Operations: 203-805-6092
 	
www.ct.gov/dmv
	Telephone Center 860-263-5700
	Suspension/Restoration 860-263-5720
	Driver Improvement..860-263-5720
	Vehicle and Driver Record Information 860-263-5154
	State Department of Insurance 860-297-3804
	State Police..860-685-8000
	General Email Contacts at:
	   www.ct.gov/dmv/cwp/view.asp?a=803&q=244560
	Motor Vehicle Laws at:
	   www.cga.ct.gov/2005/pub/Title14.htm?dmvPNavCtr=|#39798
	Motor Vehicle Regulations at:
	   www.ct.gov/dmv/cwp/view.asp?a=803&q=396292

Driver License Facts

License Format
Nine numbers. The first two digits indicate, by odd or even year, the driver's month of birth and the seven additional numbers are the next available sequential numbers.

Document Appearance
Newer Documents
As of May 20, 2009, the DMV began issuing a new driver's license and identification card. The new license features a salmon-colored banner across the top and the non-driver identification cards have a green banner. The new cards will also feature more prominently the license or identification number, date of birth, and expiration date in bold letters. To view samples, visit www.ct.gov/dmv/cwp/view.asp?a=805&q=447352.

Security Characteristics 1) An embedded graphic of the Charter Oak tree within the center of the card that is only visible when held up to a bright light. 2) An image of a lighthouse that will appear as a hologram when the credential is held under ultra-violet light. 3) A special laminate with security features that will cover both sides of the card. 4) A second bar code and unique serial number located on the back of each card. The serial number, which is also contained within the bar code, will be connected to the customer's identity record.

Position of Photo Lower right, also, a smaller ghost image on lower left. Applicants under 21 years old have image in upper center on left side of card, smaller ghost image on lower right of card.

Minor Age Driver Locator The date when 16 and 17-year-old card holders will turn 18 appears in a yellow box running vertically and adjacent to the person's photo. The words "Under 21 Until xx-xx-xxxx" appear in a red box running vertically and adjacent to the person's photo or else next to the under 18 yellow box. Also, all cards for applicants under 21 years of age are printed in a vertical format.

CDL Indicator A green box appears in the top banner with class and *"Commercial Driver's License"* is printed in green under the salmon bar. If the license holder has a commercial instruction permit, the indicators are the same except the color is yellow, not green.

Older Document
This license and identification card have been in circulation since June 2002. This card has a glossy finish with a 2D barcode on the back and scenic backgrounds – a lighthouse on driver licenses and a covered bridge on identification cards. Dates of birth and expiration are printed in red. While this document was phased in over a six-year renewal period, some older cards may still be valid. The old card has a matte type finish with bar code on the front.

Security Characteristics Optical Variable Device (State of Connecticut seal and "DMVCT") embedded in

	overlay. Back laminate includes a State outline map image, visible under a black light, with the word Connecticut running through the image. *Connecticut* banner for all cards are color-coded. (CDL – Green, Permits – Yellow, Driver License – Blue, Identification Card – Red)
Position of Photo	Lower right, also, a smaller ghost image on lower left. Applicants under 21 years old have image in center right of card, smaller ghost image on lower right of card.
Minor Age Driver Locator	The words "Under 21 Until xx-xx-xxxx" appear on the lower front of card in red block. Also, all cards for applicants under 21 years of age are printed in a vertical format.
CDL Indicator	"*Commercial Driver's License*" is printed in green on upper right corner; also, "learner's" or "CD instruction permit" printed here in orange

Issue and Renewal
Age Requirements
The state has a mandatory Graduated Licensing Program for young drivers with specific restrictions in place for the first and the second three-month period of drivers aged 16 and 17. Those obtaining a Learner's Permit on or after 08/2008 have a "Photo Permit" and those who obtained the permit prior to 08/2008 have a "Paper Permit." Since 01/01/2009, all 16 and 17-year-olds seeking a driver's license need to pass a second written test called the DMV Final Exam. Passenger restrictions for 16-and-17-year-old motorcycle operators' license dictate they may not transport any passengers during the first six months they hold the endorsement. Motorcycle drivers 18 years-old or older may not transport passengers for the first three months. The web gives extensive details on all the requirements for the Graduated Licensing Program.

Renewal
Renewal is the birth date of sixth year, CDL is for four years, see below for over 65. Driver keeps same number when renewing. All renewals, including for military, require a photo. Out-of-state military personnel may began renewal process up to 4 months prior to expiration. An application, with signature of commissioned officer in charge, is required. Call 860-263-5148 for information on renewal while out of state. Renewal cannot be done online, but a driver or ID holder may request a change of address form.

Elderly-Related Restrictions
A Limited License Program for older drivers (and for those drivers whose abilities have changed since their initial licensing) is offered. The license will contain limitations (such as daylight driving only) noted as restrictions on the physical document. Vision tests are not required at renewal or for new license after age 65. If requested, a 2-year license renewal is offered for those over 65.

Residency
License must be obtained within thirty (30) days of establishing residency.

License Classes
Commercial Classifications
Class A	Any combination of vehicles with a gross combined weight rating (GCWR) of 26,001 pounds or more, provided the GVWR of the vehicles being towed is in excess of 10,000 pounds.
Class B	Any single vehicle with a GVWR of 26,001 pounds or more, or any such vehicle towing a vehicle not in excess of 10,000 pounds.
Class C	Any single vehicle not in excess of 26,001 pounds, or any such vehicle towing a vehicle not in excess, including vehicles required to be placarded for hazardous materials; or any vehicle designed to transport 16 or more passengers, including the driver. Also, vehicles designed to transport more than ten passengers (including the driver), and used to transport students under the age of twenty-one years to and from school.

Non-Commercial Classifications
Class 1	(Not issued after 01/01/2006) Any motor vehicle except a commercial motor vehicle.
Class 2	(Not issued after 01/01/2006) Any motor vehicle including a combination of motor vehicle and trailer or trailing unit used exclusively for camping or any other recreational purposes regardless of the gross weight of the trailer or trailing unit, except a commercial motor vehicle or an articulated vehicle or any other combination of motor vehicle and trailer where the gross weight of the trailing unit or trailer is more than 10,000 pounds.
Class D	(Issued as of 01/01/2006) Any motor vehicle including a combination of motor vehicle and trailer or trailing unit used exclusively for camping or any other recreational purposes regardless of the gross weight of the trailer or trailing unit, except a commercial motor vehicle or an articulated vehicle or any other combination of motor vehicle and trailer where the gross weight of the trailing unit or trailer is more than 10,000 pounds.
Class M	(Moved to an Endorsement as of 01/01/2006) Alone or combined with any other class evidence that the holder is licensed to operate a motorcycle.

HAZMAT Endorsement Procedure

The state is in compliance with the Patriot Act. All applicants applying for a new or renewal or transfer HAZMAT Endorsement (HME) must first complete the application online from https://hazprints.tsa.dhs.gov/Public/ or by calling 877-429-7746. The driver must also be fingerprinted. EMSI is the state-designated entity to process fingerprints. There is one location in the state that performs this service. Visit the web page listed above to find the address location. The cost of the fingerprint process is $89.25.

The fingerprints and application information is sent to the Federal Transportation Security Administration (TSA). TSA performs the background checks (using the FBI database) and notifies the DMV whether the application is approved or denied. When completed and approved, the HME is valid for up to five years.

The Department provides an overview of the program at www.ct.gov/dmv/cwp/view.asp?Q=289306&A=805.

Safety and Enforcement Facts

Insurance and Financial Responsibility

Connecticut requires liability insurance. Minimum financial responsibility limits are $20,000/40,000/10,000. The state does not have a security type law in effect for verification of insurance. The state's enforcement program is based on mandatory cancellation reporting by insurance companies.

Alcohol and Chemical Testing

Connecticut's legal intoxication standard is .08 percent and .02 percent for those under 21. The state has an implied-consent law as well as an administrative license-suspension law. Blood, urine, and breath tests are permissible. CDL holders are subject to a standard of .04 percent when operating a commercial motor vehicle.

Motor Vehicle Sanctions and Criminal Penalties

The license suspension periods outlined below have been recently revised and will be imposed in addition to criminal penalties (see 2nd chart below.) In most cases, the motor vehicle sanctions will be imposed much earlier.

Admin Per Se Sanctions - Drivers 21 Years and Older	First Offense	Second Offense	Third Offense
Refusal to submit to a blood, breath or urine test		1 year	3 years
Test results of .08 or higher up to .16	90 days	9 months	2 years
Test results of .16 or higher	120 days	10 months	2½ years

Admin Per Se Sanctions - Drivers 18-20	First Offense	Second Offense	Third Offense
Refusal to submit to a blood, breath or urine test		2 years	6 years
Test results of .02 or higher up to .16	6 months	18 months	4 years
Test results of .16 or higher	240 days	20 months	5 years

Admin Per Se Sanctions - Drivers 16 and 17	First Offense	Second Offense	Third Offense
Refusal to submit to a blood, breath or urine test		3 years	6 years
Test results of .02 or higher up to .16	1 year	2 years	4 years
Test results of .16 or higher	1 year	30 months	5 years

Criminal Law for Test Results of .08 or Higher

Under Connecticut's criminal law, the driver arrested for DUI will receive both a summons and court date. If the court proceedings result in a conviction, the following penalties must be imposed:

	First Offense	Second Offense	Third Offense
Fine	$500 to $1000	$1000 to $4000	$2000 to $8000
Jail	6 months, 48 hrs minimum mandatory or 6 months, suspended with 100 hrs. community service.	2 years, 120 days minimum mandatory and 100 hrs. community service.	3 years, 1 year minimum mandatory and 100 hrs. of community service.
Suspension	One year.	1 year PLUS 2 years with a Ignition Interlock Device.	Permanent Revocation, but can reapply after 6 years.

Accident Reporting

Accident reporting is not under the jurisdiction of the Department of Motor Vehicles but under the Department of Public Safety. Motorists are required to report motor vehicle accidents to police if there is an injury, death or property damage (no minimum limit designated) and if they are unable for any reason to share information with the injured party or property owner. Motorists are not, however, required to file written accident reports, which are the responsibility of the investigating police agency.

Suspensions and Revocations
The state is in compliance with the federally mandated disqualifications on CDLs. See the Appendix for details.

Violations That Will Result in a Suspension
- High Points
- Operating Under the Influence
- Evading Responsibility
- False Statements or Reports
- Improper Use of Marker, Registration or License
- Reckless Driving
- Child Restraint
- Racing
- Dishonored Check to DMV
- Operating Under Suspension
- Assault in the 2nd Degree With a Motor Vehicle
- Using Motor Vehicle or Vessel Without Owner's Permission
- Medical Qualification
- Disobeying Signal of Officer
- Manslaughter With Motor Vehicle
- Interfering or Tampering with a Motor vehicle
- 4 or More Moving Violations in 2 Year Period
- 4 or More Speeding Violations in 2 Year Period
- Failure to Complete Retraining Class

Young Drivers: 16 and 17 year old drivers receive a 48 hour suspension if cited for:
- Violating any of the driving restrictions that apply after licensure.
- Driving 20 miles per hour or more above a posted speed limit.
- Driving under the influence of alcohol or drugs.
- Driving recklessly.
- Racing a motor vehicle on a public highway.

Reinstatement Requirements
Suspension ...... $125.00 fee.
Revocation ...... $125.00 fee.

Substance Abuse Treatment Program
Prior to operator license restoration, an individual suspended for driving under the influence of alcohol or drugs, or refusal of the implied consent to test or failure to pass a BAC test, must complete an extensive Treatment Program, including a residential component. The Driver Services Division oversees the vendor-administered program and may be reached at 860-263-5723. This administrative requirement is in addition to any conditions imposed through the courts.

Point System Overview
Points range from 1 to 5. There is a 30-day suspension for more than 10 points within a 2 year period. However, the Department is not allowed to assess points if the violation is paid by mail to the Centralized Infractions Bureau, but the conviction is recorded on the driver's history record.

License Plate Facts

Registration Renewal
Plates are issued on an biannual basis. Renewal is blocked to those who have unpaid municipal property taxes or more than five unpaid parking violations. Online renewal is available at www.ct.gov/dmv (click on Online Services) for those who have no record changes, parking violations or property tax issues (and have received a PIN with the renewal notice).

New Residents
License plates must be purchased within sixty days of establishing residency.

Inspections and Emissions Testing
Connecticut has required emissions tests for gasoline and diesel powered vehicles up to 10,000 pounds (motorcycles, composite vehicles, and farm vehicles are exempt). Testing every two years is required for vehicles 4 to 24 years old. Vehicles exempt from emissions testing will require a VIN verification inspection if previously registered out-of-state. Safety inspections are required for certain vehicles including taxis, ambulances, school transportation vehicles, driver education vehicles if over 100,000 miles, homemade trailers, non-commercial trailers 10,000 GVWR and under, and certain imported vehicle over 10 years old among others. The complete list is available on the web.

Plate Descriptions
Connecticut began issuing the current, fully reflectorized tri-color blue marker plate on January 1, 2001. All classes of marker plates, except "Early American" will display the same color scheme. Early American plates remain as a white background with black letters/numerals.

Typical Plate Patterns .... Passenger and light truck plates are 6 digits, generally 3 numeric and 3 alpha, but the pattern can vary. Commercial vehicle plates are 1 alpha and 5 numeric.
County/City Codes .... The county of issuance is not indicated on the plate.
Plates and Stickers in Force .... Most vehicles are issued two plates, with the exception of Trailers and Motorcycles which are issued one plate. There is one decal (MO-YR), shown on the windshield.
Plates Remain with Car when Sold? . No. Plates can be transferred to another vehicle by the same owner, otherwise they are returned to the Department of Motor Vehicles.

Overview of Record Access

About Driving Records
Department of Motor Vehicles, Copy Records Section, 60 State Street, Wethersfield 06161-0503, 860-263-5154. The fee is $20.00 for a certified driving record, or if obtained online then $15.00 per record. Vendors may not transmit records via the Internet unless acceptable safeguards are imposed.
Request Methods – Mail, Walk-in (but only the person of record), Online, Bulk
What You Should Know – Requesters must complete Copy Record Request Form J-23. The form can be ordered by calling the Telephone Information Center at 860-263-5700 or by ordering on the Internet (www.ct.gov/dmv/J23), but cannot be downloaded. Connecticut does not report accidents on the driving record.

About Accident Reports
Reports (officer copy) of accidents occurring on a state roadway or investigated by the state law enforcement officials can be obtained from the Department of Public Safety, Reports and Records Unit, 1111 Country Club Rd, Middletown CT 06457, 860-685-8250, www.ct.gov/dps. Requests must be in writing and include the $16.00 search fee per uncertified report or $17.00 if certified, name and address of requester, date and location of incident, names of operators, and the eight digit case number if known. Use of Form DPS-96C is suggested. Forms may be downloaded from the web. Turnaround time can take as long as six weeks. The agency will not release criminal cases still pending in the court systems. Normally, records are destroyed after 10 years.

About Vehicle Records
Department of Motor Vehicles, Copy Record Unit, 60 State Street, Wethersfield 06161-1896, 860-263-5154. It takes two weeks before new records are available for inquiry. The release of vehicle title and registration information is restricted to permissible users or those who have authorization from the subject. Permissible users can search by name and vehicle plate number, or vehicle plate number and description (VIN is helpful) and must fill out DMV Form J-23. Form J-23 asks for the make, year and VIN. The standard fee is $20.00 for a title search (includes lien data), a current owner file information, a copy of Application for Title, or an original registration certificate. Certification for any document is an additional $20.00. Paper records are kept a minimum of three years after expiration.
Request Methods – Mail, Walk-in for record holder only, Bulk (limited)

About Watercraft Records
The DMV maintains the registration file for boats. All motorized boats and all boats over 19 1/2 ft must be registered. Boats are not titled. For record requests, the J-23/J23B Form must be filled out and processed by the Marine Vessel Section at 60 State Street, Wethersfield, CT 06161-5031 860-263-5151. The fee is $20.00 for a current owner print-out or for a copy of the registration or for a complete boat history. Turnaround time is 7-14 days. The SSN is not released on records. Batch and bulk delivery is available, subject to DPPA standards.

Delaware

Administration	Important Telephone and Web Contacts
Jennifer Cohan, Director Division of Motor Vehicles Safety and Homeland Security Building 303 Transportation Circle, Dover 19901 PO Box 698, Dover 19903 302-744-2510 - Fax: 302-739-3152 www.dmv.de.gov/default.shtml Note: All DMV offices have hours of operation from 8:00 am to 4:30 pm (EST), except Wednesday hours are noon to 8 pm.	Driver Licensing .... 302-744-2505 Driving Records .... 302-744-2506 Vehicle Records .... 302-744-2511 License Suspensions .... 302-744-2509 License Revocations .... 302-744-2508 Financial Responsibility .... 302-744-2513 Commercial Driver License .... 302-744-2563 State Department of Insurance .... 302-674-7300 State Police .... 302-739-5901 Email .... dot-public-relations@state.de.us Laws and Regulations http://DelCode.delaware.gov

Driver License Facts

License Format
One to seven numbers and is computer generated, there is no coding. Zeros are not placed in front if number is less than seven digits.

Document Appearance
Delaware will be transitioning to a newly formatted driver license document in early 2010. At press time of this book, the details have yet to be finalized.

Existing Format
The current card, issued since 03/03, is a digital license on a hard plastic card with a yellow strip at the top.

Security Characteristics	Caesar Rodney in laminate, bar code.
Position of Photo	Top, left hand side.
Under 21 Age Driver License	Vertical format, red rectangle with white letters stating, "21 on mm/dd/year and 18 on mm/dd/year."
CDL Indicator	Written white letters on green strip, on top.

Oldest Format
This format may still be in use by military personnel. This older digital license is a hard plastic card with blue strip on left hand side and was issued 04/1997 until 03/2003.

Security Characteristics	State seal and state outline in laminate, bar code.
Position of Photo	Top, left hand side.
Under 21 Age Driver License	Vertical format, red rectangle with white letters stating, "21 on mm/dd/year and 18 on mm/dd/year."
CDL Indicator	Written in yellow letters on blue strip on far left side.

Issue and Renewal

Age Requirements
The minimum age is 16 years. A Graduated Driver License (GDL) took effect on July 1, 1999. A permit holder who is at least 17 years old, but less than 18 years old, may obtain a Class D operator's license when the driver has held a Level One Learner's Permit for at least 12 months, the sponsor has not withdrawn his/her endorsement, and the applicant's driving privileges are not suspended, revoked, canceled, denied, or surrendered. For the first six months after issuance of a Level One Learner's Permit, the permit holder may only drive when supervised.

Renewal
Birthdate of fifth year. Driver keeps same number when renewing. Online renewal is not offered. Military may renew by mail.

Elderly-Related Restrictions
None reported by state.

The 2010 U.S. Motor Vehicle Reference Book — Delaware 47

Residency
A non-resident must obtain a Delaware license within sixty days of establishing residency.

License Classes

Code	Literal	Remarks
CA	CDL Class A	Over 26,000 pounds combination vehicle with trailer over 10,000 pounds.
CB	CDL Class B	Over 26,000 pounds single vehicle or combination vehicle with trailer 10,000 pounds or under
CC	CDL Class C	26,000 pounds or under, if used to transport sixteen or more passengers (including the driver) or any vehicle requiring placarding for HazMat.
D	Class D	All non-CDL vehicles 26,000 pounds or under or if used to transport sixteen or more passengers (including the driver) or any vehicle requiring placarding for HazMat. Includes Level 1 Learners' Permit.
DA	Denied (Admin)	Denied license in Administration Office.
DG	Denied in Georgetown	Denied license in Georgetown Office.
DN	Denied in New Castle	Denied license in New Castle Office.
DW	Denied in Wilmington	Denied license in Wilmington Office.
GDL	Level 1 LP	Learner's Permit for Graduated Driver License.
LP	DE Learners' Permit	Permit for Driver Education students, adult students and *CDL permits*.
NA	Non-CDL A	Class A vehicle under Farmer or Fire-fighter waiver.
NB	Non-CDL B	Class B vehicle under Farmer or fire-fighter waiver.
NO	None	Violations/History on file or license issue denied.
OT	Out-Of-State	Violations/History on file.
PA	Perm Non-CDL A	Permanent non-CDL A, Class NA vehicle.
PB	Perm Non-CDL B	Permanent non-CDL B, Class NB vehicle.
PD	Perm D	Upgraded from old Class A or new Class D.
T	Temporary LIC	A Temporary License, giving short term driving authority for all license classes except learner permits.

HAZMAT Endorsement Procedure
The state is in compliance with the Patriot Act. All applicants applying for a new or renewal or transfer HAZMAT Endorsement (HME) must apply online at https://hazprints.tsa.dhs.gov/Public/ or apply by calling 877-429-7746. The driver must also be fingerprinted. COMNETIX is the state-designated entity to process fingerprints. There is one location in the state that perform this service at 415 Transportation Dr in Dover. The cost of the fingerprint process is $89.25. The fingerprints and application information is sent to the Federal Transportation Security Administration (TSA). TSA performs the background checks and notifies the DMV whether the application is approved or denied. Applicants must also pass the written HME test. When completed and approved, the HME is valid for five years.
The DMV has an excellent explanation of the program at www.dmv.de.gov/services/driver_services/TSA/new_haz_req.shtml.

Safety and Enforcement Facts

Insurance and Financial Responsibility
Delaware has compulsory liability insurance requirements of $15,000/30,000/10,000. Delaware vehicle owners must carry a valid insurance identification card in the vehicle at all times. Proof of insurance must be presented to the Division at the time of registration or renewal. Vehicles are audited for proof of insurance as a result of notification of cancellation by insurance companies. Failure to comply with an audit, maintain continuous liability insurance or surrender tags prior to insurance cancellation may result in fines and registration and owner's drivers license suspensions.

Alcohol and Chemical Testing
The legal limit is .08 percent (non-commercial) and to .02 percent for drivers under 21. The CDL legal limit is .04 percent; additionally, drivers will be placed out-of-service for twenty-four hours for any measurable alcohol content. The driving-under-the-influence laws include implied-consent as well as administrative revocations. The following tests are permissible: breath, blood, and urine. Any person who has been convicted of a driving under the influence of alcohol charge may be required to have an Ignition Interlock Device installed on all vehicles owned by the offender.

Accident Reporting
Accidents involving damage in excess of $500.00, injury, death, or if it appears that a driver has been impaired as a result of drug or alcohol use, then the accident must be reported to local police, but not with the Motor Vehicle Division..

Suspensions and Revocations

The state is in compliance with the **federally mandated disqualifications on CDLs**. See the Appendix for details.

Drag Racing, Speed Exhibition
- First Offense .... One-month suspension.
- Second Offense .... Twelve-month suspension.

Driving While License Suspended or Revoked:
- Suspension or revocation period is doubled up to one year.

Passing a Stopped School Bus .... One- to twelve-month suspension.

Point Accumulation in One Year
- Fourteen Points .... Four-month suspension.
- Sixteen Points .... Six-month suspension.
- Eighteen Points .... Eight-month suspension.
- Twenty Points .... Ten-month suspension.
- Twenty-two Points .... Twelve-month suspension.

Note: Also, at twelve points a driver must complete a behavior modification/attitudinal-driving course within 90 days after notification (unless extended by DMV). A mandatory 2-month suspension will be imposed for failure to comply.

Refusal to Pay Child Support .... Suspension until matter resolved.

Failure to adhere to Level 1 Learner's Permit or Driver's Education Permit (other than using cell phone)
- First Offense .... Two-month suspension.
- Second Offense .... Four-month suspension.

Level 1 Learner's Permit or Driver's Education Permit and using a cell phone while driving:
- First Offense .... One-month suspension.
- Second Offense .... Three-month suspension.

Alcohol-Related (Any person who drives under the influence is subject to both administrative and criminal penalties.)

Driving Under the Influence (non-commercial)
- First Offense (Probable Cause) .... Three-month revocation.
- Second Offense .... Twelve-month revocation.
- Third Offense .... Eighteen-month revocation.
- Criminal Penalties include .... One- to Five-year revocation.

Driving Under the Influence (holder of CDL)
- First Offense .... One-year disqualified.
- First Offense with Hazardous Material ... Three-year disqualified.
- Second Offense .... Lifetime disqualified.

Zero Tolerance - Under 21 Administrative & Criminal Penalties:
- First Offense .... Two-month revocation.
- Second Offense .... Six-month revocation.
- Third offense .... One-year revocation.

Refusal to Submit to Chemical Test (non-commercial)
- First Offense .... Twelve-month revocation.
- Second Offense .... Eighteen-month revocation.
- Third or Subsequent Suspension .... Two-year revocation.

Refusal to Submit to Chemical Test (holder of CDL)
- First Offense .... One-year disqualified.
- First Offense with HazMat .... Three-year disqualified.
- Second Offense .... Lifetime disqualified.

Serious Offenses in a Commercial Vehicle:
- Two in three years .... Disqualified for sixty days.
- Three in three years .... Disqualified for 120 days.

Speeding Related Suspensions
- The driver will be suspended for one (1) month when convicted of driving 25 MPH over the posted speed limit. The length of suspension will increase by one month for each additional 5 MPH over the initial 25-MPH threshold. The driver may elect to attend the behavior modification/attitudinal-driving course in lieu of license suspension when driving 25-29 MPH over the posted limit. For speeding 30 MPH over the posted limit or more, the suspension is mandatory.
- One-year suspension when convicted of driving 50 MPH or more over the posted speed limit or driving 100 MPH on a highway.

Other Actions Which May Result in a Suspension Include:
- Has by reckless or unlawful operation of a motor vehicle contributed to an accident resulting in injury or death to any person or caused serious property damage.
- Is incompetent to drive a motor vehicle for serious medical or mental conditions.
- Has driven a motor vehicle without consent of its owner.
- Has issued a non-collectible check to the Division.
- Speed exhibition and spinning wheels.
- Failing to answer a court summons in any state.
- Use of fictitious, suspended, revoked or borrowed driver's license.
- Loaning a driver's license to another person
- Giving a fictitious name or address or making a false statement in applying for a license.
- Unlawful manufacture or possession of a false insurance document.
- Driving an uninsured motor vehicle
- Altering a driver's license or using a fraudulent license.

The Following Offenses Require Mandatory Revocation:
- Driving while under the influence of intoxicating liquor or narcotic drugs
- Leaving the scene of accident involving death or injury to another person or property damage
- Attempting to flee from a police officer after having received a visual or audible signal to stop your vehicle
- Three convictions for reckless driving in a period of twelve consecutive months
- Contributing to the death of anyone by operating a vehicle
- The crime of assault in which a death occurs from operating a vehicle
- Using a motor vehicle in committing any serious crime
- Making a false statement or using fraudulent information
- Underage possession/consumption of alcohol by persons under 21 years of age
- Any drug offense that results in a conviction

Habitual Offender Revocation
After an accumulation of certain types of traffic violation convictions, the driver may be declared a habitual offender and his/her license may be revoked for up to five (5) years. No work or hardship licenses are issued to those convicted of being a habitual offender. Any combination of three of the following offenses in a five (5) year period may convict driver as a habitual offender:
- Manslaughter
- Use of a motor vehicle in the commission of a felony
- Driving while under the influence of alcohol or drugs
- Driving without a license
- Driving during suspension or revocation
- Reckless driving
- Failing to stop at the scene of an accident
- Failing to identify yourself at the scene of an accident
- Making a false statement to the Division of Motor Vehicles
- Violation of an occupational license
- Failing to stop on the command of a police officer

Also, any combination of the above offenses and lesser offenses, such as speeding, that result in 10 convictions in 3 years may convict driver as a habitual offender.

Aggressive Driving
Violators committing a combination of 3 or more specific violations may, in addition to those violations or in lieu of those violations, may be charged with *aggressive driving*. Violations include: disregarding a traffic device; speeding; improper passing; improper lane change; following too close; fail to yield right of way; failing to signal; passing a stopped school bus; and, disregard a stop sign. Violators convicted of aggressive driving are required to complete a behavior modification/attitudinal driving course that is offer statewide. Failure to attend course will result in suspension.

Reinstatement Requirements

Suspension	$25.00 fee; time lapse.
Revocation	$143.75 fee; time lapse; re-examination in some cases.
Disqualification	$25.00 fee; time lapse; re-examination in some cases.

- Alcohol-related violations also require satisfactory completion in a designated alcohol education/rehabilitation program and may be required to have character background review.
- Delaware *may* issue a conditional/restricted/occupational and/or temporary license for individuals revoked, suspended or in the Ignition Interlock Program.

Ignition Interlock Program

An Ignition Interlock Program is available to DUI offenders on a voluntary basis and is mandatory for those with one or more DUI convictions. Various eligibility requirements must be met before installation of the device and issuance of a special IID license. The IID license is valid for Class "D" vehicles only.

Point System Overview

Delaware points range from 2 to 6. An accumulation of 8 or more points in a 24-month period identifies problem drivers. An advisory letter is sent at point levels of 8 to 11.5. A driver is required to complete a behavior modification/attitudinal driving course at point levels of 12 to 13.5. A point level of 14 or greater results in a mandatory suspension of 4 months to 1 year, depending on point level. The behavior modification/attitudinal driving course is offered statewide. Drivers passing an approved defensive driving course may have 3 points deducted from their points total once every three years. A speeding violation of 1 to 14 mph over the posted speed limit will not be assessed points, IF (a) it is the first violation within any three (3) year period and (b) the ticket is paid through the Voluntary Assessment Center or Alderman's Court and recorded as a "guilty mail-in."

License Plate Facts

Registration Renewal

Inspection is biennial; however, one may renew for one year or two. You cannot renew online.

New Residents

Must obtain title and registration within 60 days of establishing residency.

Inspections and Emissions Testing

Delaware requires a safety inspection, fuel tank pressure, fuel cap test, brake, emissions tests, and on-board diagnostics testing for 1996 and newer vehicles (1997 and newer if diesel powered). Inspections are performed at state operated inspection stations. Delaware exempts the first five model year vehicles (weighing less than 10,000 lbs.) from inspections. A "new" vehicle is exempted for up to five (5) years; other vehicles in this timeframe are exempted from inspection in a similar manner. All vehicles older than five (5) years can renew registrations for one or two years. All vehicles must pass inspection prior to registration. Emissions tests are required on automobiles and on trucks with a manufacturer's gross vehicle weight rating (MGVWR) of 8,500 pounds or less. Exceptions include vehicles manufactured before 1968, diesel-fueled vehicles manufactured before 1997, motorcycles, and kit cars.

Plate Descriptions

The current Delaware titles, registration cards, registration validation stickers, and motorcycle license plates have been issued since 2005. The Division eliminated the pre-printed, multi-colored validation stickers and began using stickers with silver letters on a black background for those vehicles expiring on the 15th of the month, and black letters on a silver background for those vehicles expiring at the end of the month. The Division prints the vehicle license plate number and any special license plate number on the stickers.

Typical Plate Patterns .... "THE FIRST STATE" appears on the top of all plates, in gold lettering. Passenger plates are all numbers, up to six digits. Motor vehicles weighing less than 7,000 lbs can be issued a variety of plates, all numeric or plates prefaced by "PC" "C" "CL" or "RV" with up to six digits following. Motorcycles are issued plates prefaced by "MC," trailer plates by "T," dealer plates by "D," farm trucks by "FT," recreational vehicles by "RV," recreational trailers by "RT," construction equipment by "CT," all followed by up to six digits. Delaware also offers vanity plates which can be all alpha or a combination of alpha and numeric. For additional plate descriptions and photos see the DMV web site at www.dmv.de.gov.

There is a vanity tag availability check offered from a link at the home page.

County/City Codes .... Delaware does not have such codes.
Plates and Stickers in Force .... One plate, one decal with (MO) (YR) (Day).
Plate Remains with Car when Sold? . Yes, unless individual requests to retain their tag for new vehicle.

Overview of Record Access

About Driving Records
Driver's License Unit, Division of Motor Vehicles, PO Box 698, Dover 19903, Attn: Driver Services Dept., 302-744-2506. The current fee is $15.00 per search. No fee increases are planned. Delaware charges for "no record found" reports. DMV hours of operation are 8:00 am to 4:30 pm (EST) except Wednesday hours are noon to 8 pm.
Request Methods – Mail, Walk-in, Online, Bulk
What You Should Know – Those routinely seeking information must complete an Application and a Contract for Direct Access. If requesting information on a third party, a notarized MV703 Form or valid court document is required. For more information about establishing an online account, call Mr. Larry Bryant at 302-744-2596.

About Accident Reports
Copies of accident reports can be obtained by contacting Delaware State Police, Traffic Records, PO Box 430, Dover 19903, 302-739-5931, fax is 302-739-5936. The fee is $25.00 for each report or $60.00 for a copy of a fatal accident report. It takes 2 weeks before new records are available for inquiry. Paper records maintained since 1984. Average turnaround time is 5 to 10 days; 30 to 90 days for a fatal report. Include the full name, location, date and complaint number of the incident. You cannot search by phone, but you can verify if a report exist.

About Vehicle Records
Correspondence Section, Division of Motor Vehicles, PO Box 698, Dover 19903, 302-744-2511 or 302-744-2538. The fee for VIN, lien and registration checks is $15.00 per inquiry and $20.00 for a certified copy. Those routinely seeking information must complete an Application and a Contract for Direct Access. Authorized access account holders may obtain information in accordance with their contracts. Otherwise, third-party requests must be accompanied by a valid court document or a completed, notarized Personal Information Request Form (MV703). DMV hours of operation are 8:00 am to 4:30 pm (EST), on Wednesday hours are noon to 8 pm.
Request Methods – Mail, Walk-in, Online.
What You Should Know – Those routinely seeking information must complete an Application and a Contract for Direct Access. Authorized access account holders may obtain information in accordance with their contracts. Otherwise, third-party requests must be accompanied by a valid court document or a completed, notarized Personal Information Request Form (MV703).

About Watercraft Records
Department of Natural Resources and Environmental Control, 89 Kings Highway, Dover 19901, 302-739-9916, www.fw.delaware.gov/services/pages/licenses.aspx. As a rule, every boat, vessel, jet ski, surf jet, ski craft or any other personal watercraft operated by Delaware residents on Delaware waterways must be registered. Non-resident boats/vessels using the waters of Delaware for principal use over 60 days and non-residents owning a boat docked and/or stowed in waters of Delaware for over 60 days must be registered in Delaware. Records are available from 1979 to present. Registration information is considered confidential and this agency follows stricter guidelines than DPPA standards. However, the agency will verify information over the phone with a "yes" or "no" response only. Liens are filed at the Secretary of State and are not found at this location.

District of Columbia

Administration	Important Telephone and Web Contacts
Lucinda Babers, Director Joan B. Saleh, Driver Services Administrator Department of Motor Vehicles 95 M Street, SW Washington, DC 20024 202-737-4404 http://dmv.dc.gov/main.shtm	Driver Licensing..202-737-4404 SR-22 & Financial Responsibility...............202-737-4404 Commercial Driver License.........................202-576-8278 Vehicle Information.......................................202-737-4404 State Department of Insurance ....202-727-8000 Metropolitan Police Department..................202-727-4326 Email Questions To:.....................................dmv@dc.gov DC Municipal Regulations - Title 18 vehicle & Traffic: http://www.dcregs.org/

Driver License Facts

License Format
A seven-digit number is issued. There is no numerical code sequence used to create license numbers, they are randomly generated. Previously, the SSN was used. It will take until at least 2010 for all the SSNs to be replaced.

Document Appearance
The license is plastic and became digitized in July 2000.
- **Security Characteristics**....... Overlay with a repetitive pattern in gold "The American Experience in Washington DC."
- **Position of Photo**................... Lower left corner, also ghost image is in upper right corner.
- **Minor Age Driver Locator** .. Vertical card. The statement "Under 21 until XXX" is printed in red.
- **CDL Indicator** .... "CDL" printed on license.

Issue and Renewal

Age Requirements
The DC Department of Motor Vehicles introduced its GRAD (Gradual Rearing of Adult Drivers) program on September 1, 2000. GRAD involves three stages: a supervised learner's period; an intermediate licensing phase using a Provisional License that permits unsupervised driving only in less risky situations; and a full-privilege license with conditions that can apply at age 17. No one under age 21 may have a CDL. The minimum age for a full license is eighteen. For a Learner's Permit or Provisional License the age is sixteen; under eighteen must have written permission of parent/guardian.

Renewal
Renewal is eight years, from the birthdate in the eighth year. The driver keeps the same number if the DL is the seven digit license number. If the DL was the SSN, the DL is converted to the seven-digit number. Military personnel holding a valid DC license may retain the license for 6 years while on active duty outside the District. However, application for extension must be made in each eight year period.

Renewal for regular drivers may be made online or by mail, provided there are no violations, addresses changes or a medical condition. The online site is www.dmv.dc.gov/serv/online.shtm. CDL drivers cannot renew online. If the DC driver's license has been expired over 90 days but not more than 180 days, the driver must pass a knowledge test. If the DC driver's license has been expired for more than 180 days months, driver must pass a knowledge test and a road test.

Elderly-Related Restrictions
Drivers 70 years or older must pass an eye test and have their physician complete the certification on the driver's license application.

Residency
License must be obtained within thirty days of establishing residency.

License Classes
Commercial Classifications
- Class A All vehicles except motorcycles.
- Class B Vehicles 26,001 pounds GVW or more, towing trailers under 10,000 pounds GVW, except motorcycles. Also mopeds.
- Class C Vehicles under 26,001 pounds, towing trailers under 10,000 pounds GVW, except motorcycle. Also mopeds.

Non-Commercial Classifications
- Class D Vehicles under 26,001 pounds for non-commercial and personal use, except motorcycles. Also mopeds.
- Class M Motorcycles (endorsement).
- Class N Mopeds and motor-driven cycles.

License Types
- CDL Commercial Driver's License
- LNR Learner's Permit
- RGL Regular Driver's License
- PDL Provisional Driver License.

HAZMAT Endorsement Procedure
The state is in compliance with the Patriot Act. All applicants applying for a new or renewal or transfer HAZMAT Endorsement (HME) must complete the application at https://hazprints.tsa.dhs.gov/Public/ or by calling 877-429-7746. The driver must also be fingerprinted. EMSI is the TSA Agent for HME fingerprinting. There is one location in the District that performs this service, see the site above for the address. The cost of the fingerprint process is $89.25. The fingerprints and application information is sent to the Federal Transportation Security Administration (TSA). TSA performs the background checks and notifies the DMV whether the application is approved or denied. When completed and approved, the HME is valid for five years.

Safety and Enforcement Facts

Insurance and Financial Responsibility
Minimum coverage limits are: $25,000/50,000 for bodily injury and $10,000 for property liability. Uninsured Motorist property damage minimum is $5,000 subject to $200 deductible. Insurance for personal injury is optional. Liability insurance is mandatory. Evidence of insurance is required upon registration. Proof is required after "certain" violations. DC does use SR-22 forms.

Alcohol and Chemical Testing
A level of .07 percent constitutes a driving-under-the-influence violation. A level of .08 percent or more constitutes an intoxication violation. Urine, blood, and breath tests are all legal. There is zero tolerance if driver is under 21. The District of Columbia may also suspend under Administrative Authority.

Accident Reporting
Accidents involving personal injury, death, or damage must be investigated by the Metropolitan Police. Since 12/12/03, individual reports need not be filed with the Department of Motor Vehicles.

Suspensions and Revocations
Note: It is assumed DC is in compliance with the federally mandated disqualifications on CDLs. See the Appendix for a list of these disqualifications.

Point Accumulation of Points within Two Years
- Ten or eleven points................... Suspension of ninety-days.
- Twelve or More Points............... Revocation for minimum of six months.

Repeated Convictions
If convicted of certain criminal traffic violations in DC, including driving while intoxicated or driving under the influence, the license is revoked for 6 months for the first offense, 1 year for the second offense, and 2 years for the third or subsequent offense. The driving privileges are revoked until they have been officially reinstated and the reinstatement fee is paid.

Conviction of Any of the Following Twelve Point Convictions Will Result in Automatic Revocation—
- Committing a felony crime involving the use of a motor vehicle
- Committing any violation while operating a vehicle without the permission of the owner
- Conviction for an assault or homicide committed with an automobile
- Fleeing or attempting to elude a police officer

- Leaving the scene of a collision in which personal injury occurs (hit and run)
- Making a false affidavit or statement under any law relating to motor vehicles
- Operating a vehicle after your driver's license has been suspended or revoked
- Operating a vehicle under the influence of or impaired by intoxicating liquor and/or narcotics
- Operating a vehicle with any measurable amount of alcohol if the person is under 21 years old
- Reckless driving
- Using the driver's license of another person

In addition, the Director of the Department of Motor Vehicles has the authority to suspend or revoke a driver's license (at his discretion) for just cause, including non-payment for child support and outstanding traffic tickets (uncontested and unpaid after 30 days).

Reinstatement Requirements
Suspension $98.00 fee and/or re-examination—depending on the offense.
Revocation $98.00 fee and re-examination.

Point System Overview
The point system ranges from 2 to 12 points. A suspension can occur with the accumulation of 8 or more points within a 2-year period. A driver is eligible for one safe driving point for any calendar year in which a moving violation point was not assessed. A safe driving point may be used to offset a moving violation point and expires in 5 years.

License Plate Facts

Registration & Renewal
Plates are issued annually. Registrations can only be renewed by mail, online, or by using a drop box or onsite computer kiosk at one of the DMV facilities. One may renew online at www.dmv.dc.gov/serv/online.shtm, providing there is no address change nor administrative actions pending.

New Residents
DC law requires that all vehicles housed and operated in the District be registered in the District unless the owner displays a reciprocity sticker issued by the DMV. Vehicles must be registered at expiration of time allowed by reciprocity agreement (within 30 days). A DC title and current DC insurance are required before registration.

Inspections and Emissions Testing
Any motorized vehicle that is operated in the District of Columbia must be emission tested. This includes passenger cars, taxis, buses, snowmobiles, commercial, and government vehicles. The only vehicles which are exempt from the emissions test process are new vehicles which have a Certificate of Origin (i.e., original title from the dealer), zero emission vehicles, motorcycles and trail bikes.

The District's safety inspection program for most private cars was discontinued in October 2009. Commercial vehicles are inspected annually and vehicles for hire are inspected every six (6) months. During inspection, lights, brakes, suspension, emissions, and other safety components will be checked. Sticker is on front windshield.

Plate Descriptions
Typical Plate Patterns   Passenger plates are 6 numbers or alpha numeric, e.g., AA-0000. Commercial vehicle plates are "C" followed by 5 numbers. Apportioned plates are "AP" followed by up to four numbers.
County/City Codes   None reported.
Plates and Stickers in Force   Two plates, one validation sticker placed on front windshield.
Plates Remain with Car when Sold? No, they must be surrendered to the DC DMV by the seller or may be transferred to another vehicle.

Overview of Record Access

About Driving Records
Department of Motor Vehicles, ATTN: Driving Records, PO Box 90120, Washington DC 20090, 202-737-4404. The current fee is $7.00 for a three or five-year record and $13.00 for a ten-year record. The last fee increase was in March of 2003 and there are no increases planned for this year. The District of Columbia charges for "no record found" reports.. Major credit cards (except American Express) are accepted

Request Methods – Mail, Walk-in, Online, Bulk.
What You Should Know – All convictions with points are placed on the MVR. Accidents are listed if there is a conviction, but fault is not shown.
Special Access Programs Available – DC provides a Driver's License Verification and an Identification Card Verification at: https://public.dmv.washingtondc.gov/scripts/ds/DriverLicenseVerification.asp.

About Accident Reports
Copies of accident reports are available from the Metropolitan Police, 300 Indiana Ave NW, Rm 3075, Washington DC, 202-727-4357. A report investigated by the police is known as a PD-10. The fee is $3.00 per record, use a SASE if requesting by mail. Personal checks are not accepted, but corporate checks are. The 6-digit report number is required or the exact date and location. Name searches are not performed.

About Vehicle Records
Southwest Service Center, 95 M Street SW, Washington 20024, 202-737-4404, fax is 202-673-99083. New records are available for inquiry in 24 hours. Paper records are held for thirteen years. The current fee for VIN, registration information, and vehicle lien records is $7.00.
Request Methods – Mail, Walk-in, Online (status only), Bulk (limited).
What You Should Know – The District of Columbia provides a Vehicle Registration Verification and an Out-of-State Title Status at www.dmv.dc.gov/serv/online.shtm.

About Watercraft Records
All vessels, regardless of size and with or without mechanical propulsion, must registered by the Metropolitan Police Department, Harbor Patrol - Boat Registration, 550 Water St SW, Washington DC 20024, 202-727-4582, http://mpdc.dc.gov/mpdc/site/default.asp. Liens are shown on titles. Coast Guard documented vessels are not titled, but must be registered. Records are not open to the public, although some discretionary uses are approved if they are considered to be for the public good. Verifications are available on a case-by-case basis from the Public Information Section. Bulk purchase must be arranged via a FOIA.

Florida

Administration	Important Telephone and Web Contacts
Julie L. Jones, Executive Director Dept of Highway Safety and Motor Vehicles B-443 Neil Kirkman Building Tallahassee 32399, 850-617-3100 www.flhsmv.gov	Driver Licensing and CDL ....850-617-2000 SR-22 and Financial Responsibility ....850-617-2000 Vehicle/Vessel Information.........................850-617-2000 State Department of Insurance ....850-413-3100 Motor Carrier Services ....850-617-2909 Highway Patrol..850-617-2301 Email Contact List: www.flhsmv.gov/html/contact.html Statutes at: www.leg.state.fl.us

Driver License Facts

License Format
One letter followed by twelve numbers. The letter corresponds to the first letter of the last name, and the numbers reflect a code representing the name, date of birth, and sex. The HSMV has indicated that this code is classified, and not released to the public.

Document Appearance
The current license and ID cards, issued since June 16, 2004, are laminated with a digital photo. Previously issued Florida driver licenses and identification cards remain valid until their expiration dates.

Current Format
- **Security Characteristics**: The technology includes a 2-D barcode, magnetic stripe, digitized portrait image, signature, and various security features such as ghost image, UV image and text, and overlapping data. Florida's image is depicted with a beach scene and the state seal.
- **Position of Photo**: Left side.
- **Minor Age Driver Locator**: "UNDER 21 until xx-xx-xx" in red bar on left side of photo. License and ID cards are vertical with text at the top and a vertical photo. The cardholder's 21st birthday is indicated in the photo image area.
- **CDL Indicator**: Blue bar at top of license - CDL designation under color bar at top.

Older Format
- **Security Characteristics**: The license is a digitized, photo card. The state map appears under the photo on the right side.
- **Position of Photo**: Left side.
- **Minor Age Driver Locator**: "UNDER 21 until xx-xx-xx" across the face of license.
- **CDL Indicator**: CDL class designation on left side of photo.

Issue and Renewal
Age Requirements

The minimum age is sixteen, fifteen for a Learner's License. To earn a regular Class E license, drivers under the age of 18 must have parent/guardian signature, hold Learner's Permit for 12 months, complete a Traffic Law & Substance Education Course or high school driver's education, not incur any moving traffic convictions, certified by parent or guardian to have at least 50 hours of behind-the-wheel training, 10 of which must be at night. A Learner's License is issued at age 15 with these requirements: may operate only between 6 AM and 7 PM (after 3 months may drive until 10 PM); licensed driver 21 or older must accompany and sit in closest seat to right of driver; and does not permit operation of motorcycle if age under 16. 16 year-olds cannot drive from 11 PM to 6 AM unless accompanied by an licensed driver 21 or older, or driving to or from work; 17 year olds from 1 AM to 5 AM unless accompanied by licensed driver 21 or older, or driving to or from work.

Effective July 1, 2008, anyone under 16 who operates an off-highway vehicle on public land must complete an approved safety course and have the certificate in their possession while riding. Also, all motorcyclists must pass a basic rider course before receiving a motor cycle endorsement.

The 2010 U.S. Motor Vehicle Reference Book   Florida   57

Renewal
A clear license can be renewed for 8 years for persons 79 years of age and younger, and for 6 years for persons 80 years of age and older, except non-immigrants. The driver keeps the same number when renewing. Military personnel and their dependents serving outside the state are granted an automatic extension without renewal if their driver license status is valid. The extension is valid for 90 days after return to Florida or separation from military.

Renewal and address changes can be done online at www.GoRenew.com, by all except non-immigrants. One may renew a DL one time by a convenience method (Internet or mail). However, the next renewal must be made in a driver license office. Commercial driver licenses and licenses expired over one year cannot be renewed online or by mail.

Elderly-Related Restrictions
As of January 1, 2004, all drivers 80 years of age or older must pass a vision test before renewing their driver license. The test may be administered at the driver license office or by a licensed health care practitioner, such as a medical doctor, osteopath or optometrist. A vision examination report must be completed and submitted to the department if the vision test is administered by a doctor. Effective 10/1/2008, Drivers who are 79 years of age and under will be issued eight year licenses while drivers 80 and older will continue to receive six year licenses.

Residency
Drivers must surrender an out-of-state license and secure the Florida license within thirty days of establishing residency, enrolling children in school, registering to vote, filing for homestead exemption, or obtaining employment (including part-time employment).

License Classes
Commercial Classifications
- Class A — Any Tractor/Trailer combination that has GVWR of 26,001 lbs or more, provided towed vehicle is more than 10,000 LBS.
- Class B — Any single motor vehicle that has GVWR of 26,001 lbs or more, or any such vehicle towing a vehicle of 10,000 lbs or less.
- Class C — Any motor vehicle that has GVWR of less than 26,001 lbs when endorsements "H" or "P" would be required on the driver license.

Non-Commercial Classifications
Effective July 1, 2005, Class D licenses were converted to Class E. Drivers may continue to possess valid Class D licenses until their licenses are renewed or otherwise reissued. This includes farmers and emergency vehicle operators who are exempt from commercial driver license requirements. A resident who holds a valid Florida chauffeur license may continue to operate vehicles for which a CLASS E driver license is required until the chauffeur license expires. This includes farmers and emergency vehicle operators who are exempt.

- Class E — Regular operator's license. Any non-commercial motor vehicle with GVWR less than 26,001 lbs. A resident who holds a valid Florida operator license may continue to operate vehicles for which a Class E driver license is required, until the operator license expires.
- Class E-L — Learner's license. A resident who holds a valid Florida learner license may continue to operate vehicles for which a Class E Learner license is required, until the license expires.
- MTCYALSO — Authorized to also operate motorcycle.
- MTCY ONLY — Authorized to only operate motorcycle.

HAZMAT Endorsement Procedure
Fingerprinting must be done in a Driver License office at the same time the application for a HAZMAT endorsement is made. An application form must be completed and turned in at the time of fingerprinting to be sent to TSA. The application is available on this site and at the Driver License offices. One may download the application from www.hsmv.state.fl.us/hazmat or complete online, except for signature, before reporting to the Driver License office for fingerprinting.

The fee for a commercial driver license (CDL) is $75 and the hazardous-materials endorsement is $7. Applicants seeking a commercial driver license with a hazardous-materials endorsement must also pay $91 to cover the costs for the required background checks. License office locations are found at www.flhsmv.gov/hazmat_map.html. TSA performs the background checks and notifies the DDL whether the application is approved or denied. When completed and approved, the HME is valid for four years. Also, applicants can check the status of their HAZMAT endorsement at https://idave.flhsmv.gov. Non-immigrants are not eligible to apply for a Commercial Driver Licenses with a HAZMAT endorsement.

Safety and Enforcement Facts

Insurance and Financial Responsibility
The Florida No-Fault law was re-enacted on January 1, 2008; the minimum mandatory requirements are $10,000 each of personal injury protection and property damage liability coverage. This is required throughout the registration period and whenever asked for by a law enforcement officer. Bodily Injury liability with limits of $10,000 per person, $20,000 per occurrence and $10,000 property damage coverage are required when: a crash is caused resulting in injury; or for some types of convictions; or when there is a judgment pursuant to a law suit. Commercial vehicles require bodily injury liability coverage at all times with higher limits. Since 10/01/2007, the minimum mandatory requirements for a motorist convicted of a DUI after that date must be able to provide coverage of the higher bodily injury liability limits of $100,000 per person, $300,000 per occurrence and $50,000 property damage on the date of the arrest for a DUI conviction.

Alcohol and Chemical Testing
The unlawful alcohol level is .08 BAC for an Administrative Suspension. CMV operators who have any alcohol in their system may not drive or be in actual physical control of a commercial motor vehicle. A BAC of .04 in a CMV is considered impairment, and the driver will be arrested for DUI. An administrative suspension is ordered if the operator's BAC is .08 or higher while operating a motor vehicle or a CMV, or is a CDL holder and operating a motor vehicle, or for DUBAL, or refuses an approved test. Further, the CMV driver/CDL holder will also be disqualified from operating a CMV. Persons under 21 years of age who have a BAC of .02 will be administratively suspended. If their BAC level is higher than .02, they can be arrested and charged with DUI. If their BAC is above a .08 they can be administratively suspended as an adult. The determination is made by the police officer. Alcohol testing includes urine, blood, and breath. Blood and urine tests are used for chemical and controlled substances. Operating any vehicle under the influence is also a violation that results in revocation of the driving privilege, if convicted. Effective 07/01/05, drivers are required to install and use an ignition interlock if convicted of multiple DUIs, or if a first-time offender with a BAC of 0.15 or more (law changed from .20 to .15 effective 10/01/2008), or a minor was in the vehicle at the time of the offense.

Crash Reporting
Crashes involving death, personal injury, or $500.00 or more in damage require a written report be filed with the Department of Highway Safety and Motor Vehicles in Tallahassee within ten days—unless reported by the police or highway patrol. A reporting form is found at www.flhsmv.gov/fhp/misc/CrashReport/. There are no special reporting requirements for commercial drivers.

Suspensions and Revocations
The state is in compliance with the federally mandated disqualifications on CDLs. See the Appendix for a list of these disqualifications.

Point Accumulation

Twelve Points in Twelve Months	Thirty-day suspension.
Eighteen Points in Eighteen Months	Three-month suspension.
Twenty-four Points in Thirty-six Months	One-year suspension.

Note: Three points will be deducted from the driving record of any person whose driving privileges have been suspended only once under the point system and reinstated, if such a person has complied with all other requirements.

Teen Drivers

Six Points in Twelve Months	Restricted driving privileges until eighteen or for 12 months.
DUI	revocation.
Truant in School Attendance	suspension.
Possession of tobacco products	suspension.

Note: Drivers under the age of 21 with a blood alcohol level of .02 or more will have their license immediately suspended for six months. This administrative action is for a first offense; a second offense will result in a one year suspension. Refusal to submit to testing (first offense) results in a suspension of twelve months; eighteen months on a second offense.

Giving False Information or Identification .... Fraudulent license is cancelled, privilege suspended for one year.

Violations Which May Result in Suspension
- Admin Per Se .08 and above or .02 and above for CDL
- Allowing License to be Used for Illegal Law
- Child Support Delinquency
- Court-Ordered Suspension
- Dropping Out of School
- Failure of Road Test (5 attempts)

- Driving Without Insurance
- Failure to Pay Fine or Appear in Court
- Judged Mentally/Physically Incapacitated
- Loaning Vehicle to person who has Suspended License, and Crash Results with Injury or Death
- Making a Fraudulent License Application
- Point Accumulation
- Possession of Tobacco and Misrepresent Age to Obtain Tobacco, by a Minor
- Pending outcome of court conviction of incident which resulted in death and driver was charged
- Refusal to Submit to Breath, Blood or Urine Test
- Violation of Restriction

Violations Which May Result in Revocation
- An Immoral Act in Which a Motor Vehicle was Used
- Driving Under the Influence of Alcohol or Controlled Substance
- Failure to Stop and Render Aid in an Accident Resulting in Death or Personal Injury
- Felony Conviction of Drug Possession
- Felony Involving the Use of a Motor Vehicle
- Fleeing or Attempting to Elude a Police Officer
- Other Medical Problems
- Perjury or Misrepresentation of Truth in Ownership or Operation of a Motor Vehicle
- Three Convictions of Reckless Driving in One Year
- Theft of Motor Vehicle parts or Components
- Three Major Convictions, or Fifteen Pointable Convictions in Five Years (Habitual Offender Law)
- Vision Worse Than Standard Minimum Requirements
- Youthful Offender: Possession of Alcohol by a Minor, Gun Control, Criminal Mischief, Violation of Chapter 893 Controlled Substance

Other Violations Causing Revocations
DUI Resulting in Death.............. Minimum three-year revocation.
DUI Manslaughter...................... License revoked permanently.
Driving Under the Influence
    First Conviction.................. Revocation of 180 days to one-year.
    Second Conviction .... Revocation minimum five years (if within five years of a prior conviction).
    Third Conviction .... Revocation minimum ten years (if within ten years of prior conviction).
    Four or More Convictions in Lifetime (chronic offenders) ... License permanently revoked.

Violations Which May Result in a Disqualification
- Driving any vehicle, as a CDL holder, and arrested for DUI (post arrest they may have a BAC of .08 or above or refuse.)
- Driving a commercial vehicle without obtaining a CDL.
- Driving a commercial vehicle without the proper class of license or proper endorsement.
- Driving a commercial vehicle without having the driver license in possession, however drivers may produce proof of having had a license to the clerk of court and be found not guilty of the offense.
- Driving a commercial vehicle while the operator's license is suspended, revoked, or canceled.
- Causing a fatality through the negligent operation of a commercial motor vehicle.
- Providing false information when applying for CDL results in a 60-day disqualification.
- A person who operates a commercial motor vehicle bearing a false or fraudulent identification commits a misdemeanor of the 1st degree

Note: Drivers are required to install and use an ignition interlock if convicted of multiple DUIs, as well as those first-time offenders with a BAC of 0.15 or more, or those who had a minor in the vehicle at the time of the offense.

Reinstatement Requirements

Suspension	$45 fee; time lapse and completion of Advanced Driver Improvement Course.
Revocation	$75 fee.
DUI Revocation	$75 fee; plus administrative fee for DUI of $130; completion of DUI school.
DUI Administrative Suspension	$45 fee; plus administrative fee for DUI of $130; DUI school enrollment.
For Insurance Suspensions	$150 up to $500 for No-Fault and DUI cases and $15 for liability cases.
For Worthless Checks	55 fee.

Point System Overview
Points range from 3 to 6, and points are assessed based on Florida law. Accumulation of 12 or more points in a 12 month period, 18 points in an 18 month period or 24 points within 36 months will result in a suspension.

License Plate Facts

Registration Renewal
Renewal and address changes can be done online at www.GoRenew.com. Drivers have the option of renewing for one year or two years.

New Residents
Non-residents must register vehicles within ten days of obtaining employment or placing children in public school.

Inspections and Emissions Testing
Florida has no statewide regulation concerning safety inspections or emission testing. The emissions inspection program became obsolete July 1, 2001.

Plate Descriptions
Typical Plate Patterns	Commercial vehicles always have 6 characters; 1 or 2 alpha, numerals, then 1 alpha. Passenger cars, lightweight trucks and trailers have 4 applicable ranges as follows: AAA00A - XZZ99Z H0000A - L9999Z (Note: The letter "O" is not used in any series.) AA000A - IZ999Z A00AAA - X99ZZZ
County/City Codes	The name of the county of issuance, the words *In God We Trust* or the words *Sunshine State* appear on bottom of license plate.
Plates and Stickers in Force	Passenger cars and light trucks display one plate, one decal (MO/YR). Commercial vehicles with GVW exceeding 26,000 pounds display two plates.
Plate Remains with Car when Sold?	No, the license plate remains with the original owner.

Note: Florida Off-Highway Vehicle (OHV) Titling Law requires OHV owners to apply for a Certificate of Title and obtain an OHV decal to be affixed on his/her OHV for use on OHV trails.

Overview of Record Access

About Driving Records
Division of Driver Licenses, Bureau of Records, PO Box 5775, Tallahassee 32314-5775, 850-617-2000. The fee for a three-year record is $8.00 and for either a seven-year record or a complete record the fee is $10.00.

Request Methods – Mail, Walk-in, FTP/Cartridge, Online, DL & Yong Driver Check Online (see below).

What You Should Know – Requesters needing less than 5,000 records per month are called Individual Users and are directed to a commercial vendor who is a Network Provider. A list of these companies is found at www.flhsmv.gov.

Special Access Programs Available – Florida gives employers and insurers the ability to monitor drivers with a program that essentially permits approved entities to purchase in bulk based on new activity. Call the Director's office for more information and fees.

Visit https://www6.hsmv.state.fl.us/DLCheck/main.jsp for a free online check of any FL driver license number. Note this web address is case sensitive. Only the license number is used to access. No personal information is released. This site also gives parents and guardians the ability to check the driving history of their children under 18 years of age. The last four digits of the SSN and the DOB are needed to view the record. Also, applicants can check the status of their HAZMAT endorsement at https://idave.flhsmv.gov

About Crash Reports
Records are available from 1942 to present, from 1983 forward are on microfiche. Traffic crash reports are exempt from public disclosure for 60 days after the date the report is filed, except for parties involved in the crash and other specific parties outlined in the statute (Section 316.066). For crashes prior to 1983, the exact date, county, location, driver's name, and agency that investigated must be supplied with the request. After 1983, only the driver's name, date of crash, and county are needed. It takes approximately 3 to 4 weeks to receive the report. The cost is $10.00 per report.

To request a copy of a crash report that was completed by a member of the Florida Highway Patrol, please contact the local FHP station in the area where the crash occurred. For copies of crash reports dating back more than 12 months, contact Crash Records - MS-28, DHSMV, 2900 Apalachee Parkway, Room B310, Tallahassee 32399-0538, 850-617-3416 or 617-2306, fax is 850-617-5134. Homicide reports are kept in the local districts for 5 years from the date of crash. To order a traffic crash report older than 2 years, the cost is $10.00; a homicide report older than 5 years is $25.00, to order call 850-617-2306. To order traffic homicide photographs, call 850-617-3409.

About Vehicle Records

Division of Motor Vehicles, Information Research Unit, Neil Kirkman Building, Room B-335, Tallahassee 32399. The mail address is 2900 Apalachee Parkway, Neil Kirkman Building, Mail Stop 73, Tallahassee, FL 32399-0620. 850-617-2000. www.hsmv.state.fl.us/html/titlinf.html To research by name for current vehicle information, the DOB and city are required. The fee for non-certified computer printouts of VIN, registration, lien, and tag (plate) checks is $ .50 per request; $1.00 per page for non-certified photo of micrographic copies of documents; and $3.00 for certification. The fee for a copy of a title (front and back) is $2.00. A complete 10-year title history record can cost as much as $15.00 or more. For electronic access, Florida has contracted to release information from the various Department of Highway Safety and Motor Vehicle's databases through several approved vendors. The SSN is not released.

Request Methods – Mail, Walk-in, Online, Status Check Online, Bulk.

What You Should Know – A free status check is provided. Enter title # or VIN to check the vehicle status at https://www6.hsmv.state.fl.us/rrdmvcheck/mvchecking. The vehicle status lets customer know if the plate is renewable. Online access is only for approved requesters, fees vary by type of record and how purchased.

About Watercraft Records

Department of Highway Safety and Motor Vehicles, Bureau of Titles and Registrations, 2900 Apalachee Room MS68, Tallahassee 32399, 850-617-2000. www.flhsmv.gov/dmv/faqboat.html All motorized vessels must be titled and registered, regardless of size. Non-motor powered vessels less than 16 ft in length and any non-motor powered canoe, kayak, racing shell, or rowing scull, regardless of length are not required to be registered, however non-powered vessels 16 ft and over must be titled. A written request is required for all searches. Florida works with the local county tax collectors' offices in recording titles and registrations; this permits real-time connection.

Name searches should include DOB and county. Use Form HSMV 85054 as mentioned above. The fees are: $.50 per computer printout page; $1.00 per photo copy of record; $3.00 per certification. Liens show on all records. Turnaround is 10 days to 3 weeks. The Bureau also offers a program of bulk purchase for all or part of the database. Records are available for 10 years to present.

Florida recognizes valid registration certificates and numbers issued to visiting boaters for a period of 90 days. An owner who intends to use his vessel in Florida longer than 90 days must register it with a county tax collector. However, he may retain the out-of-state registration number if he plans to return to his home state within a reasonable period of time.

Georgia

Administration	Important Telephone and Web Contacts

Alan Watson, Director
Department of Driver Services
2206 East View Parkway, PO Box 80447
Conyers, GA 30013
678-413-8400
 	
Douglas Hooper, Director
Department of Revenue, Motor Vehicle Division
PO Box 740381
Atlanta, GA 30374-0381
404-362-6500
 	
www.dds.ga.gov (driver)
https://etax.dor.ga.gov/ (vehicle)
	All Driver License Related Questions are Directed to
	                                                 678-413-8400/8500/8600
	Vehicle Information 404-968-3800
	Tag and Title 404-968-3690
	Commercial Vehicle Registration.................... 404-968-3850
	State Commissioner of Insurance 404-656-2056
	Georgia State Patrol, North Adjutant............... 404-624-7451
	                        South Adjutant 404-624-7718
	
	General Email Vehicle motorvehicleinquiry@dor.ga.gov
	
	Rules and Regulations www.dds.ga.gov/rules/index.aspx
	  and www.dds.ga.gov/business/

Driver License Facts

License Format
The current format is nine numbers or Social Security Number (SSN), but the state indicated that a new DL format may be released sometime in the near future. The SSNs are being phased out. There is no code or sequential arrangement that determines the characters making the license number.

Document Appearance
Georgia began issuance of new DL and ID card in November 2009. All previously issued Georgia licenses and IDs will remain valid until the expiration date when they will be exchanged for the newly-designed card. Both versions, which have digital imaging, a hologram, and a barcode on the back are described below.

Current Documents
- **Security Characteristics** — Security features include ghost photos, a laser-engraved signature over the primary photo to minimize alterations and a tamper resistant coating placed over the card. The cards feature machine-readable barcodes that can be used by banks, retailers and other businesses to verify the information printed on the front. The State Seal over the front of the card responds to ultra-violet light.
- **Position of Photo** — Left edge, with a double ghost photo in lower right corner.
- **Minor Age Driver Locator** — This vertical card has photo on middle left edge and a double ghost image photo on lower right corner. The words "Under 21" is printed in read to the right of the photo. The DL and ID cards do NOT specifically show the date that a teen under 21 reaches age 21.
- **CDL Indicator** — The new Commercial DLs and permits are labeled with the word "Commercial" and are printed in a distinctive blue text.

Older Documents
Since November 2006, these driver's licenses issued by the DDS show "Issue Date" instead of "Exam Date" on the face of the license.
- **Security Characteristics** — Barcode on back. Hologram in laminate "Georgia" on new cards. Small state seal on top to left of photo next to governor's signature. "Georgia" appears upper left corner.
- **Position of Photo** — Right side, governor's signature is on top.
- **Minor Age Driver Locator** — "UNDER 21" appears vertically on the left edge of photo, in brown.
- **CDL Indicator** — CDLs have the word Georgia in yellow, while non-CDL is in green. "Commercial Driver's License" is stated on top of the license in yellow..

The 2010 U.S. Motor Vehicle Reference Book — Georgia

Issue and Renewal
Age Requirements
The minimum age is eighteen for Class C; sixteen for Class D; fifteen for a Learner's License (Class CP). All teenagers wishing to obtain a Class D license when turning 16 must have completed driver's education from a DDS approved provider, the Class D license must be obtained at age 17.

Renewal
Birth date of fifth or tenth year. The driver keeps the same number when renewing unless SSN, then driver must change to the computer-generated number. If there is no address change, non-CDL licenses may be renewed online at www.dds.ga.gov/ or by mail, but by invitation only. Military personnel may renew by mail.

Elderly-Related Restrictions
The Dept. of Driver Services is required by Georgia law to administer a vision test to customers age 64 or older prior to renewing or issuing a Georgia driver's license. Because the vision test can only be taken in person at a Customer Service Center, customers age 64 or older are not eligible for auto-renewal services.

Residency
New residents must obtain license within thirty days.

License Classes
Commercial Classifications
- Class A — Any combination of vehicles with a GVWR of 26,001 pounds or more, provided the GVWR of the vehicle(s) being towed is in excess of 10,000 pounds. Includes vehicles in Classes B and C.
- Class B — Any single vehicle with a GVWR of 26,001 pounds or more, or any such vehicle towing another vehicle not in excess of 10,000 pounds. Includes vehicles in Class C.
- Class C — Can also be non-commercial. Any single vehicle with a gross vehicle weight rating not in excess of 26,000 pounds, or any such vehicle towing a vehicle with a gross vehicle weight rating not in excess of 10,000 pounds, any such vehicle towing a vehicle with a gross vehicle weight rating in excess of 10,000 pounds, provided that the combination of vehicles has a gross combined vehicle weight rating not in excess of 26,000 pounds, and any self-propelled or towed vehicle that is equipped to serve as temporary living quarters for recreational, camping, or travel purposes and is used solely as a family or personal conveyance. Class C commercial licenses are issued only if the vehicle is designed to carry sixteen or more passengers (including the driver), or utilized to transport hazardous materials in quantities that require placarding.

Non-Commercial Classifications
The non-commercial A and B Licenses are for drivers who operate certain larger vehicles which are not classified as Class C vehicles or commercial vehicles. Applicants for a driver's license in Classes A or B (non-commercial) must submit a DS Form #36. This affidavit must show a minimum driving experience of 3 months and/or 3,000 miles in the type of vehicle for class of license being applied for.
- Class A — Any combination of vehicles with a GCWR of 26,001 or more pounds provided the GVWR of the vehicle(s) being towed is in excess of 10,000 pounds.
- Class B — Any single vehicle with a GVWR of 26,001 or more pounds, or any such vehicle towing a vehicle not in excess of 10,000 pounds GVWR.
- Class C — See above.
- Class D — Provisional License for Class C vehicles, with restrictions an driving hours and passengers.
- Class M — Motorcycles.
- Class P — Instructional Permit. Note that CP, MP, AP, and BP are all instructional permits issued with the class designation followed by the letter P. Applicants under 18 years of age must hold a Class CP a minimum of 12 months before obtaining a Class D license.

HAZMAT Endorsement Procedure
The state is in compliance with the Patriot Act. All applicants applying for a new or renewal or transfer HAZMAT Endorsement (HME) must first complete the electronic application at www.hazprints.tsa.dhs.gov or by calling 877-429-7746. The driver must also be fingerprinted. EMSI is the TSA-designated entity to process fingerprints. There are seven locations in the state that perform this service. Visit https://hazprints.tsa.dhs.gov/Public/ or the web page listed above to find the address locations. The cost of the fingerprint process is $89.25. The fingerprints and application information is sent to the Federal Transportation Security Administration (TSA). TSA performs the background checks and notifies the DMV whether the application is approved or denied. When completed and approved, the HME is valid until the CDL is renewed. For more information visit www.dds.ga.gov/Commercial/HazMatDriverGuidanceFaq.pdf.

Safety and Enforcement Facts

Insurance and Financial Responsibility
Georgia has compulsory-insurance laws. Failure to comply with compulsory-insurance laws may result in vehicle registration (not driver license) suspension. Minimum financial responsibility limits are $35,000/50,000/25,000. Proof of insurance must be carried in the vehicle or proof must reside in the Department of Revenue database. Georgia employs SR-22 forms.

Alcohol and Chemical Testing
The prohibitive alcohol level is .08% or excess of .05%, .04% for CDL, and .02 % if under 21 years. Legal testing means include blood, urine, and breathe testing.

Accident Reporting
Georgia requires accidents involving death, injury, or damage in excess of $250.00 to be investigated upon request by the Department of Transportation. The DOT Crash Reporting Unit is at PO Box 80447, Conyers, GA 30013, 678-413-8647. Not that the DOT web page (www.dot.state.ga.gov) has a accident reporting form that is downloadable. However, the form is for personal use only. The DOT states that it will throw away any such reports mailed to them.

Suspensions and Revocations
Although suspensions and revocations are designated for specific time periods, many convictions require that the license physically be held for the specified period before the licensee is eligible to reinstate.
Also, the state is in compliance with the federally mandated disqualifications on CDLs. See the Appendix for details.

Suspensions
Administrative License Suspension (40-5-67.1)	One to five years.
Failure to Appear	Indefinite.
Implied Consent (CDL or regular DL)	One year.
Safety Responsibility	Until requirements of 40-9-33, 5, and 61 are complied with.

Suspensions (First Conviction in Five Years)
DUI, Under 21 if Alcohol Level less than .08%	Six months.
DUI, Under 21 if Alcohol Level .08% or More	Twelve months.
Driving Without Insurance	60 to 90 day suspension.
Driving While Suspended or Revoked	Six months, beginning at conviction date.
Driving Under Influence (1st Offense)	Minimum 120 days from disposition date.
Eluding a Police Officer (1st Offense)	Minimum 120 days from date of conviction.
Fraudulent or fictitious use of, or application for a license	Varies.
Homicide by Vehicle (1st Offense)	Three years from date of conviction.
Homicide by Vehicle (2nd degree)	Minimum 120 days from date of conviction.
Leaving Scene of Accident; Hit-and-Run; Failure to Stop and Give Aid	Minimum 120 days from date of conviction.
No Proof of Insurance	Sixty days from date of conviction.
Racing (1st Offense)	Minimum 120 days from date of conviction.
Serious Injury by Vehicle	Three years from date of conviction.

Suspensions (Second Conviction in Five Years)
Driving Under Influence	Not eligible for permit for twelve months, reinstatement for eighteen months; Installation of ignition interlock device then required and completion of alcohol/drug risk clinical treatment; All license plates registered in driver's name must be surrendered to the court.
Homicide by Vehicle (second degree)	Three years from conviction date.
No Proof of Insurance	Ninety days.

Point Accumulation
First Fifteen Points in Twenty-four Months	One year with early return option.
Second Fifteen Points in Twenty-four Months	Three years with early return option.
Third Fifteen Points in Twenty-four Months	Two years from SD; no permits or early reinstatement options.

Revocations
Habitual Violator	Any third conviction of a mandatory offense within five years is a five-year revocation from surrender date.
Medical Revocation	Indefinite from surrender date.
Under 21, If Four Point Offense	Six months first offense; one year second or subsequent offense;

Under 21 DUI	.02-.07 alcohol level, six month suspension; .08 or higher, one year suspension.
Under 18, If Four Points Accumulated in Twelve Months	Six months first offense; one-year second or subsequent; if .02-.07 alcohol level, six-month revocation; if .08 or higher one-year suspension.

Additional Mandatory Suspensions for Drivers Under 21
- Any offense for which four or more points are assessable
- Aggressive driving
- Exceeding the speed limit by 24 mph or more
- Hit and run
- Improper passing on a hill or a curve
- Leaving the scene of an accident
- Misrepresenting age for purpose of illegally obtaining any alcoholic beverage
- Misrepresenting identity or using false identification for purpose of purchasing or obtaining any alcoholic beverage
- Purchasing an alcoholic beverage
- Racing on highways or streets
- Reckless driving
- Unlawful passing of a school bus
- Using a motor vehicle in fleeing or attempting to elude an officer

Note: All "Under 21" revocations require that the license be held by the agency for the specified revocation period before the licensee will be eligible for reinstatement.

Other Mandatory Revocations Include:
- Any third conviction of a suspendable offense within 5 years.
- Refusal to submit a reexamination of driving skill or knowledge of driving rules after receiving notice giving reasonable grounds for such a request.
- Sufficient evidence of incompetence or unfitness to drive, due to incapabilities by reason of disease, mental or physical disability, or by alcohol or drug addiction.

Reinstatement Requirements

Suspension   Any mandatory suspension is $200 fee by mail, $210 fee in-person; approved DUI or defensive driving course certificate. If for Insurance, then $50 fee by mail, $60 fee in person; proof of insurance required.

Revocation   HV is $200 fee by mail, $210 fee in-person; time lapse and possible DUI course certificate.

Point System Overview

The Georgia point system ranges from 2 to 6. A driver with 15 points in a 24 month period will be suspended

License Plate Facts

Registration & Renewal

There are three (3) different types of registration systems in Georgia: year-round registration (in the majority of counties); four-month staggered registration (Talbot county); and a four-month non-staggered registration system. The registration period depends upon what county the primary owner resides. Tag renewals are available at https://mvd.dor.ga.gov/tags/index.aspx. A "RIN" (registration ID) is needed and the address must be correct.

New Residents

Non-resident visitors may stay in Georgia on a reciprocal basis for ninety days. New residents must register their vehicle within thirty days.

Inspections and Emissions Testing

There are no statewide laws governing either safety inspections or emission testing. However, the following thirteen counties in the Metro Atlanta area do require an annual emissions test: Cherokee, Clayton, Cobb, Coweta, DeKalb, Douglas, Fayette, Forsyth, Fulton, Gwinnett, Henry, Paulding, and Rockdale. The three most recent model years are exempt each year.

Plate Descriptions

Typical Plate Patterns   The standard plate for passenger cars and light truck plates has seven characters. Private trucks 14,000 to 18,000 lbs and 18,000 to 26,000 lbs use six characters. These plates indicate the weight limit vertically on the left side.

County/City Codes	County codes are not necessary as county of issue appears on the plate for typical plate patterns. However, certain license plates do not have county designation per legislative statute.
Plates and Stickers in Force	One plate, one decal for the year.
Plate Remains with Car when Sold?	The plate remains with the owner.

Overview of Record Access

About Driving Records

Customer Services, Licensing and Records, PO Box 80447, Conyers 30013, 678-413-8400. The current fee is $6.00 for a three-year history or $8.00 for a seven-year history. Personal checks are not accepted. Georgia charges for "no record found" reports.

Request Methods – Mail, Walk-in, fax, Online.

What You Should Know – There are five purposes for requesting Motor Vehicle Reports: insurance, employment, credit, rental car agency and limited rating information. For each purpose and use, a requester will be assigned a separate user-Id and password in order to log onto the Motor Vehicle Reports web page.

Special Access Programs Available –The Limited Rating Information (LRI) is a specific type of record, but only available to the insurance industry. A LRI report, which is $1.40, gives the license status and a summary of the number of violations relating to: driving under the influence of alcohol, drugs, or other intoxicating substances; and the number and type of other moving traffic violations committed by the subject. No withdrawal information is included on a LRI.

About Accident Reports

Copies of accident reports may be obtained from Department of Transportation, GDOT Crash Reporting Unit, PO Box 80447, Conyers 30013, 678-413-8647. Normally, new records are available for inquiry in 30 days. The requester must have a letter from the subject or proof of legal representation to obtain a record. Records are available for 10 years to present. Include the following in the request; full name, date and location of accident. The fee is $5.00 per report. There is no charge for a no-record found. Turnaround time is 1 week to 10 days.

About Vehicle Records

Attention: Research Unit, DOR/Motor Vehicle Division, PO Box 740381, Atlanta, GA 30374-0381, for Tag and Title - 404-968-3690; for CDL Registration 404-968-3850; fax is 404-362-2729. Certified copies and microfilm histories can be obtained from this department. The fee for a printout of tag or title or lien information is $1.00 per vehicle or name. For a microfilm search (title history) of five years the fee is $5.00. Certification is an additional $10.00. Major credit cards are accepted. Fees still apply if no record found. Due to the strict public access laws, vehicle information is not available in bulk or batch mode for any type of commercial purpose. It takes about 2 weeks before new records are available for inquiry on microfilm histories. For those public entities that qualify, records are available going back for only 5 years. General questions can be directed to motorvehicleinquiry@dor.ga.gov.

Request Methods – Mail, Walk-in, Online.

What You Should Know – Georgia does not offer a general online inquiry access program; however, there are online systems for specific groups. The Division provides a free vehicle insurance status check at https://mvd.dor.ga.gov/vincheck/VinCheck.aspx. Also, there is a web inquiry program for GA dealers only. In addition, email requests may be sent to motorvehicleinquiry@rev.dor.ga.gov.

About Watercraft Records

Georgia Department of Natural Resources, Boat Registration Office, 2065 U.S. Highway 278 SE, Social Circle 30348-5310, 800-366-2661, www.georgiawildlife.com. All motorized boats and all sailboats over 12 ft must be registered. Exceptions include canoes, kayaks and rubber rafts with no mechanical propulsion, and boats operated exclusively on private ponds or lakes. Titles are not required on watercraft, and for boat trailers. Records are available from 1986 and are computerized since 1994. Paper records are maintained for three years. Access by phone or mail. Requests should include name, registration # or hull number. There is no fee to do a name or registration search. Turnaround time is one week or longer. Liens are filed at the county level and do not show on records found at this agency. It takes 30-45 days before new records are available for inquiry.

Hawaii

Administration

Hawaii does not have a central agency that manages and regulates motor vehicle and driver functions. The Hawaii Department of Transportation, Motor Vehicle Safety Office is responsible for the program co-ordination of five separate county-responsible agencies that oversee driver licensing matters and vehicle registration or titling matters.

The Traffic Violations Bureau in Honolulu is the centralized agency that processes most of the manual record requests. Electronic access to driving records is through the Hawaii Information Consortium (HIC).

Motor Vehicle Safety Administrator
Motor Vehicle Safety Office
601 Kamokila Blvd #511, Honolulu 96707
808-692-7650
http://hawaii.gov/dot/highways/hwy-v/mvso.htm

Traffic Violations Bureau
1111 Alakea St, 2nd Floor, Honolulu, HI 96813
808-538-5500,   www.courts.state.hi.us

Administrative Rules governing Driver Licensing at:
http://hawaii.gov/dot/highways/admin-rules/ruleshwy.htm
Chapter 286, Hawaii Revised Statutes, sections 101-140, that govern Driver Licensing found at:
www.capitol.hawaii.gov/site1/docs/docs.asp?press1=docs

Important Telephone and Web Contacts

County of Hawaii
www.hawaii-county.com/vrl/dlgeninfo.html
    Driver Licensing.................................808-961-2222
    Vehicle 808-961-8351
    Traffic Court.......................................808-961-7470

City and County of Honolulu
www.co.honolulu.hi.us/csd/vehicle/dlinformation.htm
    Driver Licensing.................................808-532-7730
    Vehicle 808-532-7700
    Traffic Court.......................................808-538-5500

County of Kauai
www.kauai.gov. (click on Licenses & Permits)
    Driver Licensing.................................808-241-6550
    Vehicle 808-241-6577
    Traffic Court.......................................808-482-2355

County of Maui
www.mauicounty.gov/index.asp?nid=554
    Driver Licensing.................................808-270-7363
    Vehicle 808-270-7840
    Traffic Court.......................................808-244-2800

State Department of Insurance.................808-586-2790
Consumer Protection Office 808-586-2636

The district traffic courts in each county manage that county's driving record convictions.
County police agencies handle all law enforcement duties. There is no Central Highway Patrol or DPS-type agency.

Driver License Facts

License Format
Since 01/01/2001, a nine-character license is issued to all new and renewal drivers. This number consists of the letter "H" followed by eight numbers, selected on a random basis. Previous license numbers formatted by using the Social Security Number are valid until expiration. There is no "code" for the nine digit users.

Document Appearance
The current digital document has been in use since 03/2005.

Current Document
- **Security Characteristics**: Pink stripe on top containing "USA" and the Hawaii state flag. 2D barcode on rear. Hologram includes the state seal and a rainbow.
- **Position of Photo**: Top left with ghost image on the right.
- **Minor Age Driver Locator**: "UNDER 21 UNTIL..." is indicated under the top bar. The document is vertical.
- **CDL Indicator**: "CDL" appears on the lower right corner, as do the endorsement and restriction fields.

Old Document
- **Security Characteristics**: Since 06/01, this document was issued with a 2-D barcode below address along bottom of license. The graphics show "Aloha State" with hibiscus.
- **Position of Photo**: Top left (also, barcode below photo).

Minor Age Driver Locator   "UNDER 21 UNTIL..." appears in red and is under the license number.
CDL Indicator   A red "CDL" appears next to the endorsement/restriction fields.

Issue and Renewal
Age Requirements
A Graduated Driver License Program (GDL) was implemented in 09/2006. The minimum age to obtain an Instruction Permit is 15 1/2 years of age. A Provisional License may be issued at 16 years of age and must be held a minimum of 180 days. A Class 3 Driver License may be issued at 17 years of age. Other factors in the program include a driver education certification, and while operating a motor vehicle be seated next to a person who is at least 21 years of age and licensed to operate the same type of motor vehicle. However, between the hours of 11:00 p.m. and 5:00 a.m., the supervising parent or guardian must be seated next to the minor driver.

Renewal
Since November 3, 2008, HI driver's licenses issued to applicants age 24 thru 71 expire in eight years. Applicants under 25 expire in 4 years except provisional licenses expire on the applicant's 19th birthday. Previously, if the driver was under 18 years of age, the license was issued for four years and for drivers between 18 and 71 the license was issued for 6 years. The driver keeps the same number when renewing. Each license holder is limited to two consecutive renewals by mail. Resident military personnel and their immediate family may request for renewal by mail as many times as necessary if they reside outside the state of Hawaii on official military duty.

Elderly-Related Restrictions
If the driver is 72 or older the license is issued every two years, this includes CDL.

Residency
Non-residents (eighteen and over) from any state, U.S. territory, or Canada are permitted to drive on Class 1, 2 or 3—as long as home-state license remains valid.

License Classes
Commercial Classifications
Class A   Any combination of vehicles with a GCWR of 26,001 pounds or more; GVWR of vehicles towed is in excess of 10,000 pounds.
Class B   Any single vehicle with a GVWR of 26,001 pounds or more; the GVWR of a towed vehicle is 10,000 pounds or less.
Class C   Any single vehicle or combination of vehicles that meets neither the definition of A nor B and is designed to transport sixteen or more passengers, or used to haul hazardous materials requiring placards.

Non-Commercial Classifications
Class 1   Mopeds or Motor scooters 5hp or less.
Class 2   Motorcycles over 5hp and motor scooters.
Class 3   Any single vehicle with a GVWR of 15,000 pounds or less and vehicles designed to transport fifteen or fewer passengers (including the driver).
Class 4   Any single vehicle with a GVWR of 15,001 to 26,000 pounds.

HAZMAT Endorsement Procedure
The state is in compliance with the Patriot Act. All applicants applying for a new or renewal or transfer HAZMAT Endorsement (HME) must first obtain the application from https://hazprints.tsa.dhs.gov/Public/ or by calling 877-429-7746. The driver must also be fingerprinted. EMSI is the state-designated entity to process fingerprints - there are four locations, visit the web listed above to find the address locations. The cost of the fingerprint process is $89.25. The fingerprints and application information is sent to the Federal Transportation Security Administration (TSA). TSA performs the background checks and notifies the DMV whether the application is approved or denied. When completed and approved, the HME is valid for five years. For more information, visit the county web pages that describe licensing procedures. The Hawaii Department of Transportation does not provide an overview of the program and refers users to the TSA.

Safety and Enforcement Facts

Insurance and Financial Responsibility
Hawaii has mandatory no-fault insurance. Minimum financial responsibility limits are $35,000/10,000. Proof of insurance is required as part of the annual vehicle inspection program and after reportable accidents and after "certain" violations. Hawaii uses SR-22 forms.

Alcohol and Chemical Testing
Hawaii's alcoholic content provision is .08 %, .04 % for CDL, and zero tolerance if driver under 21 years old. Testing is

done by breath or blood. There is an implied-consent law and administrative revocation provisions.

Accident Reporting
Hawaii has a security-type law for accidents involving death, personal injury, or damage in excess of $3,000. Accidents within Hawaii County must be reported immediately to the Police Department at 349 Kapiolani Street, Hilo HI 96720. Reports are filed by the police and need not be filed by those involved. In the City and County of Honolulu, accident reports must be filed if no report is made at the scene. Reports should be filed with the Honolulu Police Department, 801 South King Street, Honolulu 96813. For Kauai County, accidents must be reported immediately to the Kauai Police Department, 3060 Umi Street, Lihue 96766. Reports must be filed only if the earlier reports were insufficient in the opinion of the Police Dept. Within Maui (Islands of Maui, Lanai, and Molokai) accidents must be reported immediately to the Police Department at 55 Mahalani Street, Wailuku 96793. No reports need to be filed by those involved in the accident, the police will collect all necessary information.

Suspensions and Revocations
It is assumed HI is in compliance with the **federally mandated disqualifications on CDLs** per MCSIA. See the Appendix for details.

Under the Influence of Intoxicant ....Ninety-day suspension.
Under the Influence if .15% or above ....Six-month to one-year revocation.
Second DUI Offense Within Five Years ....One-year suspension.
Third DUI Offense Within Five Years ....One- to five-year revocation.
Driving While License Suspended or Revoked for DUI ....Suspension or revocation for an additional year.

Periods of Administrative Revocation of Driver License and Criteria
1. No prior alcohol contacts during five-year period preceding the date of arrest .... Three months.
2. If one prior alcohol enforcement contact within a five-year period .... One year.
3. If two prior alcohol enforcement contacts within a five-year period .... Two years.
4. If three or more priors in the ten years preceding .... Lifetime.
5. Refusals under (1), (2), and (3) are revoked for respective periods of one, two, and four years.

Penalties for Driving While License is Suspended or Revoked for DUI
1. For a first offense, or any offense not preceded within a five-year period by a conviction under this section:
    a. A term of imprisonment at least three consecutive days, but not more than thirty days;
    b. A fine not less than $250, but not more than $1,000; and
    c. License suspension or revocation for an additional year.
2. For an offense which occurs within five years of a prior conviction under this section:
    a. Thirty-days imprisonment;
    b. A fine of $1,000; and
    c. License suspension or revocation for an additional two years.
3. For an offense that occurs within five years of two or more prior convictions under this section:
    a. One-year imprisonment;
    b. A $2,000 fine; and
    c. Permanent revocation of the person's license

Reinstatement Requirements
Suspension or Revocation $10.00 or higher fee; time lapse; SR-22.
To be eligible for re-licensing after a period of administrative revocation has expired, the person shall:
1. Submit to the Director proof of compliance with all conditions imposed by the Director or by the court;
2. Obtain a certified statement from the director indicating eligibility for re-licensing;
3. Present the certified statement to the appropriate licensing official;
4. Pay all applicable fees; and
5. Successfully complete each requirement for obtaining licensure in the state.

Point System Overview
Hawaii has no point system. Years ago an existing point system was repealed by the legislature.

License Plate Facts

Registration & Renewal
The registration of all vehicles in Hawaii must be renewed every year in the county where the vehicle is registered and being driven. Three counties - Kauai, Oahu, and Maui - offer online registration renewal at https://mvr.ehawaii.gov/renewals/index.html.

New Residents

Non-residents must register vehicles within ten days after arrival. However, an Out-of-State Permit is available. The permit has to be applied for within 30 days of arrival, proof of arrival (bill of lading), and the vehicle has to pass a safety check. This permit is good for 12 months or until the out-of-state plates expire, which ever comes first.

Inspections and Emissions Testing

Hawaii requires a yearly safety inspection, but no emission testing.

Plate Descriptions

Typical Plate Patterns	Passenger and light truck plates are LLLNNN. Commercial vehicles, trailers and motorcycles are NNNLLL.

County/City Codes	The first alpha digit on a plate refers to the county of issue as follows:
	   H Hawaii
	   K Kauai
	   M Maui
	   All other alpha Honolulu

Plates and Stickers in Force	2 plates, 1 decals (MO & YR) on rear plate.
Plates Remain with Car when Sold?	Yes.

Overview of Record Access

About Driving Records

Traffic Violations Bureau (TVB), 1111 Alakea Street, Honolulu 96813, 808-538-5500, www.courts.state.hi.us/. Also, Hawaii Information Consortium (HIC) provides access to records on behalf of Traffic Violations Bureau. The TVB and the traffic courts in each county issue two types of certified documents that report a person's traffic history: traffic abstracts and traffic court reports. The driver's license number, full name, and date of birth are needed when ordering.

1) **Traffic Abstract** (sometimes called a "public" or "abbreviated" abstract), shows moving violations and alleged moving offenses, but does not show juvenile records unless a Juvenile Information Release Form is signed by the juvenile and a parent or legal guardian]. If an adult has a juvenile traffic record and would like it displayed on the public record, a signed consent form must be provided. The fee is $7.00 per record and $9.00 per CDL record if processed by mail or in-person. The fee is $10.00 if accessed electronically (see below).

2) **Traffic Court Report** (sometimes called a "complete" or "court" abstract) shows all cases including juvenile (with signed release form), parking, miscellaneous, dismissed and found not guilty cases. A photo ID is required from the individual requesting this abstract. If an individual has juvenile record but release form is not provided, an abbreviated abstract without juvenile record will be issued. The fee is $1.00 plus $.50 per page. Since this record can go back as far as 55 years, the record of drivers with extensive activity can be quite costly to obtain. This document can only be ordered in-person (by the person for whom the record is for) with a photo ID.

Request Methods – Mail, Walk-in, Online.

What You Should Know – Traffic Abstracts are normally used for insurance purposes. Traffic Court Reports, which are essentially internal court records, are normally provided to government agencies and attorneys or to the subject person. Note that walk-in requesters may purchase abstracts with a VISA or MasterCard.

Online ordering of driving records by DPPA compliant requesters is available from the state's designated entity - Hawaii Information Consortium (HIC). Visit www.ehawaii.gov/dakine/docs/subscription.html or call 808-695-4620 for more information.

About Crash Reports

There is no centralized agency that handles accident reports. The police department in each county must be contacted. For example, in Honolulu reports are available from the Records Division (808-529-3271) 7 days after the accident. For the addresses please refer to the *Accident Reporting* section earlier this chapter.

About Vehicle Records

Hawaii does not have a statewide Department of Motor Vehicles. Vehicle Registration is managed by each county government. For information please contact:

County of Hawaii
   East: Aupuni Center, 101 Pauahi Street, Suite 5, Hilo, HI 96720

West: 75-5706 Kuakini Hwy, Suite 107, Kailua-Kona, HI 96740
Phone: (East) 808-961-8351; Phone: (West) 327-3543

City & County of Honolulu
Division of Motor Vehicles and Licensing, PO Box 30320, Honolulu, Hawaii 96820-0320; 808-532-7700
www.co.honolulu.hi.us/csd/vehicle/mvehicle.htm

County of Kauai
www.kauai.gov. (click on Licenses & Permits)
Phone: 808-241-6577

County of Maui
Department of Finance, Division of Motor Vehicles & Licensing, Maui Mall Shopping Center, 70 E. Kaahumanu Avenue, Suite A-17, Kahului, HI 96732-2176; Phone: 808-270-7363 Fax: 808-270-7858
http://www.mauicounty.gov/index.asp?nid=554
E-mail: maui.dmvl@co.maui.hi.us

What You Should Know – Honolulu provides online title inquiry at www4.honolulu.gov/mvrtitleinq/. Must provide last four digits of VIN and plate number.

About Watercraft Records

Land and Natural Resources, Div. of Boating & Recreation, 333 Queen Street Room 300, Honolulu 96813, http://hawaii.gov/dlnr/dbor/dbor.html, *808-587-1966.* Requests must be in writing and describe reason for the search. Liens are filed at the Bureau of Conveyances, but information is made available from this agency. There is no fee to do a registration or lien search. Records are maintained since the 1950s; on microfiche from 1987-1994, and on computer and hard copy from 1994 forward (records are dropped from computer when not renewed). A boat or hull number is needed, but they can do a name search on the computer. Online renewal is available.

Idaho

Administration	Important Telephone and Web Contacts
Motor Vehicle Administrator Idaho Transportation Department P.O. Box 7129 Boise 83707-1129 208-334-8000 www.itd.idaho.gov/dmv/ http://trucking.idaho.gov/ General Email: DMV-info@itd.idaho.gov	Driver Licensing & CDL..................................208-334-8736 Driver Services..208-334-8735 SR-22 and Financial Responsibility ....208-334-8736 Motor Carrier...208-334-8611 Vehicle Titles ....208-334-8663 Vehicle Registrations ....208-334-8649 Highway Patrol..208-884-7200 State Department of Insurance ....208-334-4250 Motor Vehicle Laws: www3.state.id.us/idstat/TOC/49FTOC.html Administrative Rules: http://adm.idaho.gov/adminrules/

Driver License Facts

License Format
Idaho law Code 49-306(2) prohibits disclosing the Social Security Number. Effective May 1, 1993, the "Current License Format" below is used as new licenses are issued. Note that old formats may still be valid for certain license holders.
  Current License Format.................................9 characters—2 alpha, 6 numeric, 1 alpha.
  Old License Format - 1/1/93 to 5/1/93 ....9 numeric beginning with 910, 920, 930 or 940.
  Old License Format - Prior to 1/1/93 ....9 numeric beginning with 910, 920, or SSN.

Document Appearance
  Security Characteristics   A plastic card with laminate. A gold, repetitive design is embossed in the laminate.
  Position of Photo   Bottom left.
  Minor Age Driver Locator   Licenses issued to individuals under 21 are in a vertical format. "UNDER 21 UNTIL XXXX" or "UNDER 18 UNTIL XXXX" is printed below the date of birth line. Under 21 licenses have a red border around the photo. Under-18 licenses have a green border around the photo.
  CDL Indicator   A CDL is indicated by the class code and the designation "CDL" or the words "Commercial Drivers License" appear on the top of the card.

Issue and Renewal
Age Requirements
The minimum age is fifteen with Driver Education; otherwise seventeen. For an Instruction Permit, driver must be accompanied by an licensed adult (eighteen or older).
Renewal
Birth date of fourth year. The driver keeps the same number when renewing (new cycle). Out-of-state military personnel can extend by mail for four years. The HAZMAT endorsement cannot be extended by mail. Upon discharge or return to Idaho, the license must be renewed within 60 days.
Elderly-Related Restrictions
None, unless the Department is notified in writing by a family member, physician, law enforcement officer or driver license examiner about an individual's inability to safely operate a motor vehicle.
Residency
Persons residing within the state for a continuous ninety days are considered residents.

License Classes
Commercial Classifications
  Class A   Enables a driver to operate combination vehicles with a GCWR over 26,000 pounds—provided the GVWR of the vehicle(s) being towed is greater than 10,000 pounds. A driver with a Class A license is properly licensed to operate Class A, B, C, and D vehicles.

Class B	Enables a driver to operate single vehicles with a GVWR of over 26,000 pounds, or any such vehicle towing a vehicle not in excess of 10,000 pounds GVWR. A driver with a Class B license is properly licensed to operate Class B, C, and D vehicles.
Class C	Enables a driver to operate vehicles that do not fall in Class A or B, but are designed to carry sixteen or more passengers (including the driver) or carry hazardous materials in quantities which require placards. A driver with a Class C license is properly licensed to operate Class C and D vehicles.
Class NA	Non-resident Class A CDL.
Class NB	Non-resident Class B CDL.
Class NC	Non-resident Class C CDL.

Non-Commercial Classifications

Class D	Enables a driver to operate a vehicle that is not a commercial vehicle.

HAZMAT Endorsement Procedure

The state is in compliance with the Patriot Act. All applicants applying for a new or renewal or transfer HAZMAT Endorsement (HME) must first obtain the application from https://hazprints.tsa.dhs.gov/Public/ or by calling 877-429-7746. The driver must also be fingerprinted. EMSI and COMNETIX are the state-designated entities to process fingerprints. There are three locations in the state that perform this service. Visit the web page listed above to find the address locations. Also, the state has an excellent site explaining the program at www.itd.idaho.gov/dmv/DriverServices/HazMatFactSheet.pdf. The cost of the fingerprint process is $89.25. The fingerprints and application information is sent to the Federal Transportation Security Administration (TSA). TSA performs the background checks and notifies the DMV whether the application is approved or denied. When completed and approved, the HME is valid until the expiration date of the driver license.

Safety and Enforcement Facts

Insurance and Financial Responsibility

Idaho has a compulsory insurance law. Minimum financial responsibility limits are $25,000/50,000/15,000. Proof of insurance must be carried at all times and is required to be shown when an officer asks for it under registration law. SR-22 forms are used.

Alcohol and Chemical Testing

Idaho's alcoholic content level law is .08 percent, for CDL is .04 percent, and for under 21 is .02 percent. It is possible that a driver's CDL privileges are disqualified while the operator's privileges are not. The following tests are legal: urine, blood, and breath. There is an implied-consent violation provision.

Accident Reporting

Accidents resulting in death, personal injury, or damage in excess of $1,500 must be reported immediately to the local police; however, written reports do not have to be filed by the driver. Idaho reports no variations in this method for commercial drivers.

Suspensions and Revocations

The state is in compliance with the **federally mandated disqualifications on CDLs**. See the Appendix for details.
Point Accumulation
    Twelve or more points in twelve months .... Thirty-day suspension.
    Eighteen or more points in twenty-four months .... Ninety-day suspension.
    Twenty-four or more points in thirty-six months .... Six-month suspension.
Conviction of Driving Under the Influence of Alcohol, Drugs or any Other Intoxicating Substance
    First Offense.. May include up to 180-day suspension.
    Second Offense Within Ten Years .... May include one-year suspension.
    Third Offense Within Ten Years... May include one- to five-year suspension.
Conviction of Aggravated Driving While Under Influence of Alcohol, Drugs
   or any Other Intoxicating Substance .... May include one- to five-year suspension.
Leaving the Scene of an Accident Resulting in Death or Injury .... One-year revocation.

Other Reasons for Suspension
Judges and the Idaho Transportation Department are authorized under state statute to suspend, disqualify, deny, cancel, or revoke the license of drivers convicted of violating certain laws, no matter what the driver's point-system count. Those violations include:

- Alcohol-age violation (possession, use, or procurement).
- Administrative license suspension (for failing a breath, blood, or urine test when tested for DUI).

- Any court or the Department of Health and Welfare may order the Idaho Transportation Department to suspend the driver license and privileges of any person who fails to pay child support, fails to comply with visitation rights, or fails to comply with a subpoena for a paternity suit or child support proceeding.
- Conviction or action in another state for an offense that, if committed in Idaho, would be grounds for suspension.
- Driving while under the influence of alcohol or other drugs.
- Driving with a suspended license (driving without privileges).
- Failing to pay a fine for conviction on an "infraction" charge. (Infractions are a step below misdemeanors and include such minor violations as parking tickets.)
- Failing to pay a judgment for damages in an accident.
- Failure to carry motor vehicle insurance.
- Fleeing from or eluding a peace officer.
- Leaving the scene of an accident in which you were involved, when the accident caused property damage.
- Leaving the scene of an accident resulting in injury or death.
- Making false statements, oral or written, to the Transportation Department while under oath.
- Reckless driving.
- Refusal to Submit to an evidentiary test for DUI.
- Repeat violations under age 17.
- School districts may order the Idaho Transportation Department to suspend the driver's license and privileges of a minor who fails to attend school or does not comply with school requirements.
- Underage possession of marijuana or drug paraphernalia.
- Unlawful use of a driver's license or ID card.
- Using a motor vehicle to commit a felony.
- Violation of restriction.
- Violation of restrictions of supervised instruction permit.
- Violations from other states that, if committed in Idaho, would require license withdrawal.

Reinstatement Requirements
Suspension .... $25.00 to $85.00 fee most cases; time lapse; SR-22 in some cases.
Revocation .... $85.00 fee most cases; time lapse; SR-22 in some cases.
In State DUI conviction .... $285.00 fee most cases; time lapse; SR-22 in some cases.
Out of State DUI Conviction .... $245.00 fee; time lapse; SR-22 in some cases

Point System Overview
The Idaho point system ranges from 1 to 4 points. A driver can be suspended for accumulating 12 or more points in a 12 month period; 18 or more points in a 24 month period; or 24 or more points in a 36 month period. Once every three (3) years, drivers may reduce their point total by three points if they complete an approved defensive driving course. The course must be taken before a suspension for accumulation of points takes place. A point reduction can only be applied on an Idaho driver's license record. The conviction is not removed from the record, only the points.

License Plate Facts

Registration & Renewal
Online renewal is available online at https://www.accessidaho.org/secure/itd/vehicle/renewal.html for registrants in the following counties: Ada, Adams, Bannock, Bear Lake, Bingham, Blaine, Boise, Bonneville, Camas, Canyon, Cassia, Custer, Elmore, Fremont, Gem, Gooding, Idaho, Jerome, Kootenai, Latah, Madison, Minidoka, Oneida, Payette, Twin Falls, and Washington County residents. This web service is currently not available for the renewal of the following registration programs: Boats, Classic, Dealer, Exempt, Legislative, Loaner, Off-Road, Old Timer, Repossession, Snowmobiles and Transporter. Additional counties may participate in this program in the future.

New Residents
Persons whose primary home has been in the state for ninety days are considered residents for the purpose of driver's license, title, and registration. Persons may apply for the Idaho drivers license, title or registration earlier than ninety days and then be considered a resident.

Inspections and Emissions Testing
Idaho has no statewide, passenger vehicle-safety inspection program or emission-testing program, except in ADA county emission testing is required for vehicles owned by Ada county residents.

Plate Descriptions
Typical Plate Patterns   Passenger and light truck plates have a 1, 2, or 3-digit prefix (either L, NL or NNL) followed by 1 to 6 numbers. In more populous counties, an alpha numeric mix may be used for the sequential portion of the plate. Commercial vehicles are LLNNNN.

County/City Codes	The prefix to the passenger plates designates the county of issuance. The code is the numeric sequence of the first initial of the county with that initial (i.e. Butte is the 10th county starting with "B", so the prefix is "10B").
Plates and Stickers in Force	2 plates, 1 decal (MO & YR) on each plate.
Plates Remain with Car when Sold?	No, they remain with the seller.

Overview of Record Access

About Driving Records

Drivers Services, PO Box 34, Boise 83731-0034, 208-334-8736, fax 208-334-8739. The state refers to the driving record as a DLR (Driver License Record). The fee is $7.00 if processed manually or $9.00 if online. Certification of a single record is an additional $14.00. If a DLR is requested plus copies of file documents (i.e., Citations, Suspension Orders, etc.) the fee is $14.00. The MVA accepts MasterCard and Visa for payment of records. Idaho charges for "no record found" reports for mail and fax requests. Records are reported for the last 3 years, unless an "all year" record is requested.

Request Methods – Mail, Walk-in, Fax, Online, Bulk.

What You Should Know – Driver Services and Access Idaho refer to driving records as Driver License Records (DLRs) and refer to records related to vehicle title or registration as MVRs.

Special Access Programs Available – At https://www.accessidaho.org/secure/itd/reinstatement/index.html there is a free DL Status Check. Access Idaho provides the online service for records.

Also, Access Idaho (https://www.accessidaho.org/online_services/) provides a driver monitoring program for a subscribers that wish to monitor driving records for violations and suspensions. The program works on a monthly basis. The user supplies a driver list for a fee of $.14 per driver for each month checked (the check can go back in time). If there is activity, the system automatically generates a driving record for the $9.00 fee. Activity includes moving violations and withdrawal actions. The program is available for DPPA permissible user clients including employers and insurance companies. Access Idaho also offers a Youthful Driver check that operates on a similar basis. For more information on either program, call 208-332-0102.

About Vehicle Records

Vehicle Services, Idaho Transportation Department, PO Box 34, Boise 83731-0034, 208-334-8649 or 8663. Idaho maintains title, registration, and lien records for vehicles and mobile homes not declared real property. This agency also maintains title records since 01/2000 on watercraft for model year 2000 or if there is a permanently attached mode of propulsion or if longer than 12 feet unless exempt. If a lien is placed on a vessel that is older than model year 2000, that vessel must be titled. Note that vessels are registered with the Parks and Recreation Department (see below).

The fee for obtaining a hard copy of a title record, lien record, or registration record is $7.00. A complete title history is $14.00 (often using microfilm). The certification of a record (per vehicle) is an additional $14.00. Fees for online access is $9.00. Medical information and SSNs are not released. The same fees for vehicle ownership searches apply to vessel ownership searches.

Request Methods – Mail, Walk-in, Fax, Online, Bulk.

What You Should Know – The counter on State Street is closed except for motor carrier and commercial trucking needs. However, records may be requested from any county assessor auto licensing location, statewide.

About Watercraft Records

Idaho Parks & Recreation, PO Box 83730, Boise 83720-0065, 208-514-2480, ext 306, fax is 334-2639, www.parksandrecreation.idaho.gov/recreation/boating.aspx. **See above about titles.** All boats with either a motor or permanently attached sail must be registered. Registration records are open to the public but address information is not released. Record information can be verified or provided; however state statutes forbid the release of commercial lists. Access is by mail and in-person only, but verification can be done over the phone. Turnaround time by mail is within 10 working days. Phone numbers and addresses are not released, unless written consent given. Simple ownership and registration verification are provided for no fee, but fees are charge for custom data searches. Requesters must provide name or hull number or registration number. Lien record information must be searched at the UCC Division of the state for liens recorded prior to 01/01/00, or recorded against vessels exempt from titling after 01/01/00 (call 208-334-3191) or at vehicle services for liens recorded against title-able vessels since 01/01/00. Note there is a $6.00 fee for UCC data.

Illinois

Administration	Important Telephone and Web Contacts
Michael J. Mayer, Director Drivers Services Department 2701 S Dirksen Parkway Springfield, IL 62723 Ernie Dannenberger, Director Vehicle Services Department 501 S 2nd Street Room 312 Springfield, IL 62756 www.sos.state.il.us www.cyberdriveillinois.com	Driver Licensing............................217-782-6212 SR-22 & Financial Responsibility..............217-782-3720 Mandatory Insurance..................217 524-4946 Driver Services...........................217782-2720 PDPS Help Desk........................217-785-3108 Commercial Driver License.........................217-524-1350 Vehicle Information.......................217-782-6992 State Police (Springfield District)................217-786-7107 State Department of Insurance.....................217-782-4515 Rules of the Road Laws: www.cyberdriveillinois.com/publications/motoristpub.html#trafficsafety

Driver License Facts

License Format
One letter and eleven numbers. The format is coded, however the coding "translation" is not available to the public

Document Appearance
Two recent changes (01/01/2005 and 01/01/2008) were made to the DL and ID documents. Older licenses are being phased out as new licenses are issued.

Documents Phased in Since 10/2007

Security Characteristics — Security features include kinetic movement and color shifting designs, a UV feature, microtext, a ghost image of the photo and incorporation of the date of birth in two locations on the cards.

Overall Description — The photo with blue background is on the upper left, a ghost image is found in the lower right corner. Colors across the card tops indicate card types. Red is used for standard DLs and CDLs. ID cards are in green and Temporary Visitor DLs are in purple.

Minor Age Driver — All Illinois Under 21 driver's licenses, identification cards, and commercial drivers licenses (DLs, IDs, and CDLs) are a vertical design. The "Under 21 until MO/DAY/YR" and "Under 18 until MO/DAY/YR" text appears in red and yellow bars next to the photo. The header bar above the photo is blue and identifies the card type (DL, ID or CDL).

Temp Visitor — Known as the TVDL (Temporary Visitor Driver's License), the standard card and under 21 card look like the associated DL or ID card, except the color header across the top is purple. Front has text "Not Valid for Identification" in red under purple header bar and TVDL in a blue bar.

CDL Indicator — "CDL" appears in a blue bar on right side under the header.

Documents Issued 2005 Through Fall 2007

Security Characteristics — The appearance of the digital license is similar to a credit card. There is a hologram across the bottom of license and a "Safer State with .08" 1-D bar code on back contains driver's license number. A 2-D bar code on the back contains data from the front. Blue header is above photo for drivers over 21.

Position of Photo — Photo with blue background is on right.

Minor Age Driver — These Illinois Under 21 driver's licenses, identification cards, and commercial drivers licenses (DLs, IDs, and CDLs) are a vertical design with a blue pattern across much of the card. The actual text that appears on the card remains the same. The card back is unchanged from the pre-2005 document. The "Under 21 until MO/DAY/YR" and

	"Under 18 until MO/DAY/YR" text appears in red and yellow bars next to the photo. The header bar above the photo is blue and identifies the card type (DL, ID or CDL). The DL/ID number, issue date and expiration date appear in a blue block beneath the signature. The date of birth appears beneath an image of the State Seal. The retro-reflective "Safer State with .08" optical variable device runs through the side of the card lengthwise, over part of the photo and signature and DL/ID number.
Temp Visitor Under 21	The Under 21 Temporary Visitor Driver's License looks like other Under 21 cards, but the background color is green. The header bar above the photo is green instead of blue and includes the text "Temporary Visitor Drivers License". The bar containing the text "Under 21 until MO/DAY/YEAR is green instead of red. The block containing DL number, issue date and expiration date is green instead of blue. The text "Not Valid for Identification" is in red above the name. The expiration date will indicate either 3 years from date of issuance, or less if the authorized length of stay in the U.S. is less.
CDL Indicator	"CDL" appears at top of the photo.

Pre-2005 Documents

Security Characteristics	State's outline in data area; hologram in laminate which covers portions of both the data and photo areas; a three digit security plate number appears vertically in top left of photo area.
Position of Photo	Lower right
Minor Age Driver	Red header above photo, red printing and borders on license laminate and red background. Minor's license is indicated by "under 21 until xx/xx/xx" (or under 18 if applicable), across top. Photo position is in lower right.
CDL Indicator	"CDL" in blue background appears in data area of lic., and directly above photo area.

Issue and Renewal

Age Requirements
Illinois has a graduated licensing system for young drivers with strict standards for drivers under 21. The minimum age is eighteen; sixteen with completion of approved driver education course (minimum of 50 hours including 10 hours of night-time practice) holding Learner's Permit nine months. Unless emancipated, all applicants under eighteen must have parent/guardian consent. A Learner's Permit, which is required first, is valid for two years. Driver must be accompanied by parent or licensed adult age 21 or older with one year of driving experience.

Renewal
Normally, birthday of fourth year. Driver keeps same number when renewing unless change of name, DOB, and/or gender. The Safe Driver Sticker Renewal Program allows Illinois residents whose driving records contain no convictions or accidents to renew their driver licenses over the telephone, Internet or through the mail. Participants receive a sticker to attach to the back of their current license, which extends the expiration period by four years. Active military personnel serving outside IL may obtain a Military Deferral Card to be carried with the expired license. The card is also available for spouses and dependents. The card, which can be secured from the Driver Services Department (217-782-2720), is valid for 90 days after discharge or reassignment to a military base in IL.

Elderly-Related Restrictions
All persons aged 75 or older must take a driving test at each renewal. Drivers aged 81-86 must have their licenses renewed every two years, while persons aged 87 and older must renew annually

Residency
Non-resident's home-state license honored on a reciprocal basis; must secure Illinois license within 90 days of establishing residency. CDL holders must obtain an Illinois CDL within 30 days of becoming an Illinois resident.

License Classes

Commercial Classifications

A	Any combination of vehicles with a GCWR of 26,001 pounds or more, provided the GVWR of the vehicle(s) being towed is in excess of 10,000 pounds.
B	Any single vehicle with a GVWR of 26,001 or more pounds, or any such vehicle towing a vehicle not in excess of 10,000 pounds GVWR.
C (1)	Any single vehicle with a GVWR of 16,001 or more pounds, but less than 26,001 pounds GVWR, or any such vehicle towing a vehicle not in excess of 10,000 pounds GVWR;
C (2)	Any vehicle less than 26,001 pounds GVWR designed to transport sixteen or more people (including the driver) or used in the transportation of Hazardous Materials (HazMat) which requires the vehicle to be placarded;

C (3)   Any vehicle less than 26,001 pounds GVWR designed to transport sixteen or more people (including the driver) or used in the transportation of HazMat which requires the vehicle to be placarded, towing a vehicle with a GVWR of 10,000 pounds or less or with a GCWR of less than 26,000 pounds.

R-CDL   A Restricted CDL is available to drivers employed by farm retail outlets and suppliers, agri-chemical business, custom harvesters and livestock feeders. The R-CDL can be issued for no less than 90 days and no more than 180 days within a 12 month period and is valid only within 150 miles of the employer's place of business. The R-CDL must be accompanied by an Illinois Class B driver's license and letter of employment verification.

Non-Commercial Classifications

D (1)   Any single vehicle with a GVWR of 16,000 pounds or less that is not designed to transport sixteen or more people, or not used in the transportation of HazMat which requires such vehicle to be placarded.

D (2)   Any single vehicle with a GVWR of 16,000 pounds or less that is not designed to transport sixteen or more people, or not used in the transportation of HazMat which would require such vehicle to be placarded, towing any vehicle providing the GCWR is less than 26,001 pounds.

L   Any motor driven cycle with less than 150 cc displacement.

M   Any motorcycle.

HAZMAT Endorsement Procedure

The state is in compliance with the Patriot Act. Applicants should complete the TSA HAZPRINT application on the IBT website at https://hazprints.tsa.dhs.gov/Public/, or by calling the IBT Driver Service Center at 1-877-429-7746). The operator at the IBT Driver Service Center will guide the applicant through the process and ensure the application is completed correctly. The applicant can also call the IBT Driver Service Center at any time if he or she has any questions about the website. It is important to note that the application must be completed either online or via telephone through the IBT Driver Service Center prior to arriving at the fingerprint capture location. It cannot be completed at the fingerprinting site. The cost of the security threat assessment is $89.25. For more information, visit www.cyberdriveillinois.com/departments/drivers/cdl/hazmat.html. Once approved, the driver will be notified to visit an Illinois Secretary of State CDL facility to obtain the endorsement.

Safety and Enforcement Facts

Insurance and Financial Responsibility

Minimum financial responsibility limits are $20,000/40,000/15,000. Mandatory insurance laws apply to all vehicles operated within the state. Proof of financial responsibility is required after an uninsured at fault accident, revocations and mandatory insurance offenses. Proof of financial responsibility (SR-22 Certificate) is required for three years on: unsatisfied judgment suspensions related to an accident; and safety responsibility suspensions and revocations. Since 01/01/2008, proof of financial responsibility is required for three years as a condition of supervision for violations of the mandatory insurance law and those receiving three convictions for mandatory insurance violations. A circuit court may request the Secretary of State suspend the driving privileges of a parent who is 90 days behind on child support payments. The court ordered suspension will appear as a FR (Family Financial Responsibility) on the driving record.

Alcohol and Chemical Testing

Illinois' alcoholic provision limit is .08% with .04% for CDL and .00% (zero tolerance) if under 21 years of age. Legal testing means include urine, blood, and breathe. Illinois has provisions within its laws for an implied-consent violation and an administrative suspension. Effective 2009, certain individuals convicted of a DUI are required to have an ignition Interlock device installed in their vehicles. See Public Act 095-0400.

Accident Reporting

Accidents resulting in property damage in excess of $1,500, injury, or death must be reported in-person or by phone to the nearest law enforcement agency. Within ten days, form "SR-1" must be filed with the Department of Transportation, Accident Report Office, 1340 North 9th Street, Springfield 62766. The "SR-1" form is for both personal and commercial vehicles. A box on the form is checked for "driving in the course of employment." Drivers at fault in the crash must also meet the requirements of Safety Responsibility Law. This law requires a security (a guarantee of payment) if there is no insurance coverage or another acceptable form of payment.

Suspensions and Revocations

Point Accumulation: If three or more point assessed violations are committed within a 12-month period, or two or more point assessed violations are committed by a driver under the age of 21 within a 24-month period, the driver's record is reviewed for possible suspension or revocation. If the driver's record shows no prior suspensions or revocations in the previous seven-year period, the following tables are used to determine the length of the suspension or whether revocation is to be entered:

Point Accumulation - Under Age 21
- 10 thru 34 points .... One-month suspension.
- 35 thru 49 points .... Three-month suspension.
- 50 thru 64 points .... Six-month suspension.
- 65 thru 79 points .... Twelve-month suspension.
- 80 or more points .... Revocation.

If the driver is under the age of 21 and has previously been suspended for being convicted of 2 or more point assigned violations within a 24 month period and is convicted of another point assigned violation... OR... If a person under the age of 21 is convicted of the violations illegal possession or consumption of alcoholic beverages, the driving privileges shall be suspended or revoked as follows—
- First offense .... Six-month suspension.
- Second offense .... Twelve-month suspension.
- Third of subsequent offense .... Revocation.

If the driver was previously revoked and is convicted of another point assigned violation, driving privileges will be revoked.

If the driver is under age 21 and is placed on Court Supervision for a violation of illegal possession or consumption of alcoholic beverages the driving privileges shall be suspended for three months.

Point Accumulation - Over Age 21
- 15 thru 44 points .... Two-month suspension.
- 45 thru 74 points .... Three-month suspension.
- 75 thru 89 points .... Six-month suspension.
- 90 thru 99 points .... Nine-month suspension.
- 100 thru 109 points .... Twelve-month suspension.
- 110 or more points .... Revocation.

DUI Convictions - Under Age 21
- First Offense .... Minimum two-year revocation.
- Second Conviction .... Minimum five year revocation.
- Third Conviction .... Minimum ten-year revocation.
- Fourth Conviction .... Lifetime revocation.

DUI Convictions - Age 21 or Older
Same as above except if 2nd conviction in twenty years ... Minimum five-year revocation.

Statutory Summary Suspension for Refusal to Submit to Chemical Test Indicating .08 BAC or higher
- First Offense (prior to 01/01/2009) .... Six-month suspension.
- First Offense (01/01/2009 or thereafter).... Twelve-month suspension.
- Subsequent Offenses within five years...... Twelve-month suspension.

Statutory Summary Suspension for Refusal to Submit to Chemical Test
- First Offense (prior to 01/01/2009) .... Three-month suspension.
- First Offense (01/01/2009 or thereafter).... Twelve-month suspension.
- Subsequent Offenses within five years...... Thirty-six-month suspension.

Illegal Transportation of Open Alcoholic Beverages-Drivers Under Age of 21
- First Offense .... Twelve-month suspension.
- Subsequent Offenses .... Revocation.

Illegal Transportation of Open Alcoholic Beverages-Drivers Over Age of 21
- First Offense .... No action.
- Second Offense within one year................ Twelve-month suspension.
- Third or Subsequent Offense..................... Revocation.

Zero Tolerance Law Under 21 with BAC of more than .00%
- First Offense .... Three-month suspension.
- Subsequent Offenses .... Twelve-month suspension.

Zero Tolerance Law Under 21--Refusal to Submit to Chemical Test
- First Offense .... Six-month suspension.
- Subsequent Offenses .... Twenty four-month suspension.

Zero Tolerance Law School Bus Drivers BAC of more than .00 - Any Offense .... Cancellation of Permit.

Driving While License Suspended or Revoked
Extension of revocation or suspension or loss of full driving privileges, if privileges have been reinstated.
- Felony DUI .... Minimum one-year revocation.

Reckless Homicide Class 2 Felony .... Minimum two-year revocation.
Leaving the Scene of a Fatal or Personal Injury Accident.... Minimum three-year revocation.
Graduated Drivers License Denials:.................................. One serious violation (majors plus speeding 30+ over) means a denial for six months or until the 18th birthday, which ever is shorter. A moving violation conviction results in nine months waiting period before applying for a driver's license. Driving with no valid license or committing an offense that would result in a mandatory revocation of a license or permit will deny the applicant until 18 years of age.

These additional violations may trigger a revocation or suspension. Termination dates vary according to offense.

Revocations:
- Aggravated DUI (minimum revocation lengths vary according to type of offense and previous history)
- Aggravated Fleeing the Police
- Auto Theft
- Drag Racing or Street Racing
- Felony Offense (vehicle used when serious crime committed)
- Fraudulent ID
- Perjury (gave false information to the Secretary of State)
- Reckless Conduct (involving a vehicle resulted in injury or danger to another person)
- Reckless Driving (convicted of three reckless driving offenses in 12 months)
- Second or Subsequent Conviction of Driving While Revoked When Already Revoked for Reckless Homicide

Suspensions:
- Drug or Sex Offense (committed a drug or sex crime while operating or in direct physical control of an automobile)
- Failure to Appear (failed to appear for any traffic citation)
- Failure to Pay Child Support
- Failure to Pay Five or More Automated Traffic Law Violations
- Failure to Pay Five or More Tollway Violations
- Failure to Yield and Proceed with Due Caution Upon Entering a Construction Zone or When Workers are Present
- Failure to Yield Right of Way to Emergency Vehicles
- Failure to Obey a Railroad-Crossing Signal (second violation)
- Fraudulent License/ID Application
- Illegal Transportation of Alcohol (convicted of illegally transporting alcohol twice in 12 months)
- Obstructing Railroad Crossing For Use by Trains or Railroad Equipment
- Parking Violations (failure to pay fines or penalties for 10 or more unpaid parking violations)
- School Bus Violations (failed to stop as required by law for a school bus that was picking up or dropping off children)
- Speeding in a Construction Zone (second or subsequent violation within two years)
- Theft of Motor Fuel
- Traffic Crashes (convicted for refusal or neglect to report a traffic accident)
- Uninsured Crashes

Illinois is in compliance with the mandatory CDL disqualifications. See the Appendix for these disqualifications.

Reinstatement Requirements

Suspension — $70 fee; time lapse. If under 21, may be required to attend remedial education and be re-examined.

Admin "Per Se" — $250 fee, first offense; $500 subsequent offenses.

Revocation — $500 fee; $10 license fee; time lapse (at least one year); proof of financial responsibility (SR-22) insurance for three years; application for renewal of license; re-examination; formal/informal hearing required.

Point System Overview

Illinois employs two point systems. Refer to Point Accumulation sub-section above for more information.

License Plate Facts

Registration Renewal

License plate registrations are renewed annually. Online renewals are available for motorists using a Renewal Code and Personal Identification Number (PIN) printed on the renewal notice. Renewals can also be processed via a touch-tone phone system by calling 866-545-9609 using a major credit card.

New Residents
Non-residents must register vehicles within thirty days of establishing residency.

Inspections and Emissions Testing
Although Illinois has no mandatory statewide emission testing program, certain counties and parts of counties require emissions testing including all of Cook, DuPage and Lake counties, and parts of Kane, Kendall, Madison, McHenry, Monroe, St. Clair, and Will counties. All cars and trucks are tested every two years beginning when four years old, except vehicle model year 1995 or older and diesel-powered vehicles, must be tested. There is no cost to the vehicle owner.

The Secretary of State does not require a safety inspection except for all salvage vehicles that are eight model years old or newer before a rebuilt title may be issued. However, a safety inspection on certain commercial vehicles is required by the IL Dept. of Transportation. See 625 ILCS 5/13-100.1 for the standards. Be warned - the law is confusing.

Plate Descriptions
The state began issuing current license plates to all renewals on 08/01/01.

Typical Plate Patterns	Passenger plates can be all numeric or LNNNNNN, LLNNNN, LLLNNN, or LLLNNNN. Light trucks are normally NNNNLL or NNNNNL. Commercial vehicle plates are typically 3, 4 or 5 numbers followed by 1 or 2 coded letters. The letters signify gross weight and type of vehicle. Over 50 codes are used. Commercial year is figured July-June for intrastate plates, April-March for interstate plates.
County/City Codes	There is no county coding on the plates.
Plates and Stickers in Force	2 plates, 1 decal on rear with MO-YR.
Plates Remain with Car when Sold?	No, they remain with seller.

Overview of Record Access

About Driving Records
Abstract Information Unit, Driver Analysis Section, Driver Services Department, 2701 S. Dirksen Parkway, Springfield 62723, 217-782-2720. The current fee is $12.00, certification included if paper record purchased. The state does charge for "no record found" reports

Request Methods – Mail, Walk-in, Cartridge, Online.

What You Should Know – When accessing records online, the driver's license number is the only information needed when ordering; however, a secondary search can be made using the driver's name, sex, and date of birth. The driver's address is provided as part of the record. The minimum order is 200 requests per day.

Special Access Programs Available – The parents or guardians of persons under 18 years of age may view the teen's record for free online at https://www.ilsos.gov/parentalaccess/. Some of the data appearing on the record is not included on the public driving record. Therefore, there are multiple levels of security involved.

About Vehicle Records
Vehicle Record Inquiry, Vehicle Services Department, 501 S. 2nd Street Room 408, Springfield 62756, 217-782-6992 or 217-785-3000. The database also contains registration information on unattached mobile homes, but not on watercraft. Off-road motorcycles and ATVs are titled but are not registered. In general, records are available for last 10 years. There is a $5.00 fee for either a title search or a registration search and $10.00 for a certified document.

Request Methods – Mail, Walk-in, Online, Bulk (limited).

Special Access Programs Available –A free Title and Registration Status Inquiry is at www.ilsos.gov/regstatus. Enter either the license plate number to check registration status or enter VIN to check the status of a vehicle title.

About Watercraft Records
Department of Natural Resources, Records and Legal Services, One Natural Resources Way, Springfield 62702-1270, 800-382-1696, 217-557-0180, http://dnr.state.il.us. All watercraft must be registered and titled unless non-motorized craft is only used on one's own property. Liens are recorded with this agency. The watercraft and snowmobile records are maintained on computer from 1982 to present. A title history record costs $5.00 and can take up to 6 weeks. The record will include any lien. Snowmobile records are also available. It can take as long as 6 to 8 weeks for new records received by this office on paper format to be input into the system. Bulk information may be purchased only on a FOIA basis.

Indiana

Administration	Important Telephone and Web Contacts
Andrew J. Miller, Commissioner Bureau of Motor Vehicles (BMV) 100 North Senate Avenue Indianapolis, IN 46204 317-232-6000 www.in.gov/bmv/	Driver Licensing.............................. 317-233-6000 or 233-0766 SR-22 & Financial Responsibility..........................317-232-2840 Commercial Driver License ....317-615-7335 Title Tracing for Government and Law Enforcement Agencies Only.....................317-234-3712 State Dept of Insurance ....317-232-2385 State Police, General Operations............................317-232-8248 State Police, Motor Carrier Enforcement ....317-615-7373 General Email contacts at www.in.gov/bmv/3193.htm State Statutes www.in.gov/legislative/ic/code/

Driver License Facts

License Format
Ten numbers. Since July 1988, the first 3 digits denote the License Branch where issued on applications since July 1988. Otherwise, Indiana reports that no codes or sequential arrangements are used to determine license number.

Document Appearance
Effective June, 2007, the state began issuing new driver licenses and ID cards. The previous digital format had been issued since July 1, 1999. It will be at least 2012 before the new license is completely phased in.

Current License
Effective 01/01/2010, IN began issuing new SecureID documents. Permit holders renewing, amending, or replacing their current Indiana driver's license, permit, or identification card, must bring original versions or certified copies of documents so they can obtain this a new SecureID credential. Those who do not need to renew their licenses, permits, or identification cards in 2010 will follow these procedures on their normal renewal dates.

The color strip across the top is a pinkish dusty rose, unless an ID card then strip is green. Different types are indicated by different header colors of map icon in upper left corner. Brown is an Operator Driver License, Motorcycle Only License, Public Passenger Chauffeur License, and Chauffeur License. Purple is a Driver Education Learner Permit, Learner Permit or Learner Permit with a DE permit restriction.

  Note: Since 11-19-2009, IN no longer issues a Driver Education Learner Permit. If the driver is attending a driver education program, the DE Permit restriction is added to the Learner Permit. Red designates a CDL and Green an ID.

Security Characteristics	Security features include printed variable data only detectable with a black light, IDMarc, a security feature only detectable by a validation device offered by Indiana's vendor, UV ghost portrait, and 2D Barcode on back.
Position of Photo	The picture is placed in the mid to upper left hand corner.
Minor Age Driver	In vertical format. "Under 21 until..." or "Under 18 until ..." appears vertically to the right of the photo.
CDL Indicator	CDL is indicated with a red state icon in upper left corner.

Old License
Different licenses are indicated by different header colors. Green indicates for Ids, purple for all learner and driver education permits, red for CDLs, and gold for operators.

Security Characteristics	Indiana torch and stars are embedded as an OVD, 2 dimensional bar code on rear.
Position of Photo	The picture is placed in the lower left hand corner.
Minor Age Driver Locator	"Under 21 until..." or "Under 18 until ..." appears in red, the DOB is also in red. If under 18, "Probationary" is printed under the license type on front.
CDL Indicator	CDL is indicated with a red band across the top, as well as by classification.

Issue and Renewal
Age Requirements
The minimum age is 16 years and 30 days with completion of driver education course; otherwise, 16 years and 180 days. Effective 07/01/2010, the minimum age will be 16 years and 180 days with completion of driver education course; otherwise, 16 years and 270 days. A Driver's Education Lerner Permit or Learner Permit with the DE Permit restriction can be issued at age 15 (15 years and 180 days on or after 07/01/2010), if enrolled in approved driver education course; upon completion, learner must be accompanied by parent, guardian or relative 21 or older with a valid license. A Learner's Permit can be issued at 16; must be accompanied by parent, guardian or relative 21 or older with a valid license.

Changes to the state laws on July 1, 2009 affected probationary drivers who get an Indiana driver's license on or after that date. Changes included expansion of prohibited driving times and restrictions on driving with passengers for those with a probationary driver's license. Also those drivers who obtain a probationary driver's license on or after July 1, 2009, will not qualify for court diversion programs.

Renewal
The validity period of an operator's license is 6 years; for a CDL the period is 4 years. Older drivers have different periods (see below). Driver keeps same number when renewing. Military personnel stationed out of Indiana may renew by mail every 6 years. When the operator's license of an Indiana operator who is in the military and stationed outside of Indiana's license has expired, the license remains valid for 90 day following the person's discharge. Renewal is not available online.

Elderly-Related Restrictions
Licenses issued after December 31, 2005 for drivers 75 to 84 years old expire at midnight on the birthday of the holder three years following the date of issuance. Licenses issued after June 30, 2005 for drivers at least 85 years old expire at midnight on the birthday of the holder two years following the date of issuance.

Residency
Non-residents must obtain Indiana license within sixty days of establishing residency; exceptions are persons attending an institution of higher learning or active-duty military personnel.

License Classes
Commercial Classifications
- Class A — Any combination of vehicles with a combined GVWR of 26,001 or more pounds, provided vehicle(s) being towed is in excess of 10,000 pounds.
- Class B — Any single vehicle with GVWR of 26,001 or more pounds, or any such vehicle towing a vehicle not in excess of 10,000 pounds GVWR. Also, buses 26,001 or more pounds, 16 passengers including the driver.
- Class C — Any single vehicle less than 26,001 pounds GVWR or any such vehicle towing a vehicle not in excess of 10,000 pounds GVWR, which is placarded for hazardous material or designed to transport 16 or more persons, including driver.

Non-Commercial Classifications
- OPR — Operator
- CH — Chauffeur (15 passengers or less)
- PPC — Public Passenger Chauffeur (taxi, horse drawn carriage) (also PPCH)
- MC — Motorcycle

Note: One may operate a moped (motorized bicycle) without a DL or MC endorsement or motorcycle MC as long as driver has a state-issued form of identification at all times.

HAZMAT Endorsement Procedure
The state is in compliance with the Patriot Act. All applicants applying for a new or renewal or transfer HAZMAT Endorsement (HME) must be fingerprinted. For a list of eleven branch offices that provide fingerprint services visit www.in.gov/bmv/4915.htm. The Threat Assessment Fee is $100.00. This fee will cover the costs charged by the Transportation Security Administration, Indiana State Police, Federal Bureau of Investigations, as well as the additional costs incurred by the Bureau of Motor Vehicles. The fingerprints and application information is sent to the Federal Transportation Security Administration (TSA). TSA performs the background checks and notifies the DMV whether the application is approved or denied. When completed and approved, the HME is valid for four years.

Safety and Enforcement Facts

Insurance and Financial Responsibility
Insurance is mandatory, minimum limits for financial responsibility are $25,000/50,000/10,000. Proof of financial responsibility must be shown on these occasions:
- if involved in a traffic accident;
- have more than two traffic ticket convictions within a twelve month period;
- is convicted of a misdemeanor or felony involving a motor vehicle; or
- has been previously suspended for having no insurance.

If proof of insurance information is not provided, a Certificate of Compliance must be signed by the insurance agent verifying proof of insurance for the date of the incident. The penalty for non-compliance is a 90-day license suspension and a graduated reinstatement fee. 1st offense $150.00, 2nd offense $225.00, 3rd offense $300.00, each additional $300.00. In addition, if there is a second occurrence within three years, there is an additional one-year license suspension. After the suspension period ends the driver must show current proof of insurance (SR50) and pay the appropriate reinstatement fee.

Alcohol and Chemical Testing
Indiana's illegal intoxication level is .08 %, .02 % for drivers under 21, and .04% for drivers of CMVs. Urine, blood, and breath testing are used. Indiana has an implied-consent violation, as well as a provision for an administrative suspension. Operating a horse or bicycle under the influence is also considered illegal.

Accident Reporting
Any accident involving death, injury or damage in excess of $1,000 must be reported to the local police. Accident reports should be filed within ten days with the Indiana State Police, Vehicle Crash Records Section, Room N301, Indiana Government Center, Indianapolis 46204, 317-232-8286. Also, since 01/01/2006, written accident reports must be sent by the driver to the Bureau of Motor Vehicles. Forms are not available on the web, but they can be obtained from the BMV, Safety Responsibility, Room N402, 100 N Senate, Indianapolis, IN 46204.

Suspensions and Revocations
Note: Indiana does not have a "Revocation" status.

- Altering a Driver's License — Ninety-day suspension.
- Allowing Another Person to Use Your License — Ninety-day suspension.
- Criminal Reckless — Sixty-day to two-year suspension.
- Driving While Intoxicated — 180-day probationary license, or ninety-day to two-year suspension.
- Driving While Suspended — Ninety-days to two-years suspension.
- Failure to Pass Chemical Test (DUI) — 180-day suspension *(minimum thirty-days)*.
- Failure to pay Child Support — Indefinite Suspension Until Payments Made Satisfactorily to Court or Administration.
- Financial Responsibility (Accidents or conviction of a violation of a law relating to motor vehicles.)
  - First Offense — 90 day suspension; $150.00 fee.
  - Second Offense — 90 day suspension; $225.00 fee.
  - Third or Subsequent Offense — 90 day suspension; $300.00 fee.
  - If Twice Within Three Year Period — Additional one-year suspension.
- Graffiti — Up to one-year.
- Habitual Traffic Violations
  - 1 Major and 9 Minor Traffic Offenses — Five-year suspension.
  - 3 Major Traffic Offenses — Ten-year suspension.
  - 2 Major Traffic Offenses Resulting in Injury or Death — Ten-year suspension.
- Leaving the Scene of an Accident — Six-month suspension.
- Perjury or Making a False Affidavit — Up to one (1) year suspension.
- Possession, Use or Sale of Controlled Substances Involving Use of Motor Vehicle — Six-month suspension.
- Reckless Homicide or Manslaughter Resulting from Operation of a Motor Vehicle — Two to five-year suspension.
- Refusal to Take Chemical Test — One-year suspension.
- Suspension or Expulsion from School (Under 18) — Minimum 120 days suspension.
- Three Convictions of Criminal Recklessness in Twelve Months — Six-month suspension.
- Using a Motor Vehicle to Commit a Felony — Six-month suspension.
- Writing a Bad Check to the License Bureau — Indefinite suspension.

Note: Any person who, within a 12-month period, commits two or more traffic offenses that result in convictions will be required by the BMV to attend a BMV-approved driver safety program. Failure to complete the course or pay the fee within the specified time period will result in the suspension of the individual's driving privileges.

For Points: Motorists who accumulate 18 or more active points during a 2-year period will be notified and required to attend an administrative hearing conducted by the BMV. At the hearing, the presiding officer will make a determination whether to place the driver on probation; suspend the person's driving privileges for 30 days to 1 year; or impose additional requirements beyond the order of probation or suspension such as requiring attendance at a BMV-approved Driver Safety Program.

CDL & MCSIA Compliance
The Indiana BMV is in compliance with the provisions of the Motor Carrier Safety Improvement Act (MCSIA). See the Appendix for more information about all of the mandatory CDL disqualification sanctions.

Reinstatement Requirements
Administrative or SR-22 Suspension $10.00 fee. If for financial responsibility, see above.

Point System Overview
Points can range from 2 to 8. Indiana law states that, within a 12-month period, any driver who has been convicted of at least 2 traffic misdemeanors, 2 traffic judgments or a combination of both may be required to attend the Defensive Driving Course. Failure to complete the course and/or pay all applicable fees will result in suspension until completion or payment. As an added incentive to those who have completed the course in order to improve their driving habits, a four point credit will appear on the driving record for a period of 3 years.

License Plate Facts

Registration Renewal
Vehicle registration is staggered by month corresponding to owner's last name initial. Corporate vehicles are always registered in January. Registrants can renew online at via "myBMV" at www.in.gov/bmv/4893.htm. No PIN number is required. The license plate number, plate type, Social Security Number and insurance information are needed. Renewal is not available with this system if additional documentation is required, such as with many special recognition plates.

Note: Since 01/01/06, Indiana Code specifies that all "off road" vehicles with a model year of 2001 or later purchased or brought into the State of Indiana be titled with the BMV.

New Residents
Non-residents must title and register vehicles within sixty days of establishing residency.

Inspections and Emissions Testing
Indiana has no provision for statewide vehicle safety inspections or statewide emissions testing. Vehicles registered in Lake and Porter counties are required to undergo emissions tests and tampering inspections every two years from 1976 and newer passenger vehicles with a gross vehicle weight rating (GVWR) of 9,000 pounds or less. The four newest model year vehicles are exempt.

Plate Descriptions
The state began issuing a new standard plate effective 01/01/2008. The previous standard plate were issued since 01/01/2002.

Current Plates
The background is blue, with white lettering and a torch on the left side.

Typical Plate Patterns	Commercial vehicles and light trucks are 1-6 numbers followed by 1 letter. Effective 01/01/2008, standard passenger plates are NNNLLL (101 AAA to 999 ZZZ)
County/City Codes	For standard passenger plates, the name of the county of issuance appears on the top of the plate along with a corresponding number from 1 to 98 per an alphabetical list of the 92 counties. Thus 1 is Adams, 2 is Allen, etc. Two counties have additional assigned numbers—Marion County has 93, 95, 97, 98, and 99 while Lake County has 94 and 96 assigned.
Plates and Stickers in Force	One plate, registration sticker has different coloring indicating which date of expiration (7th, 14th, 21st or 28th).
Plate Remains with Car when Sold?	No, it remains with the seller.

Older Plates
The background consists of grassy fields and a rural farmhouse scene.

Typical Plate Patterns	Passenger plates are 1-2 numbers followed by 1 letter followed by 1-4 numbers. Commercial vehicles and light trucks are 1-6 numbers followed by 1 letter.

County/City Codes	The code for the originating county of issuance (first two numbers on passenger plate) for a vehicle license plate corresponds to 1 to 98 to an alphabetical list of the 92 counties. Thus 1 is Adams, 2 is Allen, etc. Two counties have additional assigned numbers—Marion County has 93, 95, 97, 98, and 99 while Lake County has 94 and 96 assigned.
Plates and Stickers in Force	One plate, two decals
Plate Remains with Car when Sold?	No, it remains with the seller.

Overview of Record Access

About Driving Records

Bureau of Motor Vehicles, Driver Records, 100 N Senate Ave, Room N405, Indiana Government Center North, Indianapolis 46204, 317-233-6000. There are three general types of driver related records available: driver's driving record (ODR/MVR); SR 21-Proof of insurance at the time of an accident or ticket; and driver's license history. The driver's license history includes a driver's driving record plus photocopies of specified underlying documents. The current fee for a driving record or SR-21 is $4.00 (or $7.50, if online), or $8.00 for a driver's license history. A record can be certified for an additional $4.00. The state does not charge for "no record found" reports. There is no "license status only" report available. Electronic request accounts must obtain records through www.in.gov/accounts.

Request Methods – Mail, Walk-in, Mail, Online.

What You Should Know – Indiana does not report non-moving violations on the public record. Indiana displays all accidents as received by the Indiana State Police on the Official Driving Record. Electronic request accounts must obtain records through www.in.gov/accounts.

About Accident Reports

Records have been privatized. Copies of accident reports may be obtained from Portal Solutions at 374 Meridian Parke Lane, Ste B, Greenwood, IN 46142, 317-215-8300, fax is 317-234-2041, www.buycrash.com. Records are available from 20 years back to present. It takes from 2 hours to 2 weeks before new records are available for inquiry. The fee is $12.00 per report. If a search must be performed, add $25.00 per hour. Major credit cards are accepted. Items required include; full name, specific date and location of the incident. Normal turnaround time is 10 days. If only a name is given, then turnaround time can be 4-6 weeks. The agency will not disclose SSNs or driver license numbers. The agency will sell a downloaded pdf of records.

About Vehicle Records

Bureau of Motor Vehicles, Vehicle Records, Government Center North, 100 N Senate Ave., Room N404, Indianapolis 46204, 317-233-6000. The search fees are $4.00 per "inquiry" and $8.00 per "history." Certification is an additional $4.00. The online access fee is $5.00. One of the following is required when requesting a record: make of vehicle and VIN; SSN or Federal ID#; plate number, plate type and plate year; or title # (accesses title file only).

Request Methods – Mail, Walk-in, Online.

What You Should Know – There are four general types of vehicle records available: **title inquiry**, **title history**, **registration inquiry**, and **registration history**. A title inquiry contains information pertaining to the current owner and includes information regarding liens; vehicle make, model, year, and VIN; odometer reading; and vehicle purchase date. A title history includes information pertaining to all prior Indiana owners. A registration inquiry contains: information pertaining to the current registrant and includes county and township of registration; registration fees and county tax paid; vehicle purchase date; vehicle make, model, year, VIN, type and color; and plate number with expiration date. A registration history includes the registration inquiry information for the previous four years.

About Watercraft Records

Indiana is a title and registration state: all motorboats (and jet skis) that were valued over $3,000 when new must be titled and registered. All sailboats must be registered. Watercraft that must be registered in Indiana do not need to be titled if: you purchased the watercraft before January 1, 1986; the watercraft was valued under $3,000 when new; or the watercraft was home built and not intended for resale. One can search by name, hull # or registration number. The Watercraft Titles phone number is 317-233-2513. Fees and required form are described above.

Iowa

Administration	Important Telephone and Web Contacts
Tim Snook, Office Director Kathy Ohorilko, Records Manager Department of Transportation, PO Box 9204 Des Moines 50306-9204, 515-237-3153 Tina Hargis, Office Director Office of Vehicle Services, PO Box 9278 Des Moines 50306-9278, 515-237-3110 www.iowadot.gov/mvd	General Number for Driver Licensing, Accidents, Financial Responsibility, Commercial Driver Licensing is: 515-244-8725 or 800-532-1121 Vehicle Information..........................515-237-3055 or 3049 Iowa State Patrol .... 515-281-5824 State Department of Insurance .... 515-281-5705 General Email ods@dot.iowa.gov For Iowa Codes and Administrative Rule see www.legis.state.ia.us/

Driver License Facts

License Format
Since July 1, 2001, an assigned nine-digit number has been issued. Prior to this date, the nine digit driver's license number was primarily the Social Security Number or nine characters alpha-numeric combination (fourth and fifth were alpha characters).

Document Appearance
The state changed the license document effective November 1999, again July 2001 (although only for minor licenses), and again in 2005. We will report the older document types until they are rotated out.

Appearance — Tamper resistant laminated coating. The document as a pinkish colored header, ID cards have a green header. In early 2010 2009, the state will begin a Central Issuance program for all Dls and Ids. Temporal cards are issued at the DL station, the permanent card is mailed within 30 days. At central Issuance, an individual's photo is compared to others on file before issuance.

Security Characteristics — 2-D barcode and magnetic stripe on back contains all the data on the front of the license. The photo has an issuing office number and Director's signature overlapping the edge. A ghost image of photo is on front. The front has an optical variable pattern that changes color when the document is tilted.

Position of Photo — Left edge in middle. Ghost image on lower right.

Minor Age Indicator — Vertical format. A red bar with "Under 21 until dd/mm/yyyy" in yellow wording appearing to the right of the photo.

CDL Locator — The license class and associated restrictions or endorsements are indicated in the "class" section of the license. There is no special heading or color.

Older Version
Appearance — Digitized photo on heavy plastic.

Security Characteristics — License header and picture border in blue for license, maroon for ID. Iowa seal under characters in data field. DOB & expiration date printed in red with other characters printed in black. Iowa DOT in security overlay across face of license. "IOWA" printed in ultra violet sensitive ink on license face. Director's signature and station number overlap photo and date area. Repeating DOT logo and Iowa Department of Transportation on license face.

Position of Photo — Top left.

Minor Age Indicator — "UNDER 18/21 until mmddyy" printed in red under photo. As of 2001, printed Vertically, "UNDER 18/21 until mmddyy" in white on red border under photo.

CDL Locator — "IOWA COMMERCIAL DRIVER LICENSE" written in header. License header and border in green.

Issue and Renewal
Age Requirements
Iowa initiated a Graduated Driver's License (GDL) program on January 1, 1999, for drivers age 14 to 18.

- **Instruction Permit** — Eligible at age 14, must be held at least 6 months to be eligible for Intermediate License. The driver is required to: limit the number of passengers to the number of seatbelts; log 20 hours of supervised driving of which 2 must be between sunset and sunrise; driving accident-free (at fault) and conviction-free for 6 months prior to obtaining the Intermediate License; and complete Driver Education.
- **Intermediate License** — Eligible at age 16 after meeting all conditions of the Instruction Permit. This license must be held at least 12 months with the limitations of: same number of riders as seatbelts; log 10 hours of supervised driving of which 2 must be between sunset and sunrise; driving accident-free (at fault) and conviction-free for 12 months; and able to drive between 5am and 12:30am without supervision. The Intermediate driver must be accompanied between the hours of 12:30am and 5am unless carrying a waiver.
- **Full Privilege License** — Eligible at age 17 after all previous conditions met. Beginning drivers over 18 are exempt from GDL requirements..

Renewal
As of July 1, 2002, the license is renewed on a five year basis, except if age 18 or under then two years. Previously the renewal was the licensee's option of the birth month of second or fourth year. At present, renewal is not available online. There are two six (6) month extensions available if temporarily absent from Iowa. The driver keeps the same number when renewing. A vision screening test each time license is renewed. If license has been expired for more than one year, the driving test and written knowledge are both required. Military extensions are available by mail and are valid until six months following initial separation from active service.

Elderly-Related Restrictions
If the driver is age 70 or older, the license is renewed every two years. IDs for those non-drivers over 70 do not need to be renewed.

Residency
A person is considered an Iowa resident for the purposes of driver licensing and vehicle registration when at least one of the following happens: registered to vote; enrolled children in public school; accepted a permanent job; or resided in Iowa for 30 continuous days.

License Classes
Commercial Classifications
- A Vehicle with 26,001 pounds GCWR or more. Towed unit(s) is 10,001 pounds GCWR or more.
- B Vehicle with 26,001 pounds GVWR or more. Towed unit(s) is less than 10,001 pounds GVWR.
- C Vehicle with 26,000 pounds GVWR or less, and either sixteen passenger design or placarded for Hazardous Materials.

Non-Commercial Classifications
- C Non-commercial vehicle
- D Chauffeur
- M Motorcycle.

HAZMAT Endorsement Procedure
The state is in compliance with the Patriot Act. All applicants applying for a new or renewal or transfer HAZMAT Endorsement (HME) must first obtain a federally mandated application form from a DL station. The form is mailed for renewals. This application must be signed in the presence of DOT personnel. The applicant is then referred to a county sheriff for fingerprinting in one of 17 counties. The list is found at https://hazprints.tsa.dhs.gov/Public/. Visit www.iowadot.gov/mvd/ods/hazmat.htm for general information. The cost of the process is $89.25. The fingerprints and application information is sent to the federal Transportation Security Administration (TSA). TSA performs the background checks and notifies the DMV whether the application is approved or denied. When completed, approved, and issued the HME is valid for five years.

Safety and Enforcement Facts

Insurance and Financial Responsibility
Iowa does not have a compulsory insurance law, but has a Financial & Safety Responsibility Act with the following criteria:

- Suspends the operating and registration privileges of a driver or owner who hasn't been able to show immediate financial responsibility following an accident; and,
- Requires anyone whose driver's license has been suspended or revoked because of a conviction, unsatisfied judgment or violation of the OWI law to prove financial responsibility for any future damages or injuries that driver may cause.

Thus, any suspension as a result of moving convictions or revocation for OWI and implied consent (Chapter 321J) requires compliance with Iowa's financial responsibility law. This requirement is normally met by filing proof of at least $55,000 insurance coverage. Otherwise, the driver must post security of $55,000 by certified check, cashier's check, money order, or surety bond. This filing must be maintained for two years.

Iowa law requires minimum financial responsibility limits of $20,000/40,000/15,000. Future proof is required for two years from the first day of a suspension or revocation for a conviction, unsatisfied judgment or violation of OWI law.

Alcohol and Chemical Testing

Iowa uses blood, breath or urine tests to determine alcohol content. Iowa statutes contain an implied-consent law and also allow for administrative revocations for .08 or more or test refusal. Implied consent affects CMV operators if .04 or higher and persons under 21 who test .02 or more but less than .08. Operating a motorized bicycle under the influence is also illegal. Iowa uses urine and blood tests to determine drug content. The same penalties apply for drugged driving as drunk driving.

Accident Reporting

An accident occurring anywhere within the State of Iowa causing death, personal injury, or total property damage of $1,000 or more must be reported on an Iowa Accident Report Form #433002 to the Department of Transportation, Driver Services, PO Box 9204, Des Moines IA 50306-9204. The form is found at www.iowadot.gov/mvd/ods/accidentform.htm. Failure to return an accident report form within 72 hours may result in suspension of driving privileges. If the accident is investigated by law enforcement and the investigating officer files a report, the driver then is not required to file a report. There are no special reporting requirements for commercial drivers.

Suspensions and Revocations

The state is in compliance with the **federally mandated disqualifications on CDLs**. See the Appendix for details.

The Following Can Cause a Suspension

Conviction of six moving violations committed within a two-year period may cause driver to be barred for one year from the date of judgment. Includes all moving violations except the first two speed convictions within a 12-month period which occur in speed zones between 34 and 56 mph and if convicted of speed 10 mph or less over the posted speed limit.

Driving While Suspended	Suspension may be doubled.
Drug or Drug Related Conviction	180 days.
Failure to Attend School	Until Age 18.
Failure to Pay College Fees	Indefinite until satisfied.
Habitual Recklessness or Negligence	
Three or more tickets or accidents in twelve months	Sixty days to one year.
Habitual Violator Bars	Ninety days to six years.

Three or more of any combination of the following convictions in a six-year period may cause a two-year to six-year bar: manslaughter with a motor vehicle; conviction of operating while under the influence of alcohol or drugs (Iowa Code Chapter 321J); conviction for driving while your license is suspended, revoked or barred; eluding or attempting to elude pursuing law enforcement vehicles; or serious injury by vehicle; failure to stop and leave information or render aid at the scene of an accident as required by Iowa Code 321.263.

Juvenile Actions:

Purchase or Attempt to Purchase Alcohol	One year.
Possession of a Controlled Substance	One year.
Public Intoxication or Public Consumption	One year.
Juvenile Possession of Alcohol - Second or Subsequent Violation	One year.
Non-Resident Violator Compact	Indefinite until satisfied.
Non-Payment of Fines	Indefinite until satisfied.
Operating While Under the Influence; Administrative Test Result	180 days to one year.
Operating While Under the Influence; Administrative Test Refusal	One year to two years.
Operating with Alcohol Content of .02 or more person under age 21	Sixty days to ninety days.
Serious Violation (twenty-five miles or more over limit)	Sixty days to one year.
Unlawful Use of License or Falsifying Information	Thirty days to one year.
Violation of License Restriction	Thirty days to one year.
Violation of Minor's Restricted License	Thirty days.

Violation of School License .... Thirty days.
Violation of School License (second conviction) .... One year.

The Following Can Cause a Revocation With License Revoked for Thirty Days to Six Years
- Alcohol Concentration of .08 Percent or More in a Chemical Test
- Drag Racing
- Driving Under the Influence of Alcohol or Drugs
- Eluding or Trying to Elude a Marked Law Enforcement Vehicle
- Failure to Stop and Give Aid at the Scene of an Accident Involving Death or Injury in Which You Were Involved
- Homicide by Vehicle if Operated while Intoxicated
- Manslaughter Resulting From Driving a Motor Vehicle
- Perjury or Making False Affidavit About the Ownership or Operation of a Motor Vehicle
- Refusing a Chemical Test Requested by Peace Officer
- Second Conviction for Reckless Driving
- Using a Motor Vehicle When Committing a Felony.

Reinstatement Requirements

When the Department suspends, revokes, or bars a person's motor vehicle license or non-resident operating privilege under chapter 321A and 321J; or suspends, revokes, or **bars** a person's motor vehicle license or non-resident operating privilege for a conviction under Chapter 321, the department shall assess the person a civil penalty of $200.00. However, for persons under age twenty, the civil penalty assessed is $50.00 for sanctions under 321A & 321 only.

Suspension $20.00 fee; knowledge and vision test; $1.00 duplicate license; and—in most cases—proof of financial responsibility. A driving test is required if license was not valid for more than 12 months.

Revocations $20.00 fee plus fee for new license; knowledge and vision test; and—in most cases—proof of financial responsibility. OWI requires payment of $200.00 civil penalty. A driving test is required if the license was not valid for more than one year.

Point System Overview

While Iowa does not have an overall point system, certain major convictions are assigned points to determine if a driver can be declared *a habitual offender* and thus barred from operating a motor vehicle. Speeding convictions for 10 MPH or less over the limit are not considered

License Plate Facts

Registration & Renewal
Renewal is annual. At present, online renewal is available in some counties, but not from the Department of Transportation.

New Residents
One is considered an Iowa resident for the purposes of driver licensing and vehicle registration when one of the following takes place: register to vote; enroll children in public school; accept a permanent job; or reside in Iowa for 30 continuous days.

Inspections and Emissions Testing
The state of Iowa has no mandatory safety inspections or emission testing programs; however, commercial vehicles are subject to the Federal Motor Carrier Safety Laws.

Plate Descriptions
The state began issuing the current standard plates on 1/2/97.
Typical Plate Patterns:
    Passenger. 3 numbers/3 alpha....123 LLL
    Light Truck. 3 numbers/3 alpha....123 LLL
    Non-commercial trailers, travel trailers, motorcycles (only one plate issued). 4 numbers/2 alpha ... 1234 LL
    Commercial Vehicle. 2 alpha/4 number, apportioned.
County Codes .... County name will appear on plate.
Plates and Stickers in Force .... 2 plate, 1 decal rear only (MO & YR).
Plates Remain with Car When Sold? No, plates remain with seller.

Overview of Record Access

About Driving Records
Driver Services Records Section, Department of Transportation, PO Box 9204, Des Moines 50306-9204, 515-244-9124 or (800) 532-1121 (IA). The current fee for a certified record is $5.50 and for an electronic record the fee is $8.50.
Request Methods – Mail, Walk-in, Online.
What You Should Know – Use of the state's form is required unless approved ongoing requester. The form is the 431069, Privacy Act Agreement for Request of Motor Vehicle Records(s). All IA forms can be found at www.iadotforms.dot.state.ia.us/iowadotforms/Library.aspx. For more information about online access, call 515-323-3468 or 866-492-3468. Information about this service is not available on the web.

About Accident Reports
Accident reports filed by law enforcement are only available to persons involved in the accident, the person's insurance company, or the person's attorney. However, the agency will provided limited information such as date, time, location, circumstances. Records are usually available within 3 days receipt by this office. To obtain a copy of the report, send $4.00 with a written request with the date of the accident, time, location, and names and driver license numbers of the drivers involved. Records are maintained for 5 years. The state's accident report form provides an excellent explanation of all the codes and abbreviations found on an accident report - go to www.iowadot.gov/mvd/ods/accidentform.htm. Accident reports filed by drivers are confidential. Individuals may obtain a copy of their own accident report for a fee of $.50. To obtain a copy of the report filled out by the driver (called Driver's Report), the fee is $.50 unless the accident was pre-1993 then the fee is $3.20.
Requests for either report can be submitted to Department of Transportation, Office of Driver Services, PO Box 9204, Des Moines 50306-9204, 515-244-9124. Courier address is 6310 SE Convenience Blvd, Ankeny 50021. Also, direct questions to ods@dot.iowa.gov. Turnaround time is 2 to 3 weeks. County sheriffs in Iowa are authorized to furnish copies of accident reports, but not all do.

About Vehicle Records
Office of Vehicle Services, Department of Transportation, PO Box 9278, Des Moines 50306-9278, (6310 SE Convenience Blvd, Ankeny 50021), 515-237-3049 or 237-3148. Vehicle histories, liens, title research, registration research and owner name research are available on vehicles, mobile homes, motorcycles, and trailers. A search fee of $5.00 per quarter-hour or a fraction thereof is applied. Computer printouts are $1.00 each; photocopies are $.10 each, and certified copies are $.50 each. No fees applied if records not found. Ongoing, approved requesters may establish an escrow account. Requests on plate information are subject to Statute 321.11 and personal information is blocked. Registration and titles records are indexed on computer and are retained for seven years.

Although Iowa titles are recorded at the county level, the title, registration, and liens are updated immediately on the DOT system and are thus provided from this office.
Request Methods – Mail, Walk-in, Fax, Online, Bulk.
What You Should Know – The web service is limited to specific users that are privacy act qualified including vehicle dealers, Iowa licensed private investigators, and security companies. To set up an account, one must first write to the Office of Vehicle Services and explain the need for the records. Upon approval, access is free of charge.

About Watercraft Records
Boats, snowmobiles, and all-terrain vehicles are registered and titled at the county recorders' offices. Boats with liens must be titled. The Iowa Department of Natural Resources permits the public to search for title and registration records, but not lien records. Call 515-242-5818 or 515-281-5918.

Kansas

Administration	Important Telephone and Web Contacts
Carmen Alldritt, Director of Vehicles Christy Weiler, Official Custodian Department of Revenue Division of Vehicles Topeka 66626-0001 785-296-3601 http://ksrevenue.org/dmvdrivercontrol.htm www.ksrevenue.org/dmv.htm	Suspension/Reinstatement............................785-296-3671 Financial Responsibility................................785-296-3671 Title and Registration Information ....785-296-3621 Commercial Driver License..........................785-296-3963 Motor Carrier Service Bureau ....785-271-3145 State Department of Insurance ....785-296-3071 Highway Patrol..785-296-6800 Email contacts www.ksrevenue.org/contactus.htm Policy Information Library http://165.201.62.139/

Driver License Facts

License Format
Since July 1, 2004, all KS licenses are issued an assigned number consisting of the letter "K" plus eight numbers. Until that date the SSN was also used as a license number. The SSN could still show as a valid number until July 2010.

Document Appearance
Effective July 2004, Kansas drivers' licenses and identification cards adopted a new license design features with an image of the state capitol under a blue sky with golden stalks of wheat waving in the foreground.

Other minor changes in the document include: the font style for the "KANSAS" heading on all documents is in black, block letters, rather than blue script lettering; and the signature of the Secretary of Revenue has been updated to reflect Joan Wagnon's appointment to the post. The license is laminated. Licenses are centrally produced and applicants receive temporary receipt at the time of the application.

Other Security Characteristics (after 07/04)	Guilloche printing, microprint, ghost image, UVR security features.
Security Characteristics (prior to 07/04)	Wheat pattern and Advantage™ transparent coating security feature.
Position of Photo	Left side.
Minor Age Driver Locator	Vertical format; under 21 has red strip under photo that states "Not 21 until MM-DD-YYYY". Under 18 has green strip under photo that states "Not 18 until MM-DD-YYYY".
CDL Indicator	"CDL" indicated in red letters at top of license.

Issue and Renewal

Age Requirements
A new GDL law that took affect 01/01/2010 placed additional driving restrictions on young drivers, added a Lesser Restricted License, and changed the minimum age for having an unrestricted license from 16 to 17. An excellent overview is found at www.ksrevenue.org/pdf/GDL_public.pdf. An Instruction Permit can be secured by a fourteen year old, and a Restricted License can be secured by a fifteen year old. The Restricted License allows driving to and from work/school; must be accompanied by a licensed driver at all other times; cannot operate vehicle with a minor passenger(s) who is not a member of the immediate family. An Instruction Permit or Farm Permit can be obtained at age fourteen.

Renewal
Non-commercial drivers 21 years of age or over but less than 65 years of age are issued a valid license for 6 years from the DOB nearest application date. Drivers under 21 or over 65 and all commercial license holders are issued a license valid for 4 years from DOB nearest application date. At present, renewal is not available online but change of address is at https://www.kdor.org/dl/default.aspx. The driver keeps same number when renewing (unless SSN used, then a new number is issued). Military personnel may renew by mail; current copy of a military ID is required. If driver is out of state, but not in military, a 6-month extension is available with form DEMI-1.

Elderly-Related Restrictions
If over 65, then license renewed every 4 years.
Residency
Non-residents (sixteen or older) may use home-state license; however, a Kansas license must be obtained if driving Kansas-registered/plated vehicle in excess of ninety days.

License Classes
Commercial Classifications
- Class A Motor Vehicles which include any combination of vehicles with a GCWR of 26,001 pounds or more, providing the GVWR of the vehicle or vehicles being towed is in excess of 10,000 pounds and all other lawful combinations of vehicles with a GCWR of 26,001 pounds or more.
- Class B Motor Vehicles which include any single vehicle with a GVWR of 26,001 pounds or more, or any such vehicle towing a vehicle not in excess of 10,000 pounds GVWR.
- Class C Motor Vehicles include any single vehicle less than 26,001 pounds GVWR, or any such vehicle towing a vehicle not in excess of 10,000 pounds GVWR, provided the GCWR of the combination is less than 26,001 pounds comprising:
    - (A) Vehicles designed to transport sixteen or more passengers (including the driver); or
    - (B) Vehicles used in the transportation of hazardous materials which require the vehicle to be placarded.

Non-Commercial Classifications
- Class A Motor vehicles which include any combination of vehicles with a GCWR of 26,001 pounds or more, provided the GCWR of the vehicle or vehicles being towed is in excess of 10,000 pounds, and all other lawful combinations of vehicles with a GCWR of 26,001 pounds, or more; except that Class A does not include a combination of vehicles that has a truck registered as a farm-truck under subsection (2) of K.S.A. 8-143, and amendments thereto.
- Class B Motor vehicles which include any single vehicle with a GVWR of 26,001 pounds or more, or any such vehicle towing a vehicle not in excess of 10,000 pounds GVWR. Class B motor vehicles do not include a single vehicle registered as a farm-truck under subsection (2) of K.S.A 8-143, and amendments thereto, when such farm-truck has a GVWR of 26,001 pounds or more, or any fire truck operated by a volunteer fire department.
- Class C Motor vehicles which include any single vehicle with a GVWR less than 26,001 pounds, or any such vehicle towing a vehicle not in excess of 10,000 pounds GVWR, or any vehicle with less than a 26,001 pound GVWR towing a vehicle in excess of 0,000 pounds GVWR, provided the GCWR of the combination is less than 26,001 pounds, or any single vehicle registered as a farm-truck under subsection (2) of K.S.A. 8-143, and amendments thereto, when such farm-truck has a GVWR of 26,001 pounds or more.
- Class M Motor vehicles which include motorcycles.
- Note: Effective July 1, 2000, a person with a suspended driver's license can get a class C license valid ONLY for operation of motorized bicycles (which includes mopeds), unless suspension is for DUI.

HAZMAT Endorsement Procedure
The state is in compliance with the Patriot Act. All applicants applying for a new or renewal or transfer HAZMAT Endorsement (HME) must first obtain the application from https://hazprints.tsa.dhs.gov/Public/ or by calling 877-429-7746. The driver must also be fingerprinted. EMSI is the state-designated entity to process fingerprints. There are eight sites authorized to collect fingerprints for Kansas residents only. Visit the web page listed above to find the address locations. The cost of the fingerprint process is $89.25. The fingerprints and application information is sent to the Federal Transportation Security Administration (TSA). TSA performs the background checks and notifies the DMV whether the application is approved or denied. When completed and approved, the HME is valid for four years.

Safety and Enforcement Facts

Insurance and Financial Responsibility
Kansas has compulsory no-fault insurance. Evidence of insurance is required at registration, renewal, upon suspension and after an accident, or certain violations. Minimum financial responsibility limits are $25,000/50,000/10,000. A driver (including a driver licensed in another state) may be required to provide proof of insurance to any law enforcement officer. SR-22 forms are used.

Alcohol and Chemical Testing
The Kansas illegal intoxication level is .08 percent and above for non-commercial drivers and .04 percent for commercial drivers and .02 for under 21 years of age. Urine, blood, and breath testing are used. Kansas has an implied-consent

violation, as well as the provision for an administrative suspension.

Accident Reporting
Any accident resulting in death, injury, or total damage in excess of $1000.00 must be reported immediately to the nearest law enforcement agency. It is not necessary to file a separate accident report with the state. The Motor Vehicle Division may request that the vehicle owner submit insurance information, if the data is incomplete on the police report. Motor Carriers licensed by the state Corporation Commission must file a report with the Commission at 1500 SW Arrowhead Road, Topeka, KS 66604. There are no special state reporting requirements for commercial drivers.

Suspensions and Revocations
The state is in compliance with the **federally mandated disqualifications on CDLs**. See the Appendix for these disqualifications.

Conviction of Any of the Following May Result in Suspension or Revocation
- Aggravated Vehicular Homicide
- Failure to Stop and Give Aid When Involved in an Accident
- Reckless Driving
- Committing a Felony While Using a Car
- Attempting to Elude a Police Officer
- Three or More Moving Violations in Twelve Months
- Refusal to Submit to a Chemical Test
- Failure to Appear in Court
- Failure to Maintain Liability Insurance
- Driving Under the Influence of Alcohol or Drugs
- Transporting an Open Container of Liquor
- Testing .08 Percent or Above for Blood Alcohol
- Minor Testing .02 to .0799 Percent Blood Alcohol

Note: Kansas laws do not allow the issuance of a hardship license, that would allow a person to drive during the length of their suspension, revocation, cancellation or disqualification period

Reinstatement Requirements
Suspensions and Revocations
Failure to Comply $59.00 fee; comply with citation.
Insurance $100.00 to $300.00 fee; file evidence of insurance for one year; obtain release of liability.
DUI Reinstatement fee varies, depending on number of alcohol occurrences; $25.00 reexamination fee

Point System Overview
Kansas does not have a point system.

License Plate Facts

Registration Renewal
Renewal is annual and handled locally by the county treasurer's motor vehicle offices. Renewal is available online at www.kswebtags.org.

New Residents
New residents must secure KS plates within thirty days. Non-residents may drive vehicles without Kansas registration on a home-state reciprocal basis for ninety days (exceptions to this rule are military and students).

Inspections and Emissions Testing
Kansas does not have a provision for mandatory statewide emission testing or annual safety inspection of vehicles. Kansas does require VIN inspections of vehicles that request to be titled in Kansas from another state. Additionally, inspections are required for specially constructed vehicles such as street rods and assembled vehicles.

Plate Descriptions
Typical Plate Patterns — Kansas began issuance of a new plate in 2007. Passenger and light truck plates are now issued as NNNLLL or LLLNNN; previously issued plates were normally LLL-NNN (ABC123). Commercial vehicles are also LLL-NNN, except for apportioned trucks that are six numeric characters (123456).
County/City Codes — The county designation is applied to the plate by decal only. It is not part of the plate.
Plates and Stickers in Force — One plate, three decals (MO) (YR) (County).

Plate Remains with Car when Sold?	The license plate stays with the registrant when the county of residence changes. One plate is displayed on the back of the vehicle. One or two personalized plates may possibly remain with owner, at owner's option.

Overview of Record Access

About Driving Records
Division of Vehicles, Driver Control Bureau, PO Box 12021, Topeka 66612-2021, 785-296-3671. The physical location is at the Docking State Office Building, 915 SW Harrison Room 100. The current fee is $10.00 per record and $20.00 for a driver's license folder for mail or in person searches, $6.00 for online batch, and $6.50 for online interactive. Kansas does charge for "no record found" reports. The last fee increase was effective 07/01/09.

Request Methods – Mail, Walk-in, Online, Bulk.

What You Should Know – The state does not report violations of: ten mph or less over in a fifty-five to seventy zone, six mph or less in a thirty to fifty-four zone, diversion agreements, or expungements on the driving record.

Special Access Programs Available – For online access, go to www.kansas.gov, click on Subscriber Center or call 800-452-6727. Kansas offers a monitoring system or notification program to insurance companies to track driver status.

About Accident Reports
Copies of accident reports may be obtained from Driver Control Bureau, First Floor, Docking State Office Building, Topeka 66612-0001. Request items required include the full name, DOB and/or driver license number, and date of incident. If the requester was not involved, Form DL302 is required. The fee is $10.00 per record.

About Vehicle Records
Division of Vehicles, Title and Registration Bureau, Verification Section, Docking State Office Bldg, 915 SW Harrison Rm 155, Topeka 66626-0001, 785-296-3621, fax is 785-296-3852. The current fee per vehicle registration or motor carrier registration record is $10.00 (except online, see below). A vehicle title history is $25.00, a certified title history is $30.00. Requests should be submitted by completing Form TR/DL 302 or 301. Records are computerized since 1988. Records from 1970-1987 are stored on microfiche and microfilm. The state maintains registration and lien information on vehicles and mobile homes (if unattached). It generally takes eight weeks from the date of application before new records are available for inquiry. Kansas charges for "no record found" reports. For apportioned vehicle records, call the Motor Carrier Services at 785-271-3127.

Request Methods – Mail, Walk-in, Online.

What You Should Know – For online access, go to www.kansas.gov, click on Subscriber Center or call 800-452-6727.

About Watercraft Records
Kansas Department of Wildlife and Parks, Boat Registration, 512 SE 25th Ave, Pratt 67124-8174 620-672-5911, www.kdwp.state.ks.us. All vessels powered by gasoline, diesel, electric or sail must be registered, including sailboards and personal watercraft. Boats are not titled in this state. Liens are recorded at the county level with the Register of Deeds. Registration requests must be in writing with an explanation of why the information is needed. There is no fee for single requests, multiple request fees depends on volume and information needed. Turnaround time is 3 to 5 days. Records are maintained on computer from 1967 to present. New records are available for inquiry in 2 to 3 weeks. Records are not released for solicitation purposes. Liens are not filed here and can be found by searching at the county level.

Kentucky

Administration	Important Telephone and Web Contacts
Cindy Vanhoose, Director Doug Sutton, Assistant Director Division of Driver Licensing 502-564-6800 Willie Payton, Director Godwin Onodu, Assistant Director Division of Motor Vehicle Licensing 502-564-5301 Transportation Office Building, 2nd Fl 200 Mero Street 40622 http://dmc.kytc.ky.gov/home_vr.htm	Driver Licensing................................. 502-564-6800 or 0280 Reinstatement...502-564-0278 Commercial Driver License ....502-564-0279 Vehicle Title Information.....................................502-564-2737 Vehicle Registration Information ....502-564-5301 Motor Carriers..502-564-4540 State Police..502-695-6300 Motor Vehicle Enforcement................................502-564-3276 General Email: kytc.ddlwebservices@ky.gov Statutes: www.lrc.state.ky.us/krs/titles.htm Title 601 Regs: www.lrc.state.ky.us/kar/TITLE601.HTM

Driver License Facts

License Format
The DL or ID consists of a combination of a single alpha and eight numerals. The alpha corresponds to the first initial of last name, but if name changes license number does not. The state no longer uses the Social Security Number as the DL.

Document Appearance
Kentucky began issuing the current license and permit documents in December 2001. The older license is a photo paper card that is laminated after picture is developed. Some may still be in use.

Current Documents

Security Characteristics	KY Transportation Cabinet logo is optical variable device across front.
Position of Photo	Horizontal on left edge, bluish background for regular documents, red if an ID document, and purple if a permit.
Minor Age Driver Locator	Vertical format, date when age 18 and age 21 in upper right.
CDL Indicator	New Green background color, indicated under license type and class.

Older Documents

Security Characteristics	A 1/4 inch clear laminate border, "KENTUCKY DRIVER LICENSE" is across top in blue.
Position of Photo	Lower right, bluish background.
Minor Age Driver Locator	Special laminate "UNDER 21" printed vertically on sides.
CDL Indicator	Indicated under license type and class.

Issue and Renewal

Age Requirements
The minimum age for non-commercial is sixteen. An Instruction Permit is required of operator, motorcycle, and CDL applicants; must be accompanied by licensed driver 21 years or older (except motorcycle). Kentucky has a Graduated Driver's License program for drivers under 18 years of age. This program defines driving privileges and responsibilities using three phases: Permit, Intermediate License, Full Unrestricted License. Extensive changes were made to the GDL in 2007 regarding the Intermediate Stage. Intermediate License holders are not allowed to drive between the hours of 12 midnight and 6 a.m. unless the driver can demonstrate a good cause for driving such as emergencies, school or work related activities.

A commercial driver's license may be issued to an individual 18 years of age who holds a valid automobile Class D driver's license who has passed the vision and knowledge test required for a commercial driver's license of the class vehicle to be driven, if the individual only drives a commercial motor vehicle in intrastate commerce and does not drive a school bus or a vehicle hauling hazardous material. The license shall be class specific and shall contain an "I" restriction noting that the commercial driver is limited to Kentucky intrastate commerce. For school bus or hazardous materials endorsements, the minimum age is 21.

Since May 18, 2009, a CDL permit/license cannot be issued until the applicant has provided a copy of the CDL application to the Division of Driver Licensing and DDL has posted the application to the driver's record. This process could take up to 48 hours. It is the applicant's responsibility to provide the Division of Driver Licensing a copy of the 10 Year History Application prior to the issuance of the CDL permit/license.

Renewal
Birth date of 4th year, under 21 license expires 90 days after 21st birthday. Driver keeps same number when renewing even if last name changes. If the license is expired for more than one year, a vision and written test is required. Military personnel stationed out-of-state must renew by mail from the county where the license was issued. The county will issue an ID w/o photo. This must be done every 4 years.

Elderly-Related Restrictions
None are reported.

Residency
Non-resident's home-state license honored on a reciprocal basis; Kentucky license must be secured upon establishing residence.

License Classes
Commercial Classifications
- Class A Any combination of vehicles with a GVWR of 26,001 or more pounds, provided the GVWR of the vehicle(s) being towed is in excess of 10,000 pounds.
- Class B Any single vehicle with a GVWR of 26,001 or more pounds, or any such vehicle towing a vehicle not in excess of 10,000 pounds GVWR.
- Class C Any single vehicle less than 26,001 pounds GVWR, or any such vehicle towing a vehicle not in excess of 10,000 pounds GVWR. This group applies to vehicles that are placarded for hazardous materials or designed to transport sixteen or more people (including the driver).

Non-Commercial Classifications
- Class D Operator.
- Class E Moped.
- Class M Motorcycle.

HAZMAT Endorsement Procedure
All CDL drivers applying to obtain a HME must summit to a Background Threat Assessment check. 1st time applicants are provided a toll-free line for the KY State Police (KSP). The KSP schedules an appointment at one of eight fingerprinting stations. The HME application is completed electronically at the time of an appointment by a KSP license examiner then printed for the applicant to sign, witnessed by the KSP personnel. The fingerprints are sent to the FBI, the application to the Transportation Security Administration (TSA).

For renewal, CDL drivers with the HME, the Transportation Cabinet, Division of Driver Licensing CDL Section mails a notification to the driver 60+ days prior to expiration. The letter instructs the driver how to start the security threat assessment. All applicants will receive a letter from the TSA and the Transportation Cabinet informing them of the TSA decision. All CDL holders with the HME are required to repeat the Background Security Threat Assessment check every four years prior to renewing the CDL.

Safety and Enforcement Facts

Insurance and Financial Responsibility
Kentucky has compulsory liability and no-fault insurance laws. Insurance cards must be kept in the vehicle. Compulsory insurance limits are $25,000/50,000/10,000. Proof of insurance is required at registration and renewal of the vehicle. SR-22 forms are not used in this state.

Alcohol and Chemical Testing
Kentucky's illegal intoxication level is .08 BAC and .04 BAC for drivers of commercial vehicles. All drivers under the age of 21 are subject to Zero Alcohol Tolerance (defined as .02 Blood Alcohol Concentration). Urine, blood, and breath testing are used. Operating a horse, bicycle or any non-motor vehicle under the influence is also considered illegal.

Accident Reporting
Any accident resulting in property damage in excess of $200.00—which is not investigated by a law enforcement agency—must be reported in writing within ten days to the State Police, Records Section, 1250 Louisville Road, Frankfort 40601 502-227-8700. Form: www.kentuckystatepolice.org/word/KSP_232_Civilian_Collision_Report.dot.

Suspensions and Revocations

The state is in compliance with the mandated disqualifications on CDLs per MCSIA. See the Appendix for details.

Attempt to Elude a Peace Officer, First Offense	3-month suspension discretionary.
Failure to Answer Court Summons	Indefinite.
Failure to Enroll in or Complete State Traffic School	Indefinite.
Failure to Maintain Liability Insurance, Second Offense	1-year suspension.
Driving While License Suspended or Revoked	Fine and/or jail and 6-month suspension.

(If under the influence: fine and/or jail and suspension is doubled.)

Third/Subsequent Offense	2-year suspension.
False Application	6-month suspension.
Leaving Scene of an Accident, First Offense	6-month suspension.
Racing on a Public Highway, First Offense	3-month suspension discretionary.
Speeding Twenty-six mph or More Over Limit, First Offense	3-month suspension discretionary.

Alcohol-Related Withdrawals

Driving Under the Influence of Alcohol or Other Substance Which May Impair Driver Ability, if Within 5 Year period

Over Age Eighteen
- First Offense .... 30 to 120 days suspension, 2 to 30 days jail time, education program.
- Second Offense .... 12 to 18 months suspension, 7 days to 6 months jail time, education program.
- Third Offense .... 24 to 36 months suspension, 30 days to 12 months jail time, education program.
- Fourth Offense .... 60 months suspension, Class D felony, education program.

Under Age Eighteen
 Suspensions for first, second, and third offenses are identical to the periods of time listed above *or* until the eighteenth birthday, whichever is longer.

Under Twenty-One with BAC .02 to .08 ... Thirty days to six months.

Refusal to Submit to Breathalyzer Test -- The court of jurisdiction imposes a pre-trial suspension for refusal to submit to breathalyzer test. Suspension periods for pre-trial suspensions and/or refusal convictions are:
- First Offense .... Up to 6-month suspension.
- Second Offense .... Up to 18-month suspension.
- Third Offense .... Up to 3-year suspension.
- Fourth or Subsequent Offense .... 5-year suspension.

DUI with Aggravating Circumstances - mandatory jail time if convicted of DUI while:
- .18 BAC or higher
- Causing accident resulting in death or serious physical injury
- Going wrong way on limited access highway
- In excess of 30 mph above posted speed limit
- Refusal to take blood, breathe or urine test
- Transporting a passenger under 12 years of age

Notes: Regarding CDL Drivers...If a driver tests from .01% BAC to .039% BAC, that driver shall be put out of service for 24 hours. Drivers testing at .04% BAC or higher will be disqualified for one year. A second conviction carries a penalty of disqualifying a commercial driver for life. Penalties apply to the commercial driving privileges only. *Also:*

- A driver under the age of 18 who accumulates more than 6 points, or a driver age 18 and over who accumulates 12 points may have their driving privilege suspended.
- Drivers convicted of a second or subsequent DUI will forfeit their license plates to the courts during the period in which the driver license is suspended.
- The court may order an ignition interlock device to be installed on the violator's vehicle after the driver serves a statutory suspension period. The ignition interlock device prevents a driver from operating that vehicle if the driver's BAC is .02 or greater.
- A "No Pass/No Drive Law" (KRS 159.051) is in effect. The law states that all students ages 16 or 17 can be denied a driver's license or have a license revoked for academic deficiency. The statute only affects drivers who obtain a permit or license after August 1, 2007.

Reinstatement Requirements

Suspension $40.00 fee; re-examination if suspended for one year or more.
Revocation $50.00 fee; re-examination if suspended for one year or more.

Point System Overview

The point system ranges from 3 to 6 points. If a driver over eighteen years of age accumulates 12 or more points in a 2-year period, or 7 or more points if under eighteen, an administrative hearing will be held.

License Plate Facts

Renewal
Renewal is annual. Vehicles registered with standard issue passenger car plates can renew online from the home web page as long as the address on the renewal notice is correct.

New Residents
Non-residents must register vehicles within 15 days upon establishing residency.

Inspections and Emissions Testing
Kentucky has neither a mandatory safety inspection nor emission testing required with a vehicle registration; however, some local jurisdictions do have emissions testing.

Plate Descriptions

Typical Plate Patterns	Passenger plates are NNNLLL, light trucks NNNNLL. Commercial vehicle plates are NLL-NNN.
County/City Codes	Passenger plates have county of issue printed on bottom; commercial plates do not.
Plates and Stickers in Force	One plate, one decal (MO & YR)
Plate Remains with Car when Sold?	Yes.

Overview of Record Access

About Driving Records
Attention: MVRs, Division of Driver Licensing, Transportation Office Building, 200 Mero Street, Frankfort 40622, 502-564-6800, ext. 2250. The current fee for commercial or non-commercial driver records is $3.00, the fee for electronic access is $5.00. Credit cards are accepted. The last fee increase was December 2006 when the electronic record fee increased from $4.50 to $5.00. The driver's license number or SSN, or name and DOB must be submitted with request

Request Methods – Mail, Walk-in, Online (Batch or Public), Bulk.

What You Should Know – Kentucky reports all moving violation convictions, and all out-of-state convictions except non-CDL speeding violations. Electronic access in batch mode is available to approved, ongoing requesters with a permissible use. The system, run by Kentucky.gov, is open 24/7 and provides immediate results after requests are sent. For more information, call Kentucky.gov at 502-875-3733 or email to: support@kentucky.gov

Special Access Programs Available – A three-year driving record without personal information may be obtained at http://dhr.ky.gov/DHRWeb/. This website allows anyone to request Driving History Records for Kentucky drivers.

About Accident Reports
Accident reports can be obtained from the Kentucky State Police, Criminal Identification and Records Branch, 1250 Louisville Road, Frankfort 40601 502-226-2175, fax 502-226-7418. Records are maintained from 1998. Requests must be in writing and include the exact date, county, roadway, and the driver's name. Requesters must have a permissible use per DPPA. The cost is $5.00 per report. The report may also be accessed using the microfilm number appearing on the driving record entry. In-person and fax searching are available. Turnaround time is normally 1 to 2 weeks. Statistical reports are available to the general public.

About Vehicle Records
Division of Motor Vehicle Licensing, Transportation Office Building, 200 Mero Street 2nd Fl, Frankfort 40622, 502-564-2737 for Title History, 502-564-5301 for Registration, 502-564-3298 for other requests. Email questions to KYTCMVLHelpDesk@ky.gov. The current fee for VIN, registration, ownership, vehicle information, and lien checks is $2.00. Certification is an additional $2.00. Records include those of boats and mobile homes. Records are computerized or microfilm since 1992 for title histories, 1999 to present for current titles only. Please note that this agency will not do a search using only the name and DOB. Also, this agency will not search using a SSN.

Request Methods – Mail, Walk-in, Online, Bulk.

What You Should Know – The same system for online driving records provides access to vehicle record data. Fee is only $.44 per record.

About Watercraft Records
Records can be obtained from the Division profiled above. Only motorized boats must be titled and registered. Title and registration information is available from 1992 to present. Prior records are kept by county clerks. Direct questions to 502-564-2737.

Louisiana

Administration	Important Telephone and Web Contacts

Commissioner
Office of Motor Vehicles
PO Box 64886, Baton Rouge 70896
225-925-6335
http://omv.dps.state.la.us/
Laws and Statutes
    www.legis.state.la.us/searchlegis.htm
Policies and Procedures:
    https://web01.dps.louisiana.gov/omv1.nsf/
	Driver Licensing..225-922-1175
	Driving Records/Record Discrepancies..............877-368-5463
	Financial Responsibility.....................................877-368-5463
	Suspensions & Revocations 877-368-5463
	                                              or 225-925-6388
	Commercial Driver License 225-925-6277
	Vehicle Information 225-925-6146
	State Dept of Insurance 225-342-5900
	State Patrol 225-925-6006
	    Email Contacts www.dps.state.la.us/omv/email.html

Driver License Facts

License Format
The format is eight digits preceded by one zero (e.g., 012345678). Louisiana reports there is no code or sequential arrangement which determines the characters making the license number other than the double zeros at the beginning.

Document Appearance
Horizontal licenses are issued to license holders age 21 and over. Class I (ID cards) and H (Handicap) cards will specify "THIS IS NOT A DRIVER'S LICENSE." The state capitol drawing coordinates with the header bar with blue for Class E (personal), green for Class D (chauffeur), blue of all ID cards and Handicap Placards, gold for CDL, and red as indicated below for under 21. A duplicate license is shown by "DUP" in the license header.

Security Characteristics	The license has a reflective security strip in the shape of the state, across the text.
Position of Photo	The photo is on the right side, a signature is above the photo.
Minor Age Driver	Vertical licenses are issued to those under 21. Text will indicate "Under 21/18 until xxxx". There is a red border around photo.
CDL Indicator	"COMMERCIAL LICENSE" is printed across top. The header bar is gold, unless driver is under 21 then header is red.
Sex Offender	"SEX OFFENDER" is printed in orange below the photo.

Issue and Renewal

Age Requirements
Minimum ages are fifteen for Learner's Permit, sixteen for Intermediate License, and seventeen for a regular Class E License. After completing the learner's permit stage and upon reaching at least sixteen years of age, a minor may apply for a Class "E" Intermediate License. This license must be maintained for a minimum of one year from the date of issuance or until the driver has reached the age of seventeen. This license allows the minor to drive alone or with other passengers in the vehicle, but restricts him from driving between the hours of 11:00 p.m. to 5:00 AM unless he is accompanied by a licensed parent, guardian, or adult at least twenty-one or older. After the one-year period or once the driver reaches age seventeen, the minor may qualify for a regular Class E license.

Renewal
Birth month of fourth year, except sex offenders are issued driver's license/ID cards valid for one year. Driver keeps same number when renewing. Driver's License renewal and Identification Card renewal are available online. But making changes in personal information, including address, is not permitted when renewing on the web or by telephone or mail. In accordance with R.S 32:412F, any Louisiana out-of-state military personnel is not subject to renewal until 60 days after returning or discharge. Note that nothing is permanent except a Mobility Impaired Handtag or Senior ID.

Elderly-Related Restrictions
None are reported.

Residency
Non-resident's home-state license honored for ninety days; however, Louisiana license must be secured within thirty days of establishing residency.

License Classes
Commercial Classifications
Class A — Any combination of vehicles with a GCWR of 26,001 pounds or more towing a vehicle in excess of 10,000 pounds GVWR. This license also permits the operation of all other classes of vehicles.

Class B — Any single vehicle with a GVWR of 26,001 pounds or more, or towing a vehicle not exceeding 10,000 pounds GVWR. This license also permits the operation of Class C, D, and E vehicles.

Class C — Any single vehicle with a GVWR of 26,000 pounds or less, or towing a vehicle not exceeding 10,000 pounds GVWR, or designed to transport sixteen or more passengers (including the driver), which is not within Class A or B, or is utilized for the transportation of hazardous materials. This license also permits the operation of Class D and E vehicles.

Non-Commercial Classifications
Class D — Any single vehicle less than 26,001 pounds GVWR or any such vehicle designed or utilized for the transportation of passengers for hire or fee or which is not within the definition of vehicles within groups A, B, or C, including all vehicles with three or more axles or having GVW in excess of 10,001 pounds, and not utilized in the transportation of materials found to be hazardous. This license also permits the operation of Class E vehicles.

Class E — Any single motor vehicle under 10,001 pounds GVWR, excluding motorcycles or motor scooters, not utilized to transport passengers for hire. This class includes all personal use vehicles, recreational vehicles, and farm vehicles operated within 150 miles of the owner's farm. The Learner's Permit, Intermediate License and Learner's License are all Class E.

HAZMAT Endorsement Procedure
The state is in compliance with the Patriot Act. All applicants applying for a new or renewal or transfer HAZMAT Endorsement (HME) must first obtain the application from https://hazprints.tsa.dhs.gov/Public/ or by calling 877-429-7746. The driver must also be fingerprinted. EMSI is the state-designated entity to process fingerprints. There are four locations in the state that perform this service. Visit the web page listed above to find the address locations. For more information on the overall process visit www.dps.state.la.us/omv/patriotact.html. The cost of the fingerprint process is $89.25. The fingerprints and application information is sent to the Federal Transportation Security Administration (TSA). TSA performs the background checks and notifies the DMV whether the application is approved or denied. When completed and approved, the HME is valid for five years.

Safety and Enforcement Facts

Insurance and Financial Responsibility
Louisiana has a compulsory insurance law but not a no-fault insurance provision. Minimum financial responsibility limits are $15,000/30,000/25,000 (increased from $10,000/$20,000/$10,000 on 01/01/2010) for vehicles with a gross vehicle weight of 20,000 pounds or under. Vehicles with a GVW of 20,001 to 50,000 pounds must have insurance coverage of at least $25,000/$50,000 bodily injury and $25,000 property damage or a single combined limit of no less than $75,000. The limits for vehicles with GVW over 50,000 pounds is at least $100,000/$300,000 bodily injury and $25,000 property damage or a combined single limit of $300,000. Proof of financial responsibility is required following an accident wherein a judgment is rendered, or for DWI convictions and refusals. SR-22 forms are used by the state.

When applying for a license plate for any motor vehicle, the applicant must have proof of the required liability insurance or other allowable substitute. Proof of insurance must be maintained in the vehicle when the vehicle is operational and must be presented any time a law enforcement officer requests that such proof be provided. If unable to provide the proof upon request, the vehicle's license plate will be seized and the vehicle may be impounded.

Alcohol and Chemical Testing
Louisiana's illegal intoxication level for the purpose of convicting individuals of driving while intoxicated is .08 percent and above for non-commercial vehicles and .04 for commercial vehicles. In addition, individuals under the age of 21 can be convicted for underage driving while intoxicated with a .02 percent intoxication level. Blood, urine, and breath tests are all permissible for measurement purposes. Louisiana has an administrative per se suspension as well as suspensions upon being convicted of driving while intoxicated or underage driving while intoxicated. The crime of operating a vehicle while intoxicated is the operating of any motor vehicle, aircraft, water craft, vessel, or other means of conveyance.

Accident Reporting
Any accident resulting in death or injury must be reported immediately to the nearest police department. SR claim forms maybe filed, but it is not required.

Suspensions and Revocations

The state is in compliance with the federally mandated disqualifications on CDLs per MCSIA. See the Appendix for details.

    Driving While License Suspended... Suspension extended for one year.
    Driving Under the Influence (at any age)
        First Conviction .... One-year suspension; SR-22 or bond required.
        Second Conviction .... Two-year suspension; SR-22 or bond required.
        Third or Subsequent Conviction .... Three-year suspension; SR-22 or bond required.
    Refusal to Submit to a Chemical Test
        First Conviction ....Six-month suspension.
        Second or Subsequent Conviction..One and one-half-year suspension.
    Vehicular Negligent Injury 2nd ....Two-year suspension.
    Vehicular Negligent Injury 3rd ....Three-year suspension.

Driving Privileges Will be Suspended or Revoked for Any of the Following Violations

- Committing an Offense in Another State, if Committed in LA Would be Punishable by Suspension or Revocation
- Failure to Answer Traffic Violation Charge
- Failure to Comply with Financial Responsibility Law
- Failure to Maintain Liability Insurance
- Felony Conviction While Operating Motor Vehicle (Two years)
- Habitual Offender
- Hit & Run (Two years)
- Homicide Committed While Operating a Motor Vehicle, Manslaughter, Negligent Homicide, Felony with MV Used (All are two year suspensions)
- Three Convictions for Reckless Driving in Twelve Months (Two years)
- Violation of License Restrictions

Ignition Interlock and Interlock Hardship

Any restricted driver's license issued on or after August 15, 2007, for a Refusal/Submit, DWI or Vehicular Negligent Injury, including underlying Driving Under Suspension convictions, will require an ignition interlock device to be installed in the vehicle being driven prior to the issuance of an interlock hardship..

Reinstatement Requirements

    Suspension   Expiration of mandatory suspension period; SR-22 for DWI convictions/refusals; payment of reinstatement fee.
    Revocation   Expiration of mandatory revocation period; payment of reinstatement fee.

Note: Any reinstatement processed on or after August 15, 2007, regardless of the offense/conviction date, which requires an ignition interlock to be installed as a condition of reinstatement will be required for no less than 6 months or for the length of original suspension period, whichever is longer. If an interlock hardship was issued during the course of the suspension period, credit will be given for time the interlock was installed.

Point System Overview

Louisiana does not have a point system.

License Plate Facts

Registration Renewal

Online renewal is available at the home web page. Motorcycles expire after four years, motor homes two years, boat and light utility trailers four years, trucks up to 6000 GVW four years, commercial vehicles one year, and passenger cars two years (one year if commercial plate). Trailers 1500 pounds or greater can be one year, four years or permanent.

New Residents

Non-residents must register vehicles immediately upon obtaining employment or establishing residence. When applying for a license plate for any motor vehicle, the applicant must have proof of the required liability insurance or other allowable substitute.

Inspections and Emissions Testing

Every automobile, truck, trailer, boat trailer and motorcycle operated on the highways of this state must have a current motor vehicle safety inspection sticker. The City of New Orleans, the City of Kenner and the City of Westwego have their own inspection programs.

Plate Descriptions

Typical Plate Patterns	Passenger plates are LLLNNN (ABC123), light trucks LNNNNNN (W123456), and commercial vehicles LNNNNNN (A123456).
County/City Codes	The state indicates there is no coding designation on the plates.
Plates and Stickers in Force	One plate, one decal (YR).
Plate Remains with Car when Sold?	No, it is destroyed by the dealer or returned to the state, except for very special circumstances.

Overview of Record Access

About Driving Records

Department of Public Safety and Corrections, Office of Motor Vehicles, PO Box 64886, Baton Rouge 70896, 877-368-5463. Note that this agency often refers to a driving record as an ODR - which means Official Driving Record. Use of "Request for Louisiana Driver's License Information" Form is required. This may require signed release of subject. The current fee for a driving record is $15.00, $6.00 electronically for approved requesters and businesses, and $17.00 via the web for license holders. The fee for a copy of a driver license application or basic driver license information is $5.00 per record.

Request Methods – Mail, Walk-in, Online, Bulk.

What You Should Know – citation for "Speed Greater Than Reasonable and Prudent" allows the police officer to cite for speed due to conditions rather than specific miles per hour over limit. This cite is frequently used with accidents. The online subscription online system is meant only for approved high volume, ongoing requesters. For more information, contact Ms. Cecile M. Bush, MVMII, DMS 2nd Floor, PO Box 64886, Baton Rouge, LA 70896-4886, 225-922-0017.

Special Access Programs Available – An individual may view and print his/her driving record at http://omv.dps.state.la.us/odr/odr.asp. The cost is $17.00; use of a credit card or debit card is required.

About Accident Reports

Copies of accident reports may be obtained from the Louisiana State Police, Traffic Records Unit - A27, PO Box 66614, Baton Rouge 70896, 225-925-6157 or 925-3518, www.lsp.org/safety_crash.html. Records are maintained from 2000 to present. New records are available for inquiry 1-2 weeks after incident. The fee is $7.50 per record; include a SASE. Personal checks are not accepted. The driver's name, date of accident and parish (county) are needed when ordering

About Vehicle Records

Department of Public Safety and Corrections, Office of Motor Vehicles, PO Box 64886, Baton Rouge 70896, 225-925-7198 or 877- 368-5463. The state closed the walk-in counter; in person search requests are not accepted. Requesters must have a license plate number or VIN to do a search. The current fee for VIN, registration, lien or plate checks is $10.00 per record ($8.00 to search and $2.00 per page to certify). A written letter must be submitted with each mailed request.

Request Methods – Mail, Online (limited), Bulk.

What You Should Know – The online service is only offered to the contracted towing/recovery/storage related-industries.

Special Access Programs Available –Requests can be faxed to this office by pre-approved requesters.

About Watercraft Records

Department of Wildlife & Fisheries, PO 14796, Baton Rouge 70898, 225-765-2898. www.wlf.louisiana.gov/boating. All motorized boats and all sail boats over 12 ft must be registered. No titles are issued here. Records can be searched by name, hull number or registration number and from whom the boat was acquired. Records are indexed on computer since 1970. The release of records is subject stricter criteria than vehicle records. Consent must be given, including for insurance purposes. There is no fee; turnaround time is 7-10 days. Liens are filed through the parish courts.

Maine

Administration	Important Telephone and Web Contacts
Patty Morneault, Director of Driver License Svcs Garry Hinkley, Director of Vehicle Services Bureau of Motor Vehicles 29 State House Station Augusta 04333-0029 207-624-9000 www.maine.gov/sos/bmv/ Motor Vehicle Laws and Rules may be accessed from the home page. **State Statutes** are found at http://janus.state.me.us/legis/	Driver Licensing............................ 207-624-9000 x52114 Driver Records .... 207-624-9000 x52116 Financial Responsibility (SR-22) .. 207-624-9000 x52108 Commercial Driver License........... 207-624-9000 x52122 OUI.. 207-624-9000 x52104 Titles.. 207-624-9000 x52138 Registrations................................. 207-624-9000 x52149 State Police.................................... 207-624-7200 State Department of Insurance 207-624-8475

Driver License Facts

License Format
Seven numbers. Maine reports there is no code or sequential arrangement which determines the characters of the license number. Drivers convicted of an offense for OUI under drugs or alcohol will have an asterisk displayed on their license for 10 years.

Document Appearance
The current document, introduced 10/99, is a digital driver's license. It will take 9 years to completely replace all driver's licenses.

Security Characteristics	A small ghost photo image on the opposite side of photo, with an embedded hologram. Information on the front of the card is stored on a bar code on the rear. Heading is orange-ish with word "Maine" written in middle.
Position of Photo	Right edge; if only an ID Card, then on left edge.
Minor Age Driver Locator	There is a red notation in the bottom center with "Under 21 Until xx/xx/xx".
CDL Indicator	The words "CDL Operator" appears in blue lettering under the Maine Banner.
Non-Photo License	Prior to 01/03, the document is of heavy paper stock and is not laminated. Validation has date stamp on left side and signature of Secretary of State. After 01/03, non-photo licenses are issued with the same formatting as the digital driver's license with the words "valid without photo" placed where the image would appear.

Issue and Renewal
Any resident seeking to acquire or renew a Maine driver license or non-driver ID card must provide documentary evidence of legal presence. This documentary evidence must contain an actual physical address

Age Requirements
Maine's 3-step graduated drivers licensing system for new drivers who are under 18 years of age was introduced in September, 2003. The minimum age for an Intermediate License is 16 with approved driver education course. There are many driving restrictions with this license. A Learner's Permit is required for all new drivers. That person must hold the permit for 6 months before applying for a road test and is prohibited from using a cellular phone while operating with a permit. While driving, the permit holder must be accompanied by a licensed driver at least 20 years of age and has held a valid license for two years.

Proof of Authorized Presence
Individuals applying for a Maine driver license or non-driver ID card must establish that they are legally present in the U.S. and a resident if the State of Maine.

Renewal
If age less than 62, then birth month of 6th year, photo license required; if age 62 or older, then birth month of 4th year,

photo license required. In an effort to improve customer service and reduce wait times in regional branch offices, some license holders have been renewed for 8 years instead of 6. Renewals are available online for persons having already proven legal residency and legal presence. This service is available for any Maine licensed driver with an active digital license, digital motorcycle license or digital motor driven cycle restricted license and any holder of a digital Maine ID card. This service is not available for commercial driver license holders. Driver keeps same number when renewing. Active Military personnel stationed out-of-state need not renew. Upon discharge, they must renew within 30 days.

Elderly-Related Restrictions
None, other than the shorter renewal period as mentioned above.

Residency
A non-resident's home-state license honored on a reciprocal basis. A Maine license is required within thirty days of declaring or establishing residency.

License Classes
Commercial Classifications
Class A — A combination of vehicles with a GVWR or registered weight of 26,001 or more pounds, providing the GVWR or GW of the vehicle or vehicles being towed is in excess of 10,000 pounds. A Class A license is a commercial driver's license. Holders of a Class A license may—with any appropriate endorsements—operate all vehicles in Class B and Class C.

Class B — A single vehicle with a GVWR or registered weight of 26,001 or more pounds, or any such vehicle towing a vehicle not in excess of 10,000 pounds GVWR or GW. A Class B license is a commercial driver's license. Holders of a Class B may—with any appropriate endorsements—operate all vehicles in Class C.

Class C — A Class C License (see below) is a commercial driver's license if it carries a bus or hazardous materials endorsement.

Non-Commercial Classifications
Class C — A single vehicle or combination of vehicles that does not meet the definition of Class A or Class B license. Holders of a Class C license may—with any appropriate endorsements—operate all vehicles in that class.

HAZMAT Endorsement Procedure
The state is in compliance with the Patriot Act. All applicants applying for a new, renewal or transfer Hazmat Endorsement (HME) must successfully pass the hazmat written examination. Upon completion, a Hazmat Receipt Card and TSA Hazmat application is issued. The driver must be fingerprinted. To schedule fingerprinting visit https://hazprints.tsa.dhs.gov/Public/ or call 877-429-7746. Integrated Biometric Technology is the state-designated entity to process fingerprints. There are multiple fingerprint locations in the state. The cost of the fingerprint process is $89.25. The fingerprints and application information is sent to the Federal Transportation Security Administration (TSA). TSA performs the background checks and notifies the BMV whether the application is approved or denied. When completed and approved, the HME is valid until expiration of the CDL.

Safety and Enforcement Facts

Insurance and Financial Responsibility
Maine has a compulsory insurance law, but does not require no-fault insurance. Minimum financial responsibility limits are $50,000/100,000/25,000. Proof is required at registration, renewal, after an accident and after certain violations. Maine uses SR-22 forms.

Alcohol and Chemical Testing
Maine's illegal intoxication level is .08 percent and above; .04 percent if operating a CMV; and if driver is under twenty-one years or has a conditional license, the level is any amount. Blood and breath testing are authorized. Maine has both an implied-consent violation and a provision for an administrative suspension.

A driver's license may be reinstated prior to the expiration of the total suspension period with installation of an approved ignition interlock device in the motor vehicle of the driver.

Crash Reporting
Crashes involving death, injury or property damage in excess of $1000.00 must be reported immediately to the nearest law enforcement agency. There are no special CDL reporting requirements.

Suspensions and Revocations
Note: The state is in compliance with the federally mandated disqualifications on CDLs per MCSIA. See the Appendix for details. See www.maine.gov/sos/cec/rules/29/250/250c006.doc. for the rules for suspension for CDL drivers.

Offense	Penalty
Aggravated Assault with a Motor Vehicle (Class B)	Three-year revocation.
Altering License/registration	Thirty-day suspension.
Assault with a Motor Vehicle (Class C)	Three-year revocation.
Assault with a Motor Vehicle (Class D)	Two-year revocation.
Criminal Threatening with a Motor Vehicle (Class D)	Two-year revocation.
Displaying Suspended License	Thirty-day suspension.
Drag Racing	Ninety-day suspension.
Elevated Aggravated Assault with a Motor Vehicle (Class A)	Three-year revocation.
Eluding a Police Officer	Ninety-day suspension.
Failure to Stop for Police Officer	Thirty-day suspension.
False Application for License/registration	Thirty-day suspension.
False Information to Police	Thirty-day suspension.
Illegal transportation of liquor or drugs by minor	Thirty-day suspension.
Leaving Scene of Injury Accident	Thirty-day suspension.
Loaning License	Thirty-day suspension.
Operating After Suspension	Sixty-day suspension.
Operating Alone on Permit	Thirty-day suspension.
Operating Under the Influence	
First Offense	Minimum ninety-day suspension; for refusal to take test—275 days.
Second Offense - Violation Date Prior to 09/01/2008	Eighteen-month suspension.
Second Offense - Violation Date On or After 09/01/2008	Three-year suspension.
Third Offense - Violation Date Prior to 09/01/2008	Four-year suspension.
Third Offense - Violation Date On or After 09/01/2008	Six-year suspension.
Fourth or Subsequent Offense - Violation Date Prior to 09/01/2008	Four-year suspension.
Fourth or Subsequent Offense - Violation Date On or After 09/01/2008	Six-year suspension with Restoration Requirement that Ignition Interlock Device is installed for four years.
Operating Under the Influence - CDL Holders	
First Offense	One-year suspension.
First Offense w/HAZMAT	Three-year suspension.
Second Offense	Permanent suspension.
Operating Without License	Thirty-day suspension.
Passing a Roadblock	Ninety-day suspension.
Passing Stopped School Bus	Thirty-day suspension.
Reckless Conduct with a Motor Vehicle (Class D)	Two-year revocation.
Speed Thirty Miles or More Over Limit	Thirty-day suspension.
Three License Suspensions in Three Years Plus Subsequent Conviction	120-day suspension.
Twelve Demerit Points within One Year Period	Fifteen-day suspension.
Unlawful Use of License	Thirty-day suspension.

Reinstatement Requirements
Suspension $50.00 fee; time lapse; state conditions.
Revocation $50.00 fee; time lapse; financial responsibility; re-examination.

Point System Overview
The Maine point system ranges from 2 to 8 points. There is a 15 day suspension due to accumulation of 12 or more points within a year. With 12 months of a clear record, a driver can "earn" a free violation credit point, with a maximum of 4 points. Also, one 3 point credit can be given to a person for successful completion of an authorized Defensive Driving Course or a Motorcycle Defensive Driver Course. The credit will be given only once in a twelve month period and the credit of points will be erased one year from the completion date.

License Plate Facts

Registration Renewal
Vehicle registration renewal is available online for passenger vehicles, commercial vehicles, and non-excisable trailers. Rapid Renewal may be accessed through www.informe.org/bmv/rapid-renewal/, the Department of the Secretary of State's site for online services. Registrations not eligible to renew online include island use, emergency/coach, vehicles

over 12,000 pounds GVW, apportioned, special mobile equipment, tractors, municipal and state vehicles which all must be renewed in person.

New Residents
Non-residents must register vehicles within thirty days of declaring or establishing residency.

Inspections and Emissions Testing
Maine requires an annual safety inspection on all vehicles. All vehicles in Cumberland County are subject to an Enhanced Auto Inspection (effective since 01/01/99).

Plate Descriptions
Typical Plate Patterns	Passenger & light trucks are NNNNLL. Commercial vehicle plates are NNNNNN or NLNNNN.
County/City Codes	There is no coding on the plate designating the county of issuance.
Plates and Stickers in Force	Two plates, two decals (MO) (YR) on both plates.
Plates Remain with Car when Sold?	No, plates remain with seller.

Overview of Record Access

About Driving Records
Driver License Services, 29 State House Station, 101 Hospital Street, Augusta 04333-0029, 207-624-9000 x52116, the fax is 207-624-9090. The current fee for a three-year record is $5.00; a ten-year record is $10.00. **Add $2.00 if requested online or faxed back.** Add $1.00 for certification. The state charges for "no record found" reports only if request is mailed.

Request Methods – Mail, Walk-in, Auto Fax Back, Online.

What You Should Know – There are two programs. Maine offers online interactive access 24 hours daily through Driver Record Check at www.informe.org/bmv/drc/. This is open to all users, no personal information is reported. A second system is available for approved requesters entitled to receive a full record with personal identifiers.

Special Access Programs Available – Driver CrossCheck is an innovative service that allows employers to automatically receive notification about changes to the driving records of employees. This program is also offered by InforME (www.maine.gov/informe/subscriber/index.htm).

Vehicle Records
Registration Section, 29 State House Station, Augusta 04333-0029, 207-624-9000 x52138-Titles, x52149-Registration). Records are held from 1982. All requests must be submitted in writing. Registration search records are $5.00 each for uncertified and $6.00 for certified. A certified title record is $33.00. Besides record on passenger and commercial vehicles, the Bureau of Motor Vehicles maintains records for certain RV vehicles—motor homes and camper trailers. All other RV (ATV and snowmobile) records as well as boat records are maintained by the Department of Inland Fisheries and Wildlife. Mobile homes are only required to be registered if they are being moved, hence the Bureau of Motor Vehicles only maintains records of those mobile homes that are registered. All mobile homes records (including lien records) are maintained by the municipality in which the mobile home is located.

Request Methods – Mail, Walk-in, Phone, Fax, Online.

What You Should Know – Besides record on passenger and commercial vehicles, the Bureau of Motor Vehicles maintains records for certain RV vehicles—motor homes and camper trailers. All other RV (ATV and snowmobile) records as well as boat records are maintained by the Department of Inland Fisheries and Wildlife. Mobile homes are only required to be registered if they are being moved, hence the BMV only maintains records of those mobile homes that are registered. All mobile homes records (including lien records) are maintained by the municipality in which the mobile home is located.

Special Access Programs Available – Maine offers online interactive access to title and registration records 24 hours daily through InforME's Interactive Services. This is a subscription service and is open only to those who qualify as permissible users. The fee is $5.00 per title or registration record.

Watercraft Records
Department of Inland Fisheries and Wildlife, 41 State House Station, Augusta 04333-0041, 207-287-5232 (certified docs), 207-287-2043 (look-ups), http://www.maine.gov/ifw/ All motorized boats must be registered, boats are not required to be titled. Registration records can be searched by name or registration number. Records go back on the computer to 1989 for those who have renewed. There is a $5.00 if searching is done by staff; $2.00 if you do-it-yourself. Turnaround time for mail requests is up to two weeks. The fee is $25.00 if the search requires accessing older records on microfiche in another building. Credit cards are accepted for payment. Liens are not shown and must be searched with the Secretary of State at 207-624-7752.

Maryland

Administration	Important Telephone and Web Contacts
John T. Kuo, Administrator Motor Vehicle Administration 6601 Ritchie Highway Glen Burnie 21062 410-768-7274 www.mva.maryland.gov	Driver Licensing.................. 301-729-4550 or 410-768-7000 Driver Records ....410-787-7758 Financial Responsibility ....410-768-7431 Vehicle Information ....410-768-7508 State Police...410-486-3101 Maryland Insurance Division ....410-468-2000 General Email: www.mva.maryland.gov/contact.htm Motor Vehicle Laws: http://mlis.state.md.us

Driver License Facts

License Format
1 letter and 12 numbers. The letter represents the first letter of the driver's last name. The twelve numbers are coded in groups of three, creating a unique total number: the first three digits are coded to the last name; the second three to the first name; third group to the middle name; and the last group is coded to the month and day of birth.

Document Appearance
Security Characteristics   Advantage transparent coating security feature, bar code of license. Magnetic strip on back contains license number and identifying information.
Position of Photo   Top left with ghost imaging technique.
Minor Age Driver   Card is vertical, "Under 21 alcohol restricted" printed in red.
CDL Indicator   Document I.D. line (under state name) states "CDL".

Issue and Renewal
Effective June 1, 2009, a new applicant for a learner's permit, license, moped operator's permit or ID card must present (1) document to prove age and identity, (1) document to prove they possess a valid, verifiable Social Security Number (SSN) or proof of ineligibility for an SSN, (1) document to prove lawful status and (2) residency documents. The applicant must bring original documents or copies certified by the issuing agency. Photocopies, notarized copies, and documents with alterations or erasures are not accepted. Under the provisions of the law, individuals holding a valid Maryland driver's license or ID card prior to April 19, 2009 but cannot provide proof that they are in the United States legally will be allowed to renew their license or identification card until June 30, 2015, but their product may not be acceptable for federal purposes. After June 30, 2015, any renewal will require all individuals to provide proof of legal presence utilizing acceptable documents outlined above.

Age Requirements
One cannot obtain a full license until reaching the age of 18. A Graduated Licensing System with three levels of licensing - learner's permit; provisional license, full driver's license - is in effect. In 2005 and 2009, modifications were made to the program. Those who hold a learner's permit must wait a full nine months before being eligible for a provisional license. The nine-month period will be restarted should the person be convicted or granted probation before judgment (PBJ) for a moving violation. The holder must be at least age 16 years and 6 months before being eligible for a provisional license after holding the learner's permit for the mandatory 9 months. Provisional License Holders must hold the provisional license for a minimum of 18 consecutive months without violation before conversion to a full license. The 18-month period will be restarted for any convictions or PBJ's for moving violations or violations of license restrictions.

Renewal
Expiration on birth day and month of 5 year; if under 21, expires 60 days after 21st birthday. Products for individuals, with temporary lawful status, will reflect an expiration date that coincides with the individual's lawful status in the U.S. Driver keeps same license number when renewing, unless name or date of birth change. There is no online renewal available. Drivers have up to one year after expiration to renew without having to take additional tests. In addition to issuing renewal licenses by mail for eligible applicants (if a current photo image is on file), MD issues a photo license for applicants who are MD residents but temporarily outside the state. Out-of-state military personnel are not required to

renew, but may do so to obtain a valid "absentee photo license." They must renew within 30 days of discharge or return to state. Renewal can be done in-person or by mail for certain drivers.

Also, Maryland's law requires individuals who are 40 and older to obtain vision certification or submit to an MVA vision screening each time a license is renewed. Individuals under the age of 40 are required to obtain a vision certification every 10 years.

Elderly-Related Restrictions
There are no restrictions in place for renewing drivers. Individuals 70 years or older who are applying for an original (first time issued anywhere) Maryland license must provide proof of satisfactory operation of a motor vehicle or a written certification from a licensed physician attesting to the general physical and mental qualifications of the applicant.

Residency
New resident's home state license is honored on reciprocal basis. New residents if currently licensed must obtain a Maryland license within sixty days of establishing residency for a non-commercial license and within thirty days for a commercial license. Applicants who have not previously held a driver's license for eighteen months or more, conviction free, will be issued a provisional driver's license.

Note: Since October 1, 2003, Maryland non-commercial drivers operating a commercial motor vehicle in intrastate commerce (within the state of Maryland) and if the vehicle weight is between 10,001 and 26,000 pounds are required to hold a valid Federal Motor Carrier (DOT) physical card in their possession. If driver is licensed prior to October 1, 2003 and has a pre-existing medical condition, and the onset was prior to that date, the driver is exempt from this requirement for a 20-year period, provided the pre-existing condition does not worsen.

License Classes
Commercial Classifications

Class	You May Drive	And May Tow	Exceptions
Class A	Any single combination of vehicles	Any trailer	Motorcycles
Class B	Motor vehicles 26,001 or more pounds (GVW)	Trailers 10,000 pounds or less	Combination of Class F (tractor) and Class G (trailer), Motorcycles
Class C	Motor vehicles under 26,001 pounds (GVW)	Trailers to 10,000 pounds or less	Motorcycles

Non-Commercial Classifications

Class	You May Drive	And May Tow	Exceptions
Class A	Any single or combination of non-commercial motor vehicles	Any non-commercial trailer	Commercial Motor Vehicles, Motorcycles
Class B	Any non-commercial vehicle 26,001 or more pounds (GVW)	Any non-commercial trailer	Commercial Motor Vehicles, Combination of Class F (tractor) and Class G (trailer), Motorcycles
Class C	Any non-commercial combination of motor vehicles with a GCW less than 26,001 pounds	Any non-commercial trailer	Commercial Motor Vehicles, Motorcycles
Class M	Motorcycles	Motorcycle trailer	Commercial & Non-Commercial Motor Vehicles - Classes A, B & C

HAZMAT Endorsement Procedure
The state is in compliance with the Patriot Act. Drivers are required to complete an electronic Maryland Hazardous Materials Endorsement application. Hazmat information is found at www.mva.maryland.gov/DriverServ/Apply/CDL/Hazmat.htm. The application can be downloaded or picked up in any MVA office. Hazmat applications are only processed at the Bel Air, Glen Burnie Headquarters (Annex Building), Salisbury, Frederick (may be limited hours), and Waldorf MVA offices. An appointment is required; call 800-638-8347. The process involves two separate transactions: the Hazmat application is processed by MVA staff; the fingerprint background record check and fee collection is processed by the Department of Public Safety & Correctional Services (DPSCS) staff at the Bel Air, Glen Burnie (Annex Building), Frederick, Salisbury or Waldorf locations. Fingerprint records will be forwarded by the DPSCS to the Criminal Justice Information Systems for a Federal and State criminal background check.

Safety and Enforcement Facts

Insurance and Financial Responsibility

Maryland law requires that all motor vehicles registered in Maryland be insured by a company licensed in Maryland and carry coverage of $20,000 for bodily injury per person, $40,000 for bodily injury for two or more people, and $15,000 for property damage. The state has optional add-on no-fault insurance (PIP coverage of $2,500) and compulsory insurance. The state does not use insurance cards; vehicle owners must self-certify when registering or upon renewal. Proof is required when the state is notified by the insurance company of a cancellation (FR-19 needed), through random selection, and when a warning letter is issued for accumulation of bad driving points.

Penalties Assessed Against Uninsured Drivers—If insurance certification Form FR-19 is not submitted to verify continuous insurance of a vehicle, penalties are assessed at the rate of $150 for the first 30 days the vehicle is uninsured and $7.00 for each additional day. Non-compliance also results in suspension of the uninsured vehicle registration and future registration privileges.

Alcohol and Chemical Testing

Maryland's illegal alcoholic levels are: .08 % or higher is "under the influence;" .10 % and above is "intoxicated." The legal limit for drivers under 21 is .02, if driving a CMV .04. Blood and breath testing are authorized. Maryland has both an implied-consent violation and a provision for an administrative suspension. Operating a horse or bicycle under the influence is also considered illegal.

Accident Reporting

Every operator involved in an accident resulting in injury or death—regardless of fault—must report the accident to the Motor Vehicle Administration (6601 Ritchie Highway, Glen Burnie 21062) within fifteen days. No report is required from the operator if the accident is investigated by a law enforcement officer and involves property damage only.

Suspensions and Revocations

Maryland completed structure testing and received CDLIS certification in 2006. See the Appendix for more information about the mandatory CDL disqualification sanctions.

Driving While Intoxicated
    First Conviction   Minimum six-month revocation.
    Second Conviction   Twelve-month revocation.
    Third and Subsequent Convictions   Eighteen-month revocation.
Driving While Under the Influence
    First Conviction   Up to sixty-day suspension.
    Second and Subsequent Convictions   Up to 120-day suspension.
Refusal to Submit to Chemical Test
    First Offense   120-day suspension.
    Second and Subsequent Offenses   One-year suspension.
Administrative Per Se (for test results .08 percent alcohol concentration or more)
    First Offense   Forty-five-day suspension.
    Second Offense   Ninety-day suspension.

The Administration May Cancel, Revoke, Refuse, or Suspend a License for any of the Following Reasons:
- Commission of an offense in another state, which would require revocation or suspension in Maryland.
- Disregard of traffic laws and the safety of others
- Making a false certification of insurance on any application for a title or vehicle registration
- Outstanding arrest warrants—law enforcement agencies notify the MV Administration which places a flags/suspends the license
- Permitting unlawful or fraudulent use of a driver license
- Provisional Driver under age 18 operating a motor vehicle while using a wireless communication device and or cell phone
- Suspension or revocation in another state
- Unfit, unsafe, habitually negligent or reckless driver
- Violation of license restrictions

Reinstatement Requirements

Suspension   Time lapse (reinstatement procedure not required for suspension.
Revocation   Time lapse and reinstatement process.
Fees $15.00 filing fee; $30.00 approval fee; $60.00 approval fee if revocation due to alcohol/drug-related

motor vehicle violation).

Reinstatement Process   Reinstatement application: $15.00 filing fee; and current close-up photograph (applicant's) signed "Authorization for Release of Information Form." May also include Driver Improvement Program; interview with Medical Advisory Board; or Alcohol Treatment or Education Program. If applicant has been involved in two alcohol incidents in preceding five years or three or more alcohol incidents during any time period, must submit evidence of current on-going satisfactory treatment, along with reinstatement application. There is a $30.00 restoration fee for those licenses flagged and suspended for outstanding arrest warrants.

Point System Overview
The Maryland point system ranges from one to twelve points. There is no automatic suspension without an opportunity for a hearing for point accumulation

License Plate Facts

Registration Renewal
Online registration renewal via the Internet is available through a program called "e-MVA." One may also renew by telephone at 888-834-7344.

New Residents
New residents must register their vehicles within sixty days of establishing residence.

Inspections and Emissions Testing
Maryland requires a safety inspection for all used vehicles at the time of transfer. Emission testing is required every two years in 23 counties and in the City of Baltimore. An On-Board Diagnostics (OBD) test is required for; 1) model year 1996 and newer passenger vehicles and light duty trucks, 2) model year 2008 and newer heavy duty vehicles up to 14,000 pounds. The Idle Tailpipe test is required for; 1) model year 1977 - 1995 passenger vehicles and light duty trucks, 2) model year 1977 - 2007 heavy duty vehicles up to 14,000 pounds, 3) model year 1977 and newer heavy duty vehicles 14,000 - 26,000 pounds. New vehicles are exempt from testing for the first two years with testing scheduled between 30 and 36 months. Senior citizens 70 years of age or older that drive less than 5,000 miles per year are also exempt.

Plate Descriptions

Typical Plate Patterns   The MVA has a brochure describing over 50 possible numeral letter combination. For example, passenger plates are issued as LNL LNN, but can be LLL NNN or NNN LLL. Light truck plates can be NNNNNN or NNLNNN or NLLNNN. Commercial vehicle plates can vary, many are NNN or 5 numeric + F.
County/City Codes   The state does not designate the county of issuance on the plate.
Plates and Stickers in Force   Two plates, two decals (MO) (YR) on rear.
Plates Remain with Car when Sold?   No, plates remain with seller.

Overview of Record Access

About Driving Records
MVA, Driver Records Unit, 6601 Ritchie Highway NE, Rm 145, Glen Burnie 21062, 410-787-7758. The current fee is $9.00 per electronic or manual record, and $12.00 for certified paper reports. The state does charge for "no record found" reports, except for walk-in requests. The fee must accompany requests except for online service which is billed monthly and magnetic tape which is pre-paid. The last fee increase was in July 2004 and no increase is planned for the near future.

Request Methods – Mail, Walk-in, Online, Bulk.

What You Should Know – The MVA implemented a plan in 2005 to phase out all non-electronic requests for record information (except for certified paper requests used for official purposes). Except for minimal mail-in requests (most of which are individual requests), the MVA has completed the migration to electronic processing. Under the **Direct Access Record System (DARS)**, participants access driver and vehicle record information via an Internet connection. For questions or to request application forms, include your mailing address in your email to: drivingrecords@mdot.state.md.us or MVRSDataRequests@mdot.state.md.us.

Special Access Programs Available – MVA implemented the **License Monitor System (LMS)** for employers and insurance companies that need to monitor their employees' or insured drivers' driving records for violations and suspension. LMS subscribing companies/agencies provide (via File Transfer Protocol) a listing of the Soundex numbers to the MVA that they want to monitor. The MVA, upon receipt of any new Soundex number submitted for monitoring, produces a 3-year public driving record for each Soundex annually, except employers receive complete record. This program runs overnight, sends the client an email notification, and makes available to the company/agency the resulting output file the next day.

After providing the initial 3-year driving record, the LMS actively monitors those same driver license numbers until removed by user and automatically creates files of any activity that has occurred on their driver records. The record activity or updates are provided to the subscriber at the frequency requested (daily, weekly, or monthly) & in the record-type requested (3-year or partial - partial record meaning individual conviction entries). 3-year records are charged at the existing statutory rate for non-certified copies (currently $9.00) and updates are charged as partial updates at the existing statutory rate (currently for non-government entities $0.05 per entry; for government agencies .025 cents per entry/update). Only those updates that have been deemed as moving violations, suspensions, cancellations, revocations, and restrictions are provided to the subscribers of LMS. By this means, subscribers only get new activity that is meaningful.

About Accident Reports

Copies of accident reports investigated by the State Police, except for occurrence in the city of Baltimore, can be requested from: Maryland State Police, Central Records Division, 1711 Belmont, Woodlawn 21244, 410-298-3390. Requests should include report number, date of incident, driver(s) names, self-addressed stamped envelope, and $4.00 check or money order for each record. If there was a fatality involved, please state so since these records are handled by a different unit. In can take 20 days before new records are available for inquiry. Turnaround time can take 3 to 4 weeks. Records are kept for 5 years plus present year. For reports in Baltimore, call 410-396-2378 or 2663.

About Vehicle Records

Vehicle Registration Division; 6601 Ritchie Highway NE, Room 204; Glen Burnie 21062; 410-768-7508, fax 410-768-7529. The fee for VIN, plate, ownership, title histories and lien searches (including unattached mobile homes/house trailers) is $9.00 per non-certified record and $12.00 per certified record. Medical information is not released. Title service agents (private businesses) may also supply certified copies of title and registration documents.

Request Methods – Mail, Walk-in, Fax, Online, Bulk.

What You Should Know – Title service agents offer services related to MVA certificates of title, registrations, drivers' licenses, certified copies of records, and other related documents. Fees may vary. The MVA does not maintain information of the services each agent provides, but provides a list of agents at www.mva.maryland.gov/VehicleServ/REG/titleagents.htm

About Watercraft Records

Department of Natural Resources, Licensing & Watercraft Division, 1804 West St #300, Annapolis 21401 410-260-3220, fax 410-260-4339, www.dnr.state.md.us. All motorized boats must be titled and registered. Vessels 16 feet in length or less and/or propelled by a motor of 7.5 hp or less must display a 2-year registration decal but are exempt from the registration fee. The 2-year registration decal is valid for the calendar year in which it is issued and the subsequent year, expiring on December 31. Boat trailers are registered with the Maryland Motor Vehicle Administration. Records are maintained since 1962; paper records kept 5 years before conversion to digital imaging. Three types of records are released: certified true copy for $10.00; microfiche history file for $5.00; and a current computer file copy for $5.00. Lien records are blocked and are not released. However, when asked the Department will indicate with a yes or no if a lien exists. A Maryland boat number, tidal fish license number, or name and address of boat owner or tidal fish license holder is needed for look-up. At most, it takes about 2 weeks to process a request. The home address, phone and DOB of a subject will not be released. There are 6 additional Regional Service Centers in the state that will process in-person record requests.

Massachusetts

Administration	Important Telephone and Web Contacts
Rachel Kaprielian Registrar of Motor Vehicles 10 Park Plaza, #3170, Boston, MA 02116 617-973-7969 www.massdot.state.ma.us/rmv/ Mary Ann Mulhall Director of the Merit Rating Board PO Box 55889, Boston 02205-5889 617-351-4400 www.mass.gov/mrb	Merit Rating Consumer Service Section .....617-351-4400 Driver Licensing..617-351-4500 Suspensions/Revocations ....617-351-7200 Current Insurance Carrier............................617-351-4500 Commercial Driver License.........................617-351-9350 Vehicle Information......................................617-351-9384 State Police..508-820-2300 State Division of Insurance..........................617-521-7794 For Motor Vehicle Laws: www.mass.gov/legis General Email: www.mass.gov/rmv/feedback/index.htm

Driver License Facts

License Format
A computer generated number of one letter (usually an "S") and eight numbers is automatically issued.

Document Appearance
The current driver license and ID format has been in use since 2004. The background color is greenish, previous licenses with a white background.

Appearance — State-of-the-art security features include: ghost imaging; multiple date of birth placement; security laminate; UV security and barcodes designed to protect against counterfeiting and fraud. The front and back of the license has ultraviolet UV security protection.

Security Characteristics — Ghost imaging on all licenses and cards, 2D barcode, multiple repeats of the DOB in multiple colors.

Position of Photo — Flush right with ghost image to the left for both License and ID card. Previous ID card if only adult ID was bottom left.

Minor Age Driver Locator — The Under 21 license is printed vertically. "UNDER 21" is in bold red lettering with date printed under message indicating when driver turns 18 or 21.

CDL Indicator — "CDL Driver's License" is printed on upper portion; class description and any endorsements or restrictions are printed on the reverse side. If under 21, is vertical format.

Issue and Renewal

Age Requirements
The state has a Graduated Licensing Law. The minimum age is 18 years old without Driver Education; 16 1/2 with the completion of an approved driver education course. The Junior Operator License (JOL) is subject to all persons under the age of 18. A driver must first have had a Learner's Permit for a period of at least 6 months. JOLs are restricted from carrying passengers under the age of 18 for the first 6 months after receiving the JOL, unless it is an immediate family member or are accompanied by a licensed driver 21 years of age or older and is occupying the seat beside them. Driving is prohibited between 12:00 am and 5:00 am, unless accompanied by parent/guardian. Effective 09/01/2007, JOL education requirements were increased, and penalties and reinstatement fees were increased for certain violations. Also, certain offenses will require the Junior Operator to complete retraining courses including a Driver Attitudinal Retraining Course and State Courts Against Road Rage (SCARR) program.

Renewal
Birth date of fifth year. Driver keeps same number when renewing. Drivers may renew their license and make address changes from the web page under a program called RMV Express Lane. One cannot renew DL online if license photo

was taken before age 21 or is more than nine (9) years ago, or if holding a CDL. Military personnel are not required to renew, but can do so by mail. A non-photo license is issued until their discharge or return to Mass.

Elderly-Related Restrictions
None is reported by RMV.

Residency
Home-state license honored on a reciprocal basis; Massachusetts license must be secured immediately upon establishing legal residence.

License Classes
Commercial Classifications
- **Class A** Any combination of vehicles with a GCWR of 26,001 or more pounds—provided the GVWR of the vehicle(s) being towed is in excess of 10,000 pounds, except a school bus, (includes Class B and C with appropriate endorsements).
- **Class B** Any single vehicle with a GVWR of 26,001 or more pounds, or any such vehicle towing a vehicle not in excess of 10,000 pounds GVWR, except a school bus, (includes Class B and C with appropriate endorsements).
- **Class C** Any single vehicle that is less than 26,001 pounds GVWR, or any such vehicle towing a vehicle not in excess of 10,000 pounds GVWR that is placarded for hazardous materials or designed to transport sixteen or more persons (including the operator), except a school bus.

Non-Commercial Classifications
- **Class D** Any motor vehicle or combination, except a semi-trailer unit, truck trailer combination, tractor, or truck having a registered gross weight in excess of 26,000 lbs., a bus or a school bus.
- **Class M** A motorcycle or any other motor vehicle having a seat or saddle for the rider and designed to travel with no more than three wheels in contact with the ground.

HAZMAT Endorsement Procedure
The state is in compliance with the Patriot Act. All applicants applying for a new or renewal or transfer HAZMAT Endorsement (HME) must first obtain the application from https://hazprints.tsa.dhs.gov/Public/ or by calling 877-429-7746. The driver must also be fingerprinted. EMSI is the state-designated entity to process fingerprints. At this time, there is only one location in the state that performs this service. Visit the web page listed above to find the address. The cost of the fingerprint process is $89.25. The fingerprints and application information is sent to the Federal Transportation Security Administration (TSA). TSA performs the background checks and notifies the DMV whether the application is approved or denied. When completed and approved, the HME is valid for the term of the license. For more information, see the brochure at www.mass.gov/rmv/rmvnews/2005/hazmatbrochure.pdf.

Safety and Enforcement Facts

Insurance and Financial Responsibility
The state has compulsory financial responsibility laws which state that a motor vehicle insurance policy or bond, or security deposit in lieu of a motor vehicle insurance policy or bond pursuant to M.G.L. c. 90, § 34D, must be in force for any vehicle. See M.G.L. c. 90, § 34A, et seq. Massachusetts also has a no-fault insurance provision. Minimum financial responsibility limits for motor vehicle policies and bonds are $20,000/40,000 per person/per accident for bodily injury liability coverage. Proof of compliance with the financial responsibility provisions of M.G.L. c. 90 must be electronically present on the Registry's file or must be provided at the time a vehicle is registered or renewed.

Alcohol and Chemical Testing
Massachusetts' illegal intoxication level is .08 percent and above, .02 for under age 21 drivers, and .04 for CDL drivers. Blood (by registered physician, nurse, or certified medical technician only), and breath (breathalyzer or infra-red) testing are used. Massachusetts has an implied-consent violation as well as the provision for an administrative suspension. Operating a horse, boat or bicycle under the influence is also considered illegal.

Accident Reporting
All accidents must be reported to the Police Department in the jurisdiction where the accident occurred. Any accident resulting in death, personal injury, or over $1,000.00 in property damage must be reported within five days to the Registry of Motor Vehicles at the address above. A driver does not need to file a report if the crash occurred on a private road, driveway, private parking lot or other private way. Forms are available from the police, the Registry, and at www.mass.gov/rmv/forms/21278.pdf. There are no special reporting requirements for commercial drivers.

Suspensions and Revocations

The RMV provides an excellent overview of suspensions and revocations at www.mass.gov/rmv/dmanual/chapter2.pdf. The state is in compliance with the federally mandated disqualifications on CDL related infractions. See the Appendix for a list of these disqualifications.

Three Speeding Offenses in Twelve Month Period	Thirty-day suspension.
Junior Operator One Speeding Offense in Twelve Month Period	Six-month suspension.
Failure to Make Court Ordered Child Support Payments	Indefinite suspension.
Habitual Traffic Offender	Four-year suspension.
Leaving Scene of Accident with Property Damage Only, First Offense	Sixty-day suspension.
Leaving Scene of Accident with Property Damage Only, Second Offense	One-year suspension.
Leaving Scene of Injury Accident, First Offense	One-year suspension.
Leaving Scene of Injury Accident, Second Offense	Two-year suspension.
Motor Vehicle Homicide	Fifteen-year to permanent suspension.
Operating MV Without Owner's Authority, First Offense	One-year suspension.
Operating MV Without Owner's Authority, Second Offense	Three-year suspension.
Seven Surchargeable Events	Sixty-day suspension.

OUI (See text on Melanie's law www.mass.gov/rmv/dmanual/chapter2.pdf for a complete review of all penalties.)

First Offense within 10 Years	One-year suspension.
Alternative First Offense within 10 Years	45 to 90-day suspension, plus Alcohol Program.
First Offense (under twenty-one)	210-day suspension, plus Alcohol Program.
Second Offense in Life of Operator	Two-year revocation.
Third Offense in Life of Operator	Eight-year revocation.
Fourth Offense in Life of Operator	Ten-year revocation.
Fifth Offense in Life of Operator	Lifetime revocation.
OUI Homicide by Motor Vehicle OUI or Neg. Operation Fatality	Ten-year revocation.

Note: If previous OUI or Fatality, then lifetime revocation.

Chemical Tests

Failures (.08 BAC or more)	30-day suspension.
Failures - Under Age 21 (.02 BAC)	30-day suspension.

Refusals with:

No Prior OUI offenses	180-day suspension; three-year if under 21.
One OUI Prior in Life of Operator	Three-year suspension.
Two OUI Prior in Life of Operator	Five-year suspension.

About Ignition Interlock Devices

Since January 1, 2006, any driver with a second or subsequent OUI offense who is eligible for a hardship license or is eligible for a license reinstatement is required to have an Ignition Interlock Device (IID) on all associated vehicles. A driver with a hardship license must use the IID for the entire period of the hardship license and fro an additional two years after the license has been reinstated. If a driver with two or more OUI offenses is eligible for license renewal, the IID will be required for a mandatory two years.

Reinstatement Requirements

Minor Suspension	$100.00 fee.
Major Suspensions (Criminal Moving Violations, HTO)	$500.00 fee.
OUI	$500.00 first offense, $700.00 2nd offense, $1,200.00 third+.

Point System Overview

The state of Massachusetts does not have a point system for license suspensions or revocations; suspensions and revocations are in accordance with specific statutes.

License Plate Facts

Registration Renewal

Vehicles registration may be renewed from the home page at www.massdot.state.ma.us/rmv/ under a program called Online Branch.

New Residents

Non-residents must register vehicles at expiration of period granted by home-state reciprocity agreement.

Inspections and Emissions Testing
Massachusetts has an annual safety inspection. Vehicles 1996 and newer will be tested for emissions (On Board Diagnostic test) every year along with the annual safety inspection.

Plate Descriptions

Typical Plate Patterns	Passenger plates are 6 characters-6 numbers or 3 numbers 3 alpha or 4 numbers 2 alpha, or 3 alpha-3 number - LLLNNN. Commercial vehicles and some light trucks are LNNNNN or NNNNNN or the letters "BB" followed by 1-3 numbers.
County/City Codes	There are no county code numbers designated.
Plates and Stickers in Force	One plate (green and white) is no longer issued; currently 2 plates (red and white) are issued. One sticker (YR) only applied to rear plate.
Plates Remain with Car when Sold?	No, they remain with seller.

Overview of Record Access
Driving Records

Two Agencies Provide Driving Records
In Massachusetts there are two agencies that provide motor vehicle records - Registry of Motor Vehicles (RMV) and the Merit Rating Board (MRB). The Merit Rating Board is responsible for, among other services, providing driving records to the insurance industry. The Registry provides driving records to employers and the general public. The MRB and RMV use the same master conviction table when reporting convictions on their respective records record. However, the extent of the content and to whom the record is provided is different. Both agencies are described in detail in this chapter.

1. Registry of Motor Vehicles (RMV) Driving Records
Two different types of driving records provided by the Registry and are used for employment or personal use. The Registry's **Driving History** is a printed list of an operator's complete (active and non-active) license and registration activity over the life of an individual. The Registry's **Driving Record** is a printed list of an operator's active license and registration activity for a minimum of the past ten years including the current year. This record includes specified convictions for a minimum of ten years and all other convictions and accidents for a minimum of three years. The Registry can be reached at Registry of Motor Vehicles, Driver Control Unit, PO Box 55889, Boston 02205-5889, www.mass.gov/rmv.

Request Methods – Mail, Walk-in, Telephone, Electronic

What You Should Know
Walk-in public service for the RMV is at 630 Washington St, Boston 02108; however, a driver can request an MVR at any full service RMV branch

Special Access Programs Available
The Registry provides a License/Permit and ID Inquiry at https://secure.rmv.state.ma.us/LicInquiry/intro.aspx. One may use this no fee transaction to verify the status of a MA License/Permit or ID. This screen indicates the class/type and status, expiration date, method of next renewal (online or in person), and if the licensee has outstanding obligations associated with the MA License/Permit or ID number provided. No personal information is ever displayed.

2. Merit Rating Board (MRB) Driving Records
The Merit Rating Board's primary responsibility is the maintenance and update of operator driving history record information for Massachusetts auto insurers as well as other government agencies involved in transportation and public safety. The MRB's operator driving history records contain surchargeable incidents, such as at-fault accidents and traffic violations as defined in 211 CMR 134.00 Safe Driver Insurance Plan. Merit Rating Board's address is PO Box 55889, Boston MA 02205-5889. The physical address is 25 Newport Avenue Extension, Quincy, MA 02171. The home page is www.mass.gov/mrb.

Request Methods – Mail, Walk-in, Online.

What You Should Know
The Merit Rating Board manages The Safe Driver Insurance Plan (SDIP), a state designated rating system that outlines specific surcharges for certain traffic violations and accidents, and applies specific credits for clean driving records. Each operator is assigned an Operator SDIP Rating based on the operator's driving history record within the 6-year policy experience period. The Merit Rating Board is the only authorized source of Safe Driver Insurance Plan (SDIP) driving records for all insurance companies. As of April, 2008, Massachusetts auto insurers may elect to either use the SDIP as

their Merit Rating Plan or they may elect to develop their own rating system. Automobile policies that are assigned through the Massachusetts Auto Insurance Plan (MAIP) are subject to the SDIP. Detailed information about the Safe Driver Insurance Plan (SDIP) is available on the Merit Rating Board's website at www.state.ma.us/mrb. Below is an explanation of the rating portion of the SDIP.

A "surchargeable incident" defined in 211 CMR 134.00 (SDIP) may result in an increase in auto insurance premium as a:

At-Fault Accident
A claim payment for damage to someone's property, bodily injury liability, collision or limited collision, of more than $500. An "at-fault" accident is one in which the insurance company determines that the operator is more than 50% at fault.

Major Traffic Law Violation
Includes violations such as: vehicular homicide, driving under the influence (including assignment to a driver alcohol or drug education program), driving to endanger or reckless driving, leaving the scene of an accident, refusing to obey a police officer, driving after license suspension or revocation.

Minor Traffic Law Violation
Includes violations such as: speeding, operating a vehicle without a valid inspection sticker, failure to obey traffic lights.

Out-of-State Incidents can be classified in any of the above categories. For additional information, Massachusetts advises contacting the Merit Rating Board at 617-351-4400 or by visiting the website at www.mass.gov/mrb.

About Accident Reports

Copies of accident reports may be obtained from the Registry of Motor Vehicles, Accident/Crash Reports, PO Box 55889, Boston 02205, 617-351-9434 for a fee of $20.00 per report. Request items include full name, date of incident, location and license or registration number. An online request for accident/crash report is available at www.mass.gov/rmv/forms/accrecform.pdf. Records are available from 2 years to present. Criminal offender record information will not be released. Allow 4 weeks after the incident before new records are available. Normal turnaround time is 7 to 10 days; however, it can take as long as 4 weeks. In-person searches are available while you wait. Quarterly or yearly electronic updates are available for $2,500.

About Vehicle Records

Registry of Motor Vehicles, Document Control, PO Box 55889, Boston 02205-5889 617-351-9458. The Title Department can be reached at PO Box 55885. The current fee for a computer printout of a VIN or registration record, or a history search is $5.00. A photocopy of an original RMV-1 Applications is $10.00. Credit cards are accepted for payment. Lien information is automatically provided as part of registration and title information. Records are available from 30 years to present. Use of the forms described above is needed to obtain personal information. Personal information is not released, when requested by non-permitted users. Note that fax requests are accepted from government agencies only.

Request Methods – Mail, Walk-in, Online, Bulk.

What You Should Know
Permissible use requesters such as Massachusetts-based insurance companies and some Massachusetts insurance agents are online to the Registry's computer, for whom there is no cost beyond the line charge. However, this availability is restricted solely to such users and is not open to the general public.

About Watercraft Records

Massachusetts Environmental Police, 251 Causeway St, #101, Boston 02114 617-626-1610 www.mass.gov/dfwele/dle/elereg.htm
Records maintained from 1998 to present. State law requires all boats 14 ft or over to be titled. State law requires the registration of any boat that is powered by a motor and operated on public waterways in Massachusetts. Registration is required even if the motor is not the primary means of propulsion for that boat. Examples of boats requiring registration include fishing boats with motors, recreational motorboats, canoes or sailboats that use motors (includes electric motors), and personal watercraft such as jet skis or wet bikes. Boats exempt from registration requirements include those that do not use motors, and documented vessels (large boats that are issued a marine document and registration through the U.S. Coast Guard). Vessels used solely by a city, county, state, or federal agency will be issued a certificate of registration and number at no charge. All motor powered boats and jet skis must be registered.

There is no charge for a record search. Name searches may be conducted by fax at 617-626-1630. Records from 2000 forward are available by telephone. SSNs, DOBs, and subject phone numbers are not released. This agency maintains lien record information and will release lien holder names and addresses.

Michigan

Administration	Important Telephone and Web Contacts
Fred Bueter, Director Driver and Vehicle Records Division Department of State 7064 Crowner Drive, Lansing 48918 www.michigan.gov/sos Send questions to: soswebmaster@michigan.gov	Driver Licensing..888-767-6424 Driving Records ....517-322-1624 Financial Responsibility & SR-22 ....517-322-6406 Commercial Driver License.........................888-767-6424 Vehicle Information.......................................888-767-6424 State Police...517-332-2521 State Department of Insurance ....877-999-6442 Motor Compiled Laws can be viewed at: www.legislature.mi.gov/

Driver License Facts

License Format
The format is one letter followed by twelve numbers. The numbers are coded as follows: three numbers for the last name, three numbers for the first name, three numbers for the middle name, and three numbers for the birth month and day. Because a small number of drivers' names and birth dates have the same number, MI began using the first initial of the last name with the code 726 or 727 to assign drivers a unique driver license number.
Note: Michigan will be changing the numbering system with the implementation of the Business Application Modernization (BAM) project. No BAM implementation date is set at this time

Document Appearance
The SOS Office now provides an enhanced driver's license and ID as an alternative to the standard license and ID. The enhanced driver's license or ID card contains a Radio Frequency Identification chip to facilitate border crossings and homeland security efforts. The unique reference number assigned to the RFID chip allows the Customs and Border Protection agent to quickly and accurately verify identity and citizenship.

To apply, a person must present documentation of:
- A valid Social Security number, such as a Social Security card
- U.S. citizenship, such as an original or certified birth certificate
- Identity, such as a Michigan license or state ID card
- Residency, such as a Michigan license or state ID card

Appearance	A digital image document with signature.
Security Characteristics	Magnetic strip and bar code with PolaPrime UV security feature only visible under black light.
Position of Photo	Bottom left, since 07/01/03 a ghost image appears in upper right.
Minor Age Driver Locator	"Under 21 Until dd/mm/yy" appears above photo. Effective 07/01/03 those under the age of 21 are issued a vertical (portrait) style driver license.
CDL Indicator	"COMMERCIAL DRIVER LICENSE" printed in green above license number.

Issue and Renewal

Age Requirements
A graduated licensing for drivers up to 18 years old includes three levels:

Level 1	**Learner's License**	A driver must be at least 14 years 9 months, completed an approved Segment 1 driver education course, pass a vision test and meet physical and mental standards, and obtain written approval from a parent, or legal guardian. **Restrictions** Allows operation of a motor vehicle only when accompanied by a licensed parent or legal guardian, or with a licensed driver 21 years of age or older whom is given permission by the parent or legal guardian.
Level 2	**Intermediate License**	Driver must be at least 16 years of age, possessed a Level 1 for a minimum of 6

	months, completed Segment 2 of an approved driver education course, have no convictions/civil infractions, suspensions, or at-fault crashes for the 90-day period immediately preceding application. Driver must accumulate a minimum of 50 hours behind-the-wheel practice driving, including 10 hours of nighttime driving. Certification of such is required by parent or legal guardian. Driver must pass a road test conducted by an independent testing agency and meet physical and mental standards.
Level 3 **Full License**	Driver must be at least 17 years of age, held a Level 2 license for not less than 6 months, and completed 12 consecutive months of driving without a moving violation, an at-fault crash, a suspension or violation of graduated license restrictions.

Renewal
Birth month of fourth year. Driver keeps same number when renewing, unless there is a change in name or date of birth that would require issuing a new license number. (When the DL format changes with the implementation of the Business Application Modernization project, drivers will no longer be assigned a new license number if there is name change.) A driver's license can be renewal by mail or in-person at a branch, but renewal is not available online.

Elderly-Related Restrictions
None reported by the state.

Residency
Michigan license must be secured immediately upon establishing residency. Since December 13, 2004, proof of residency is required at driver's license application.

License Classes
Commercial Classifications
A	Operation of vehicle towing a vehicle or trailer with a GVWR over 10,000 pounds.
B	Operation of a single vehicle with a GVWR of 26,001 pounds or more, **or** a combination of vehicles having a GCWR of 26,001 pounds or more, with the vehicle being towed having a GVWR of 10,000 pounds or less.
C	Operation of a small vehicle or combination of vehicles (with a GVWR of 26,000 pounds or less) designed to carry sixteen or more people (including the driver), **or** a small vehicle carrying hazardous materials in amounts requiring the display of a placard.

Non-Commercial Classifications
O1	Operator, Level 1		O	Operator or Level 3 Operator
C1	Chauffeur Level 1		C	Chauffeur or Level 3 Chauffeur
O2	Operator, Level 2		M	Moped
C2	Chauffeur Level 2			

Note: A Chauffeur License is required if the driver is not required to obtain a commercial classification but is employed for the principal purpose of one or more of the following:
- Operate a motor vehicle with a gross vehicle weight rating (GVWR) of 10,000 pounds or more.
- Operate a motor vehicle as a carrier of passengers or as a common or contract carrier of property.
- Operate a pupil transportation vehicle used for the regularly scheduled transportation of pupils between school and home, a bus or a school bus if a CDL with the S endorsement is not required.
- Operate a taxi or limousine.

HAZMAT Endorsement Procedure
The state is in compliance with the Patriot Act. All applicants applying for a new or renewal or transfer HAZMAT Endorsement (HME) must first obtain the application from https://hazprints.tsa.dhs.gov/Public/ or by calling 877-429-7746. The driver must also be fingerprinted. Integrated Biometric Technologies (IBT) is the state-designated entity to process fingerprints. There are seven locations in the state that perform this service. Visit the web page listed above to find out more details, including the addresses of locations. The cost of the fingerprint process is $89.25. The fingerprints and application information is sent to the Federal Transportation Security Administration (TSA). TSA performs the background checks and notifies the DMV whether the application is approved or denied. When completed and approved, the HME is valid for five years. The five-year validation must end later than the license expiration date or new fingerprints must be obtained before license renewal.

Safety and Enforcement Facts

Insurance and Financial Responsibility
The state has a compulsory no-fault insurance law. Proof of insurance must be presented when purchasing a registration and must be shown at the request of a law enforcement officer. About 80% of proofs of insurance are obtained through an Electronic Insurance Verification (EIV) program. Customers whose insurers participate in this program receive a Personal Identification Number (PIN) as proof of insurance. Minimum financial responsibility limits are $20,000/40,000/10,000. A driver's license may be suspended if the driver fails to satisfy a Financial Responsibility (FR) court judgment within thirty days for damages arising out of the ownership, maintenance, or use of a motor vehicle. A suspension becomes effective thirty days after preparation of suspension order, and remains in effect until the driver satisfies the judgment. A restricted license may be issued to the driver if the court approves a partial-payment agreement and proof of financial responsibility insurance is provided.

Alcohol and Chemical Testing
Michigan intoxication levels are as follows: Less than .08 percent is "operating while impaired;" .08 percent or greater is "operating while intoxicated." Urine, blood, and breath testing are authorized. For CDL holders the threshold is .04 percent, for drivers under 21 the threshold is .02 percent. Michigan has an implied-consent violation, but not an administrative suspension.

Accident Reporting
The driver in an accident involving death, injury or damage in excess of $1,000 must immediately report that accident to the nearest or most convenient police agency. Accidents in excess of $1,000 require completion of a written report by the police officer receiving a report. There are no state special requirements for commercial drivers.

Suspensions and Revocations
The state is in compliance with the **federally mandated disqualifications on CDLs** per MCSIA. See the Appendix for details. Extensive information about suspensions and revocations including corresponding statutes is found at: www.michigan.gov/documents/offensecode_73877_7.pdf

Habitual-Offender Revocation
Persons who repeatedly operate a motor vehicle during periods of suspension, revocation, and/or denial or who repeatedly violate the state's drinking/driving laws are subject to repeat offender penalties. These penalties may include plate confiscation, vehicle immobilization, registration denial, ignition interlock, and vehicle forfeiture.

First revocation is for a minimum of one year; second revocation is for a minimum of five years.

- First revocation is for a minimum of one year; second is for a minimum of five years.
- *Two convictions in seven years for DUI alcohol or drugs, unlawful blood alcohol level, or impaired driving.
- Two convictions in seven years for reckless driving.
- Two convictions in seven years for felonies involving a motor vehicle.
- *Three convictions within ten years for any alcohol violation.
- One conviction of DUI or impaired driving causing injury or death.
    * =One conviction of child endangerment will count same as alcohol conviction.

Child Support Suspension
The driver and occupational licenses of parents in arrears in their child support are suspended. This suspension is identified as an FCJ and requires an $85.00 reinstatement fee.

Reinstatement Requirements
Suspension or Revocation $125.00 fee ($85.00 if Child Support); re-examination.

Point System Overview
Points range from one to six and remain on driving record for two years after the conviction or adjudication date. Michigan operates on a twelve point system for non-probationary drivers. Four points in any two-year period triggers an initial letter and the need to be careful. At eight points, drivers receive a warning letter that advises they will be scheduled for a re-examination if driving habits do not improve. At twelve points, a driver re-examination is scheduled at which time driving privileges could be suspended.

Also, points **assessments** are assessed once annually for drivers who accumulate and maintain seven or more points on their driving record. Drivers are assessed each year in which seven or more points remain. The fees begin at $100 for seven points and increase by $50 for each additional point on the record. In addition, Category 2 Fees are imposed for specific offenses as defined by law. This fee is assessed for two years in a row. Fees range from $150 to $1,000.

License Plate Facts

Registration Renewal
Renewal for passenger vehicles is set at one year. Trailers and trailer coaches are registered with a permanent, non-expiring trailer plate based on the unit's weight. These trailer plates are non-transferable. Renewal is available online 24/7 at www.michigan.gov/sos. Owners can use this service if the renewal notice contains a PIN (proof of mandatory insurance) and if the owner's name, address, and vehicle information are all correct. If not, renewal must be done at a branch office. Renewal can also be done by mail or telephone.

New Residents
Non-residents must register vehicles after ninety days; plates must be purchased immediately upon establishing residency.

Inspections and Emissions Testing
Michigan has no statewide provisions for annual emission testing or vehicle safety inspections.

Plate Descriptions

Typical Plate Patterns............................	Passenger and light truck plates are NNN-LLL, LLL-NNNN or NLL-LNN or LLL-NN or NN-LLL; commercial vehicles are LL-NNNN or NNNN-LL or LNN-NNL or LLL-NN or NN-LLL or LLNNNNN for the newer Blue Bar plate.
County/City Codes............................	Although county codes, used to designate where the owner resides and for redistribution of registration fees, show on the vehicle registration, they do not show on the plate. An owner may purchase a plate in any county.
Plates and Stickers in Force	One plate, one decal with the plate number and both expiration month and year. Current renewals are issued one decal with expiration month and plate number.
Plate Remains with Car when Sold? .	No.

Overview of Record Access

About Driving Records
Department of State, Record Lookup Unit, 7064 Crowner Drive, Lansing 48918, 517-322-1624, fax 517-322-1181. The current fee is $7.00 per record. If information needs to be certified, there is an additional $1.00 fee. The state charges for no record found reports. The last fee increase was effective October 1, 2003; fee increases are determined by the legislature. If the requester anticipates a high volume of requests (15 or more records per month), call 517-322-6714 or 877-570-6714 to establish an account with the Department of State.

Request Methods — Mail, Walk-in, Phone, Fax, Online Batch, Online Interactive, Bulk.

What You Should Know — Same day service is only available for walk-in customers who are requesting their own driving records. If requesting another person's record, requests will be available for pick-up 24 hours after submitting a request. Phone service is available for pre-approved, established accounts or for those obtaining their own records. Results are returned by mail. Major credit cards are accepted. For online access, call Commercial Services Section, 517-322-6281.

Special Access Programs Available — The Commercial Services Section (517-322-5281) provides a program that sends driving records to employers and insurance companies annually or whenever there is activity on the driving record. There is no set-up cost for this Subscription Service, but a fee of $7.00 per record generated is charged. Government agencies are not charged for this service.

About Crash Reports
Copies of crash reports are available from the Department of State, Record Lookup Unit for drivers convicted of a violation in conjunction with the accident, call 517-322-5509, fax 517-322-5350. It will take 6 to 8 weeks for a new incident to be available for a search. Requests will be accepted in-person, but responses will be mailed. Procedures for obtaining the accident report are the same as described under *Accessing Driving Records*. Fax requests are also accepted. The Traffic Crash Purchasing System (TCPS) makes records available online at: https://mdotwas1.mdot.state.mi.us/TCPS/login/welcome.jsp. The fee is $10.00; a credit card may be used unless billing arrangements are made. Records are available from 1983 to present or 10 years using the TCPS. Online requests are viewable when ordered, mail requests take up to 10 days.
For specific questions email CrashPurchaseTCPS@michigan.gov.

About Vehicle Records

Department of State, Record Lookup Unit, 7064 Crowner Drive, Lansing 48918, 517-322-1624, Fax 517-322-1181. Alpha-searches can be made with complete name and street address. Title records are available for 10 years to present and 4 years to present for registration. The current fee for VIN, registration, and lien holder searches is $7.00 per transaction. For a complete title history, there is a $7.00 fee incurred for each title change or correction. There is an additional $1.00 fee if the record must be certified. If both a registration and current title record are ordered, you will be charged for 2 records ($14.00). There is a full charge for a no record found. Records are available on vehicles, mobile homes, and watercraft.

Request Methods – Mail, Walk-in, Phone, Fax, Online, Bulk.

What You Should Know – Walk-in customers may request their own vehicle records at the address above and receive same-day service. If requesting another person's record, must go through the Crowner Drive address and requests will be available for pick-up 24 hours after submitting a request. Lengthy lists or unusual circumstances may take longer. Phone requests are available for pre-approved, established accounts. Call Record Look-up Unit at 517-322-1624. For online service, call Commercial Services Section, 517-322-6281. Plate, VIN, and registration information is available via a program called Direct Access.

About Watercraft Records

All motorized boats must be registered; if 20 ft or over they must also be titled. Vessel records can be searched by either name or MC number or registration number with same restrictions as vehicle record requests. Vessel records can be obtained in the same manner as described above for vehicle records. One may do a search at the registration renewal site https://www.ms.gov/gf/boating/renewRegistration.jsp. There is no name searching; both the MI Number and Serial (VIN) must be input.

Minnesota

Administration	Important Telephone and Web Contacts
Driver and Vehicle Services Patricia McCormack, Director Minnesota Department of Public Safety 445 Minnesota St St. Paul 55101, 651-296-6911 www.mndriveinfo.org	Driver Licensing ....651-297-3298 Records ....651-215-1335 Financial Responsibility..............................651-296-2015 Commercial Driver License ....651-297-5029 Driver Evaluation..651-296-2025 Vehicle Information ....651-296-2126 State Patrol...651-201-7100 State Department of Insurance ....651-296-2488 GeneralEmail motor.vehicles@state.mn.us Minnesota Statutes at: https://www.revisor.mn.gov/ DVS Rules www.dps.state.mn.us/dvs/rules.html

Driver License Facts

License Format
The driver license number is one letter followed by twelve numbers. Until 12/2004, the letter represents the first letter of the last name; the numbers represent a coding of the last name, the first name, the middle name and date of birth. Since that date with the issuance of the newer current driver's license document, the assigned DL# is NOT based on the driver's name, including the first letter.

Although the DVS cannot release the pattern of the coding information on the older license number, they do report that the pattern is nearly the same as used by Michigan.

Document Appearance
The current license document is issued to new drivers and renewals since 12/12/2004.

Current Document
Security Characteristics
- **Front**: A holographic state seal that appears only under ultraviolet light. A virtual image of a loon appears to float above or sink below the surface as the viewing angle changes. A digital image of the cardholder is fused with heat into the card plastic with fine print over the image and a rainbow print pattern.
- **Back**: A 1-D bar code, 2-D bar code, and a magnetically encoded strip.

Position of Photo — Always on left.

Minor Age Driver Locator — A red border around photo image indicates "Under 21." Age 18 birth date (if applicable) is printed in red to the right of the date of birth.

CDL Indicator — The word "Commercial" is printed under the driver's license in the header area.

Older Document
The license card issued in 1999 through late 2004 has a polymer core with a front and back laminate.

Security Characteristics
- **Front**: An encrypted 2-D bar code, holograms depicting snowflakes and the word Minnesota, loons printed with ultraviolet sensitive ink and micro-printing in the shape of a star. Digital image and ghosted image of the card holder. No embossing.
- **Back**: A 1-D bar code and magnetically encoded strip.

Position of Photo — 21 and over - right side; under 21 - left side.

Minor Age Driver Locator — Photo on left. "Under 21" is printed in the header and 21st birth date is printed directly underneath 2-D bar code. Beginning 02/01/00, 18th birth date is printed directly underneath 21st birth date.

CDL Indicator — The letters "CDL" printed directly under colored header.

Issue and Renewal
Age Requirements
The state's Graduated Driver's License law (effective 01/01/99) provides for three phases of licensing for persons under 18 years of age: Phase I-Instruction Permit; Phase II-Provisional License; and Phase III-Full License. More limitations were put into effect as of 08/01/2008. Limitations on teens in the first 6 months of licensure include a nighttime driving prohibition between midnight and 5am, and only one passenger under the age of 20 permitted, unless driver accompanied by a parent or guardian. During the second 6 months of licensure, 3 passengers under 20 are permitted (family members exempted).

Instruction Permit	Must be at least 15 years of age and pass vision and written test. If under age 18, must have completed 30 hours of classroom instruction and be enrolled in behind-the-wheel instruction.
Provisional License	Must be at least 16 years of age, have completed driver education, held an instruction permit for 6 months with no convictions for moving violations or convictions for alcohol/controlled substance violations, and pass road test.
Under 21 Full License	Must be at least 18 years of age or must have held a provisional license for at least 12 consecutive months with no convictions for alcohol/controlled substance violations or crash-related moving violations, and with not more than one conviction for a moving violation that is not crash-related. If under 18, the person who approves the application also certifies that the applicant has driven under the supervision of a licensed driver at least 21 years of age for not less than 10 hours on the provisional license. If age 18, must have held an instruction permit for 6 months. If age 19 or older, must have held an instruction permit for three months. License expires at age 21 and may be renewed without additional written or road tests.

Renewal
Birthday of fourth year. Driver keeps same new format number for life, regardless of name change. At present, renewal is not available online. MN law states that military personnel need not renew their license, but after discharge renewal must be secured within 90 days. Those MN drivers who are temporarily out-of-state may renew by mail, but must appear for a new photo within 30 days of their return to the state.

Elderly-Related Restrictions
None indicated.

Residency
Non-resident's home-state license honored if age 15 or older, but must secure Minnesota license within sixty days (within thirty days if CDL) of establishing permanent residency.

License Classes
Commercial Classifications
- A Valid for any vehicle or combination.
- B Valid for any Class D/C single unit motor vehicle, including with passengers endorsement buses. May tow only vehicles with GVW of 10,000 pounds or less.
- C Valid for Class D vehicles with hazardous materials, passenger and/or school bus endorsement. May tow vehicles with GVW of 10,000 pounds or less. Towed vehicles may exceed 10,000 pounds only if combined weight 26,000 pounds or less GVW.

Non-Commercial Classifications
- D Valid any single unit 26,000 pounds GVWR or less; emergency equipment operated by firefighters on-duty; all farm-trucks and recreational vehicles, except buses or vehicles requiring hazardous material endorsement. May tow vehicle with GVW of 10,000 pounds or less. Towed vehicles may exceed 10,000 pounds only if combined weight 26,000 pounds or less GVW.

HAZMAT Endorsement Procedure
The state is in compliance with the Patriot Act. All applicants applying for a new or renewal or transfer HAZMAT Endorsement (HME) must first obtain the application from https://hazprints.tsa.dhs.gov/Public/ or by calling 877-429-7746. The driver must also be fingerprinted. There are several approved vendors in the state that perform this service. Visit the web page listed above to find the address locations. The cost of the fingerprint process is $89.25. The fingerprints and application information is sent to the federal Transportation Security Administration (TSA). TSA performs the background checks and notifies the DVS whether the application is approved or denied. When completed and approved, the HME is valid until the CDL expires. For more information, visit www.dps.state.mn.us/dvs/DriverLicense/HazMat/HME.htm.

Safety and Enforcement Facts

Insurance and Financial Responsibility
Proof of insurance must be provided upon request of a law enforcement officer. Liability limits are $30,000/60,000/10,000. Insurance is compulsory and the state has no-fault insurance provisions.

Alcohol and Chemical Testing
Minnesota's illegal intoxication level is an alcohol concentration of .08 percent and .04 percent for CMV drivers. There is zero tolerance for drivers under 21. Urine, blood, and breath testing are authorized, and there is a one-year revocation for refusal to submit to a test. Minnesota does have provisions for administrative revocation.

Accident Reporting
Accidents involving death, injury or damage to an apparent extent of $1000 or more must be reported immediately to the local or state police. Drivers must file a written report of the accident with the Department within ten days of the accident. Reports can be filed online at www.driveinfo.org or send to Department of Public Safety (DPS), Driver and Vehicle Services, 445 Minnesota St, Ste 181, St. Paul 55101, 651-296-3279. If a commercial driver is issued a citation in another state, they must report it to DPS per the Commercial Motor Vehicle Safety Act of 1986 - Federal Statute 383.31.

Suspensions and Revocations
The Minnesota DPS is in compliance with the provisions of the Motor Carrier Safety Improvement Act (MCSIA). See the Appendix for more information about these mandatory CDL disqualification sanctions.

Any Misdemeanor Offense Resulting in Fatality .... 180-day suspension.
Any Misdemeanor Offense Resulting in Class A Injury to Another .... 90-day suspension.
Criminal Vehicular Operation .... One- to 10-year revocation.
Driving While License Revoked, Suspended, or Cancelled .... 30-day to one-year suspension.
DUI - Under 21 Years of Age
    First Offense .... 6-month revocation if BAC <.20; One-year revocation if BAC >.20.
    Second Offense in 10 years .... 180-day revocation if BAC <.20; One-year revocation if BAC >.20.
Failure to Maintain or Provide Proof of Insurance
    No other violations .... 30-day revocation.
    One other violation .... 90-day revocation.
    Two other violations .... 180-day revocation.
    Three or more other violations .... One-year revocation.
Felony Involving Motor Vehicle .... One-year revocation.
Fleeing a Police Officer .... One- to 10-year revocation.
Habitual Offender
    Four violations in 12 months .... 30-day suspension.
    Five offenses in 12 months .... 90-day suspension.
    Five offenses in 24 months .... 30-day suspension.
    Six offenses in 24 months .... 90-day suspension.
    Seven offenses in 24 months .... 180-day suspension.
    Eight or more offenses in 24 months .... One-year suspension.
Leaving the Scene of an Accident .... 6-month to one-year revocation.
Multiple Misdemeanors Revocations
    Two misdemeanors in 12 months .... 30-day suspension.
    Three misdemeanors in 12 months .... 30-day revocation.
    Four misdemeanors in 12 months .... 90-day revocation.
    Five or more misdemeanors in 12 months .... One-year revocation.
Perjury or False Statement .... 180-day revocation.
Refusal to Submit to a Drug or Alcohol Test .... One-year revocation.
School Bus Stop Arm Violation
    One gross misdemeanor or more .... 90-day to one-year revocation.
    Two petty misdemeanors (or 1 petty misdemeanor + 1 misdemeanor) in 5 years .... 30-day suspension.
    Three petty misdemeanors in 5 years .... 90-day suspension.
    Four or more petty misdemeanors in 5 years .... 1-year suspension.
    Two misdemeanors in 5 years .... 30-day revocation
    Three misdemeanors in 5 years .... 90-day revocation.
    Four misdemeanors in 5 years .... 180-day revocation.
    Five or more misdemeanors in 5 years .... 1-year revocation.

Editor's Note: The Minnesota legislature structured the stop arm violation law in response to a public outcry that sanctions were too harsh or not harsh enough. As a result, a stop arm violator's conviction (from the courts) is based on the nature of his/her violation. For example, passing a bus on the right with a child present gets a higher sanction than passing on the left with no child present. It is rare for someone to gets more than three petty misdemeanors of this violation in 5 years.

Speed in Excess of 100 mph .... 6-month revocation.
Theft of Gas .... 30-day suspension.
Unlawful/Fraudulent Use of Driver's License .... 90-day to 180-day suspension

Reinstatement Requirements
Suspension $20.00 fee.
Revocation   30.00 or $680.00 (for alcohol-related offenses) fee; time lapse; reapply for license, written test required

Point System Overview
Minnesota does not have a point system.

License Plate Facts

Registration Renewal
Owners may renew vehicles online at https://www.mvrenewal.state.mn.us/ with a credit card or ACH. Registration stickers will be mailed within 10 days of the Internet transaction.

New Residents
New residents have a 60-day grace period in which to register a passenger vehicle. If the registration displayed on the vehicle expires before the 60-day grace period ends, the owner must apply for Minnesota registration immediately.

Inspections and Emissions Testing
There are no provisions for statewide safety inspections or emission testing.

Plate Descriptions
License plates issued to passenger automobiles and dealer license plates are replaced at seven (7) year intervals; all other license plates are issued for the life of the vehicle.

Typical Plate Patterns	Normal passenger and light truck plates are NNNLLL or LLLNNN. Commercial vehicle plates are LLNNNNN or LLLNNNN.
County/City Codes	Counties are coded in alphabetical order respectively from 01 to 87. The coding is as follows: 01 is Aitkin, 02 is Anoka..... and 87 is Yellow Medicine. Code 88 is used for Foreign.
Plates and Stickers in Force	2 plates, 2 decals (MO) (YR) on both plates for normal passenger plates, but the number of plates and stickers vary based on the class of registration.
Plates Remain with Car when Sold?	Yes, except certain specialty and unique symbol plates, restricted use plates, and prorate class plates are retained by owner. Note that passenger plates are replaced at seven-year intervals

Overview of Record Access

About Driving Records
Driver and Vehicle Services Division; Driver License Record Requests, 445 Minnesota St, #161 St Paul 55101, 651-215-1335, fax: 651-282-5512. Unless otherwise noted below, fees are $9.50 per motor vehicle record display ($9.00 if the requester is subject of the data). There is a $1.00 fee per printed page of material when mailed. An additional $1.00 fee is charged to certify the record copy. The fee for each online inquiry is $5.00.

Request Methods – Mail, Walk-in, Telephone (by person of record), Online, Online Status, Bulk.

What You Should Know – Convictions not reported include speeding 10 mph or less in a 55 mph zone and certain non-moving violations as determined by statute and department rules and regulations. Also accidents are not shown on the driving record. For more information on online access call 651-297-5352

Special Access Programs Available – Driver license status information is available from the web page (www.mndriveinfo.org). The requester must submit the DL#, there is no fee. Only public information is disclosed.

About Crash Reports
The current fee for copies of police reports obtained with authorization from individual(s) involved in the accident is $5.00 per record. Records are indexed from 1998 forward, electronically imaged. Request should be submitted to Driver & Vehicle Services; Crash Records, 445 Minnesota St. #161, St Paul 55101.

A request form may be downloaded from the web at www.dps.state.mn.us/dvs/PDFForms/FormFrame.htm. Turnaround time is 1 week. Records are usually available 3 weeks after the incident. A driver can obtain, upon written request, a free copy of his own citizen report. For questions, email to crash.records@state.mn.us or call 651-215-1335 or fax 651-282-5512.

About Vehicle Records

Driver and Vehicle Services Division, Record Requests, 445 Minnesota St., Ste 161, St Paul 55101-5161, 651-297-5352, fax: 651-282-5512. Records released include ownership and vehicle information and are available for the past 7 years. Fees are $9.50 per motor vehicle record display ($9.00 if requester is subject). Plus, there is a $1.00 fee per printed page when mailed. The fee to certify a copy is an additional $1.00 per document. The online fee is $5.00 per request.

Request Methods – Mail, Walk-in, Online, Online Status, Bulk.
What You Should Know – For online access, the fee for each inquiry is $5.00. The account balance is displayed at time of log on. For more information call 651-297-5352.
Special Access Programs Available – Enter a MN plate or registered VIN at www.mndriveinfo.org to get a status report. Only public information is released. There is no fee.

About Watercraft Records

Department of Natural Resources, License Center, 500 Lafayette Rd, St. Paul 55155-4026, 651-296-2316 (Registration); 296-7007 (Watercraft Titling), also 877-348-0498. Records are maintained 15 years for watercraft, snowmobiles, and off-highway vehicles (all terrain) and off-highway motorcycles. A watercraft must be titled if over 16 feet and 1980 model or newer. All motorized and sailboats must be registered. Non-motorized boats and duck hunting boats are exempt. Record searches follow DPPA; permissible use must be shown to obtain address information. Use of DNR ELS Records Request Form is advised. One or two names/vehicles may be done over the phone. Lists with more than 2 requests must be mailed; turnaround time is usually 2 weeks or less. Ongoing requesters may fax requests to 651-297-8851. Lien record information is available on titled watercraft vessels only. Operators of off-highway vehicles (all terrain) and off-highway motorcycles must have a separate license issued through this department.

Mississippi

Administration	Important Telephone and Web Contacts
Captain Jason Jennings Director of Driver Services Driver Services Bureau PO Box 958, Jackson 39205 601-987-1206 Barbara Ford, Director Motor Vehicle Licensing Division PO Box 1140, Jackson 39215 601-923-7131 www.dps.state.ms.us (driver) www.mstc.state.ms.us/mvl/main.html (vehicle)	Driver Licensing..601-987-1206 Financial Responsibility/SR-22 ....601-987-1230 Reinstatements..601-987-1269 MVR...601-987-1275 Commercial Driver License........................601-987-1334 Vehicle Registration ....601-923-7100 Vehicle Title..601-923-7200 Highway Patrol..601-987-1212 State Department of Insurance ....601-359-3569 There is no general email for Driver License questions. For Vehicle questions, use the email submission form at www.mstc.state.ms.us/perl/ContactUs.pl#email Motor Vehicle Laws: www.mscode.com/free/statutes/63/index.htm

Driver License Facts

License Format
The license number is a randomly generated nine-digit number in the same format as a Social Security Number with the first three digits assigned as 800 (i.e. 800-11-1111). Until several years ago the Social Security Number was used as the DL unless the license holder specifically requested an assigned number. Now DPS issues an assigned number to all new license holders and renewals.

Document Appearance
Mississippi began issuing the current driver's license and ID cards in November 2002. Since some older cards may remain in force if used by military personnel both old and new are described below.

Current Format
- **Security Characteristics** — These digital documents are highly durable plastic with a laminate security coating. The coating contains a hologram of the state seal and the letters DPS. There is a "ghost" photo image in the lower right corner. A 2D bar code and magnetic stripe is on the back of the card containing the bearer's demographic data and medical codes if pertinent. State outline in green indicates regular operator; blue indicates an ID card.
- **Position of Photo** — Left side, smaller ghost image in lower right corner.
- **Minor Age Driver** — The DL and ID documents are in a vertical format. "Under 21 Until---" appears in red under photo, "Under 18 Until---" appears in yellow under photo.
- **CDL Indicator** — Red indicates CDL. "COMMERCIAL LICENSE" in red box appears above personal information.

Old Format
- **Security Characteristics** — The **old** documents are laminated with digital image photo. The Commissioner's signature is shown.
- **Position of Photo** — Left.
- **Minor Age Driver** — The document is in a vertical format. "Under 21 Until-------" appears.
- **CDL Indicator** — "COMMERCIAL DRIVER LICENSE" is at top of document in state heading.

Issue and Renewal
Age Requirements
The minimum age for a Class R is fifteen years and six months of age or older and applicant must have held a Learner's

Permit for a minimum of six months. Twenty-one is the minimum age for Class A, B, and C Commercial, except for persons aged seventeen authorized to operate a vehicle transporting sixteen or more passengers within the state. For an Intermediate License, the age is fifteen years and must have six months of 6AM-10PM restrictions. For a Learner's Permit the age is fifteen years; age fourteen can drive but only when in driver education car.

Renewal
On birthday every four years. Sixteen and seventeen year-olds are good for 1 year or until their birth date. The driver is assigned the 9-digit license number at renewal, if the previous license was using the driver's SSN. Driver keeps same number when renewing. Online renewal is available but only to holders of a Class R license. One can renew the license online every other time when the card is up for renewal. To renew online, driver must live at the address that is printed on current license that is expiring. One may renew a license online up to one year after the expiration date. Out-of-state military personnel can renew every 4 years by mail as long as a copy of current military ID is submitted.

Elderly-Related Restrictions
None, unless state personnel at the renewal station detect a reason the a person is unfit to drive.

Residency
A non-resident must secure Mississippi license after sixty days, unless a tourist, out-of-state student, or a military person.

License Classes
The driving record abstract will show "Regular" and "Class R" for a non-commercial; and "Commercial" with appropriate class for commercial.

Commercial Classifications
- A   Any Combination of vehicles with a gross vehicle weight rating of 26,001 pounds or more, or towing a vehicle with a GVWR of 10,001 pounds or more.
- B   Any single vehicle with a gross vehicle weight rating of 26,001 pounds or more.
- C   Any single vehicle less than 26,001 pounds GVWR with placard for hazardous materials or designed to transport sixteen or more people.
- D   All persons not requiring a Class A, B, or C license, but requiring a commercial license under Mississippi law.

Non-Commercial Classifications
- R   Regular Operator license.
- LP   Learner's Permit
- Y   Intermediate License

HAZMAT Endorsement Procedure
The state is in compliance with the Patriot Act. All applicants applying for a new or renewal or transfer HAZMAT Endorsement (HME) must first obtain the application with instructions from a state CDL office.

The driver must also be fingerprinted by one of thirteen state offices that perform this service. The cost of the fingerprint process is $89.25. The fingerprints and application information is sent to the Federal Transportation Security Administration (TSA). TSA performs the background checks and notifies the DMV whether the application is approved or denied. When completed and approved, the HME is valid for four years.

Safety and Enforcement Facts

Insurance and Financial Responsibility
Mississippi has compulsory insurance laws, but not no-fault insurance laws. Financial security minimum limits are $10,000/20,000/5,000. SR-22 may be required. Proof is required after a reportable accident and certain violations. Proof is not required when vehicle registrations are renewed.

Alcohol and Chemical Testing
Mississippi's illegal intoxication level is .08 percent and above, for drivers of CMVs the level is .04 percent and above, for drivers under 21 years old the level is .02 percent. Urine, blood, and breath testing are authorized. Mississippi has an implied-consent violation, as well as the provision for an administrative suspension.

Accident Reporting
Accident reports should be filed with the nearest law enforcement agency when damage is in excess of $500.00. For accidents involving death, personal injury, or damage in excess of $1,000.00, an individual accident report must be filed with the Highway Patrol, Safety Responsibility Branch, PO Box 958, Jackson 39205, 601-987-1256. There are no special state reporting requirements for commercial drivers.

Suspensions and Revocations
The state is in compliance with the federally mandated disqualifications on CDLs per MCSIA. See the Appendix for details. Below are listed suspensions associated with driving under the influence.

Driving Under the Influence
  First Conviction .... One-year suspension.
        (Ninety-days, if driver completes MASEP; not less than thirty days with hardship order.)
  Second Conviction in Five Years .... Two-year suspension.
        (This can be reduced to one year with completion of alcohol and/or drug abuse treatment.)
  Third or Subsequent Conviction in Five Years .... Five-year suspension.
        (This can be reduced to three years with completion of alcohol and/or drug abuse treatment.)
  DUI Conviction with Refusal to Submit to a Chemical Test
    First Refusal .... Ninety-day administrative suspension.
        (In addition to any other suspensions upon conviction of DUI.)
    Second or Subsequent Refusal .... One-year suspension.
        (In addition to any other suspensions upon conviction of DUI.)
  Driving While License Suspended for DUI .... Six months added to original suspension

Reinstatement Requirements
Suspension — 25.00 fee; time lapse of thirty days to five years; SR-22 filing required for three years from date of DUI and three years from date of accident, if driver was uninsured on accident date and could be held liable for property damages or injuries.

Revocation — $100.00 reinstatement fee on DUIs or Drug-Related Convictions

Point System Overview
Mississippi does not have a point system.

License Plate Facts

Registration Renewal
Motor vehicle with a Gross Vehicle Weight (GVW) of 10,000 lbs or less must be registered receive tags from the local county tax collector's office where the vehicle is garaged or domiciled. For motor vehicles with a Gross Vehicle Weight (GVW) of over 10,000 lbs and which travels in Mississippi only, register in the local county tax collector's office and receive their tags from the State Office. For motor vehicles with a Gross Vehicle Weight (GVW) of over 10,000 lbs and which travels across state boundaries, register at the State Office in Clinton, Mississippi. Online renewal is offered for the following counties through www.ms1stop.com/: Alcorn, Attala, Desoto, Hancock, Harrison, Jackson, Lafayette, Lauderdale, Lee, Madison, Pearl River, Rankin, and Warren. Also, renewal for Hinds County is found at https://hinds.ms.ezgov.com/eztags_text/index.jsp.

New Residents
New residents must register vehicles within thirty days.

Inspections and Emissions Testing
Mississippi has a required annual safety inspection for vehicles. There is no statewide provision for emission testing.

Plate Descriptions
Typical Plate Patterns	Passenger plates are LLLNNN; light trucks LLNNNN; and commercial vehicles NNNNNLL.
County/City Codes	The county name of issuance is indicated at the bottom of the plate.
Plates and Stickers in Force	One plate, two decals (MO) (YR).
Plates Remain with Car when Sold?	The tag is issued to both the vehicle and the owner. If one or the other changes, the tag must be removed and surrendered to the issuing authority.

Overview of Record Access

About Driving Records
Driver Records Branch, PO Box 958, Jackson 39205, 601-987-1275. The fee for all request methods is $11.00 per record. The fee is $6.00 for a copy of a driver license application; a copy of a suspension/reinstatement letter is $5.00. The last fee increase went into effect October 13, 2004 and no increases are planned for the near future. Direct questions regarding driving records to acline@mdps.state.ms.us.

Request Methods – Mail, Walk-in, Online.

What You Should Know – Accidents and non-moving violations do not appear on driving records. Drivers may view their own record at https://www.ms.gov/hp/drivers/license/motorVehicleReportBegin.do. The fee is $11.00 plus a $2.14 convenience fee for using a credit or debit card. Mississippi offers interactive online access and some limited batch access to approved high volume vendors only. Hook-up is through the Advantis System.

About Accident Reports

Accident reports require authorization for release. Records may be obtained through written request by any person involved in the accident, the legal counsel, or representative of the insurer. Requests should be sent to Safety Responsibility, PO Box 958, Jackson 39205 601-987-1255 or 967-1254. The fee is $10.00 per copy. No personal checks accepted. Turnaround time is 5 working days. Only the name is needed to search recent records. For records prior to 2004, the driver's DL# must be submitted. All requests must be in writing, in-person requests are mailed back if more than two records sought. Mail requests must include a SASE with $.65 postage. Original records are destroyed after 5 years, after being placed on microfiche

About Vehicle Records

Tax Commission, Motor Vehicle Licensing Bureau, PO Box 1140, (Title Bureau is PO Box 1033), Jackson 39215, 601-923-7100 for Registration, 601-923-7200 for Titles. Please note there are two bureaus—Title Bureau and Motor Vehicle Bureau (MVLB)—within the Tax Commission which furnish information. They are both located at 1577 Springridge Rd, Raymond 39154. Be sure to address mail requests accordingly. Records are available from July 1, 1969. Record information can also be obtained at the county level. For vehicle related questions, there is an email submission form at www.mstc.state.ms.us/perl/ContactUs.pl#email.

Request Methods – Mail, Walk-in, Fax, Online, Bulk.

What You Should Know – The MVLB provides VIN and registration checks for $3.00 per inquiry. Recent records have a turnaround time of 2 days. Note that records over 4 or 5 years old must be searched in a different history file and will take up to 14 working days to process.

Title Bureau data (i.e., title history, lien data) is available by written request only. The fee is $8.00 per document of each title issued for a particular vehicle and $5.00 per lien history. Records are available on microfiche from July 1, 1969 to present, images are available from June 2005 forward.

Special Access Programs Available – Online access is available for approved, DPPA-compliant users at www.mstc.state.ms.us/, click on Records Inquiry.

About Watercraft Records

Wildlife, Fisheries and Parks Department, PO Box 451, Jackson MS 39205, 601-432-2186 http://home.mdwfp.com/fishing.aspx. All motorized boats and all sailboats must be registered. Since 07/98, boats are titled at the option of the owner. The department will do a record search with a boat number or name at no fee; however, they will screen calls to insure that the purpose of the request complies with DPPA. Liens are shown on this database. One may do a search at the registration renewal site at https://www.ms.gov/gf/boating/index.jsp. There is no name searching, use the "MI" number or Hull number.

Missouri

Administration	Important Telephone and Web Contacts
Jackie Bemboom, Director Motor Vehicle and Driver Licensing Division 301 W High Street, Jefferson City 65101 573-526-1827 Phil Reed, Chief Information Officer Office of Administration - Revenue Office of Information PO Box 41, Jefferson City 65105 573-526-1824 http://dor.mo.gov/mvdl/drivers (Drivers) http://dor.mo.gov/mvdl/motorv (Vehicles)	Interactive Voice Response System..................573-526-2407 Points, Tickets, Revocations, Suspensions ......573-526-2407 Driver Licensing..573-751-2730 Financial Responsibility, Accidents ....573-751-7195 Administrative Alcohol ....573-751-4833 Vehicle Information ....573-526-3669 or 4509 Commercial Driver License.............................573-751-2730 Highway Patrol...573-751-3313 State Department of Insurance ....573-751-4126 General Email................................dlbmail@dor.mo.gov Motor Vehicle Laws.......................www.moga.state.mo.us Driver License Bureau Rules: www.sos.mo.gov/adrules/csr/current/12csr/12c10-24.pdf

Driver License Facts

License Format
Effective 12/17/05, Missouri implemented the requirements of the Federal Intelligence Overhaul Legislation (S2845) which prohibits all states from displaying the Social Security Number (SSN) on any driver license or personal identification card. The change over takes place at renewal for those that still have a SSN. Prior to 12/17/05, the SSN or an assigned number consisted of one alpha and five to nine numbers or nine numbers only.

Document Appearance
In April 2003, the Missouri Department of Revenue began issuing the current driver license, permit, and non-driver license documents with upgraded format and enhanced security features.

Current Format
- **Security Characteristics** The most evident new feature is a "ghost" portrait of the applicant at the bottom of the license. Other security features include an outline of the state of Missouri and the words "Show Me" across the front of the license visible under ultraviolet light, printed data overlapping the ghost portrait, and a two dimensional barcode on the back of the license.
- **Position of Photo** Lower right.
- **Minor Age Driver Locator** The photo appears on the left side of the card and the license indicates "Under 21 until MM-DD-YY" in red on upper right.
- **CDL Indicator** "Missouri Commercial Driver License" appears in green on the heading.
- **Anatomical Gift** Red donor heart with green ribbon in lower left corner (right corner for minor licenses).

Older Format
This license is made of polyester for flexibility with a 3M retro-reflective laminate on the front.
- **Security Characteristics** A pattern of red-colored state seals, easily visible under normal light, appears across the identifying data on the bottom of the card. These seals shift in color as the card is tilted. The front contains an outline of the state and the word "Missouri" slanted through the outline that is visible only under ultraviolet light.
- **Position of Photo** Lower right.
- **Minor Age Driver Locator** The photo appears on the left side of the card and the license indicates "Under 21 until MM-DD-YY."
- **CDL Indicator** "Missouri Commercial Driver License" appears in green on the heading.

Missouri

Issue and Renewal

Age Requirements
The minimum age for Class F or M is sixteen. For Classes A, B, C, or E it is eighteen. A Graduated Drivers License Law went into effect 01/01/01 as follows:

Instruction Permit An individual who is at least 15 years of age can obtain a Temporary Instruction Permit. The holder of a temporary instruction permit who is less than 16 years of age may only operate a motor vehicle with a licensed parent, grandparent, legal guardian, or certified driving instructor. The holder of a temporary instruction permit who is 16 years of age or older may operate a motor vehicle with any licensed driver who is 21 years of age or older. Under any condition, the licensed driver riding with the permittee must occupy the seat next to the driver.

Intermediate License For ages 16 to 18, must have driven with an instruction permit for a minimum of 6x months. The parent, grandparent, legal guardian or certified instructor with a federal residential job training program must certify the driver has received 40 hours of behind-the-wheel instruction with a minimum of 10 hours of nighttime driving. The applicant must have no alcohol-related offenses in the last 12 months, no traffic convictions in last six months. Seat belts required for all passengers and no driving alone between 1 a.m. and 5 a.m. During the first six months, intermediate driver is limited to only one passenger who is under 19 and who is not a member of their immediate family. After the first 6 months, the intermediate driver is limited to less than 3 passengers who are under 19 and who are not members of the driver's immediate family.

Renewal
Intermediate license expires in 2 years or less based on proof of identity verification. Drivers 18-20 years or driver age 70 and over receive a license expiring in 3 years or less based on proof of identity verification. Drivers 21-69 years of age receive a license expiring in 6 years or less based on proof of identity verification. Applicants for CDL with a hazmat endorsement are limited to a license term of 5 years or less based on federal regulations. Driver keeps same assigned license number when renewing. Active-duty armed forces members (temporarily mobilized and deployed outside of Missouri) may obtain a new, renewal, or duplicate permit/driver/non-driver license via a mail-in process or through a power of attorney when required documentation is submitted.

Elderly-Related Restrictions
Ages 70 and over renew on DOB of third year.

Residency
Non-resident's home-state license honored on a reciprocal basis.

License Classes

Commercial Classifications
- Class A — Combination vehicle 26,001 pounds GVWR or more with trailer over 10,000 pounds GVWR.
- Class B — Single vehicle 26,001 pounds or more GVWR.
- Class C — Vehicle under 26,001 pounds GVWR or placarded for hazardous materials or designed to transport sixteen or more people, including the driver.

Non-Commercial Classifications
- Class E — Operator for hire not required to have Class A, B, or C - single vehicle under 26,001 GVWR.
- Class F — Operator.
- Class M — Motorcycle.
- Class ND — Non-Drivers (ID Card).

Also, a Limited Driving Privilege (LDP) hardship license is issued for those in work or alcohol programs, medical treatments, school, etc.

HAZMAT Endorsement Procedure
The state is in compliance with the Patriot Act. All applicants applying for a new or renewal or transfer HAZMAT Endorsement (HME) must first complete the application at https://hazprints.tsa.dhs.gov/Public or by calling 877-429-7746. The driver must also be fingerprinted. Visit the web page listed above to find the fingerprint processing locations. The cost of the assessment process is $89.25. The fingerprints and application information is sent to the Federal Transportation Security Administration (TSA). TSA performs the background checks and notifies the DMV whether the application is approved or denied. When completed and approved, the HME assessment is valid for up to five years. For more information about the state's program, visit http://dor.mo.gov/mvdl/drivers/commercial/hazmat/index.htm.

Safety and Enforcement Facts

Insurance and Financial Responsibility
Missouri has compulsory insurance and requires all vehicle owners and drivers to be financially responsible and show proof of financial responsibility to the Department of Revenue or to any law enforcement officer when requested. Minimum limit amounts are $25,000/50,000/10,000. Proof must be carried in the vehicle at all times. The state does not have a no-fault insurance provision. Anyone renewing license registration for their vehicle must present their insurance card or other acceptable proof of insurance. Proof is required normally for reinstatement after suspension or revocation and for "certain" violations. SR-22 forms are normally used, but in some instances insurance companies send this information electronically. If the suspension/revocation is for not having insurance and an accident is not involved, a copy of the insurance card is also accepted as proof.

Alcohol and Chemical Testing
Missouri's illegal intoxication level is .08 percent and above, .04 percent if CDL. If blood alcohol content is .08 percent or higher (.02 if under 21), a provision for "license withdrawal" is instituted. Saliva, urine, blood, and breath testing are authorized. Missouri has both an implied-consent violation and a provision for an administrative suspension. Minors arrested or stopped with a .02 or more blood alcohol content are also subject to administrative sanctions.

Accident Reporting
All accidents resulting in damage, injury, or death must be reported to the Missouri Highway Patrol within 20 days by the local police or investigating jurisdiction. Reports are made to Missouri Highway Patrol, P.O. Box 568, Jefferson City, MO 65102. In addition, all accidents occurring in Missouri that result in property damage in excess of $500, death or personal injury and which involve an uninsured motorist must be reported to the Department of Revenue. Reports are accepted for up to one year after the accident occurs. Copies of statements from the attending physician or an appraiser's estimate of damage must accompany reports involving personal injury or property damage. The form is found at http://dor.mo.gov/mvdl/drivers/forms/1140.pdf.

Suspensions and Revocations
The state is in compliance with the federally mandated disqualifications on CDLs per MCSIA, see Appendix for details.

Point Accumulation
- Eight or More Points in eighteen Months:
    - First Suspension .... Thirty days.
    - Second Suspension .... Sixty days.
    - Third or Subsequent Suspension .... Ninety days.
- Twelve or More Points in Twelve Months .... One-year revocation.
- Eighteen or More Points in Twenty-Four Months .... One-year revocation.
- Twenty-four or More Points in Thirty-Six Months .... One-year revocation.
- Three years with No New Points Added .... Points reduce to zero.

Failure to Have Financial Responsibility:
- First Offense .... Zero days.
- Second Offense .... Ninety-days.
- Third Offense .... One year.

Other Reasons for Suspensions or Revocations:

Abuse and Lose	Fraud Suspension
Administrative Fraud Suspension	In-State or Out-of-State Failure to Appear Suspension
Child Support Arrearage Suspension	Mandatory Insurance
Citation Revocation	Minor in Possession
Court Ordered (i.e. fail to stop for school bus, FTY)	Misrepresentation
Failure to File an Accident Report	Motor Fuel Theft
Failure to Appear in Court or Pay Fine when Operating a CMV in One of these States- AK, CA, MI, MT, OR, WI	Motor Vehicle Accident Judgment
	Out-of-state Accident
	Refusal for Not Taking Alcohol or Drug Test
Failure to Maintain Insurance or Having False Insurance	Security Accident
Failure to Failure to Maintain Ignition Interlock Device (IID)	Zero Tolerance or Administrative Alcohol

About Alcohol-Related Offenses
- Any person convicted of two intoxication-related traffic offenses within a five-year period is denied all driving privileges for five years.

- Individuals with more than one alcohol offense on their driving record must have an ignition interlock device (IID) installed prior to reinstatement of their driving privileges OR issuance of a Limited Driving Privilege (LDP) or Restricted Driving Privilege (RDP). The IID must be maintained for six months following the reinstatement date, and the driver is required to report to a certified IID vendor each month for maintenance to ensure the device is working properly. Failure to maintain the device during the six-month period will result in a re-suspension of driving privileges.

Notes: 1) The Department issues **Restricted Driving Privileges** only for first-time alcohol-related point suspensions. The driver must serve the first 30 days of the point suspension and file proof of liability insurance and proof of installation of an IID (if required) with the Driver License Bureau (i.e., SR-22 form). A person cannot obtain an RDP to drive a commercial motor vehicle.

2) The Department provides a **Limited Driving Privilege (LDP)** to those who have lost their driving privilege, but need to drive for employment or other important matters. Eligible drivers may obtain an LDP unless they have certain convictions or losses of license on the driver record. Some convictions or loss of license are so serious that an LDP may not be granted. Details are found at http://dor.mo.gov/mvdl/drivers/ldp.htm#whatis. A person cannot obtain an LDP to drive a commercial motor vehicle.

Reinstatement Requirements
Reinstatement information is available by telephone at 573-526-2407. Reinstatement fees may also be paid by telephone with use of a major credit card.
  Suspension $20 fee; proof of financial responsibility.
  Revocation $20 fee; proof of financial responsibility; re-examination (except for a alcohol/drug test revocation).

If For Financial Responsibility Suspension
  First Offense $20 fee; proof of financial responsibility.
  Second Offense $200 fee; proof of financial responsibility.
  Third or Subsequent Offense $400 fee; proof of financial responsibility.

Note: An additional $25 fee is assessed when the suspension/revocation is alcohol related (unless it was based on an out-of-state alcohol conviction). Successful completion of a Substance Abuse Traffic Offender Program or comparable program is also required. If more than one alcohol offense is showing on the record, an IID will be required.

Point System Overview
The Missouri point system ranges from 1 to 12 points. Drivers could be suspended with an accumulation of 8 or more points in 18 months or revoked for an accumulation of 12 or more points in 12 months, 18 or more points in 24 months and 24 or more points in 36 months.

License Plate Facts

Registration Renewal
Drivers are eligible to renew vehicle registration online with the Missouri Online Registration Exchange (MORE), if a PIN (Personal Identification Number) is recorded on the renewal application. The web page is http://plates.mo.gov. A vehicle can be operated for 30 days beyond the vehicle's registration date if it is being driven to reset the vehicle's readiness monitors in order to pass the on-board diagnostic (OBD) emission inspection.

New Residents
Non-residents must register (and title) vehicles within thirty days of establishing residency.

Inspections and Emissions Testing
A vehicle safety inspection is required statewide. Effective Jan. 1, 2010, vehicles with a manufacture model year of five years or less are exempt, as well as vehicles registered in excess of 24,000 pounds for a period of 12 months or less. The exemptions do not apply to salvage vehicles.

Certain areas require an emissions inspection. Vehicles 1995 and older are exempt from emissions testing requirements. All inspections are good for two years, unless the vehicle is sold in that two-year period. Even model year vehicles must be inspected when the registration expires in even years and odd model year vehicles when the registration expires in odd years. Emissions inspections only apply to residents of St. Louis, St. Charles, Franklin and Jefferson counties, and the City of St. Louis. The program, known as the Gateway Vehicle Inspection Program (GVIP) combines safety inspections and emission testing into one program.

Note: Franklin County vehicle owners are not required to have emissions inspections every year. Instead, emissions inspections are good for two years and due in conjunction with safety inspections. Registration renewal will require an emissions test for odd model years only in odd years and even model year vehicles only in even years. A number of different vehicles are exempt from an emissions inspection for a variety of reasons. See the web page for details.

136 Missouri　　　　　　　　　　The 2010 U.S. Motor Vehicle Reference Book

Plate Descriptions

Typical Plate Patterns........................Passenger plates are 2 alpha, 1 numeric, 1 alpha, 1 numeric, and 1 alpha. Light trucks are 1 numeric, 2 alpha, and 3 numerics. Commercial Vehicles above 24,000 lbs are 2 numerics, 1 alpha, 1 numeric, and 2 alphas.
County/City Codes............................No such coding is used.
Plates and Stickers in Force ....The current license plate issued has been in effect since 6/15/2008. The current plate features a blue stripe across the bottom fading upward to the white. "Missouri" and "Show Me State" are centered at the top. The outline of Missouri is in the middle of the plate, centered behind the configuration. A bluebird is centered at the bottom of the plate below the configuration. Month of expiration is embossed in the upper left-hand corner and year tab is located in the center of the plate.
Plates Remain with Car when Sold? . No, plates remain with owner.

Overview of Record Access

About Driving Records

Motor Vehicle and Driver Licensing Division, Record Sales, PO Box 2167, Jefferson City 65105 [301 W High Street Rm 370] 573-751-4300. Fee is $5.88 for manual processed records and those accessed through the Dialing for Records process. There is a surcharge to use a credit card or debit card. Frequent requesters of driving records should establish an account with the Record Sales area and obtain records through the Dialing for Records process. As mentioned above, a Security Access Code assignment is required. The fees for electronic access fees vary, see below.. For questions about driving records, email dlrecords@dor.mo.gov.

Note: One may request driver records by mail or walk-in that do not contain the personal information of an individual. Non-personal information includes the driving history showing speeding tickets and other violations.

Request Methods – Mail, Walk-in, Phone, Fax, Online, Email, FTP, Bulk.

What You Should Know – The electronic access of driving records in Missouri is very unique. Approved users and vendors may purchase electronic records in either a batch or database mode. The fee schedule is not based the traditional method used in other states of using a per record cost per the specific names submitted in a request. Call for details or see *The MVR Access and Decoder Digest*.

Special Access Programs Available – Requests for driver records may be emailed to dlrecords@dor.mo.gov. Customers request must include all credit card information (type, number, expiration date, etc.) in order for the request to be processed.

About Vehicle Records

Department of Revenue, Motor Vehicle Bureau, PO Box 100, Jefferson City 65105, 573-751-4509, 573-526-3669; fax is 573-526-7367. The Department of Revenue maintains record information on boats, motors, mobile homes, trailers, and motorcycles as well as passenger and commercial vehicles. Lien information shows on title records. Current registration/title records are on computer. Records are purged from the computer files after two years of no activity and placed on microfiche. Records are available from 1968 to present. All requestors of personal information must qualify to receive such information under the DPPA. The SSN is not shown on records. As of June 2005, the Department of Revenue no longer takes vehicle record requests by phone, nor does it offer billable accounts for customers.

Request Methods – Mail, Walk-in, Online, Bulk.

What You Should Know – Record searches are $5.88 search, certification is no extra charge. There is a surcharge to use a credit or debit card. When returned by fax is an additional $.50 per page.

Special Access Programs Available – Vehicle lienholder data, registration and ownership information is available to registered requesters. There is an approval process since records are only released per permissible use. The $.0382 record fee is automatically debited from the requestor's ACH (Automated Clearing House) account or credit card account. For more information, call 573-751-4300.

About Watercraft Records

Records are available from the Motor Vehicle Bureau, see http://dor.mo.gov/mvdl/motorv/watercraft/. Missouri law requires that all motorized boats/vessels and any boat/vessel more than twelve feet in length powered by sail alone be titled and registered, unless exempt by law. This includes jet skis and motorized water bikes. Any vessel regardless of length which is solely propelled by oars or paddles is not required to be titled or registered. Also, trolling motors are exempt from title and registration requirements.

Montana

Administration	Important Telephone and Web Contacts
Greg A Noose, Bureau Chief Motor Vehicle Division, Department of Justice Records and Driver Control 303 N Roberts, Helena 59620-1430 406-444-3288 Joann Loehr, Bureau Chief, Title and Registration Bureau 1003 Buckskin Drive, Deer Lodge, MT 59722 406-846-6000 www.doj.mt.gov/driving/default.asp	Driver Licensing..406-444-3933 Financial Responsibility/SR-22..................406-444-3288 Commercial Driver License 406-444-3244 or 444-3667 Vehicle Information......................................406-846-6000 State Department of Insurance ....406-444-2040 Highway Patrol...406-444-3780 General email for vehicle questions mvdtitleinfo@mt.gov General email for driver licensing mvd@mt.gov The Montana Code is found at http://data.opi.mt.gov/bills/mca_toc/61.htm

Driver License Facts

License Format

Since October 2005, all Montana driver licenses and IDs are issued with a system generated 13 numeric number. For individuals licensed prior to 2005 who requested to use their SSN as a driver license number, the electronic system would pre-fill four zeros (0000) at the end of the SSN. Prior to this, the SSN or a nine digit (*made-up number*) was used.

All previously issued licenses and ID cards remain valid until the card expiration date or another transaction that would provide for the opportunity to change the customer's driver license number. Since October 2005 05 driver licenses and ID cards are not issued using the SSN as the license number or ID card number. Below is a description of prior card numbering systems.

Issued From October 2000 to Present. Below example is of a system generated 13 numeric license number 0100019544114.

> First 2 digits: .... Month of birth (01)
> Next 3 digits:..................... Sequence numbers assigned by Driver License Application System (000)
> Next 4 digits: .... Year of birth (1954)
> Next 2 digits: .... Montana statehood (41)
> Last 2 digits:...................... Day of birth (14)

Issued July 1994 to October 2000. Now only applicable for military personnel.
(Made-Up Number) When a made-up number comes up on-terminal as belonging to someone else, the same number is used, but at the end of the number (male/female) a "2" is placed instead of the "0" or "1"; if the "2" is also a duplicate, succeeding numbers are used (i.e., "3" or "4", etc.) The following describes the construction of made-up numbers for Angela Rae Olson, DOB 07-02-68, whose license number is F8702ANG1.

> Position 1: .... An alpha character (A-L) corresponding to the decade in which the year of birth falls: i.e., 1910=A, 1920=B, 1930=C, 1940=D, 1950=E, 1960=F, 1970=G, 1980=H, 1990=I, 1900=J, 1890=K, 1880=L
> Position 2: .... A number corresponding to the year of birth within the decade. (8)
> Position 3: .... A number or alphabetic character (1-9, A-C) corresponding to the month of birth: January=1, February=2, etc. to September=9, then October=A, November=B, December=C. In the example above "7" is used.
> Positions 4 & 5: .... Numbers (01-31) corresponding to the day of birth. (02)
> Positions 6, 7 & 8: .... Alpha characters representing the first three letters of the individual's first name (use a dash where there is no letter). (ANG)
> Position 9: .... A number designating sex; 0=male, 1=female.

Document Appearance

Since 1994, Montana has issued digital licenses and ID cards.

Security Characteristics — Licenses issued between Jan 1994 and July 1995 - a state seal hologram covers name, DOB, and a portion of the photo. Licenses issued after July 1995 - the security feature changed to a series of grizzly bears. driver licenses produced between October 2000 and July 2008 contain a ghost image as well as previous security features.

In July 2008, Montana introduced New-Style driver licenses and ID cards. The card formats and security features on the New-Style cards comply with AAMVA standards. These include: color-coded banners; custom lettering; quick reference codes; repeated, overlapping data and photos; a retro reflective surface with a "Grizzly Bear" design that sinks and floats within the card overlay; and special ultraviolet and shadow features that appear within the card stock. A pamphlet that full describes New-Style card security features is available and may be obtained by emailing mvd@mt.gov. Driver licenses and ID cards with the previous design are valid until their expiration date.

Position of Photo — **Old–Style:** Regular license, CDL and over 21 ID card-lower left; under 21 ID card and under 21 driver license-lower right. **New–Style:** Regular license, CDL and over 21 ID card- left side; under 21 ID card and under 21 driver license card printed vertically- photo upper left; all cards have ghost photo image-lower right.

Minor Age Driver Locator — **Old-Style:** Photo position as described above and the date the driver turns 21 is printed under the license number. **New-Style:** Minor age cards have yellow or red banners next to portrait with *Under 18 OR Under 21 until...*

CDL Indicator — **Old-Style:** Text is printed in red, "COMMERCIAL DRIVER'S LICENSE" appears under number. **New-Style:** Gold-colored upper banner - Quick Reference Code "CDL" and adjacent Class A, B or C.

Motorcycle Only — Effective October 2000, Montana began issuing a new license valid only for the operation of a motorcycle. It follows the same expiration pattern as any other license. Old-Style: header is black and contains the words "MOTORCYCLE ONLY". **New-Style:** Quick Reference Code "ML" with adjacent Class M.

Issue and Renewal

Age Requirements

In 2006 Montana adopted a Graduated Licensing Program with three stages. The minimum age for the first stage - an Instruction Permit -is 14 1/2. The next step is the Restricted License, then a Full Privilege License is issued on or before the age of 18. As part of the program, the driver must participate in an approved driver education course.

Renewal

Effective 10/1/1995, renewal is the birth month of eighth year for all applicants aged 21-67 years old receive an 8 yr license. New applicants 15-21 receive license pro-rated to 21st birthday. Qualified military personnel are exempted from DL expiration (as long as it is not suspended or revoked) and need not renew their license. For exempted military personnel, a driver license is valid for 30 days following separation from military service. Driver license renewal is not available online. Those who live in a county that does not provide driver license services - Carter, Garfield, Golden Valley, Jefferson, Judith Basin, Madison, Petroleum, Prairie, Treasure and Wibaux – or those who are temporarily out-of-state may apply for a renewal of a regular Class D Montana driver license through the mail. Driver license mail-in renewal forms are available online at www.doj.mt.gov/driving/forms.asp.

Elderly-Related Restrictions

Applicants aged 67-75 receive license pro-rated to 75th birthday. All applicants 75 and over receive four-year license.

Residency

Non-resident's home-state license honored; Montana license must be secured within 120 days, commercial license within 30 days.

Proof of Authorized Presence

Since December 2005, individuals who apply for a Montana driver license must provide proof that their presence in the United States is authorized under federal law. Applicants must prove that they are either a U.S. citizen or that they are legally authorized to be in the U.S. In the case of authorized non-citizens, the card expiration date is concurrent with the documented end date for lawful presence. More detailed information is available at: www.doj.mt.gov/driving/requireddocuments.asp#proofauthorizedpresence.

License Classes

Commercial Classifications

Class A — Any combination of two or more vehicles, including trailer(s) in excess of 10,000 pounds, articulated buses

The U.S. Motor Vehicle Reference Book Montana 139

	with a GVWR exceeding 26,000 pounds, and all vehicles authorized to be driven under Class B, C, or D.
Class B	Any single vehicle in excess of 26,000 pounds GVWR, or any such vehicle towing a vehicle not in excess of 10,000 pounds GVWR, or any school bus and any vehicle designed to carry and capable of carrying more than sixteen passengers (including the driver), and all vehicles under Class C or D.
Class C	A single vehicle under 26,000 pounds GVWR which may tow a trailer under 10,000 pounds GVWR which hauls hazardous materials in an amount sufficient to require placarding under "CFR391," and any such vehicle which transports sixteen or more passengers (including the driver), and all school buses.
Type 1	Allows a driver to operate a commercial motor vehicle in interstate commerce.
Type 2	Allows a driver to operate a commercial motor vehicle in intrastate (only within the state of Montana) commerce.

Non-Commercial Classifications

Class D	A regular non-commercial license.

Notes:
- A Learner Licensee allows an individual who has paid the license fees and passed the vision and written tests to operate a vehicle when accompanied by a driver who has a valid license of the same class and type as that of the vehicle being driven. A learner's license is valid for up to six months from the date fees are paid.
- "Motorcycle; motor-driven cycles" is shown as an endorsement (M), not as a class. One can get a motorcycle license only, but there is no separate license class indicated.
- Seasonal CDL is valid 03/15 to 09/10—180 day period of the current year.

HAZMAT Endorsement Procedure

The state is in compliance with the Patriot Act. All applicants applying for a new or renewal or transfer HAZMAT Endorsement (HME) must first pass a hazardous endorsement test and then complete an application from https://hazprints.tsa.dhs.gov/Public or by calling 877-429-7746. The driver must also be fingerprinted. EMSI is the state-designated entity to process fingerprints. There are two locations in the state that perform this service. Visit the web page listed above to find the address locations. The cost of the fingerprint process is $94.00. The fingerprints and application information is sent to the Federal Transportation Security Administration (TSA). TSA performs the background checks and notifies the DMV whether the application is approved or denied. When completed and approved, the HME is valid for five years. For more information visit www.doj.mt.gov/driving/driverlicensingcommercial.asp.

Safety and Enforcement Facts

Insurance and Financial Responsibility

Motor vehicle liability insurance is mandatory; it is unlawful to operate a vehicle without a valid motor vehicle liability insurance policy. Minimum financial responsibility limits are $25,000/50,000/10,000. Whenever the Motor Vehicle Division revokes the driver license of any person, proof of financial responsibility (SR22) is required to be provided prior to reinstatement. The Division will suspend license plates for up to 180 days following multiple convictions of either failure to have or failure to provide proof of required motor vehicle liability insurance.

Alcohol and Chemical Testing

Montana's illegal intoxication level is .08 percent and above, .02 percent if under 21 years old, and .04 percent if operating a commercial vehicle. Blood and breath testing are authorized. Montana has an implied-consent violation. Since October 2003, drivers convicted of a second or subsequent offense of driving under the influence of alcohol or drugs shall, in addition to other punishments imposed in accordance with law, have their motor vehicle seized and subjected to forfeiture or equipped with an ignition interlock device for a twelve-month period following reinstatement.

Accident Reporting

Accidents resulting in death, injury, or property damage in excess of $500 to any one person must be reported immediately. Written reports should be filed when an accident results in injury or property damage in excess of $1,000. Reports should be filed with Montana Highway Patrol, 2550 Prospect Ave, Helena 59620. No written report is needed if the accident is investigated by a law enforcement officer.

Suspensions and Revocations

The state is in compliance with the federally mandated disqualifications on CDLs. See the Appendix for details.

Suspensions

Under Montana law, the following are examples of suspensions:
Driving Under the Influence or Operating a Motor Vehicle with a Blood Alcohol Content of 0.08% or Greater:
First Offense...................................Six-month suspension

    Second or Subsequent Offense......One-year suspension
  Refusal to Submit to Alcohol Testing (Implied Consent or Preliminary Alcohol Screening Test):
    First Refusal ....Six-month suspension
    Second or Subsequent Refusal ......One-year suspension
  Operation of a Vehicle by a Person Under 21 Years of Age with an Alcohol Concentration of 0.02% or More:
    First Conviction.............................90-day suspension
    Second Conviction ....Six-month suspension
    Third Conviction ....One-year suspension
  A Commercial Driver Operating a Commercial Motor Vehicle with an Alcohol Concentration of 0.04% or More:
    First Violation - 1 Year Suspension (3 Year Suspension if Transporting Placardable Hazardous Materials)
    Second or Subsequent Violation Suspension for Life (Reinstatement May be Reconsidered After Ten Years)
  Minor in Possession of Alcohol (MIP):
  MIP convictions are not recorded on an individual's Montana Driving Record. However, as part of the penalty for an MIP, judges have the authority to order the suspension of an offender's driver license. If a judge sends notice of a license suspension resulting from an MIP conviction, the MVD will suspend the offender's driver license for the number of days ordered by the court and permanently record the withdrawal action on the offender's driving record.

Note: As provided by law, all alcohol-related suspensions may also include jail time and fines.

Other Suspensions that may mandate a driver's license will be suspended for varied periods lasting from 30 days to 1 year (or in some cases, even indefinitely) include, but are not limited to:

- 3 reckless driving offenses committed within a period of 12 months
- Altering a driver's license or ID card to obtain alcohol
- Any unlawful use of a driver's license
- Authorizing another to use ones license or ID card to obtain alcohol
- Default on a student loan
- Driver medically unable to safely operate a motor vehicle
- Failure to pay child support
- Failure to obtain required medical evaluation or submit to testing
- Falsifying a date of birth on a driver's license application
- Fraudulent application for a license to drive
- Non-Payment of fines or non-appearance on a notice to appear
- Unsatisfied judgment
- Use a motor vehicle in the theft of motor vehicle fuel

Revocations

Upon receiving notice of a conviction from a court for any of the following violations, a driver's license will be revoked for one year:

- Conviction for negligent homicide resulting from the operation of a motor vehicle
- Conviction for any felony in the commission of which a motor vehicle is used (including 4th offense DUI / BAC violations)
- Failure to stop and render aid as required from motor vehicle accident resulting in the death or personal injury of another
- Negligent vehicular assault involving a motor vehicle
- Perjury or the making of false affidavit or statement under oath relating to the ownership or operation of motor vehicles

For Habitual Traffic Offenders:

- Any person who accumulates 30 or more conviction points within a three-year period - license revoked for three years

Cancellations - Examples Include:

- Death of a person signing a minor's application
- Fraud and/or falsifying information on an application for a license to drive
- License is suspended or revoked in another state
- Paying for a driver's license service with a non-sufficient funds check
- Removal of parental consent
- Voluntary surrender of a license.

Reinstatement Requirements

Driver's license reinstatement is based upon time lapse for periodic suspension requirements and payment of reinstatement fees ranging from $100 (non-alcohol) to $200 (alcohol). Montana law authorizes that a person who submits a certificate of completion from a department-approved driver rehabilitation program must receive a 50% reduction on a driver license reinstatement fee. Other requirements may include substance abuse treatment, proof of financial responsibility, application fees, and taking tests for new licenses.

License Plate Facts

Registration Renewal
Registration must be renewed annually for passenger cars and trucks unless eleven years old or older and registered permanently. Permanent registration is used for motor cycles, trailers, boats, and quads. At present, renewal is not available online. The MVD plans to begin offering online registration renewal for cars, motorcycles, RVs, and boats. The program is expected to go into affect in May 2009. This is part of a new computer system that will link the driver and vehicle databases.

New Residents
New residents must apply for a Montana vehicle title and register their vehicles within 60 days of establishing residency. Non-resident military personnel stationed in Montana may register their vehicles in their home jurisdictions or in Montana, unless they are gainfully employed in Montana outside of their military duties. If they are gainfully employed outside those duties, they must title and register their vehicles in Montana.

Inspections and Emissions Testing
Montana has neither an emissions test provision nor an annual safety inspection provision. Drivers may only use studded tires on Montana roads from October 1 until May 31.

Plate Descriptions

Typical Plate Patterns	Passenger and truck plates are 1C through 9C-NNNNN or NN-NNNNN. Organizational specialty plates have this patter - LLLNNN.
County/City Codes	The first two digits of the plate represent the county of issuance. These numbers range from 1 to 56. The counties are not assigned in alphabetical order and are assigned a random number. Please contact the Title and Registration office for an exact listing of these codes.
Plates and Stickers in Force	Two plates, one decal (MO & YR) on rear plate.
Plates Remain with Car when Sold?	No, they remain with seller.

Overview of Record Access

About Driving Records
Motor Vehicle Division, PO Box 201430, Helena 59620-1430, 406-444-3292, fax 406-444-7623. The current fee is $4.00 per record or $10.00 for a Certified Driver Record, and $7.25 if record is secured electronically. There may be additional fees to fax or mail back a driving record. Montana charges for "no record found" reports.

Request Methods – Mail, Fax, Walk-in, Online.

What You Should Know – Accidents are not reported unless the damage is over $500 and a conviction is rendered.

Special Access Programs Available – Both *Public User* and *Registered User* interfaces are offered at https://app.mt.gov/dojdrs. The **Registered User** system is for ongoing, pre-approved accounts. There is an annual $75.00 registration fee for 10 users. Subscribers must sign a Restricted Use Agreement for Driving Record Information stating agreement to use the information only for allowable purposes. The fee is $7.25 per record. The web portal offers many other services including vehicle history searches and business entity searches. Address information is not released. To find out more about this driving records program, call 406-449-3468.

The **Public User** system is available to anyone who is licensed to drive in Montana. Licensed drivers who establish a permissible use may obtain their own driver record or the record of another Montana driver. Personal information, including SSN or address is not released.

Also, Montana has a **License Status Conviction Activity (LSCA)** process that enables requesters to track lists of drivers on a monthly basis. The requester submits an electronic file each month, the fee is $.15 per driver submitted. The MVD, through Montana Interactive portal, checks the database and responds with a Y/N indicator. The Y/N is based upon a conviction of an ACD Code-related violation. For each "Y", the requester is sent a driver record and charged $7.25. The MVD is not monitoring the list; a list must be re-submitted each month.

About Accident Reports
In accordance with the provisions of MCA § 61-7-114, the Montana Highway Patrol regulates who may receive a copy of a Crash Report in Montana. Reports by individuals (the requestor filled out the crash report themselves) may be released only to the person who submitted the original report or by someone designated in writing by that person. Reports completed by an officer may be released to the following individuals:

1. Any person named on the report (including companies, businesses, etc.);

2. Any driver, passenger or pedestrian involved in the crash, or any person whose property was damaged in the crash;
3. A party to a civil action arising from the crash;
4. If the person is deceased, his executor or administrator or the attorney representing his executive or administrator designated in writing;
5. Anyone designated in writing by persons in categories a. and b;
6. Any insurance carrier for categories a. and b. Insurance carrier includes life, health, auto and workers compensation carriers.

To request a copy of a Crash Report, requestors must read and complete the required form and submit to 2550 Prospect Ave., Helena, MT 59620. Download form at www.doj.mt.gov/enforcement/highwaypatrol/forms/default.asp. Information about obtaining crash photos can also be found at this website. Requests are generally processed in 10 to 14 days from the date of crash. A $2.00 non-refundable search fee is required

About Vehicle Records

Title and Registration Bureau, Dealer and Specialized Services Section, 1003 Buckskin Dr, Deer Lodge 59722, 406-846-6000. The Title and Registration Bureau regulates the titling and registration of motor vehicles. Under state law, all motor vehicles including motor homes; motorcycles and quad-cycles; travel trailers; utility trailers; all-terrain vehicles; sailboats over 12 feet in length; motorboats, jet skis and other motorized vessels; and snowmobiles must be registered with the state. The fee for a VIN, registration or lien check is $6.00 per request, this includes records on mobile homes and vessels. The Bureau cannot look up information by plate alone and must have second identifier. A complete title history is $25.00. To have pages returned by fax, the fee is $3.00 for the first 5 pages and $1.00 each additional page. (Note - There is no cost for the registration history or current information for obtaining data on requester's own vehicle.) Oldest records are available back to 1976 (microfiche).

Request Methods – Mail, Walk-in, Online, Bulk.

What You Should Know – Requesters must use Form MV210. For the purposes of Form MV210, "motor vehicle" includes all passenger cars, trucks, trailers, campers, off-highway vehicles, snowmobiles and boats/vessels/personal watercraft. The requester must provide the reason for the request, a SSN of federal tax ID number, and agree to indemnify and hold harmless the state of Montana.

Special Access Programs Available – Both Public User and Registered User interfaces are offered at https://app.mt.gov/dojvs. The Registered User system is for ongoing registered accounts approved by the Motor Vehicle Division. The Public User system is designed for Montana citizens or users with an occasional need to know the ownership history of a pre-owned car.

About Watercraft Records

All boats must be titled and registered. Records, including liens, are maintained at the agency above. Online access is available (see above), otherwise the $6.00 search fee must be included with requests. All requests in writing must be on the state form. Turnaround time is normally 10 to 12 days. Lien information shows on the title. Records are available from 1988 to present.

Nebraska

Administration	Important Telephone and Web Contacts

Beverly Neth
   Director of Motor Vehicles
Betty Johnson
   Driver & Vehicle Records Administrator
301 Centennial Mall South
Lincoln, NE 68509
 	
www.dmv.ne.gov
	Driver Licensing..402-471-3861
	Financial Responsibility/SR-22 402-471-3985
	Commercial Driver License.........................402-471-3861
	Driver Records 402-471-3918
	Vehicle Information.....................................402-471-3918
	State Department of Insurance 402-471-2201
	Highway Patrol..402-471-4545
	Rules and Regulations are found at:
	   www.dmv.ne.gov/rulesandregs.html
	General Email Address dmv.dvrweb@nebraska.gov

Driver License Facts

License Format
One letter (A, B, C, E, G, H, or V) and 3 to 8 digits make up the license number.

Document Appearance
The current driver licensing document has been in production since July 2009. Until July 20, 2009, the DMV used an over-the-counter process to produce the driver licenses and state ID cards. Since that date, the cards are issued from a central issue location and mailed within 5 to 7 days.

Current Document
The background of the driver license contains an image of the Nebraska State Capitol on both the adult and minor license designs. The current identification card design contains a background image of the Sower and the State Seal.

    Security Characteristics   Security features include a ghost photo image imprinted over vital information to minimize alterations, a tamper resistant coating placed over the card and machine readable technology via a barcode printed on the back of the card. The tamper resistant coating contains an optically variable image of the state that changes color as the license is tilted and an ultraviolet image of the state seal visbale under a UV light source. The back of the card also includes an ultrviolet ghost photo image on the right-hand side. The advantages of the this document include increased fraud protection, added security features, machine-readable technology and increased readability.

    Position of Photo   Middle, left-hand side.

    Minor Age Driver Locator   Printed vertically and will include cardholder specific items such as, "Under 21 until xx/xx/xx" and Under 18 until xx/xx/xx".

    CDL Indicator   Commercial or non-commercial designation is printed in a solid colored header bar directly under "Nebraska." All possibilities include: "Commercial Driver's License," "Commercial Learner's Permit," or "Operator's License," "School Permit," etc.

Old Document
The background of the driver license contains an image of the Nebraska State Capitol on both the adult and minor license designs. The current identification card design contains a background image of the Sower and the State Seal.

    Security Characteristics   Security features include a ghost photo image imprinted over vital information to minimize alterations, a tamper resistant coating placed over the card and machine readable technology via a barcode printed on the back of the card. The tamper resistant coating contains an optically variable image of the state seal that changes color as the license is tilted. The advantages of the this document include increased fraud protection, added security features, machine-readable technology and increased readability.

Position of Photo	Upper right-hand corner
Minor Age Driver Locator	Printed vertically and will include cardholder specific items such as, "Under 21 until xx/xx/xx" and Under 18 until xx/xx/xx".
CDL Indicator	Commercial or non-commercial designation is printed in a solid colored header bar directly under "Nebraska." All possibilities include: "Commercial Driver's License," "Commercial Learner's Permit," or "Operator's License," "School Permit," etc.

Issue and Renewal
Age Requirements
A graduated driver's licensing program regulates the age and licensing requirements of the first three permits listed below.

Learner's Permit	Fifteen; not-required.
Provisional Operator's Permit	Sixteen but less than eighteen.
Regular License Permit	Eighteen or after Provisional Permit held one year.
School Permit	Fourteen.

Renewal
On birthday of fifth year. The driver keeps same number when renewing. At present, online renewal is unavailable but paying reinstatement fees can be done. Military personnel and their spouses or dependents who are stationed out-of-state may renew two times by mail. Proof of active duty is required. "Military" will be indicated on driving records.

Elderly-Related Restrictions
None reported by the state.

Residency
Non-resident's home-state license honored for up to thirty days of continuous residence.

License Classes
Commercial or non-commercial designation is printed in the header bar. Possibilities include: "Commercial Driver's License," "Commercial Learner's Permit," or "Operator's License," "School Permit," etc. Driving record abstracts have a "CDL Status" area with classes and CDL restrictions listed.

Commercial Classifications
A	Vehicle with 26,001 pounds GVWR or more; towed unit is 10,001 pounds GVWR or more.
B	Vehicle with 26,001 pounds GVWR or more; towed unit is less than 10,001 pounds GVWR.
C	Vehicle with 26,000 pounds GVWR or less, and either sixteen-passenger design or for hazardous material.

Non-Commercial Classifications
O	Represents a regular license for automobiles and small trucks.
M	Motorcycle qualified only.

Permits
BUS	School Bus Driver's Permit		MHP	Medical Hardship Permit
FHP	Farm Husbandry Permit		POP	Provisional Operator's Permit
ID	Identification Card		SCP	School Permit
IIP	Ignition Interlock Permit		SEP	Seasonal Permit
LPC	Commercial Learner's Permit		TPL	Temporary Permit
LPD	Class O/M Learner's Permit		WRK	Work Permit
LPE	School Learner's Permit			

Notes: The **Employment Drive Permit** is available to driver's who have forfeited their regular driving privileges under the Nebraska Point System, Administrative License Revocation and for a three (3) month time period for Violating a Support Order. This permit can be used to drive from home to work and return, and strictly in reference to the terms of employment.

The **Medical Hardship Permit** is available to driver's who have forfeited their regular driving privileges under the Nebraska Point System. This permit can be used to drive from home or place of employment to a specified hospital, clinic, doctor's office, or similar location and return. This permit cannot be used for employment, shopping, probationary meetings, school, etc.

HAZMAT Endorsement Procedure
The state is in compliance with the Patriot Act. All applicants applying for a new or renewal or transfer HAZMAT Endorsement (HME) must first obtain the application from https://hazprints.tsa.dhs.gov/Public/ or by calling 877-429-7746. The driver must also be fingerprinted. EMSI is the state-designated entity to process fingerprints. There is 1 agent plus 13 Nebraska County Sheriffs have also agreed to collect fingerprints for Nebraska residents only. Visit the web page listed below to find the address locations. The cost of the process is $89.25. The fingerprints and application

information is sent to the Federal Transportation Security Administration (TSA). TSA performs the background checks and notifies the DMV whether the application is approved or denied. When completed and approved, the HME is valid for five years. For more information, visit www.dmv.ne.gov/examining/patriotact-hazmat.html.

Safety and Enforcement Facts

Insurance and Financial Responsibility
Minimum limits of financial responsibility are $25,000/50,000/25,000. Liability insurance is compulsory, no-fault is not. Nebraska's financial responsibility laws provide that proof of insurance can be required by the Motor Vehicle Department for liability reasons. Proof may be required at registration, renewal, upon an accident or certain violations. SR-22 forms are used.

Alcohol and Chemical Testing
Nebraska's illegal intoxication level is .08 percent and above; .02 for drivers under 21 years of age, and .04 for drivers of CMVs. Urine, blood, and breath testing are authorized. Nebraska does have an implied-consent violation.

Accident Reporting
If involved in a crash one must complete a Driver's Motor Vehicle Accident Report and send to the Department of Roads within ten (10) days if any person is injured or killed, or if damage appears to exceed $1,000 for any vehicle of piece of property. Accident Records Bureau, PO Box 94669, Lincoln 68509. There are no requirements for immediate notification. If the DMV determines a reasonable possibility of a judgment being rendered against a driver involved in an accident - they are required to provide the DMV with proof of financial responsibility. If the financial responsibility requirements are not met, the individual will be suspended.

Suspensions and Revocations
Note: The state is in compliance with the federally mandated disqualifications on CDLs. See the Appendix for details.
Point Suspensions
For the accumulation 12 or more points within a two (2) year time period is a revocation for six (6) months. Subsequent revocations within a five (5) year time period are for a three (3) year time period. The subject can apply for an Employment Drive Permit if there are no other open suspensions/revocations/impoundments on the record.
Other Violations That Could Result in Suspension or Revocation:

- No Proof of Insurance (owner only)
- No Proof of Insurance (when involved in accident)
- Failure to Submit to a Chemical Test
- Reckless Driving
- Falsifying/Withholding Information on License Application
- Allowing Another Person to use Your License
- Failure to Comply with a Child or Alimony Support Order
- Failure by Individuals Under 21 to Complete a Driver Improvement Course After Accumulating 6 Points in One Year
- Leaving the Scene of an Accident
- Failure to Settle Citations or Court Judgments
- Alcoholism or Drug Addiction
- Fleeing to Avoid Arrest
- Administrative License Revocation (ALR)— Immediate seizure of license for refusal or failure of alcoholic content testing.

Reinstatement Requirements

Court Suspensions/Revocations	$125.00 fee; re-examination; SR-22 for three years.
Point Revocations	$125.00 fee; re-examination; SR-22 for three years; completion of approved driver improvement course.
Failure to Settle Citation	$50.00 fee; proof of court settlement.
Accident Related Suspensions	$50.00 fee; proof of damage/injury settlement.

Point System Overview
Points range from 1 to 12, accumulation of 12 or more points in a two-year period can result in a suspension. If an individual who has less than 12 points assessed against his/her driving record completes a Driver Improvement Course for a 2-point credit, it will appear on the record as "Driver Improvement Credit" with the date of completion. This program can only be utilized once every five years.

License Plate Facts

Registration Renewal
Renewal is annual. Registrations may be renewed online at www.clickdmv.ne.gov.

New Residents
Non-residents must register vehicles upon expiration of time period granted by home-state reciprocity agreement.

Inspections and Emissions Testing
Nebraska has no provisions for a mandatory annual vehicle-safety inspection or for statewide emission testing.

Plate Descriptions

Typical Plate Patterns	Passenger plates are 1-2N followed by 1-2L followed by 1-4N). Light truck and commercial vehicle plates are 1-2N followed by 1-5N. Effective 01/01/02, residents of Douglas (1), Lancaster (2), and Sarpy (59) counties are issued plates (passenger and commercial) as LLL-NNN.
County/City Codes	First number(s) of the plate designate county of issuance, except in Douglas, Lancaster and Sarpy counties. The list of the 93 numbers and counties can be obtained from the DMV.
Plates and Stickers in Force	Two plates, one decal (MO & YR) on both plates. Note that there is a single plate for trailers, motorcycles, semi-tractors, buses, dealers, and pull types of mobile homes.
Plates Remain with Car when Sold?	No, they remain with the seller.

Overview of Record Access

About Driving Records
Driver & Vehicle Records Division, 301 Centennial Mall South, PO Box 94789, Lincoln 68508, 402-471-3918. Questions regarding driving record requests may be addressed to dmv.dvrweb@nebraska.gov. The fee is $3.00 for manual or online requests. The last fee increase was 1997 and no increases are planned for the near future. The state charges for "no record found" reports.

Request Methods – Mail, Walk-in, Online, Bulk, NDR Access

What You Should Know – Electronic access of driving records in Nebraska is through a designated third party—Nebraska.gov. The online system is interactive and open 24 hours a day, 7 days a week. There is an annual fee of $50.00 plus the record fee. For more information, call Nebraska.gov at 800-747-8177 or visit www.nebraska.gov and click on Subscriber Portal.

Special Access Programs Available – Check another online service offered is the License Status Check. Enter the full name, DOB and either the DL or SSN. Results include DL reinstatement requirements if any, license status including points, and ending date for SR-22 Insurance Form. There is no fee. Visit www.clickdmv.ne.gov and click on *Check Your Points Total*.

Also, Nebraska offers a monitoring system to employers or insurance companies to track incidents of drivers. Subscribers submit an electronic list of drivers to be monitored. The charges for program include a monthly fee of $.06 per driver involved plus a $3.00 fee for each record provided when a change or incident occurs. Call Nebraska.gov at 800-747-8177 for more information or sign-up.

About Accident Reports
Accident reports may be obtained by writing the Department of Roads, Accident Records Bureau, Box 94669, Lincoln 68509, 402-479-4645, www.transportation.nebraska.gov. The current fee is $6.00. Records are available from 1978 to the present and the index is computerized since 1988. Hard copies are kept for 1 year then placed on a document imaging system (1998 to present). Microfilm records are from 1978 to 1994, on CD 1995 to 1997. Requests may be faxed to 402-479-3637. It takes about 6 weeks for new record to become available. Individual driver reports are not released. The name, date and county of location are needed when ordering.

About Vehicle Records
Driver & Vehicle Records, 301 Centennial Mall South, Lincoln 68509, 402-471-3918. The state maintains current title, registration and lien record database for vehicles and mobile homes. Title information is available from 1939 to present. To complete a search on vehicle license plate number, vehicle identification number, title number or name of person(s)

on the title/registration, the *Application for Copy of Vehicle Record* (or use the form for multiple records, see above) must be submitted. The applicant must sign the application and give the reason the information is needed. If reason is a permissible use, consent is not required. The applicant's signature must be notarized. If not for a permissible purpose, consent is needed with the notarized signature of record holder required.

Request Methods – Mail, Walk-in, Online, Bulk.

What You Should Know – The online system is the same used for driving records. For more information, call Nebraska.gov at 800-747-8177 or visit www.nebraska.gov.

About Watercraft Title Records

Watercraft titles are held by the DMV (www.dmv.ne.gov/dvr/mbtitles/title.html), see above. All motorized boats manufactured after 11/01/72 must be titled and registered. All motorboats are required to have a 12-digit Hull Identification Number. Watercraft registration records are held by the Nebraska Game and Parks Commission (see below). Lien records, including liens on vessels, are maintained by the County Treasurer in the county where the owner resides.

About Watercraft Registration Records

Nebraska Game and Parks Commission, 2200 North 33rd Street, Lincoln, NE 68503, 402-471-5579, www.ngpc.state.ne.us/boating/. Nebraska motorboat registrations are issued only from the county treasurer of the boater's county of residence, but this agency is responsible for the records. All vessels powered by any mechanical device capable of propelling the vessel over any public or private waters in NE must be registered, except the following:

1. Vessels not powered by machinery at any time
2. Motorboats registered in another state and housed in Nebraska less than 60 consecutive days
3. Vessels owned by any government or political subdivision
4. Racing-type motorboats when competing in state-approved races and during trial runs 48 hours prior to or 48 hours after competition
5. Vessels documented by U.S. Coast Guard

Requesters are asked for reason of request. If purpose is termed legitimate, then record is released. The SSN is not entered into the database. The DOB has not been entered into the database since late 2006. There is no fee for searching or copies, unless extensive lists provided. Verifications and simple requests are handled by phone, if the reason for request is valid

Nevada

Administration	Important Phone and Web Contacts
Edgar J. Roberts, Director Diane Mays, Record Manager 555 Wright Way Carson City 89711 www.dmvnv.com General Email info@dmv.state.nv.us Traffic Laws www.leg.state.nv.us/NRS/NRS-484.html Motor Vehicle Laws www.dmvnv.com/codebook.htm	Driver Licensing - Las Vegas ....702-486-4368 Driver Licensing - Reno/Carson City ...775-684-4368 SR-22 and Financial Responsibility......775-684-4368 Help Line (Toll free)..............................877-368-7828 CDL Carson City ....775-684-4368 Elko..775-753-1126 Ely..775-289-1620 Las Vegas ....702-486-5655 Sparks ....775-688-2327 Winnemuca ....775-623-6515 Vehicle Information ....775-684-4368 State Insurance Division ....775-687-4270 Highway Patrol 775-687-5300

Driver License Facts

License Format
Since 1/1/98, Nevada has issued a ten-digit number and reports the number is made randomly:, there is no specific code.

Document Appearance
New driver license and ID documents were introduced in October 2008. These new documents contain numerous security features and will replace all existing cards upon renewal. The new documents are issued using facial recognition software, allowing the Department to compare new photos with other photos in the database as a further guard against identity theft. The previous document was initially issued in April 2002. Both the older and current cards are described below.

Current Documents

Security Characteristics	Micro-printing, ghost images, Guilloche security design, laser perforation, overlapping data, and a laser-engraved outline of the state. A 1D bar code and 2D bar code appear on the backside of the card.
Position of Photo	For adult licenses, the photo is positioned on the left with a ghost image on the right side.
Minor Age Driver Indicators	The minor cards are vertical. The photo is on the upper left side and the ghost image on the upper right. Underneath the ghost photo appears "Under 18 or 21 until xx/xx/xxxx" in red ink. The location of the laser perforation is in a different location than the adult card.
CDL Indicator	License header shows "Nevada Commercial Driver License."

Older Documents

Security Characteristics	State seal on laminate; see above.
Position of Photo	Old - bottom right: Current - top right.
Minor Age Driver Locator (since 04/02)	"Nevada Minor Driver (Under 21)" is laminated on license; photo is side profile. If under 21 is a vertical license with no side view photo, yellow bar indicates "Under 21 until xx."
Minor Age Driver Locator (prior 04/02)	"Nevada Minor Driver (Under 21)" is laminated on license; photo is side profile. If under 18 the license header is light blue, "Under 21" written in yellow. If under 21 but over 18 the license header is yellow, "Under 21" written in red.
CDL Indicator (since 04/02)	Gold bar header shows "Commercial Driver License."
CDL Indicator (prior 04/02)	License header shows "Nevada Commercial Driver License."

Issue and Renewal
Age Requirements
The minimum age for a learner's or instruction permit is fifteen and one-half. Nearly all Nevada beginning drivers under 18 must complete a driver education course. The course is not a requirement to obtain an instruction permit; it is a requirement for a driver license. Young drivers can enroll at age 15. Exceptions are not made for home-schooled students. Young drivers are required to complete 50 hours of behind-the-wheel experience (10 hours of which completed in darkness) and must have a licensed driver, who is 21 or older and has been licensed for at least one year, seated next to them at all times. An excellent description with complete details of the program is found at www.dmvnv.com/nvdlteens.htm.

Renewal
A Nevada driver's license is valid for 4 years and expires on the birthday of the 4th year unless immigration documents are presented as evidence of the name and date of birth. If immigration documents are used, the expiration of the license will coincide with the departure date on the immigration documents, or in 4 years, whichever is sooner. Driver keeps same number when renewing unless the driver has an X number. NV allows active military personnel, federal government employees, and dependents of either, to renew by mail unless the document has been expired 2 years.

Drivers may renew online once every 8 years. To qualify for web or mail renewals, a driver must have obtained or renewed in person within the last 4 years and be at least 25 years old on the next birthday, and must not have had more than two moving violations or any license suspension, revocation, cancellation or denial within the last 4 years.

Elderly-Related Restrictions
Upon driver reaching age 65, the examiner must determine if the driver has good vision and physical condition.

Residency
New residents must secure Nevada license within thirty (30) days of establishing residency. New residents under 21 must take a written test.

License Classes
Commercial Classifications
    A   Any combination of motor vehicles with a GCWR of 26,001 pounds or more, provided the vehicle being towed has a GVWR of more than 10,000 pounds.

    B   Any single vehicle with a GVWR of 26,001 or more pounds, or any such vehicle towing a vehicle weighing 10,000 pounds GVWR or less.

    C   Any single vehicle or combination of vehicles that does not meet the definition of Group A or Group B. Commercial Class C vehicles are either designed to transport sixteen or more passengers (including the driver) or placarded for hazardous materials.

Non-Commercial Classifications
Non-commercial vehicle classifications are defined the same as above, except non-commercial classifications apply to vehicles which are not used in commerce to transport passengers or property. For example, the Drivers' Handbook states that Class C "is for cars, vans, pickups, and other vehicles with a GVWR of 26,000 pounds or less; allows towing of a vehicle with a GVWR of 10,000 pounds or less, without an endorsement."

M for Motorcycles will be shown as an *endorsement* on another class of license, if a valid A, B or C license is held. Also, there is a restricted Class M license for mopeds, tri-mobiles, and motorcycles that are less than 90cc and do not exceed 6 1/2

HAZMAT Endorsement Procedure
The state is in compliance with the Patriot Act. All applicants applying for a new or renewal or transfer HAZMAT Endorsement (HME) must first obtain the application from https://hazprints.tsa.dhs.gov/Public/ or by calling 877-429-7746. The driver must also be fingerprinted. EMSI and Comnetix are the state-designated entities that process fingerprints. There are three locations in the state that perform this service, plus a site in Elko may be added in near future. Visit the web page listed above to find the address locations. The cost of the fingerprint process is $89.25. The fingerprints and application information is sent to the Federal Transportation Security Administration (TSA). TSA performs the background checks and notifies the DMV and the applicant whether the application is approved or denied. When completed and approved, the HME is valid for five years.

For more information, visit www.dmvnv.com/dlhazmat.htm.

Safety and Enforcement Facts

Insurance and Financial Responsibility
A Nevada Evidence of Insurance card must be carried in the vehicle at all times and presented to any law enforcement officer upon request. Minimum automobile liability insurance coverage is $15,000 for bodily injury or death of one person in any one accident; $30,000 for bodily injury or death or two or more persons on any one accident; and $10,000 for injury to or destruction of property of others in any one accident. Coverage must be reported by an insurance company authorized to do business in the State of Nevada. Motorists with driver license suspensions or revocations may be required to file a SR-22 with the DMV to regain driving privileges. The state does not have a provision for no-fault insurance.

Alcohol and Chemical Testing
Nevada's illegal intoxication level is .08 percent blood alcohol level or any detectable amount of a controlled substance; .02 if under 21; and .04 for anyone driving a commercial motor vehicle. Urine, blood, and breath testing are authorized. Nevada has an administrative license revocation provision. This provision also applies to juveniles with .02 - .08 percent intoxication level.

Accident Reporting
A written report is required when: an accident was not investigated at the scene by law enforcement; damage occurred in excess of $750 to any one person; the accident resulted in an injury or death. Reports must be filed within ten days with the Department of Motor Vehicles, Central Services & Records Division, Driver License Division, 555 Wright Way, Carson City NV 89711-0400. There are no additional state reporting requirements for commercial drivers at this time.

Suspensions and Revocations
The state has implemented the federally mandated disqualifications for offenses occurring in a CMV. See the Appendix for a list of these disqualifications. Below are examples of driver license suspensions and revocations. Juveniles may have additional offense that can suspend or delay their licenses.

Possible Suspensions
- Accumulation of Twelve or More Points in Twelve Months
- Aggressive Driving First Offense- Court Order
- Various CDL Disqualifications
- Child Support Arrearage
- Court Recommendations due to Traffic Violation Conviction
- Failure to Appear in Court or Pay Fines
- Failure to Maintain Insurance
- Failure to Pay Delinquent Fine
- Failure to Properly Secure a Child
- Firearm - Juvenile
- Graffiti
- Illegal Per Se - Juvenile .02-.08%
- Out-of-State Offense Which in this State Would Require Suspension
- Street Racing
- Passing a School Bus
- Truancy

Possible Revocations
- Aggressive Driving Second Offense- Court Order
- Conviction of Three Charges of Reckless Driving Within Twelve Month
- Failure to Stop When Involved in an Accident Resulting in Death or Personal Injury
- Felony Involving the Use of a Vehicle or Car Theft
- Manslaughter

DUI Revocations
- First Violation in Seven Years   Ninety days.
- Second Violation in Seven Years   One year.
- Third or Subsequent Violations   Three years.

Cancellations
- Failure to Give Correct or Required Information When Applying for a Driver's License or to Meet Department Requirements
- Fraud Committed When Applying for a Driver's License
- If the Driver is Under Eighteen, a Parent or Guardian May Request Cancellation of the License
- If the Driver Voluntarily Surrenders his/her Driver's License for Medical Reasons

Reinstatement Requirements
Suspension .... $40.00 to $120.00 fee; re-examination.
Revocation .... $75.00 to $125.00 fee; re-examination; SR-22.

Nevada

Point System Overview
The Nevada DMV operates an extensive demerit point system as part of their driver improvement program. When a conviction notice is received from a court, the offense is entered on the driving record and demerit points are assigned based on the traffic violation. When 12 months have elapsed from the date of a conviction, the demerits for that violation are deleted from the total demerits accumulated. Convictions remain part of the driver's permanent driving record.

Drivers receive a mailed notification from the DMV's Driver License Review Section when they reach three or more points and if they have accumulated between 3 and 11 points, they may have 3 points removed by completing a DMV-approved traffic safety course only if the course is not part of a plea-bargain agreement with a court of law. When drivers receive 12 or more points in any 12-month period, a 6-month suspension is automatically placed on the driver license.

License Plate Facts

Registration Renewal
Online registration is available as a limited pilot project if a vehicle is purchased from a Nevada dealer and the control number on the Dealer Report of Sale (DRS) begins with the letters "EDRS". Otherwise, registration must be completed at a Full Service DMV office. If a smog check is required the vehicle registration may be renewed online if the Department received an electronic record stating the vehicle passed. The URL is https://dmvapp.state.nv.us/vr_ren/vr_ren_input.aspx Also, online renewal is now available through Motor Carrier's MVS Express system. Carriers that wish to participate are encouraged to read the program requirements for more information and Tomi Blevins at 775-684-4896 or tblevins@dmv.state.nv.us.

New Residents
New residents must register (and have inspected) vehicles within thirty (30) days of establishing residency.

Inspections and Emissions Testing
Nevada has no annual vehicle-safety inspection, but does have provisions for annual emission testing in Clark and Washoe counties. The following vehicles are exempt from emission testing: new motor vehicles on their first and second registration; 1967 or older; motorcycle or moped; vehicles based in remote areas of Clark and Washoe counties and all other Nevada counties; alternative fuel vehicles; Diesel vehicles with a gross vehicle weight up to 14,000 pounds; vehicles registered with Classic Vehicle or Classic Rod license plates and driven 2,500 miles or less per year. A vehicle identification number inspection is required for all vehicles not previously registered or titled in Nevada.

Plate Descriptions

Typical Plate Patterns	Passenger and light truck plates are either 3 alpha - 3 numeric or 3 numeric -3 alpha (newest). Commercial vehicle plates are 5 numeric - 1 alpha. Personalized plates are available for an additional fee.
County/City Codes	Pre-1982 plates, some of which are in use, are coded with the alpha(s) designating the county. Since 1982, there are no codes.
Plates and Stickers in Force	2 plates, 1 sticker (MO & YR) on rear plate. If a vehicle is not equipped by the manufacturer for a front display, then one plate is okay.
Plates Remain with Car when Sold?	No, they remain with seller.
Note:	Any motorized vehicle which does not have the normal safety equipment such as lights and mirrors or is not built to federal vehicle standards is an off-road vehicle and is restricted to off-road use only. This includes all-terrain vehicles, pocket bikes, and snowmobiles. There is no driver license or minimum age requirements for off-road vehicles. Nevada does not issue or require titles on these vehicles. DMV issued titles on ATVs and similar vehicles up until August 15, 2005.

Overview of Record Access

About Driving Records
Department of Motor Vehicles, Records Section, 555 Wright Way, Carson City 89711-0250. For Reno/Sparks/Carson City use 775-684-4590; for Las Vegas use 702-486-4368; For rest of state or out-of-state use 877-368-7828. The fax number is 775-684-4899. Three records are available: 3-year, 10-year, and School Bus records. Only the 3-year record is available online. The current fee for a driving record is $7.00; for driver's license information the fee is $5.00; certification is $4.00; and a photo copy of a document is $3.00. The last fee increase was in July 2003 and no increases are planned for the near future. The state charges for "no record found" reports.

Request Methods — Mail, Walk-in, Online, Telephone, Bulk.

What You Should Know – Withdrawal actions and accidents are not released on a three-year record, but show on a ten-year record. Non-moving violations (except for commercial drivers) are not listed on the driving record. Accident information does not appear on the driving record. For information about online access, call 775-684-4702.

Special Access Programs Available – Individuals may obtain their own 3-year driving record by mail, fax, in person from any DMV Office or online. Go to https://dmvapp.state.nv.us/OL_DH/Drvr_Usr_Info.aspx. The fee is $7.00. Nevada offers a retrieval phone-in system at 775-684-4590. Callers must have an assigned five-digit account number for access. Pre-approved callers can request up to 5 MVRs at a time over the phone. The driver's license number or name and date of birth are needed when ordering. NV will also mail-back phone-in requests, if requested. Billing is monthly, and must be paid within 30 days. Pre-approved accounts may fax requests.

Online License Status – Check another online service offered is the License Status Check. Enter the full name, DOB and either the DL or SSN. Results include DL reinstatement requirements if any, license status including points, and ending date for SR-22 Insurance Form. There is no fee. Visit www.clickdmv.ne.gov and click on *Check Your Points Total*.

About Accident Reports

There is no centralized database of Highway Patrol investigated accident reports; the reports must be ordered from one of the three regional offices. Note that the Nevada Highway Patrol headquarters will accept orders, but sends all requests to the appropriate office. The fee to obtain an accident report is $3.50 for a non-fatality and $5.00 if fatality involved. The addresses and phone numbers of the regional office and of headquarters are listed below;

- Headquarters, 555 Wright Way, Carson City, NV 89711, 775-684-4867
- Las Vegas Div., 4615 Sunset, Las Vegas, NV 89118, 702-486-4100
- Reno Div., 357 Hammell Lane, Reno, NV 89511, 775-688-2500
- Elko Div., 3920 E Idaho St, Elko, NV 89801, 775-753-1111

About Vehicle Records

Department of Motor Vehicles, Motor Vehicle Record Section, 555 Wright Way, Carson City 89711-0250, 775-684-4590. The current fee for vehicle title or registration information is $5.00; for a vehicle history the fee is $7.00; and a title verification letter or vehicle history is $7.00. Certification of any document is an additional $4.00. A photocopy of each page of a document is an additional $3.00 per page. Records requested for insurance purposes from an insurance company or agent must provide the NAIC number of the insurance company. Note that 2009 legislation mandates that owners of off-road vehicles (ORVs) must now register their vehicles with the DMV.

Request Methods – Mail, Walk-in, Telephone, Online Status, Bulk.

What You Should Know – The same phone-in request system offered for driving record searches (see above) is available for vehicle and ownership information at 775-684-4590

Special Access Programs Available – Although full title and registration records cannot be accessed online, the DMV offers an online registration status inquiry. The requester must submit the license plate number and last four digits of the VIN to display the record information. There is no fee.
Go to https://dmvapp.state.nv.us/dmv/vr/vr_reg/vr_reg_default.aspx.

About Watercraft Records

Department of Wildlife, Attn: Boat Registration, 4600 Kietz Lane #D-135, Reno 89502 775-688-1511 www.ndow.org. All motorized boats must be registered and titled. The boat registration, hull number, or name of owner is needed to do a search. The SSN is blocked. Records are available from 1972 to present on microfilm and computer. There is a $5.00 fee per boat or person which includes computer printout. Photocopies are $.50 per page. The information will include current lien-holder name and address. Turnaround time is within 1 week. Bulk lists, labels and tapes are available for purchase. Fees depend on the media type and can be $1,000 or more.

The 2010 U.S. Motor Vehicle Reference Book   New Hampshire   153

New Hampshire

Administration	Important Telephone and Web Contacts
Virginia Beecher, Director Arthur Garlow, Assistant Director Division of Motor Vehicles 23 Hazen Drive, Concord 03305-0002 603-271-2484 www.nh.gov/safety/divisions/dmv Administrative Rules and a link to Title XXI - Motor Vehicle Laws are found under *Laws & Rules* at the home page.	Driver Licensing, CDL ....603-271-2371 Driving Records ....603-271-2322 SR-22 & Financial Responsibility ....603-271-3101 Registration Information ....603-271-2251 Title Information ....603-271-3111 State Police..603-271-3636 State Department of Insurance ....603-271-2261 Contacts: www.nh.gov/safety/divisions/dmv/contactus.html

Driver License Facts

License Format
Two numbers, three letters, and five numbers. The license number is coded as follows: birth month (two digits); the first letter of the last name; the last letter of the last name; the first letter of the first name; the year of birth (two digits); day of month (two digits); and a computer "twin" number (usually one, never a zero).

Document Appearance
The current license and ID card documents have been in circulation since May 30, 2008 and are issued to all first-time drivers and renewal licensees. Presently, all DMV card customers are issued a temporary license or non-driver ID card while their permanent license or ID card is being processed and then mailed. It will take at least five years to replace the older documents. Both document types are listed below.

Current Document
- **Security Characteristics**   Features holographs, small windows and a bar code with the driver's description and license restrictions.
- **Position of Photo**   Left side, ghost image on right.
- **Minor Age Driver Locator**   Vertical, photo on top, ghost photo on bottom, statement shows date when driver is 21.
- **CDL Indicator**   The fact that the driver is CDL qualified is indicated.

Older Document
- **Security Characteristics**   Hologram of New Hampshire, license is laminated.
- **Position of Photo**   Top left.
- **Minor Age Driver Locator**   Red border around photo, also statement on card showing date when driver is 21.
- **CDL Indicator**   "CDL" appears next to the class designation.

Issue and Renewal

Age Requirements
One must be at least 16 years of age to get a New Hampshire driver license. Persons 16 and 17 years of age may get a New Hampshire driver license only with successful completion of an approved driver education program. Persons under 18 years of age cannot get a commercial driver license. Any person 16 years of age or older and under 21 years of age will be issued a Youth Operator license. All youth operator licenses expire on the holder's 21st birthday. A Learner's Permit is required for motorcyclists only. Non-licensed learners must be accompanied by a licensed parent, guardian, certified driving instructor, or responsible adult aged twenty-five or older.

Renewal
Birthdate of fifth year for regular drivers; for commercial drivers renewal is the birthdate of the fifth year. The driver keeps same number when renewing. Renewal by mail is available for New Hampshire residents temporarily living out-of-state. The online renewal system permits non-commercial drivers to renew a five-year license once every ten years. Visit www.nh.gpv/dmv and click on "online driver license renewal."

Elderly-Related Restrictions
A driving test is required when drivers renew at age 75 or older.

Residency
Non-resident's home-state license honored on a reciprocal basis; New Hampshire license must be secured within sixty days of establishing residency. Note NH law requires the DMV be notified within ten days of a change of address.

License Classes
Classifications Overview

Code	License	Description
A	CDL-A	Class A - CDL
A M1	CDL-A MC	Class A - CDL with motorcycle
A M2	CDL-A MDC	Class A - CDL with motor-driven cycle
B	CDL-B	Class B - CDL
B M1	CDL-B MC	Class B - CDL with motorcycle
B M2	CDL-B MDC	Class B - CDL with motor-driven cycle
C	CDL-C	Class C - CDL
C M1	CDL-C MC	Class C - CDL with motorcycle
C M2	CDL-C MDC	Class C - CDL with motor-driven cycle
D	OPERATOR	Regular Operator
D M1	OPR-MC	Operator with motorcycle
D M2	OPER-MDC	Operator with motor-driven cycle
M1	MOTORCYCLE	Motorcycle
M2	MTR-DRVN-CYC	Motor-driven cycle
M3	MOPED	Moped
NO	NON-DRIVER ID	Non-driver ID
YO	YOUTH OPERATOR	Youth Operator

Commercial Classifications
Class A Any combination of vehicles with a GVWR of 26,001 or more pounds provided the GVWR of the vehicle(s) being towed is in excess of 10,000 pounds. Holders of Group A licenses may—with any appropriate endorsements—operate all vehicles within groups B and C.

Class B Any single vehicle with a GVWR of 26,001 or more pounds, or any such vehicle towing a vehicle not in excess of 10,000 pounds GVWR.

Class C Any single vehicle that is less than 26,001 pounds GVWR, or any such vehicle towing a vehicle not in excess of 10,000 pounds GVWR, that is placarded for hazardous materials or designed to transport sixteen or more persons (including the operator).

Note: The DMV does not issue a hardship license.

HAZMAT Endorsement Procedure
The state is in compliance with the Patriot Act. All applicants applying for a new or renewal or transfer HAZMAT Endorsement (HME) must obtain and complete the application by visiting https://hazprints.tsa.dhs.gov/Public/ or by calling 877-429-7746. The driver must also be fingerprinted. EMSI is the state-designated entity to process fingerprints. There are five locations in the state that perform this service. Visit the web page listed above to find the address locations. The cost of the fingerprint process is $89.25. The fingerprints and application information is sent to the Federal Transportation Security Administration (TSA). TSA performs the background checks and notifies the DMV whether the application is approved or denied. When completed and approved, the HME is valid until expiration of current license.

Safety and Enforcement Facts

Insurance and Financial Responsibility
Although the state does not have a mandatory insurance law, the state requires financial responsibility proof in case of the following convictions:
1. Driving under the influence of alcohol or drugs.
2. Failing to stop and report when involved in a crash.
3. Homicide arising out of the operation of a motor vehicle.
4. The second time for reckless driving.
5. After review of a person's driver record for any traffic violation (just cause after hearing).

The DMV strongly recommends and urges all owners of motor vehicle to carry standard liability and property damage insurance with minimum requirements of $25,000/50,000/25,000. SR-22 forms are used by the state.

Alcohol and Chemical Testing

Evidence that there was an alcohol concentration of more than .03% but less than .08% is relevant evidence (not prima facie) and may be considered with other competent evidence to determine guilt or innocence. Drivers under 21 years of age have a limit of .02 percent, if driving a CMV then .04%. Urine, blood, and breath testing are authorized. New Hampshire has provisions for implied-consent and administrative license suspensions. Operating a horse, boat, ORHV, or bicycle under the influence is also considered illegal.

Accident Reporting

An accident report must be filed within fifteen days for accidents involving death, injury, or property damage in excess of $1,000.00. Reports are written and filed by the police if they investigate. The individual operator's report should be sent to the Department of Safety, Department of Motor Vehicles, 23 Hazen Drive, Concord, 03305. There are no special requirements for commercial drivers.

Suspensions and Revocations

The state is in compliance with the federally mandated disqualifications on CDLs. See the Appendix for details.

Point Accumulation
- Drivers Under Twenty Years of Age
  - Any violation .... 20-day suspension; 45-day for second offense.
  - Third violation .... 90-day suspension.
- Drivers Under Eighteen Years of Age
  - Six points in one calendar year or third violation .... Up to three-month suspension.
  - Twelve points in two consecutive calendar years .... Up to six-month suspension.
  - Eighteen points in three consecutive calendar years .... Up to one-year suspension.
- Drivers Aged Eighteen to Under Twenty-One
  - Nine points in one calendar year .... Up to three-month suspension.
  - Fifteen points in two consecutive calendar years .... Up to six-month suspension.
  - Twenty-one points in two consecutive calendar years ..... Up to one-year suspension.
- Drivers Twenty-One Years or Older
  - Twelve points in one calendar year .... Up to three-month suspension.
  - Eighteen points in two consecutive calendar years .... Up to six-month suspension.
  - Twenty-four points in three consecutive calendar years... Up to one-year suspension.

Transporting Alcoholic Beverages .... Up to sixty-day suspension.

Intoxication or Under the Influence of Drugs
- 1st Offense .... Revocation from ninety days to two years.
- 2nd offense Within a Seven-Year Period .... Revocation of driving privileges for at least three years.

Refusal to Submit to a Chemical Test or Prior NH Refusals:
- First conviction with no prior DWI convictions .... 180-day revocation.
- Prior refusal to submit or DWI conviction .... Two-year revocation.

Note: Effective 01/01/2009, drivers with outstanding E-ZPass violations will no longer be subject to suspension; however, outstanding violations will block the driver from renewing registrations.

Reinstatement Requirements

Suspension	$100.00 fee; SR-22 (in some cases).
Revocations	$100.00 fee; SR-22 (in some cases).
DUI Suspension	$100.00 fee; SR-22; successful completion of approved alcohol program; installation of Ignition Interlock Device (in some cases).

Point System Overview

The point system ranges from 1 to 6 points. 12 or more points in a calendar year may result in a suspension. The point assessment total will be reduced by 3 points if the driver shows that he/she has completed a driver improvement course. This reduction is only available once every 3 years and is only for suspendable purposes.

License Plate Facts

Registration Renewal

Registration renewal is on an annual basis. Online renewal is available at www.egov.nh.gov/Compass/ for those residents of the participating towns or cities. To renew online the address must be the same and there can be no outstanding fees, delinquencies or suspensions with any town, city or with the State of NH. Also, to renew online the gross weight of vehicle cannot be over 8,000 pounds.

New Residents
New residents must register vehicles upon the expiration of time period granted by home-state reciprocity agreement or within sixty days of establishing residency—whichever is first.

Inspections and Emissions Testing
New Hampshire's program of vehicle safety inspections is as follows: all non-commercial vehicles, annually; all commercial vehicles (over 10,000 pounds GVW) and all buses, semi-annually. Visual inspection of several emissions components is included in the annual statewide safety inspection for light-duty vehicles. The emissions inspection shall not apply to vehicles 20 or more model years old, determined by subtracting the model year of the vehicle from the calendar year in which the inspection occurs. As of October 1, 2007 all 1996 and newer model year vehicles, subject to testing, must pass the On-Board Diagnostics (OBD II) inspection. New Hampshire incorporated OBD II inspections into the safety inspection program beginning in May 2005 as a requirement of the Federal Clean Air Act. The program enables licensed inspection stations to perform OBD II inspections and allows the state to comply with Environmental Protection Agency regulations.

Plate Descriptions
Typical Plate Patterns........................... Passenger and light truck plates are up to 7 numeric digits. Commercial vehicle plates are LLNNNN.
County/City Codes............................... Counties or codes are not designated on the plate.
Plates and Stickers in Force .... Two plates, two decals (MO) (YR) both plates.
Plates Remain with Car when Sold?.... No, they remain with seller.

Overview of Record Access

About Driving Records
Driving Records, 23 Hazen Drive, Concord 03305, 603-271-2322. If a requester does not fall into one the permitted use groups, they are required to present a document notarized by the licensee in order to obtain information. There are two records available - The Insurance Report and the Certified Report. Either one is $15.00. The online record is $12.00. Credit cards are accepted for payment. The online record is $12.00. New Hampshire charges for a no record found report.

Request Methods – Mail, Walk-in, Fax, FTP, Online, Bulk.

What You Should Know – An insurance copy of a driving record has only violations and accidents. A certified copy of a driving record has detailed information regarding past history including present and/or prior suspensions, restorations, convictions, and crash involvement. NH offers interactive and batch (FTP) online inquiry for commercial accounts. For more information, call 603-271-2484.

About Accident Reports
Copies of accident reports may be obtained by written request from the Department of Safety, Attention: Crash Section, 23 Hazen Drive, Concord 03305, 603-271-2322 or 271-3101. The Fatal Crash Unit can be reached at 603-271-2554. The department follows the privacy regulations in effect per RSA 260:14. The notarized DSMV 505 Form (same form used to request a driving record) must be completed by the subject involved or an insurance representative licensed to write automobile policies in the state of NH. In-person requesters are required to have notarized paperwork if not involved in the incident. The fee is $1.00 per page, with a minimum of $5.00. Both drivers' names and dates of birth, and the date and location of the accident are needed when ordering. Records are maintained for five years.

About Vehicle Records
Bureau of **Titles**, Department of Safety, DMV, 23 Hazen Drive, Concord 03305, 603-271-3111. **Registration**, Department of Safety, 23 Hazen Drive, Concord 03305, 603-271-2251, fax is 603-271-1061. Each section has its own location counter that process record requests. The Bureau of Title oversees requests for title and lien information. The Registration Section is another department. Photos and SSNs are not released to record requesters.

Request Methods – Mail, Walk-in, Bulk.

What You Should Know – The current fee for a title search (includes lien data) is $20.00 per request. The fee for a current registration listing is $5.00 per record, a certified copy is $15.00.

About Watercraft Records
The Department of Safety also maintains the database of boat registrations. The same privacy provisions apply as those to vehicle records. All motorized boats and all sailboats over 12 ft must be registered. Mail requests should be sent to the attention of the "Boat Desk." A name or registration search is $5.00 per name (or per registration) for current year only. The direct line is 603-271-2333. Liens on boats are recorded with the Secretary of State, for more information call 603-271-3242.

New Jersey

Administration	Important Telephone and Web Contacts
Donald Boroski, Director Compliance and Safety Motor Vehicle Services 225 East State Street, PO 174 Trenton 08666 www.state.nj.us/mvc	Driver Licensing and CDL ....609-292-6500 Driver Licensing (In-State Only)....................888-486-3339 Suspensions ....609-292-7500 Vehicle Information ....609-292-6500 State Department of Insurance ....609-292-5360 State Police..609-882-2000 Email: www.state.nj.us/mvc/About/ContactEmail.htm Statutes and Laws Look-up: www.njleg.state.nj.us

Driver License Facts

License Format
First letter of last name and fourteen numbers. For example, Driver License Number "S5778-40771-01024" is interpreted as follows:

- S — first initial of last name of the driver (i.e., <u>S</u>mith)
- 5778 — coded next four letters of last name (i.e., <u>mith</u>)
- 407 — coded first name (John)
- 71 — coded middle initial (J.)
- 01 — coded birth month for males (January)
- 02 — year of birth (1902)
- 4 — coded eye color (blue)

In another example, if the driver was a female, Christine J. Smith, with the same date and year of birth and eye color, the driver license number would be "S5778-12471-51024" and would be interpreted as follows:

- S — first initial of last name of the driver (i.e., <u>S</u>mith)
- 5778 — coded next four letters of last name (i.e., <u>mith</u>)
- 124 — coded first name (Chris)
- 71 — coded middle initial (J.)
- 51 — coded birth month for females (January)
- 02 — year of birth (1902)
- 4 — coded eye color (blue).

Document Appearance
The MVC began issuing New Jersey's first generation Digital Driver License (DDL) in mid-January 2004. By 2009, the vast majority of the older driver licenses will have expired and replaced by this virtually counterfeit-proof digital license that contains nearly two dozen security features.

- **Position of Photo** Lower left.
- **Minor Age Driver Locator** Photo is side profile.
- **CDL Indicator** Indicated by class.

Issue and Renewal

Age Requirements
Since 01/01/01, New Jersey has operated a Graduated Driver License Program. The program has three steps. Step One starts with a Special Learner's Permit or Student Permit issued at age 16. Driver must be accompanied by adult at all times and can only drive from 5AM to 11PM. Next, at 17 and after 6 months of supervised driving and passage of a road test, a Provisional Photo License is issued for one year. Step Three is the basic license at 18. The minimum age for "Agricultural Pursuit" is 16, for a CDL is 18 for interstate driving and 21 to drive with a passenger and/or HAZMAT. The minimum age for a motorboat or jet ski license is 16, but if under 17 a letter with parental or guardian consent must be provided. Starting in 2010, NJ law requires new drivers aged 21 years old and younger to display identifying decals on the front and rear licenses plates of their vehicles.

Renewal
Four years from initial or renewal issue date. At present, renewal is only available in person. Driver keeps same number when renewing unless there is a change or correction to name, sex, date of birth, or eye color. Active military duty, including New Jersey National Guard and Reserve, are entitled to automatic extensions for driver license, registration and inspection requirements. The license, registration and inspection documents will remain valid for as the subject is actively serving. Once demobilized, the document must be renewed within two weeks of the demobilization date.

Elderly-Related Restrictions
None are reported.

Residency
Non-resident's home-state license honored on reciprocal basis; drivers must secure a New Jersey license within sixty days of establishing residency.

License Classes
Commercial Classifications
- A Any combination of vehicles with a GCWR of 26,001 or more pounds, provided the GVWR of the vehicle(s) being towed is in excess of 10,000 pounds.
- B Any single vehicle with a GVWR of 26,001 or more pounds; **or** any such vehicle towing a vehicle not in excess of 10,000 GVWR; **or** any vehicle with a GVWR of 26,001 pounds and designed to transport sixteen or more passengers (including the driver) whether used for hire or not.
- C Any single vehicle with a GVWR of less than 26,001 pounds, or any such vehicle towing a vehicle not in excess of 10,000 pounds GVWR provided that the vehicle is placarded to transport hazardous materials; **or** the vehicle is designed to transport sixteen or more passengers (including the driver) whether for hire or not; **or** the vehicle is designed to transport eight to fifteen passengers including the driver and is used for hire; **or** the vehicle is designed to transport eight to fifteen persons including the driver for hire on a daily basis to and from places of employment; **or** the vehicle is used for the transportation of more than 6 passengers to or from summer day camps or summer residence camps; **or** the vehicle is required to be registered as a school bus except that a person licensed as a bus driver on or before 12/31/90 may operate a bus required to be registered as a school bus but without a CDL provided the vehicle is designed to carry not more than passengers including the driver.

Non-Commercial Classifications
- D This class is for all types of motor vehicles, except motorcycles used for non-commercial transportation.
- E Motorcycle - This class is for vehicles with less than four wheels; motor bikes and scooters included.
- F Moped - This class is for drivers fifteen years and older operating a motorized bicycle. For unlicensed drivers - not needed if operator has a Class A, B, C, D or E license.
- G Agricultural - This class is for farming purposes only and may be granted to persons between sixteen and seventeen years of age. Note that this class is subject to the Graduated Driver License Program.
- I Identification - This class is for any individual seventeen years of age or older who cannot/do not want to qualify for a driver's license. This identification is valid for four years.

Boat License - Required for operating motorboats on fresh, non-tidal waters such as lakes, creeks or rivers that are not affected by tidal conditions. No license is required for tidal waters. Anyone born after December 31, 1978 must present a boating safety certificate.

HAZMAT Endorsement Procedure
The state is in compliance with the Patriot Act. All applicants applying for a new or renewal or transfer HAZMAT Endorsement (HME) must first obtain the application from https://hazprints.tsa.dhs.gov/Public/ or by calling 877-429-7746. The driver must also be fingerprinted. EMSI is the state-designated entity to process fingerprints. There are six locations in the state that perform this service. Visit the web page listed above to find the address locations or contact TSA's contracted fingerprint vendor Integrated Biometric Technology LLC (IBT) at 877-429-7746. The cost of the fingerprint process is $89.25. The fingerprints and application information is sent to the Federal Transportation Security Administration (TSA). TSA performs the background checks and notifies the DMV whether the application is approved or denied. When completed and approved, the HME is valid until renewal date. For more information, visit www.state.nj.us/mvc/Commercial/Hazardous.htm.

Safety and Enforcement Facts

Insurance and Financial Responsibility
New Jersey has compulsory insurance including no-fault insurance. Minimum financial responsibility limits are $15,000/30,000/5,000. Proof is required after certain violations and for accidents resulting in death, injury, or damage in excess of $500.00. There is no provision in force for SR-22 forms.

Alcohol and Chemical Testing
New Jersey's intoxication level is .08 % and above; .01% for drivers under 21, and .04% if driving a CMV. Urine, blood, and breath testing are authorized. NJ has an implied-consent violation, and a provision for an administrative suspension for out-of-state convictions. Operating a horse or bicycle under the influence is also considered illegal.

Accident Reporting
Immediately report any accident involving injury, death or property damage in excess of $500.00 to the nearest law enforcement agency. If no report is filed by the investigating law enforcement officer, a report must be filed within five days with the NJ Dept of Trans, Bureau of Safety Program, 1035 Parkway Ave, PO Box 600, Trenton 08625-0600. There are no special state filing requirements for commercial drivers.

Suspensions and Revocations
The state is in compliance with the federally mandated disqualifications on CDLs, an excellent overview is provided at www.state.nj.us/mvc/pdf/Violations/cdl_chart.pdf. Also, see the Appendix for details.

Alcohol- or Drug-Related Convictions
- First Offense if BAC.08% but less than .10% .... Three-month suspension.
- First Offense if BAC.10% or higher .... Seven-month to one-year suspension.
- Second Offense .... Two-year suspension.
- Third Offense .... Ten-year suspension.

DUI or Refusing Chemical Test in School Zone or Crossing
- First Offense .... One- to two-year suspension.
- Second Offense .... Four-year suspension.
- Third Offense .... Twenty-year suspension.

Under Age 21 Alcohol and Convicted for Driving or Boating with a BAC or .01 or higher:
- First Offense .... Thirty-day to ninety-day suspension or DUI sentence above.
- Second Offense .... Two-year suspension.
- Third Offense .... Ten-year suspension.

If suspended because of a DUI offense, the court may require an ignition interlock device to fully restore driving privileges.
- First DUI Offense .... Installation of interlock device for six months to one year.
- Second DUI Offense .... Installation of interlock device for one to three years or a two year suspension of registration privileges
- Third DUI Offense .... Installation of interlock device for one to three years as a condition of restoring your driving privileges or a 10 year suspension of registration privileges.
- Driving While Suspended for DWI .... Additional one- to two-year suspension.

No Insurance
- First Offense .... One-year suspension.
- Second Offense .... Two-year suspension.
- Driving With Drugs in Possession .... Two-year suspension.
- Refusal to Take Chemical or Breath Test .... First Offense   Seven-month to one-year suspension.
- Second Offense .... Two-year suspension.
- Third or Subsequent Offense .... Ten-year suspension.
- Habitual Offender .... Up to three-year suspension.

Point Accumulation Suspensions
Note: All point suspension terms listed below are proposed; discretion allowed by courts.
- Twelve to Fifteen Points in up to Two Years .... Thirty days.
- Twelve to Fourteen Points in a Period Greater than Two Years ...... Thirty days.
- Sixteen to Eighteen Points in up to Two Years .... Sixty days.
- Nineteen to Twenty-one Points in up to Two Years .... Ninety days.
- Twenty-two to Twenty-four Points in up to Two Years .... 120 days.
- Twenty-five to Twenty-seven Points in up to Two Years .... 150 days.
- More than Twenty-eight Points in up to Two Years .... 180 days.
- Fifteen to Eighteen Points in More than Two Years .... Thirty days.
- Nineteen to Twenty-two Points in More than Two Years .... Sixty days.
- Twenty-three to Twenty-six Points in More than Two Years .... Ninety days.
- Twenty-seven to Thirty Points in More than Two Years .... 120 days.
- Thirty-one to Thirty-five Points in More than Two Years .... 150 days.

Thirty-six Points in More than Two Years.. 180 days.

Other possible reasons for suspensions:
- Failure to appear in court or to pay fines
- Failure to pay surcharges
- Driving with a suspended license
- Physical or mental disqualification
- Reckless driving
- Vehicle abandonment on a public highway
- Fault in a fatal accident

Note: The MVC does not provide a conditional or special work license. If a license is suspended, the driver cannot drive for any reason until the license is restored.

The **Probationary Driver Program (PDP)** program is mandated for new (probationary) drivers who are convicted of two or more moving violations totaling four or more points in their first two years of driving. A driver who does not successfully complete the 4-hour program (that provides up to a three-point reduction on the driver's record) or does not pay the class fee will be suspended indefinitely. A driver who commits a violation within a year after finishing the class will receive a scheduled suspension; the amount of days depends on when the violation was committed: within 0-6 months will receive a 90- day scheduled suspension, 6-9 months will receive a 60-day scheduled suspension, and 9-12 months will receive a 45-day scheduled suspension.

Reinstatement Requirements
Driving License Suspension........ $100.00 fee, suspension term served, all compliance obligations satisfied.
Registration Suspension.............. $100.00 fee and compliance obligations satisfied.

Point System Overview
Points range from 2 to 8 points per violation. A record is reviewed every time points are added to it. If a driver accumulates 6 or more points within 3 years from the last posted violation, there is a $150 surcharge plus $25 for each additional point. Accumulation of 12 or more points accumulated in any period can result in a suspension. 3 points will be deducted from the point total for each year of violation and suspension-free driving. 3 points will be deducted from the point total if driver successfully completes a Driver Improvement Program. Also, 2 points will be deducted if the driver completes a MVC-approved Defensive Driving Program (option available once every 5 years).

License Plate Facts

Registration
Starting in 2010, NJ law requires new drivers aged 21 years old and younger to display identifying decals on the front and rear licenses plates of their vehicles.

Renewal
Renewal is annual. Online renewal is available at www.state.nj.us/mvc/About/mymvc_page.htm. Vehicles eligible for renewal by Web or by phone include passenger vehicles, pleasure boats, trailers under 55,000 lbs and motorcycles. All others must renew at an MVC agency.

New Residents
Non-residents must register vehicles within sixty days of establishing residency. The "touring privileges" law is no longer valid.

Inspections and Emissions Testing
New Jersey operates a bi-annual car and truck safety inspection for all gasoline-powered cars, motorcycles and trucks. The inspection cycle for new vehicles is four years. All New Jersey registered diesel-powered motor vehicles over 18,000 GVWR (heavy duty diesel vehicles) are required to be tested annually for smoke emissions.

Plate Descriptions
Typical Plate Patterns
    Passenger—Current Issued Plates............LLNNNL
    Passenger—Old ....LLLNNN or NNNLLL or LLLNNL, some 7 character plates as LLLNNNN
    Light Trucks and Commercial Vehicles.. 6 digits
County Codes.............................The county of issuance is not designated on the plate.
Plates and Stickers in Force ....Two plates, one decal (MO & YR) found on the windshield.
Plates Remain with Car when Sold? ....No, they remain with seller.

Overview of Record Access

About Driving Records
Motor Vehicle Commission, Driver History Abstract Unit, PO 142, Trenton 08666, 609-984-7771 or 609-292-0698. The fee for a driver history record is $15.00 per look-up for either a certified complete record or certified five-year record. Requests must be submitted on Form ISM/DO-21. Established accounts pay $12.00 when record is obtained electronically. For the driver's license application information, the fee is also $15.00 per record and use of Form ISM/DO-11 is required.

Request Methods – Mail, Walk-in, Online, Status Check.

What You Should Know – Records are available for 5 years for the public, 10 years if a CDL driver; complete history for attorneys. The MVC offers the Customer Abstract Information Retrieval (CAIR) program for online access, visit www.state.nj.us/mvc/Licenses/CustomerAbstract.htm. The system is meant for permissible users. Requesters submitting on Form DO-21 (Driver history Abstract Request) will be provided records with personal information.

Special Access Programs Available – At www.state.nj.us/mvc/Licenses/driver_history_page.htm New Jersey drivers may order their own record. A user ID number must be obtained first.

About Accident Reports
There are a variety of sources for accident reports, depending on who investigated the accident.

If the accident was investigated by the New Jersey State Police, then contact their Criminal Justice Records Bureau at PO Box 7068, West Trenton 08628-0068, 609-882-2000, ext. 2382. Typical turnaround time is up to 3 weeks. No counter service is offered. New records are ready for inquiry in 2 to 3 weeks. Records are maintained for past 6 years. The drivers' names, date, and location of the incident is required. A report is available from 1991 at a cost of $10.00 if 1-5 pages, $16.00 if 6 or more pages. Photographs are $5.00 each for 1-10 photos, additional photos are $3.00 each. Typical turnaround time is three weeks.

If investigated by local police, contact either the local department (costs will vary) or the MVC Abstract Unit at PO Box 142, Trenton, NJ 08666-0142. The fee is $10.00.

If the accident occurred on a toll-road, contact the following: New Jersey Turnpike Authority at 732-442-8600 ext 2908; Garden State Parkway at 732-442-8600 ext.2419; Atlantic City Expressway at 609-965-7200, ext. 108.

About Vehicle Records
There are two addresses of importance. For vehicle (and vessel) registration, *use Motor Vehicle Services, Attn: Certified Information, PO Box 146, Trenton, NJ 08666, 609-292-6500 or in-state at 888-486-3339.* For vehicle (and vessel) ownership, use *Motor Vehicle Commission, Special Titles, PO Box 017, Trenton, NJ 08666-0017.* Motor Vehicle Services maintains registration, title, and lien information on all vehicles including mobile homes, and boats. Also, the MVC issues motorboat and Jet Ski licenses for use on fresh, non-tidal waters or lakes, creeks or rivers not affected by tidal conditions. SSNs and medical information are not released. The fee for a record request is $15.00 unless processed online then fee is $12.00.

Request Methods – Mail, Walk-in, Online.

What You Should Know – There are state forms required if the requester is not an ongoing account. Requests must be submitted on Form ISM/DO-11A for registration requests, Form DO-22A for title requests, and Form DO-22 for lien searches. Forms are found at www.state.nj.us/mvc/About/Forms.htm.

Special Access Programs Available – Limited online access is available for insurance companies, bus and truck companies, highway/parking authorities, and approved vendors. The fee is $12.00 per request for registration records and $8.00 per request for an ownership history. An application must be submitted.

About Watercraft Records
The same forms and fees for access to vehicle records apply to vessels. Mail requests may take as long as 3 months to process. Boats greater than 12 feet in length regardless of propulsion means must be titled and registered at a MVC Agency. (**Exceptions:** ship's lifeboat, canoe, kayak, inflatable, surfboard, rowing scull, racing shell, tender/dinghy used for direct transportation between a vessel and shore for no other purposes.)

New Mexico

Administration	Important Telephone and Web Contacts
Michael Sandoval, MVD Director Alicia Ortiz, Deputy Director Motor Vehicle Division PO Box 1028 Santa Fe 87504-1028 505-827-2296 www.mvd.newmexico.gov/	Integrated Voice Response System ....888-683-4636 This system connects caller to specific departments. Commercial Driver License........................505-476-3093 Heavy Vehicle Registration IRP Unit..........505-827-0392 State Department of Insurance ....505-827-4601 State Police...505-827-9300 General email questions to GGarcia@state.nm.us The **NM Motor Vehicle Code (Chapter 66**) and other NM statutes can be found online at: www.conwaygreene.com/nmsu/lpext.dll?f=templates&fn=main-h.htm&2.0 Regulations can be found in **Title 18** in the **NM Administrative Code** at: www.nmcpr.state.nm.us/nmac/

Driver License Facts

License Format
Nine numbers. New Mexico reports there is no code or sequential arrangement determining the numbers in the license.

Document Appearance
In the Spring of 2008, New Mexico began issuing a new license design with new security features. Both document types are described below. The older cards have a yellow bar across the top with the words New Mexico inside.

Current Document
- **Security Characteristics** — A Guilloche security design is present in several locations on the face of the card. There is micro-print across the bottom of the card. The card has a Zia design laser perforation, which can be seen with the naked eye by holding the card up to the light or shining a light through the card from behind. The photo on left side with a ghost photo on the bottom right. There are 1-D and 2-D bar codes on the magnetic strip. The card also has UV features on the front pattern.
- **Minor Age Driver Locator** — In a vertical format. The photo is positioned in the bottom left. Across the top or under the top bar (older license) is text explaining the type of license issued.
- **CDL Indicator** — "Commercial Driver License" is printed in red lettering on top of license.

Older Document
- **Security Characteristics** — There is a slight trim around the edge in a dark color and is a combination of three technologies; a digital image that is stored as part of the driving record; a digital signature that is also captured and stored; and a magnetic stripe that encodes the printed information on the license. The Photo is found at the bottom left.
- **Minor Age Driver Locator** — In a vertical format. The photo is positioned in the bottom left. Across the top or under the top bar (older license) is text explaining the type of license issued.
- **CDL Indicator** — "Commercial Driver License" is printed in red lettering on top of license.

Issue and Renewal
First-time driver's license applicants, out-of-state driver's license applicants, renewals, replacements and ID card applicants are issued a temporary extension while their regular license is being processed and mailed. Also, all first-time New Mexico licensees age 18 to 24 are required to take the "None for the Road" self-study DWI awareness class. Written tests are required for all applicants who are applying for a first time driver's license or for those whose licenses that have been expired for one year or more. Road tests are required for first time applicants or those with licenses expired over 5 years.

Age Requirements
A Graduated Driver License System affects all drivers under 18 until they meet the requirements for an unrestricted license. Requirements vary by age and stage, as stated below:

- Stage 1 Instructional Permit, also known as a Learners Permit - 15; must be accompanied by licensed driver (while enrolled in approved driver education course), must hold 6 months and have 50 hours of supervised driving, 10 of which at night.
- Stage 2 Provisional License - Fifteen and six months; successful completion Stage 1; prohibited driving from midnight to 5 a.m.; no more than 1 passenger younger than 21 except family members.
- Stage 3 Unrestricted Drivers License - 16 and 6 months; successful completion Stage 2; under 18 must have completed driver education.

Note: All first-time licensees in New Mexico who are 18 to 24 years of age are required to take the *None for the Road* awareness class.

Renewal
Renewal is either four years or eight years after birth month (choice is based on driver's preference). Renewal is not available online. CDL drivers who have a HAZMAT Endorsement may only receive a four-year renewal. The driver keeps same number when renewing.

Elderly-Related Restrictions
At age seventy-five, the license must be renewed annually (with no fee).

Residency
Once a motor vehicle driver establishes residency in New Mexico the person is required to obtain a New Mexico Driver's License. A driver's license held by a person who is on active duty in the armed forces of the U.S. and is absent in this state, or is in this state only on leave status, remains valid beyond the expiration date of the license. This provision also applies to spouses of such military personnel.

License Classes
Commercial Classifications
- Class A Any combination of vehicles with a GCWR of 26,001 pounds or more—provided the GVWR of the vehicle(s) being towed is in excess of 10,000 pounds.
- Class B Any single vehicle with a GVWR of 26,001 or more pounds, or any such vehicle towing a vehicle not in excess of 10,000 pounds GVWR.
- Class C Any single vehicle less than 26,001 pounds GVWR, or any such vehicles towing a vehicle not in excess of 10,000 pounds GVWR. Applies only to vehicles placarded for hazardous materials or designed to transport sixteen or more passengers (including driver)..

Non-Commercial Classifications
- Class D Single vehicles weighing less than 26,001 pounds, and to tow another vehicle provided that: (1) the towing vehicle is of equal or greater weight than the vehicle being towed; or (2) if the towing vehicle weighs less than the towed vehicle, the weight in the towed vehicle does not exceed the manufacturer's rated capacity and:
    a. the towing vehicle has either a class 4 or higher equalizing hitch or a fifth wheel;
    b. the vehicle being towed is a trailer; or
    c. the vehicle combination properly displays slow-moving insignia and moves at speeds of 25 mph or less.
- Class M Authorizes licensee to drive a two- or three-wheeled motorcycle. This class of license is issued to drivers who drive only a motorcycle, and must have an endorsement of Z, Y or W to be valid.
- Class E (CDL-Exempt) Issued only to individuals who are exempt from the requirements of the New Mexico Commercial Driver's License Act, including: drivers of non-commercial recreational vehicles, farm and ranch vehicles, firefighting equipment; and military vehicles.

HAZMAT Endorsement Procedure
The state is in compliance with the Patriot Act. All applicants applying for a new or renewal or transfer HAZMAT Endorsement (HME) may obtain the application from www.mvd.newmexico.gov/, go to Commercial Drivers Section. The driver must also be fingerprinted. There are 19 locations in the state for the fingerprint process; call 505-827-1036 to find locations. The application fee with fingerprints is $125.00. The fingerprints and application information is sent to the Federal Transportation Security Administration (TSA). TSA performs the background checks and notifies the DMV whether the application is approved or denied. When completed and approved, the HME is valid for four years. For more information visit https://hazmat.dhs.gov/AIP/splash.do.

Safety and Enforcement Facts

Insurance and Financial Responsibility
Everyone who operates a motor vehicle in New Mexico must have a motor vehicle liability insurance policy. The Mandatory Financial Responsibility Act requires that proof of such insurance be carried in the vehicle at all times. Registered vehicles must have a motor vehicle liability insurance policy with minimum limits of $25,000/50,000/10,000 or evidence of financial responsibility in the amount of $60,000 cash deposit or surety bond deposited with the New Mexico State Treasurer's Office. The state does not have a no-fault insurance provision. Insurance information from insured vehicles is matched electronically between insurance companies and the Motor Vehicle Division to ensure insurance is current. Violation will result in suspension of vehicle registration. Only vehicles currently insured are eligible for registration and/or registration renewal.

Alcohol and Chemical Testing
New Mexico's illegal intoxication level is .08 % and above for persons 21 and older, .02 % for persons less than 21 years of age, and .04% for drivers of CMVs. Use of breath and blood test(s) is authorized. New Mexico has both an implied consent administrative revocation and a DWI criminal action provision.

Accident Reporting
The nearest law enforcement agency should be notified of accidents resulting in injury, death, or damage in excess of $500.00. Within five days, an accident report must be filed with the Department of Highways and Transportation, P.O. Box 1149, Santa Fe 87504. The form will be provided by the investigating officer.

Suspensions and Revocations
The New Mexico DMV is in compliance with the provisions of the Motor Carrier Safety Improvement Act (MCSIA). See the Appendix for more information about these mandatory CDL disqualification sanctions.

Alcohol or Drug Related:
Driving Under the Influence of Liquor/Drugs
- First Conviction .... One-year revocation.
- Second Conviction .... Two-year revocation.
- Third Conviction .... Three-year revocation.
- Fourth Conviction .... Lifetime revocation.

Illegal Blood Alcohol Content (21 and Over)
- First Administrative Revocation .... Six-month revocation.
- Second or Subsequent .... One-year revocation.

Illegal Blood Alcohol Content (under 21)
- First Administrative Revocation .... One-year revocation.
- Second or Subsequent .... One-year revocation.

Refusal to Submit to Chemical Test .... Administrative revocation.

Note: If a driver has been convicted of DWI before, or refused to take the breath test, the driver is not eligible for a limited license under any circumstances, including personal or family hardship.

Other Suspensions and Revocations of Note—
- Accumulation of Seven to Ten Points in a Twelve-Month Period .... Ninety-day Suspension.
- Accumulation of Twelve Points in a Twelve-Month Period .... One-year Suspension.
  (A judge may also recommend a longer suspension for accumulation of 7 to 10 points in a twelve month period.)
- Any Offense Committed in Another State, Which, If Committed in New Mexico,
  Would Result in Suspension or Revocation .... Period specified by New Mexico Statute.
- Delinquent with Regard to Child Support Obligations ....
  .... Suspension until judgment satisfied and reinstatement fee paid.
- Driving While License is Revoked .... Revocation extended one additional year.
- Failure to Appear in Court .... Indefinite suspension.
- Failure to Pay Penalty Assessed for Traffic Citation .... Suspension until terms of citation complied with.
- Failure to Pay Judgment Resulting From an Accident ....
  .... Suspension until judgment satisfied, proof of insurance, and reinstatement fee paid. (14 year time limit.)
- Manslaughter/Negligent Homicide .... One-year revocation.
- Perjury or Making a False Statement to Motor Vehicle Division .... One-year to Indefinite Suspension.
- Permitting Fraudulent or Unlawful Use of a Driver's License .... One-year suspension.

Reinstatement Requirements
Suspension ..... $25.00 fee; proof of financial responsibility if for unpaid liability in accident. If suspended for

points, must complete Driver Improvement Course.
Revocation ..... $100.00 fee.

Point System Overview
Points range from 2 to 8 points. The accumulation of 12 points in a 12 month period will result in a suspension. 7 to 10 points in a one- year period will result in a suspension if so recommended by a judge.

License Plate Facts

Registration Renewal
The Motor Vehicle Division's Integrated Voice Response (IVR) and Internet systems allow customers to renew vehicle registration on the Internet or by telephone with a credit card (MasterCard or VISA only). To access the MVD Integrated Voice Response system call 505-827-4636 or 888-683-4636, or visit www.mvd.newmexico.gov. Vehicles can be renewed for either one year or two years.

New Residents
New residents must register vehicles within thirty days of establishing residency.

Inspections and Emissions Testing
New Mexico has no statewide provisions for either an annual vehicle safety inspection or emissions test. However, residents of the Bernalillo County and others who commute into Bernalillo County 60 or more days per year are required to have their vehicles tested and to provide proof that the vehicles have passed an emissions inspection test. More information is available from the Vehicle Pollution Management Division at 505-247-2273.

Plate Descriptions
Since February, 1999, passenger car owners have had a choice between 2 different style of license plates.

Typical Plate Pattern .... Passenger and light truck plates are NNN LLL. Commercial vehicle plates are L NNNN.
County Codes .... No county codes exist.
Plates and Stickers in Force .... One plate, one decal (MO & YR).
Plate Remains with Car when Sold? .. No, it remains with seller.

Overview of Record Access

About Driving Records
Driver Services Bureau, PO Box 1028, Santa Fe 87504-1028, 888-683-4636, fax 505-827-2792. There is no fee for mail-in or over-the-counter requests. Personal information is not released except to specified groups or if subject gives notarized approval. The fee for online service is $4.95 per record.

Request Methods – Mail, Telephone, Walk-in, Online.

What You Should Know – Speeding violations of fifty-six to seventy-five mph in a fifty-five mph zone and sixty-six to seventy-five mph in a sixty-five mph zone appear on the "life" record, but may not be used for revocation/suspension or for insurance rating purposes. Accidents are not reported on the driving record.

Special Access Programs Available – The New Mexico DMV contracts with New Mexico Interactive to provide all electronic media requests of title, registration and lien searches, as well as driving records. Records are available to subscribers that meet federal and state standards. For more information call Mew Mexico Interactive at 877-660-3468 or visit the Online Services section at www.mvd.newmexico.gov.

About Accident Reports
Department of Public Safety, Attention: Records, PO Box 1628, Santa Fe 87504, 505-827-9182. When ordered by mail, the name, date, and city or county location are needed when ordering. The fee is $1.00 first page and $.25 for each additional copy. There is no charge for person directly involved. Turnaround time is about 2 weeks. It takes up to 15 days before new accident information is available. Records are available 20 years to present on computer and 25 to present if fatality involved. Arrest information is not released. Local accidents that occur within cities, such as Albuquerque, are handled by individual city police departments and record copies must be secured from those entities. Note the online access system was closed 07/08.

Vehicle Records
Vehicle Services Bureau, PO Box 1028, Santa Fe 87504-1028, 505-827-4636 or (888) 683-4636. There is no fee manually processed record requests for VIN, plates, registration or lien information, certified copies or histories from

microfilm. The online fee is $4.95 per record. The Motor Vehicle Division also maintains the record database for boat registrations; however, lien information on boats under 10 feet in length is filed with UCCs at the Secretary of State's office.

Request Methods – Mail, Walk-in, Online, Bulk.

What You Should Know – For the online search, the VIN or plate number must be submitted – a name search is not available.

Special Access Programs Available – The New Mexico DMV contracts with New Mexico Interactive to provide all electronic media requests of title, registration and lien searches, as well as driving records. Records are available to subscribers that meet federal and state standards. For more information call Mew Mexico Interactive at 877-660-3468 or visit the Online Services section at www.mvd.newmexico.gov.

About Watercraft Records

Records are available from the agency above. All motor or sail boats and jet skis over 10 ft must be titled and registered. Motor and sail boats under 10 ft must be registered. UCCs on boats are filed here and show on title searches; UCCs on jet skis are found at the Secretary of State's office.

New York

Administration	Important Telephone and Web Contacts

David J Swarts, Commissioner
Department of Motor Vehicles
6 ESP, Swan Street, Albany 12228
 	
www.nysdmv.com
 	
Administrative Codes, Rules and Regulations:
   www.dos.state.ny.us/info/nycrr.html
State Laws and Regulations:
   http://public.leginfo.state.ny.us/menugetf.cgi
	Certified Document Center..........................518-474-0710
	Suspensions & Revocations.........................518-474-0774
	Financial Responsibility 518-474-0700
	Request Driving Record 518-486-9786
	Commercial Driver License.........................518-473-9938
	State Department of Insurance
	   ... 518-474-6600, NY only 800-342-3736
	State Police...518-457-6811
	A list of Email Contacts is found at:
	   www.nysdmv.com/mailpage.htm

Driver License Facts

License Format
New York assigns randomly selected nine-digit numeric Client Identification Numbers to all driver licenses and non-driver ID cards.

Document Appearance
A current license format has been issued since 2005. It will take at least eight years for the new format to replace the old.

Current Format

Security Characteristics — A two-dimensional barcode is on the back of the document that verifies information contained on the front of the document. Prismatic or "rainbow" printing and duplex patterns within the design and fine line structures enhance the security fatuities. An "optical variable device" (OVID) is imbedded within the laminate to prevent forgery. The wavy line, a feature unique to New York State, appears to float above the surface of the license.

On September 16, 2008, NYS began issuing WHTI-Compliant Enhanced driver licenses (EDL) (includes Enhanced learner permits) and Enhanced non-driver photo ID cards (ENDID) to applicants who can prove U.S. citizenship and NYS residency. An EDL or ENDID can be used instead of a passport at U.S. land and sea border crossings between Canada, Mexico, Bermuda and the Caribbean.

Position of Photo — Left.

Minor Age Driver Locator — All documents issued to individuals under the age of 21 have "under 21" markings printed in red ink on the face of the document.

CDL Indicator — "Commercial Driver License" printed in brown above client ID. Expiration date printed in red. All other pertinent information is in black.

Color Indicators — Color coding of the title line located underneath "new york state" distinguishes the document type: driver license - blue; restricted use - purple; conditional - purple; learner permit - green; commercial - brown; identification card - gold.

Old Format

Security Characteristics — Digital Imaging is used. Signature and image are digitally stored. Light blue and green security image of the NYS Coat of Arms in background. The security CONFIRM laminate features the State Coat of Arms in a repetitive arrangement. Current license is made from "Teslin," a thick, durable material.

Position of Photo — Bottom left.

Minor Age Driver Locator — "Under 21" printed in red right of photo. Client ID, DOB, and expiration date printed in red.

CDL Indicator — "Commercial Driver License" in brown above driver name. Expiration date printed in red. All other pertinent information in black.

Issue and Renewal
Age Requirements
The minimum age for a Class A commercial driver license is 21. The minimum age for a Class B or C license is 18; however, drivers are limited to driving in NYS only and may not transport hazardous materials or operate a school bus until they reach age 21. The minimum age is 18 for an unrestricted (non-commercial) driver license, or 17 with a driver education certificate. Since September 1, 2003 a graduated licensing program is offered with three levels of permits for youthful drivers. Major changes we made to the program in February 2010. For example, a Limited Junior License was an intermediate step between the Learner Permit and a "full" Junior License, but this was eliminated 02/2010. A Junior Permit must be held for at least 6 months before a Junior or Senior license may be issued.. There are a myriad of restrictions to these levels, including regional restrictions in the New York City Boroughs and also Long Island. For details of these restrictions, visit www.nysdmv.com/license.htm#about.

Renewal
A renewal is on the birth date every 8 years for all license classes. Online renewal is available at www.nysdmv.com/licrenew/default.html is available except for learner permits, non-driver ID cards, conditional or restricted licenses, licenses with an ignition interlock restriction, and licenses that are valid without photo. An Eye Test Report (form MV-619) is required. The driver keeps the same license number when renewing. A valid NYS driver license is automatically extended for drivers on active military duty, the driver license does not expire and is extended during active service. Once notified of military status, the DMV sets an indicator on the license record and then allows the regular license to be renewed within 6 months of discharge.

Elderly-Related Restrictions
None are reported.

Residency
Non-resident's home-state license honored; must secure New York License within thirty days of establishing residency; out-of-state licensees under sixteen are not permitted to drive regardless of license type.

License Classes
Note: As of July 26, 2005, the DMV eliminated the Non-CDL Class C license. In addition, the gross vehicle weight rating (GVWR) and gross vehicle combination weight rating (GCWR) of vehicles that a driver can operate with a Class D license increased.

Commercial Classifications
- A Any vehicle or combination (such as tractor-trailer or truck trailer) with a GCWR of more than 26,000 pounds-provided the GVWR or GCWR of vehicle(s) being towed is more than 10,000 pounds. Minimum age is 21.
- B A single unit vehicle (such as a heavy single unit truck or bus) with a GVWR of more than 26,000 pounds. Class B may tow vehicles with a GVWR of 10,000 pounds or less or may tow a vehicle of more than 10,000 pounds providing the GCWR is not more than 26,000 pounds. Minimum age is 18. Drivers under age 21 are restricted to operation in NYS only and may not transport hazardous materials or operate a school bus.
- C A single unit vehicle (such as a truck or bus) with a GVWR of 26,000 pounds or less that transports fifteen or more passengers or transports passengers under Article 19-A of the "V and T" Law, or carries hazardous materials (Class C may tow vehicles with a GVWR of 10,000 pounds or less or may tow a vehicle of more than 10,000 pounds providing the GCWR is not more than 26,000 pounds). Minimum age is 18. Drivers under age 21 are restricted to operation in NYS only and may not transport hazardous materials or operate a school bus.

Non-Commercial Classifications
- C This class is in the process of being eliminated and is only issued when a Farm (F)(G) and/or Tow Truck (W) endorsement is applied for. Valid for operation of a single-unit vehicle (such as medium trucks, farm vehicles and some heavy recreational vehicles) with a GVWR of 26,000 pounds or less that does not require a CDL endorsement. Also valid for the operation of a passenger vehicle, Class B or Class C Limited Use Motorcycle, or Limited Use Automobile.
- D A single unit vehicle (such as passenger cars and light trucks with a GVWR of 26,000 pounds or less. May tow a vehicle with a GVWR 10,000 pounds or less or may tow a vehicle of more than 10,000 pounds providing the GCWR is not more than 26,000 pounds. Limited-use automobiles; Class B and/or C limited use motorcycles; Recreational vehicles with a GVWR of 26,000 pounds or less. Minimum age 18 or 17 with Driver Education.
- DJ Valid for operation of a single-unit vehicle with a GVWR of 10,000 pounds or less, a passenger vehicle, Class B or Class C Limited Use Motorcycle, or Limited Use Automobile. Issued only to drivers younger than 18 years of age; automatically becomes a Class D license on the individual's 18th birthday.
- E GVWR of 26,000 pounds or less used to transport fourteen or less passengers for hire, and does not fall under

Article 19-A of the "V and T" Law. May tow a vehicle with a GVWR 10,000 pounds or less or may tow a vehicle of more than 10,000 pounds providing the GCWR is not more than 26,000 pounds. Recreational vehicles with a GVWR of 26,000 pounds or less. Minimum age is 18.

- M   Motorcycle. Minimum age is 18, or 17 with Driver Education. Allows operation of motorcycles and limited use motorcycles (mopeds).
- MJ   Junior motorcycle (minimum age is 16). Allows operation of motorcycles and limited use motorcycles (mopeds). Subject to Junior License Restrictions.

HAZMAT Endorsement Procedure

The state is in compliance with the Patriot Act, and also with a state law requiring a criminal history review for HazMat endorsement (HME) applicants. All applicants applying for a new HME, or to renew or transfer a HME must first pass the HME test, and submit an application (HAZ-44) to any Motor Vehicles office. Applications are available at all Motor Vehicles offices. The driver must also be fingerprinted. In New York City, there are five DMV offices where an applicant can be fingerprinted. Outside of New York City, there are 35 locations where the New York State Police will fingerprint HME applicants. The cost of the background process is $140.75 plus $5.00 for the written test.

The fingerprints and application information are sent to the Federal Transportation Security Administration (TSA) and to the New York State Division of Criminal Justice Services so background checks can be conducted; the results are returned to DMV. DMV will notify applicants who are disqualified, based on either the state criminal history review or the TSA background check. When an applicant is approved and the HME is issued, the HME is valid for five years. Any questions should be directed to the HazMat Unit either by email to HazMatUnit@dmv.state.ny.us, or by calling 518-408-2997. Information can be found at www.nysdmv.com/cdl.htm#hazmat.

Safety and Enforcement Facts

Insurance and Financial Responsibility

New York has a provision for compulsory insurance; proof of insurance must be in the vehicle at all times. Insurance companies must file notices electronic notice of new insurance, cancellation and reinstatement. Minimum financial responsibility limits are $50,000/100,000 for death, $25,000/50,000 for bodily injury, and $10,000 for property damage. The state has no-fault insurance provision. Proof is required at registration, renewal of most-for-hire registrations and late renewal, when an accident occurs, and upon certain violations. All paper proof of insurance submitted must be electronically verified by the insurer.

Alcohol and Chemical Testing

NY has varying provisions for illegal intoxication levels. A level of .08 percent and above (Driving While Intoxicated) is a misdemeanor; while a level .05 to .07 (Driving While Ability Impaired), is a traffic infraction. For commercial drivers, blood alcohol content levels .04 or above will result in revocation of commercial driving privileges. For drivers under 21, BAC levels of .02 or above will result in suspension of driving privileges. NY has provisions for implied consent violations and for administrative suspensions. Urine, blood, and breath testing are authorized.

Accident Reporting

Motorists must report within 10 days any accident occurring in NY State that involves a fatality, personal injury, or damage over $1,000 to property of any one person. Motorist reports on Accident Report Form MV-104 should be sent to: Accident Records Bureau, P.O. Box 2925, 6 Empire State Plaza Albany NY 12220-0925. Police agencies are required to file reports, forthwith for any accident involving fatalities, property damage over $1,000 or personal injuries. If a fatality occurred, they must file, in addition to the Police Accident Report (MV-104A), a Police Report for Fatal Motor Vehicle Accidents (MV-104D). A Truck and Bus Supplement Police Accident Report (MV-104S) is required to be submitted for each qualified commercial vehicle involved in the accident. Currently, a police officer may indicate whether they feel there was property damage to any one vehicle that met the reporting criteria. Forms may be downloaded from www.nysdmv.com/forms.htm.

Suspensions and Revocations - Non-CDL

Penalties for Alcohol-related and Drug-Related Violations

Violation (1)	Mandatory Driver License Action (3)
Aggravated Driving While Intoxicated (A-DWI)	Revoked for at least one year
Second A-DWI in 10 years (E felony)(1)	Revoked for at least 18-months (5)
Third A-DWI in 10 years (D felony)(1)	Revoked for at least 18-months (4,5)
Driving While Intoxicated (DWI) or Driving While Impaired by a Drug (DWAI-Drug)	DWI-Revoked for at least six months, DWAI-Drugs - Suspended for at least six months
Second DWI/DWAI-Drug violation in 10 years (E felony)(1)	Revoked for at least one year

Violation (1)	Mandatory Driver License Action (3)
Third DWI/DWAI-Drug violation in 10 years (D felony)(1)	Revoked for at least one year (4)
Driving While Ability Impaired by a Combination of Alcohol/Drugs (DWAI-Combination)	Revoked for at least six months
Second DWAI/Combination in 10 years (E felony)(1)	Revoked for at least one year/18 months (5)
Third DWAI/Combination in 10 years (D felony)(1)	Revoked for at least one year/18 months (4,5)
Driving While Ability Impaired by Alcohol (DWAI)	Suspended for 90 days
Second DWAI violation in 5 years	Revoked for at least six months
Zero Tolerance Law	Suspended for six months
Second Zero Tolerance Law	Revoked for one year or until age 21
Chemical Test Refusal	Revoked for at least one year, 18 months for commercial drivers.
Chemical Test Refusal within five years of a previous DWI-related charge/Chemical Test Refusal	Revoked for at least 18 months, one-year or until age 21 for drivers under age 21, permanent CDL revocation for commercial drivers.
Chemical Test Refusal - Zero Tolerance Law	Revoked for at least one year.
Chemical Test Refusal - Second or subsequent Zero Tolerance Law	Revoked for at least one year.
Driving Under the Influence - (Out-of-State)	Suspended for 6 months. If less than 21 years of age, revoked at least one year.
Driving Under the Influence - (Out-of State) with any previous alcohol-drug violation	Suspended for 6 months. If less than 21 years of age, revoked at least one year or until age 21 (longest term).

1. Greater penalties can also apply for multiple alcohol or drug violations within a 10-year period.
2. Surcharges are added to misdemeanors ($160) and felonies ($270).
3. The driver license penalties for drivers under the age of 21, and for drivers of commercial motor vehicles and other professional drivers, are different.
4. Three or more alcohol or drug-related convictions or refusals within 10 years can result in **permanent revocation**, with a waiver request permitted after at least 5 years.
5. A driver with an Aggravated DWI violation conviction within the prior 10 years will receive a minimum 18-month revocation if convicted of DWI, DWAI/Drugs or DWAI/Combination. Also a driver with a prior DWI, Aggravated DWI, DWAI/Drugs or DWAI/Combination with the prior 10 years will receive a minimum 18-month revocation.

Other Suspensions/Revocations of Note

Operating an Uninsured Vehicle/Uninsured Accident	One-year revocation.
Operating an Uninsured Vehicle	Registration/driver's license suspension period equals length of insurance lapse.
Three Speeding and/or Traffic Misdemeanors Within Eighteen Months	Six-month revocation.
Zero Tolerance Chemical Test Refusal	One-year revocation.

Notes: Generally, persons convicted of DWI or DWAI for the first time may be eligible for a conditional license if they participate in the Drinking Driver Program. Three or more major offenses within eight years may result in a permanent revocation.

Suspensions and Revocations of CDLs and Drivers of Commercial Vehicles

The state of New York is in compliance with the federally mandated disqualifications on CDLs per MCSIA. Please review the list of these convictions and disqualifications in the Appendix for Major Offenses, Serious Offenses, Railroad Grade Crossing Offenses and Out-Of-Service Violations.

Reinstatement Requirements

Suspension	$25 to $100 suspension termination fee.
Revocation	Re-application fee of either $50 or $100; sanction time served; and payment of civil penalty fees of between $100 and $750 may apply. If out-of-state resident, $25 reinstatement fee; sanction time served, and payment of civil penalties between $100 and $750 may apply.
Suspension For Insurance Lapse	Registration must be surrendered for the length of lapse. If the lapse is 90 days or less, a civil penalty may be paid in lieu of surrender. Driver's license is suspended if the lapse is over 90 days. Suspension period is equal to the lapse and a $25 suspension termination fee must be paid..

Note: For a **Revocation for Uninsured Operation/Accident**, there is a required application for new license plus license application fees, FS-15 Affirmation form, $750 civil penalty.

Point System Overview
Points range from 2 to 11 points. The accumulation of 11 points in an 18-month time period can result in a suspension. The accumulation of 6 or more points in an 18-month time period, where the violations occurred on or after November 18, 2004, will result in an assessment payable to the DMV. Points are not added to a NY driver record for an out-of-state traffic violation, except for traffic violations occurring in Ontario or Quebec.

License Plate Facts

Registration Renewal
Renewal is available online at www.nysdmv.com or by phone at 518-402-4838.

New Residents
New residents must register vehicles within thirty days of establishing residency.

Inspections and Emissions Testing
New York requires annual safety and emissions inspections and has the authority to require an additional inspection after involvement in an accident. The emissions inspection a vehicle requires is based on the model year, fuel, weight, and the county where the vehicle is registered.
- Statewide, 1996 and newer vehicles that are registered at more than 8500 lbs or less receive an OBD II test, which is a test of the vehicles on-board diagnostic computer system.
- In the New York Metropolitan Area (NYMA), which includes the 5 boroughs of NYC, Nassau, Suffolk, Rockland and Westchester counties, vehicles 1995 or older and vehicles registered at more than 8500 lbs. receive a High Enhanced tailpipe test (Dynamometer test if 8500 lbs or less or an idle test if more than 8500 lbs.) Both the Dynamometer and Idle tests include a pressure test of the gas cap.
- Outside the NYMA (upstate), non-OBD II vehicles receive a Low Enhanced inspection which is a visual check of the emissions control devices, including a visual check of the gas cap. This visual check is also required on High Enhanced and OBD II inspections.
- In the NYMA, diesel powered vehicles registered at more than 8500 lbs. receive a Diesel Emissions Inspection. Diesel vehicles 8500 lbs or less and all diesel vehicles registered outside the NYMA are exempt from emissions testing.

Vehicles registered in New York State must also receive a safety inspection. Vehicles less than 2 model years old, or more than 25 model years old, electric-powered, motorcycles, vehicles registered as Historical, and diesel powered vehicles noted above are exempt from emissions testing. Certain vehicles, such as Special Purpose Commercial, Farm vehicles, and some Limited Use vehicles are exempt from any inspection requirement.

Plate Descriptions

Typical Plate Patterns	The new plates have 7 characters. Passenger plates are LLL-NNNN; commercial plates are NNNNN-LL; other classes are assigned plates with varying configurations. Vehicle owners had the option to keep the number that was on their previous plate. If that happened, the new Empire plate has whatever combination the customer had before plate re-issuance up to 6 characters on a passenger plate or 6 to 7 characters on a commercial plate (as listed above).
County Codes	The plates do not show where vehicle was registered.
Plates and Stickers in Force	Two plates, with one decal (MO & YR) on front windshield for regular passenger vehicles and for most commercial vehicles. But many other vehicles have only one plate and a plate sticker that is valid for one year.
Plates Remain with Car when Sold?	No, they remain with registrant to be transferred to another vehicle or must be surrendered to the DMV.

Overview of Record Access

About Driving Records
MV-15 Processing, NYS Department of Motor Vehicles, 6 Empire State Plaza, Albany NY 12228. Current fees are: $10.00 per driving record search for mail-in, over-the-counter, and website requests; $15.00 for telephone requests; and $7.00 for searches performed using the Dial-In Display (Dial-In service) or License Event Notification Service (LENS). The driver license (client identification) number or name and date of birth are required for all searches. Search fees apply whether or not a record is found.

Request Methods – Mail, Walk-in, Telephone (by person of record), Online (by person of record), Dial-in Display.

What You Should Know – Most equipment violations (except inadequate brakes) and most non-moving violations are not reported on the driving record. For those record requesters that do not have consent or qualify, a masked abstract is issued that does not show the personal information of the driver. A masked abstract is available by mail or at the DMV Customer Service Counter of the Central Office in Albany. Form MV-15 is required to obtain certified records by mail order. DMV offers a form, MV-15GC (general consent form) on which a requester may document the motorist's consent before obtaining a record. To download either of these forms, go to www.nysdmv.com and click on "Forms."

Special Access Programs Available – The License Event Notification Service (LENS) enables an organization to file with DMV a roster of employees or volunteers who drive on the organization's behalf. The LENS program will notify the organization if a new event posts to a registered driver's record. For more information, visit www.nysdmv.com/LENS/default.html, or call the Help Line at 518-486-4480, or email LENS@dmv.state.ny.us.

AboutAccident Reports

Copies of accident reports may be requested by submitting Form MV-198C at www.nysdmv.com/forms/mv198c.pdf. MV-198C Processing, PO Box 2086, Albany 12228-2086. The Agency prefers not to disclose its phone number. Record retrieval is subject to DPPA. For mail requests, there is a $10.00 search fee plus an additional $15.00 fee for each report produced per accident. In-person searching is not permitted. In general, requests take 2-3 weeks to process. Online access is also available to eligible requesters. There is a $7.00 search fee and a $15.00 report fee. Available records go back 4 years. Reports can be viewed and printed. Visit www.nysdmv.com/AIS/default.html

About Vehicle Records

The DMV maintains registration records on all vehicles. the DMV maintains lien records on all titled vehicles including boats and manufactured homes. There are two abstracts available; the Vehicle Title Record and the Registration Plate Record. The Title Record reports lienholders and odometer reading. The Registration Plate record reports all vehicles registered using that plate number and any events that affect the status (such as lapse in insurance coverage). The current fee is $10.00 per search for mail-in and over-the-counter requests, $15.00 for telephone requests, and $7.00 for searches performed using the Dial-In Display (Dial-In service.) The plate number or the registrant's name and date of birth are required for all registration searches, and the Vehicle Identification Number (VIN) is required for all title searches. Search fees apply whether or not a record is found. Requesters must complete form MV-15, attach personal identification and include the applicable fee.

Request Methods – Mail, Walk-in, Telephone (by person of record), Online, Dial-in Display, Lien/Title Status, Insurance Status, Bulk.

Special Access Programs Available – Status Check displays the date the title was issued by the DMV, number of liens (if any), and the lien holder. No personal information is displayed. You must enter the VIN, vehicle model year, and vehicle make. For more information, go to www.nysdmv/titlestat/default.html.

About Watercraft Records

The law requires any boat that is powered by a motor and operated on public waterways in New York to be registered and titled. The DMV issues titles for model year 1987 and for newer boats that are at least 14 feet long and are registered in NYS. This includes homemade boats manufactured on or after August 1, 1986 if a model year was not designated. Lien information is included on some registrations. Same fees and turnaround times for vehicle record requests apply.

North Carolina

Administration	Important Telephone and Web Contacts
Michael D. Robertson, Commissioner Joseph R. John, Deputy Commissioner Division of Motor Vehicles 3101 Mail Service Center, Raleigh 27699-3101 www.ncdot.gov/DMV/	Driver Licensing..919-715-7000 SR-22 & Financial Security.......................919-715-7000 Traffic Records Section.............................919-861-3062 Safety Responsibility..................................919-715-7000 Commercial Driver License.......................919-715-7000 Vehicle Information....................................919-715-7000 IRP Unit ....919-861-3720 State Department of Insurance ....919-807-6750 Highway Patrol..919-733-7952 General Email List www.ncdot.org/dmv/contact/

Driver License Facts

License Format
One to twelve numbers. Although DMV indicates there is no code or sequential arrangement which determines the digits on the license number, the DMV indicates most new numbers start with four zeros, such as "00008..."

Document Appearance
The creation of the license document uses a computerized process called digital imaging.

Security Characteristics — Holographic overlay on the front and bar code on the rear. Effective December 2006, a holographic security patch is added to newly issued North Carolina driver licenses. However, this patch was removed effective October 21, 2008 This security element is a foil-based holographic patch on the back of the license which carries multiple layers of design features both visible and invisible to the human eye, including a variety of 3-D fluorescent images, codes, numbers and other items.

Position of Photo — Bottom left corner and ghost image on bottom right corner.

Minor Age Driver Locator — As of October, 2008, the DMV now issues a vertical license for drivers under the age of 21. The license includes color-coded bars that highlight the driver's 18th and 21st birthdays. Drivers between the ages of 15 and 18 now receive licenses with two color bars, red and yellow, next to their photos listing the dates they turn 18 and 21. Drivers between the ages of 18 and 21 receive licenses with one red color bar listing the date they turn 21. Previously, if under 18, the picture is framed in red as is border; if age 18, 19 & 20, picture framed in yellow as is the border; if age is 21 & over, picture is framed in green as is the border.

CDL Indicator — DMV logo is printed in amber and license will indicate Commercial Driver License Number in amber.

Issue and Renewal

Age Requirements
The minimum age for Class A and B is 18, but driver would not be eligible for the Hazardous Material Endorsement and will be restricted to drive inside North Carolina only (Intrastate Restriction 4) until age 21. Minimum age for Class C is 16.

Graduated License Process is described below - all Levels require a driving eligibility certificate or a high school diploma or its equivalent.

Level I   **Limited Learner's Permit**: Must be at least 15 and completed driver education; always accompanied by supervising driver; first 6 months can only drive between 5am and 9pm; after 6 months can drive anytime with supervising driver; everyone in car must wear seatbelt or be in child restraint system; mobile telephone restriction.

Level II   **Limited Provisional License**: Must have had Level I at least 12 months with no convictions in last 6 months; pass road test; drive unsupervised from 5am to 9pm; drive anytime to and from work or with supervising driver; drive to or from an activity of a volunteer fire department, volunteer rescue squad or volunteer emergency medical service, if the driver is a member of the organization; passenger limitation restriction; everyone in car must wear seatbelt or be in child restraint system; mobile telephone restriction.

Level III   *Full Provisional License:* Must have had Level II at least 6 months with no convictions in last 6 months; mobile telephone restriction if under 18.

Note: One must be age 16 or older to operate a moped on North Carolina highways or public vehicular areas. A driving license is not required, and the moped does not have to be registered, inspected or covered by liability insurance..

Renewal
Renewal is the birth date of eight year for those 18 through 53 years old; birthdate of the fifth year for those 54 year old and older. The driver keeps same number when renewing. As of July 1, 2008, the Division implemented a central issuance of driver licenses instead of an over-the-counter issuance program. At renewal or after a new driver completes a test, the driver receives a Temporary Driving Certificate valid for 20 days. One may keep the older license to use for photo identification until the new one arrives by mail. Renewal is not available online. Military personnel may renew by mail (write to address above C/O Temporary DL Unit) every other renewal period.

Elderly-Related Restrictions
None reported other than the five-year renewal period described above for drivers 54 years old and older.

Residency
New residents must secure a North Carolina license within 60 days of establishing residency or within 30 days if transferring a commercial license. If age sixteen or older, non-resident's home state or home country license honored.

License Classes
A **Commercial Driver License (CDL)** is required for most Class A & B vehicles. Class C vehicles that transport hazardous materials requiring placarding or that are designed to carry sixteen or more persons also require a CDL.

A **Non-Commercial license** is known as a "Regular License" in this state. Each category uses the same Class A, B or C and each Regular License has the same requirements in force as long as the vehicle is exempt from CDL requirements (such as an RV trailer or farm equipment).

Commercial & Non-Commercial Classifications
Class A   Any combination of vehicles with a GVWR of 26,001 pounds or more, provided the GVWR of the vehicle(s) being towed is(are) in excess of 10,000 pounds. if the vehicle is exempt from CDL requirements—also required for combination vehicles less than 26,001 pounds if the vehicle being towed exceeds 10,000 pounds.

Class B   Any single vehicle with a GVWR of 26,001 pounds or more, and any such vehicle towing a vehicle not in excess of 10,000 pounds if the vehicle is exempt from CDL requirements.

Class C   Vehicles under 26,001 pounds that are exempt from CDL requirements, and not towing a vehicle over 10,000 pounds. Most drivers need only a Regular C License to operate their personal automobiles and small trucks.

Note: A person must have at least a Level III Class C license with a motorcycle endorsement or a motorcycle learner permit before he/she is entitled to operate a motorcycle on public roads

HAZMAT Endorsement Procedure
The state is in compliance with the Patriot Act. All applicants applying for a new or renewal or transfer HAZMAT Endorsement (HME) must first obtain the application from https://hazprints.tsa.dhs.gov/Public/ or by calling 877-429-7746. The driver must also be fingerprinted. EMSI is the state-designated entity to process fingerprints. There are five locations in the state that perform this service. Visit the web page listed above to find the address locations. The cost of the fingerprint process is $89.25. The fingerprints and application information is sent to the Federal Transportation Security Administration (TSA). TSA performs the background checks and notifies the DMV whether the application is approved or denied. When completed and approved, the HME is valid for five years.

Safety and Enforcement Facts

Insurance and Financial Responsibility
Insurance is compulsory. Minimum financial responsibility limits are $30,000/60,000/25,000. Per federal law, for CDLs the minimum liability limit is $750,000. Proof is required upon registration or renewal, when obtaining a driver's license, and when involved in an accident or "certain" violations. The state does not use SR-22 forms.

Alcohol and Chemical Testing
North Carolina's legal intoxication level is .08 percent and above, for CDL drivers or drivers of CMVs .04 percent, and if under 21 years old there is zero (.00) tolerance. Commercial drivers are also subject to sanctions if blood alcohol content level of .00 percent. Blood and breath testing are authorized. North Carolina has both an implied consent violation and a provision for an administrative suspension.

Crash Reporting
Crashes resulting in death, injury, or property damage of $1,000.00 or more must be reported immediately to the nearest law enforcement agency. If additional information is needed, it will be requested by the Division of Motor Vehicles. Written reports of crashes must be filed with the *DMV, Traffic Records Section, 1100 New Bern Avenue, Raleigh 27697*.

Suspensions and Revocations
The North Carolina DMV is in compliance with the provisions of the Motor Carrier Safety Improvement Act (MCSIA). See the Appendix for these CDL mandatory disqualifications.

Accumulation of 12 points within three years (Note: The accumulation of eight points within three years following the reinstatement of the license can result in a second suspension.)

First Offense	Sixty days.
Second Offense	Six months.
Third Offense	Twelve months.
Assault With a Motor Vehicle	One year.
Betting, Watching, or Allowing the Use of Your Vehicle for Racing	Three years.
Death by Vehicle	One year.

Driving Under the Influence of an Impairing Substance

First Offense	One year.
Second Offense	Four years.
Third Offense	Permanent.

- Failure to Stop When Involved in an Accident .... One year.
- Making False Application for License .... One year.
- Manslaughter .... One year.
- Manslaughter While Under the Influence .... Permanent.
- Pre-arranged Racing .... Three years.
- Refusal to Submit to Chemical/Breath Test .... One year.
- Second Conviction Speeding Violation Within Twelve Months .... Sixty days.
- Speeding in Excess of 55 MPH and at Least 15 MPH Over Legal Limit .... Thirty days.
- Speeding in Excess of 55 MPH and at Least 15 MPH Over the Legal Limit While Attempting to Avoid Arrest .... One year.
- Two Reckless Driving Convictions in Twelve Months .... One year.

Provisional Licensed Drivers
- Two Moving Violations in Twelve Months .... Thirty days.
- Three Moving Violations in Twelve Months .... Ninety days.
- Four Moving Violations in Twelve Months .... Sixth months.

Other Suspensions—
- A loss of license will occur if a student receives a suspension for more than 10 consecutive days or receives an assignment to an alternative educational setting due to disciplinary action for more than 10 consecutive days.
- Failure to appear or to pay fine

The DMV can also suspend a license for the following—
- Two convictions of speeding over 55 mph during the same year
- One conviction of speeding over 55 mph and one conviction of reckless driving within a year
- A conviction of willful racing with another motor vehicle, whether it is pre-arranged or unplanned
- A court ordered sentence or part of a sentence mandating that driver must not operate a motor vehicle for a specified time period
- A conviction for speeding over 75 mph
- Speeding conviction plus reckless driving conviction on the same occasion

CDL and Alcohol
Driver will lose CDL for one year for first offense, will lose for life for second offense. If the blood alcohol concentration is less than 0.04% but with have any detectable amount, the driver will be put out-of-service for 24 hours.

Reinstatement Requirements
Suspension or Revocation... $50.00 fee; $75.00, if alcohol-related.

Point System Overview
Drivers accumulating seven points may be assigned to a Driver Improvement Clinic. Upon satisfactory completion of the clinic, three points are deducted from the driving record. Accumulation of as many as twelve points within a three-year period may cause a license to be suspended. The accumulation of eight points within three years following the reinstatement of the license can result in a second suspension. When driving privilege is reinstated, all previous driver license points are canceled.

License Plate Facts

Registration Renewal
Renewal of registration is annual. Renewal is available online at www.ncdot.org/dmv/. Since 2006, North Carolina uses a staggered registration system for Apportioned Motor Carrier, Commercial Vehicles, Special Mobile, For-Hire, Transporters, Drive Away vehicles and Taxis. In the past, these vehicles were registered on an annual basis with all registrations expiring on December 31st of each year.

New Residents
Non-residents must register vehicles within 60 days (or longer, depending on reciprocity agreement with prior state of residence) or when gainful employment is accepted, which ever comes first. New residents must obtain a North Carolina Driver License prior to registering a vehicle in North Carolina.

Inspections and Emissions Testing
North Carolina requires an annual safety inspection. As of October 2008, the inspection must be completed successfully before new plates or renewal tags are issued. Since November 1, 2008, windshield inspection stickers are no longer issued when a vehicle is inspected. New residents can register a vehicle without getting an inspection, but the vehicle cannot be renewed until the inspection is passed. The Board Diagnostics (OBD II) emissions test is required in 48 counties: Alamance, Brunswick Buncombe, Burke, Cabarrus, Caldwell, Carteret, Catawba, Chatham, Cleveland, Craven, Cumberland, Davidson, Durham, Edgecombe, Forsyth, Franklin, Gaston, Granville, Guilford, Harnett, Haywood, Henderson, Iredell, Johnston, Lee, Lenoir, Lincoln, Mecklenburg, Moore, Nash, New Hanover, Onslow, Orange, Pitt, Randolph, Robeson, Rockingham, Rowan, Rutherford, Stanly, Stokes, Surry, Wake, Wayne, Wilkes, Wilson and Union.

Plate Descriptions
Typical Plate Patterns	Passenger and light truck plates are LLL-NNNN. Commercial vehicle plates are LL-NNNN.
County Codes	The state does not designate the county of registration on the plate.
Plates and Stickers in Force	One plate, two decals (MO) (YR).
Plate Remains with Car when Sold?	No, plate remains with seller.

Overview of Record Access

About Driving Records
Division of Motor Vehicles, Motor Vehicle Records Center, 3113 Mail Service Center, Raleigh, NC 27699-3113, 919-715-7000, fax 919-861-3919. The current fee is $8.00 for either the limited three-year (insurance) record or complete seven-year (employer) record. Add $3.00 for certification. The last fee increase was October 2005. The Division does not charge for "no record found" reports, except for those mailed in for processing. Complete the Driver Privacy Protection Act Form 1 (DL-DPPA-1), or use Driver Privacy Protection Act Form 2 (DL-DPPA-2) if driver wants to give someone else permission to receive record copy. Forms are downloadable.

Request Methods – Mail, Walk-in, Online Commercial, Online Public Web.

What You Should Know – The state reports only moving violation convictions on the driving record as well as driver control actions. A "Prayer for Judgment" citation means that the court reserves the right to pass judgment later. The driver is charged the cost of court, no decision is rendered, and no points are assigned (except for a third Prayer for Judgment citation within five years). The judge can finalize the citation later. All accidents are reported—regardless of fault—if there is personal injury or damage of $1,000 or more.

Special Access Programs Available – The Internet Driving Record Request service allows North Carolina citizens to purchase a North Carolina driving record online. Requesters must first apply for a PIN which is disclosed by email. Both certified and non-certified records are available, fees are the same $8.00 per record. Records may be viewed, buy certified records are returned by mail. Go to https://edmv-dr.dot.state.nc.us/DrivingRecords/DrivingRecords

About Crash Reports
Records are available on computer from 1986 to present, 1995 to present on microfiche, and 2000 forward on paper from the Division of Motor Vehicles, Traffic Records Section, 3105 Mail Service Center, Raleigh 27699-3105, 919-861-3098. Copies can be purchased for $5.00 per certified copy. There is no fee for non-certified copies. Information on minor drivers is not released. The requester should submit a request form (TR-67A) indicating at least one of the names of the drivers, the county of occurrence, approximate date, and the exception under which he/she qualifies to receive personal information in accordance with DPPA. Normal turnaround time is 5 days. For a copy of the form, call 919-861-3098 or visit www.ncdot.org/dmv/forms/crashreports/download/tr67a.pdf

About Vehicle Records
Registration/Correspondence Unit, 1100 New Bern Avenue Rm 100, Raleigh 27697-0001, 919-715-7000. The DMV maintains records for vehicles, mobile homes and boat trailers. The current fee for VIN, ownership, lien and registration records is $1.00, or $10.00 for a certified copy. There are over 8 million vehicles registered in North Carolina.

Request Methods – Mail, Walk-in, Phone, Bulk.

What You Should Know – Request Form MVR-605A is required for new requesters. The form can be downloaded at www.ncdot.org/dmv/forms/vehicleregistration/download/mvr605a.pdf Licensed private investigators must report their state PI license number on the form.

Special Access Programs Available – Subscribers who have been assigned a user code may request information by telephone.

About Watercraft Records
NC Wildlife & Resource Commission, Transaction Management, 1709 Mail Service Center, Raleigh 27699 (800) 628-3773, fax is 919-707-0293 http://ncwildlife.org. All motorized boats and all sail boats over 14 ft must be registered. Effective 01/07, titles are mandatory; previously this was optional. Paper records maintained from 2003, computerized index from 1970. Record search fee is $20.00 but can be higher if extensive research is required. All requests must be in writing. Search by name, hull ID or registration #. Turnaround time is 1-2 days. Although liens could previously be filed at the state with the UCC filings, most lenders filed liens here. Now all liens are filed here. Liens are shown on a Title Certificate.

North Dakota

Administration	Important Telephone and Web Contacts
Glenn Jackson, Director Driver's License and Traffic Safety Division 701-328-2600 Linda Sitz, Director Motor Vehicle Division 701-328-2725 608 East Boulevard Avenue Bismarck 58505-0700 www.dot.nd.gov/public/public.htm	Driver Licensing..701-328-4353 Suspensions..701-328-2604 Financial Responsibility & SR-22...............701-328-2604 Commercial Driver License........................701-328-2600 Vehicle Information......................................701-328-2725 State Department of Insurance ....701-328-2440 Highway Patrol..701-328-2455 Rules of the Road is found at www.dot.nd.gov/divisions/dlts/docs/rulesroad.pdf

Driver License Facts

License Format
An alpha numeric combination is used comprised of nine characters beginning with the first three letters of the last name (if last name is only two letters, an "X" is added). Until April 1, 2003, at the option of the driver either the Social Security Number or an assigned nine digit number starting with a "9" was used. Now, those drivers with the SSN or a nine-digit number on their license are given a new alpha-numeric number when the license is renewed.

Document Appearance
A new license document was introduced in 2006 and is replacing older documents upon renewal. Both old and new are reviewed below.

Current Document
The document is plastic non-laminated with a security overlay on front. A "blue map" with pink sky indicates a regular driver license, motorcycle permit, regular instruction permit, temporary permit, and a motorized bicycle permit.

Security Characteristics	Ghost image of the holder on the bottom of the card; state seal overlapping the portrait; transparent hologram with alternating images of a meadowlark bird and prairie rose flower.
Position of Photo	Larger image on left edge middle, smaller image lower right corner.
Minor Age Driver Locator	Vertical design on cards issued to persons under 21. The card has a red bar with the date that the person will turn 21 or a yellow bar for person under 18 that states their 18th birthday.
CDL Indicator	State map in green map with pink sky.

Older Document
The document is plastic non-laminated with a security overlay on front.

Security Characteristics	Contains security patch over DOB.
Position of Photo	Lower right, for 21 and older.
Minor Age Driver Locator	Drivers 18 to 20 years of age have image on left side with a red border, DOB printed in red. Drivers under 18 have image on left side with a yellow border and DOB printed in red.
CDL Indicator	CDL has a green header and "COMMERCIAL DRIVER LICENSE" is printed along top.

Issue and Renewal
Age Requirements
The minimum age is sixteen; fourteen (restricted) with completion of approved driver education course. A Learner's Permit is required.

Renewal
Driver license renewal is the birth month and day of fourth year. North Dakota photo identification cards issued after August 1, 2007 expire eight years from the date of issuance. The driver receives a new number (see above) when renewing. At present, renewal is not available online. Military licenses of personnel stationed out-of-state need not be renewed, but will only remain valid 30 days after discharge or return if expired.

Elderly-Related Restrictions
None indicated.

Residency
Non-resident's home-state license honored for 60 days (30 days if CDL) after establishing residency.

License Classes
Commercial Classifications
- Class A — Any vehicle or combination of vehicles, except Class M.
- Class B — Single vehicle, trailers 10,000 pounds or less, and Class C or D. Not valid for Class A or M.
- Class C — Single vehicle less than 26,001 pounds, trailers 10,000 pounds or less, must have endorsement "H" and/or "P"; all Class D vehicles. Not valid for Class A, B, or M.

Non-Commercial Classifications
- Class D — Single vehicle less than 26,001 pounds, trailers not over 10,000 pounds. Trucks towing trailers, semi-trailers or farm-trailers not over 16,000 pounds. Not valid for Class A, B, C, or M.
- Class M — Any two or three-wheeled motorcycle.

Note: To operate a motorized bicycle or scooter, one must be at least 14 years of age and must have one of the following: operators license (minimum Class D, no motorcycle endorsement required); temporary permit; instruction permit; or motorized bicycle operators permit. NDCC 39-06-14(7)

HAZMAT Endorsement Procedure
The state is in compliance with the Patriot Act. All applicants applying for a new or renewal or transfer HAZMAT Endorsement (HME) must first obtain the application from https://hazprints.tsa.dhs.gov/Public/ or by calling 877-429-7746. The driver must also be fingerprinted. EMSI is the state-designated entity to process fingerprints. There are eight locations in the state that perform this service. Visit the web page listed above to find the address locations. The cost of the fingerprint process is $89.25. The fingerprints and application information is sent to the Federal Transportation Security Administration (TSA). TSA performs the background checks and notifies the DMV whether the application is approved or denied. When completed and approved, the HME is valid for the term of the CDL. For more information, visit www.dot.nd.gov/divisions/dlts/dlhazardousmaterial.htm.

Safety and Enforcement Facts

Insurance and Financial Responsibility
Mandatory insurance requires financial responsibility minimum limits of $25,000/50,000/25,000. North Dakota also has no-fault insurance. Proof is required after judgments, DUIs, reportable accidents, and when an authorized law enforcement officer stops a motor vehicle for any statutory violation. Proof of insurance is also required at registration and renewal.

Alcohol and Chemical Testing
North Dakota's illegal intoxication level is .08 percent and above; for drivers under 21 the limit is .02 percent, for drivers of CMVs the limit is .04 percent. Urine, blood, saliva, and breath testing are authorized. North Dakota has both an implied consent violation and a provision for an administrative suspension. Operating a horse or bicycle under the influence is also considered illegal.

Accident Reporting
Any accident resulting in death, injury, or damage in excess of $1,000.00 must be reported to the nearest law enforcement agency. If insurance information is not available at the time of the accident, it should be sent to Driver License and Traffic Safety Division, 608 East Boulevard Avenue, Bismarck 58505. There are no special reporting requirements for commercial drivers.

Suspensions and Revocations
CDL Disqualifications: The state is in compliance with the federally mandated CDL disqualifications. See the Appendix for details.

Point Accumulation
- Twelve Points .... Seven-day suspension.
- Thirteen or More Points .... Seven-day suspension for each point over eleven.

Drivers under 18 accumulating six points	Cancellation.
DWI Conviction - First Offense in Five Years	91-day suspension.
If BAC .18 or Greater	180-day suspension.
DWI Conviction - Second Offense in Five Years	365-day suspension.
If BAC .18 or Greater	Two-year suspension.
DWI Conviction - Third or Subsequent Offense Within 5 Years OR Fourth or Subsequent Offense Within 7 Years	Two-year suspension.
BAC .18 or Greater	Three-year suspension.
Refusal to Submit to Chemical Test	
First Offense in Five Years	One-year revocation.
Second Offense in Five Years	Three-year revocation.
Third Offense in Five Years	Four-year revocation.
Railroad Crossing Violation by a Commercial Driver	
First Offense in Three Years	60-day suspension, CDL only.
Second Offense in Three Years	120-day suspension, CDL only.
Third Offense in Three Years	One-year suspension, CDL only.

Reinstatement Requirements

Suspension — $50.00 fee, $100.00 if alcohol-related; proof of financial responsibility; time lapse; alcohol evaluation and treatment after conviction.

Revocation — $50.00 fee, $100.00 if alcohol-related; proof of financial responsibility; time lapse; re-examination; alcohol evaluation and treatment after conviction; retesting of written and road.

Point System Overview

Points range from 1 to 24 points. As explained, if the number of points assigned to a violation is 2 or less, the violation and points is not available to the public. These points would be assessed as part of the record only for the purpose of point reduction or license suspension. A 7-day suspension can result from the accumulation of 12 or more points. Each additional point can add another 7 days. Point total can be reduced one point for every 3-month period of no point activity, and by 3 points if the driver completes an approved driver improvement course.

License Plate Facts

Registration Renewal
Online vehicle renewal is at Mvrenewal.nd.gov is available for registration renewals of existing vehicles. New vehicles, fleet vehicles, apportioned vehicles or trucks 55,000 pounds and greater may not be renewed online.

New Residents
New residents must register vehicles upon accepting employment or establishing residency; students displaying current home-state plates are exempt.

Inspections and Emissions Testing
North Dakota has provisions for neither statewide emission testing nor mandatory vehicle safety inspections.

Plate Descriptions

Typical Plate Patterns	Passenger and light truck plates are DAA001 through JBZ000, ND1 through ND9999, 1ND through 5000ND, 1A through 7000A. Commercial vehicle plates have no distinctions to those listed above.
County Codes	There is no coding depicting the county of issuance.
Plates and Stickers in Force	Two plates, one decal (MO & YR) on both plates. Decal shows assigned plate.
Plates Remain with Car when Sold?	Plates remain with the previous owner.

Overview of Record Access

About Driving Records
Driver License and Traffic Safety Division, 608 East Boulevard Avenue, Bismarck 58505-0780, 701-328-2603. The current fee is $3.00. The last fee increase was in July of 1989 and no increases are planned for the near future. Credit cards are accepted for payment. One may email questions via the home page at www.dot.nd.gov. Two types of records are available - a limited, public record and a complete record. The complete record is only available by written request.

Request Methods – Mail, Walk-in, Fax, Online, Status Check.

What You Should Know – Conviction information on two-point or less violations are only released to the driver and not other requesters including the insurance industry. Thus, the operator license records available to the general public will only show three-point and over violations and will not report accidents unless license is suspended.

Special Access Programs Available – North Dakota provides approved entities the ability to determine if there has been a serious conviction on a driver. This is on a batch method, and not on an ongoing notification basis. Typical fees involved include $1.09 per name submitted and a $12.00 fee per batch or computer run, plus programming fees for the initial set-up.

A free status check of a North Dakota driver's license is at https://secure.apps.state.nd.us/dot/dlts/dlos/requeststatus.htm. Access by DL number.

About Accident Reports

Copies of accident reports can be ordered from Driver License and Traffic Safety Division, 608 East Boulevard Avenue, Bismarck 58505-0780, 701-328-2601 or 2604. Downloaded the request form at www.dot.nd.gov/forms/sfn04901.pdf. Records are available since 1998. There are two parts of the report: 1) The front page (Officer's Report) includes the drivers, witnesses, and insurance information, the cost is $2.00 and can be ordered by anyone with a written request; 2) The investigating officer's detailed Opinion is available only to parties of a crash, their legal representatives or their insurer for $5.00. All requests must be in writing and state why this information is desired. Mail request turnaround time is typically 5 days. It can take 1 to 2 months before new records are ready for inquiry.

About Vehicle Records

Motor Vehicle Division, Business Operations, 608 East Boulevard Avenue, Bismarck 58505-0780, 701-328-2725.

Request Methods – Mail, Walk-in, Fax, Bulk.

What You Should Know – Records with personal information are only available to requesters with a permissible use. The fee is $3.00 per record (including mobile homes) or $3.00 per search. Liens are automatically shown with an ownership search. A written request on "Form SFN-51269" is required.

About Watercraft Records

North Dakota Game & Fish Department, 100 N. Bismarck Expressway, Bismarck 58501 701-328-6335, fax 701-328-6374. All motorized boats and all sailboats must be registered. No titles are issued here. This agency does not follow DPPA; records are considered open to the public. Boat registrations may be searched by mail, in-person or fax and require the VIN, hull #, or name. Records are maintained for 5 years on computer, it takes 2 weeks for new records to appear on the system. There is no fee unless lists are presented (call). Turnaround time is normally within 24 hours. Liens are filed with UCC filing locations at either the county or state.

Ohio

Administration	Important Telephone and Web Contacts

Carolyn Y. Williams, Acting Registrar
Ohio Bureau of Motor Vehicles
PO Box 16520
Columbus 43216-6520
614-752-7600
 	
www.bmv.ohio.gov/
	Driver Licensing..614-752-7600
	SR-22 & Dl Suspension......................................614-752-7700
	Commercial DL..614-752-7600
	Titles...614-752-7752
	Registration Information .... 614-752-7800 or 752-7598
	State Department of Insurance 614-644-2658
	Highway Patrol..614-466-2660
	
	Revised Code and the Administrative Code are found at
	   http://codes.ohio.gov/
	Email Contacts are found at
	   www.bmv.ohio.gov/registrar_email.html

Driver License Facts

License Format
Two letters followed by six numbers. The state reports no special sequence to the letters or numbers issued.

Document Appearance
The license is printed on standard plastic credit card stock. As of November 3, 2008, the BMV began issuance of a new format, the color and design changed significantly. The old format is valid until expiration. Both formats are described below.

Current Documents
- **Security Characteristics** — The color Hologram overlay, bar code, magnetic strip and digital signature. A state of Ohio outline logo along the top edge indicates the type of card (DL, CDL, ID, etc.) For those 21 or older, the header on an ID Card is green and the photo is on the right side.
- **Position of Photo** — Left side, with a secondary "ghost" picture on right side.
- **Minor Age Driver Locator** — The document is vertical. The header on an ID Card is red and the photo is on the left side. Photo is located on top left side.
- **CDL Indicator** — "Commercial Driver's License" shows on the top banner.

Older DLs and IDs
- **Security Characteristics** — Hologram overlay, secondary "ghost" signature, bar code, magnetic strip and digital signature. The Class, expiration and any endorsements appear in the bottom right corner.
- **Position of Photo** — Right side.
- **Minor Age Driver Locator** — The document is vertical (short sides on top and bottom). Photo is located on top left side.
- **CDL Indicator** — "Commercial Driver's License" shows on the top banner.

Issue and Renewal

Age Requirements
Ohio adopted a graduated licensing program in 1998 and additional restrictions on probationary drivers under 18 years of age were put into place 04/06/2007. A Temporary Instruction Permit can be granted at fifteen and one-half with completion of approved driver education course. A Probationary License can be issued at age 16, provided the permit is held for a period of 6 months and driver successfully completes written, vision, road and maneuverability examinations, and provides parental verification of 50 hours of driving experience. This license is good until age 21. A Probationary CDL is granted at 18 to 21 with completion of testing requirements. A Motorized Bicycle License is granted to 14 or older with completion of written, road, and vision testing. A Hardship License is granted at 14 to 15 with proof of hardship and approval of the Registrar of Motor Vehicles. A Temporary Instruction Permit is granted if driver is accompanied by licensee of same license class; valid for one year.

Renewal
Birthday of fourth year. Drivers keep the same DL number when renewing, thus making it a permanent license number. Military personnel stationed out of Ohio can renew by mail every 4 years

Elderly-Related Restrictions
Ohio's motor vehicle laws currently do not provide for mandatory retesting of elderly drivers. All drivers, regardless of age, are required to pass a vision screening prior to being issued a renewal driver license.

Residency
Non-resident's license honored on a reciprocal basis; Ohio license must be secured within thirty days of establishing residency.

License Classes
Commercial Classifications
- Class A Any combination of vehicles with a GVWR of 26,001 pounds or more—provided the GVWR of the vehicle(s) being towed is in excess of 10,000 pounds.
- Class B Any single vehicle with a GVWR of 26,001 pounds or more, or any such vehicle towing a vehicle not in excess of 10,000 pounds GVWR.
- Class C Any single vehicle, or combination of vehicles that does not meet the definition of Class A or B (as above), but that either is designed to transport sixteen or more passengers (including the driver), or is transporting hazardous materials in an amount requiring placarding; and any school bus with a GVWR less than 26,001 pounds and designed to transport less than sixteen passengers (including the driver).

Non-Commercial Classifications
- Class D   Operator.
- Class I   Identification Card
- Class M1 Motorcycle Only
- Class M2 Motorized Bicycle Only
- Class M3 3-Wheel Motorcycle Only
- Class T   Temporary ID Card.

Other License Types
- O   Original
- R   Renewal
- E   Probationary
- F   Duplicate
- G   Temporary Permit
- G1 Temporary CDL Permit

HAZMAT Endorsement Procedure
The state is in compliance with the Patriot Act. All applicants applying for a new or renewal HAZMAT Endorsement (HME) must first obtain the application from https://hazprints.tsa.dhs.gov/Public/ or by calling 877-429-7746. The driver must also be fingerprinted. EMSI is the state-designated entity to process fingerprints. There are four locations in the state that perform this service. Visit the web page listed above to find the address locations. The cost of the fingerprint process is $89.25. The fingerprints and application information are sent to the Federal Transportation Security Administration (TSA). TSA performs the background checks and notifies the BMV whether the application is approved or denied. When completed and approved, the HME is valid for five years. The HME is transferable when converting to an Ohio DL, provided an abstract or security threat assessment from the previous state is submitted. For more information, visit http://bmv.ohio.gov/driver_license/hazmat_home.htm.

Safety and Enforcement Facts

Insurance and Financial Responsibility
Licensed drivers and vehicle owners must maintain proof of financial responsibility, and liability insurance is required. A signed affidavit is a part of the license application. The minimum financial responsibility limits are $12,500/25,000/7,500. Ohio does not have a no-fault insurance provision. Future proof is required after a reportable accident and court appearances for moving violations. SR-22 forms are used. An arresting officer must verify proof of insurance and mark the citation with a "yes" or "no."

Individuals unable to provide proof are permitted 30 days to submit proof to the BMV, or driving privileges are suspended. Limited driving privileges can be given to first and second offenders only. Other penalties include loss of license plates, vehicle registration, reinstatement fees and the requirement to have proof of financial responsibility on file with the BMV for three or five years. Financial responsibility proof must also be shown at all vehicle inspection stops and upon random checks by the Registrar of the BMV.

Alcohol and Chemical Testing

Ohio's illegal intoxication level is .08 percent and above, .02 and above for drivers under 21, .04 and above for CDL. Urine, blood, and breath testing are authorized. Ohio has both an implied consent violation and a provision for an administrative suspension. Operating a horse or bicycle under the influence is also considered illegal.

Accident Reporting

The driver of a vehicle involved in a motor vehicle accident may file a report to: Ohio Bureau of Motor Vehicles, Compliance Unit, PO Box 16520, Columbus 43216-6520 within six months after the accident if both of the following apply: (1) there was any personal injury or there was property damage in excess of $400.00, and (2) the driver or owner of the other vehicle did not have insurance or other financial responsibility coverage at the time of the accident. The proper forms can be obtained from any law enforcement agency or at the address above. Carriers (operating under the authority of PUCO) must report accidents resulting in death, injury, or property damage in excess of $500.00 within fifteen days to: Public Utilities Commission of Ohio, 111 North High Street, Columbus 43215. State Form "EN-11" or the form provided by the U.S. Department of Transportation must be submitted. Ohio carriers must also submit their tax decal number and a copy of the driver's log for the day on which the accident occurred with report to the PUCO.

Suspensions and Revocations

The Ohio BMV is in compliance with the provisions of the Motor Carrier Safety Improvement Act (MCSIA). See the Appendix for more information about these mandatory CDL disqualification sanctions.

Administrative License Suspension (ALS) Positive (alcohol tests results .08% or above)	Ninety days to five years.
Administrative License Suspension (ALS) Refusal (refusal to submit to chemical test)	One to five years.
Application for Ohio Driver License While under Suspension Elsewhere	Indefinite.
Civil Action Resulting from Accidents	Indefinite.
Court Actions From Violation Convictions	Variable.
Driver License Restriction Violation	Six months.
Driving Under Suspension	One year.
Driving Under the Influence	
	First Offense Determined by court, but usually 180 days to three years.
	Second Offense One year to five years.
	Third Offense Two years to ten years.
Driving Without Insurance	Ninety days first offense; one year second offense; two years subsequent offense.
Failure to File Reports for Accidents Involving Property Damage in access of $400.00 or personal injury	Indefinite.
Failure to Pay Fine or Appear in Court	Indefinite.
Failure to Provide Proof of Financial Responsibility	Ninety days first offense; one year second offense; Two years subsequent offense.
Falsifying a Driver's License	One year.
Habitual use of Alcohol/Drugs (three convictions in three years)	Indefinite suspension.
License Forfeiture	Indefinite.
License Given as Bond; Minor Misdemeanor or Failure to Appear	One year.
Outstanding Ticket in One of the Forty-one Compact States	Indefinite.
Result From Various Suspensions	Three years.
Three Violation Convictions Before the Age of Eighteen	One year.
Third Offense with No Insurance	Forfeiture.
Two Violation Convictions Before the Age of Eighteen	Ninety days.
Twelve or More Points Accumulated Within Two Years	Six months.
Unauthorized Withdrawal From School (drop-out)	To age eighteen.
Unruly Delinquent	Until age eighteen or twenty-one.
Using License to Obtain Alcohol When Under Age	One year.
Various Medical Reasons	Indefinite.

The 2010 U.S. Motor Vehicle Reference Book   Ohio

   Weapon on School Property .... One to five years.

Reinstatement Requirements
Reinstatement fees vary based on the type of action, date and frequency of occurrence.
For an instructive, detailed overview visit http://www.bmv.ohio.gov/suspension_reinstatement.stm.
   Suspension $30.00 up to $650.00 fee; proof of financial responsibility.
   Revocation   No fee; re-examination; proof of insurance for three years.

Point System Overview
Points range from 2 to 12. Accumulation of 12 points in a 24 month period can result in a suspension.

License Plate Facts

Registration Renewal
License plates expire on the owner's birthday or if the vehicle is leased, the registration expires on the 20th of the month designated for the leasing company. There is no grace period. Registrations can be renewed by going to a Deputy Registrar license agency, mail-in registration, by logging onto www.OPLATES.com or by calling 1-866-OPLATES (1-866-675-2837). Online, one can also select specialty plates, change address, and check on renewal status.

New Residents
Ohio requires all out-of-state vehicles to be registered with Ohio plates within 30 days of becoming an Ohio resident or becoming employed in Ohio.

Inspections and Emissions Testing
Ohio does not have a statewide vehicle safety inspection program or an emissions testing program. However, the Automobile Inspection and Maintenance program is a pollution control inspection program to increase the air quality in Cuyahoga, Geauga, Lake, Lorain, Medina, Portage, and Summit counties.

Plate Descriptions
Typical Plate Pattern	Plates are LLL-NNNN and LL-NN-LL.
County Code	The owner's county of residence on bottom center for older style plates or a numerical value in the lower left hand corner for the new style plates.
Plates and Stickers in Force	Two plates, two decals (MO & YR) and County Number on rear.
Plates Remain with Car when Sold?	No, they remain with seller.

Overview of Record Access

About Driving Records
Bureau of Motor Vehicles, Abstracts, 1970 W Broad St, Columbus 43223, or PO Box 16520, Columbus 43216-6520, 614-752-7600. The fee is $5.00 for a driving record or a status record. An additional $3.50 fee is charged if the record is requested at a local Deputy Registrar or at the Customer Service Center listed above.
Request Methods – Mail, Walk-in, Telephone, Fax, Online, Bulk.
What You Should Know – Anytime an individual is involved in a motor vehicle accident and a police report is made, all parties listed on the police report have an entry of that accident placed on their driving record. When this entry is placed on the record, there are no points assessed and it does not specify who was at fault.
Special Access Programs Available – Ohio offers a "Pre-Paid Driver Search Account" for searches. There is a $200.00 minimum deposit; access is by phone or fax. Call to make arrangement.

About Crash Reports
Copies of crash reports and crash photos from crashes investigated by the Ohio State Highway Patrol going back 5 years to present may be obtained from the Department of Public Safety, Ohio State Highway Patrol, Central Records Unit, PO Box 182074, Columbus 43218-2074, 614-466-3536. The fee is $4.00 per report; normal turnaround time is 2-3 days. Reports of crashes may be ordered http://statepatrol.ohio.gov/crash.htm, use of credit card is required. SSNs are not released.

About Vehicle Records
Bureau of Motor Vehicles, 1970 West Broad St, Columbus 43223, {mail to Attn: Abstracts, PO Box 16520 Columbus 43216-6520, 614-752-7752, (Titles at 614-752-7671) fax 614-752-7001. The fee for VIN checks, registration reports and title histories is $8.50 per record, a certified copy is an additional $3.00. Registration records are available for past seven

years. The state requires the use of a special form when making these requests. Vehicle title records include the lien information. A request for a title history requires the VIN, make and year of the vehicle. All previous owners and mileage figures are reported. Bulk requests must be accompanied by a written request explaining the purpose of the order. Since September 23, 2008, Ohio titles and registers three-wheel motor vehicles as motorcycles if the Manufacturer's Certificate of Origin indicates the vehicle meets the federal specifications of a motorcycle. For questions on titles, email asktitles@dps.state.oh.us.

Request Methods – Mail, Walk-in, Telephone, Fax, Online, Bulk (limited).

What You Should Know – Vehicle title records include the lien information. A request for a title history requires the VIN, make and year of the vehicle. All previous owners and mileage figures are reported.

Special Access Programs Available – Requests by phone or fax Faxes are accepted from pre-approved accounts with funds on file.

The BMV web site at https://www.dps.state.oh.us/atps offers a free search by either title number or identification number, but the results do not include personal information.

About Watercraft Records

Natural Resources Department, Division of Watercraft, 2045 Morse Rd, Columbus 43229, 614-265-6480, fax 614-784-5987. www.dnr.state.oh.us. Ohio is a title state, all boats 14+ foot or have a 10 or greater HP motor must be titled. All boats operated on public waters must be registered. Only Watercraft Agents issue registrations (at the county level). Only Country Clerks of Court write titles. But this agency has access to all records. Lien information will be provided, but you must first request in writing. There is no fee for a registration check, but a $2.00 fee for a title search. There is limited phone searching (no more than 5 at a time). Mail requests normally are processed in one week. A serial or hull number and/or name are needed to search. SSNs are withheld. A summary of Ohio boating laws is found at www.ohiodnr.com/watercraft/opsguide/tabid/2740/default.aspx.

Oklahoma

Administration	Important Telephone and Web Contacts

Kevin Ward, Commissioner
Department of Public Safety
3600 North Martin Luther King Blvd
Oklahoma City, OK 73111
405-425-2001
 	
Russ Nordstrom, Director
Motor Vehicle Division
Oklahoma Tax Commission
2501 Lincoln Blvd, Oklahoma City 73194
405-521-2519
 	
www.dps.state.ok.us/ (Driver License)
www.tax.ok.gov/motveh.html (Vehicle)
	Driver Licensing..........................405-425-2026
	MVR Desk.....................................405-425-2262
	Financial Responsibility 405-425-2098
	Vehicle Information 405-521-3221
	Vehicle Liens................................405-521-3344
	Highway Patrol............................405-425-2424
	State Dept of Insurance.............405-521-2828
	General Email (driver) comment@dps.state.ok.us
	Title 47. Motor Vehicles:
	    www.oscn.net/applications/oscn/index.asp?ftdb=STOKST47&level=1
	Laws for Motor Carriers:
	    www.dps.state.ok.us/ohp/chapter56.pdf

Driver License Facts

License Format
Until 01/02, the Social Security Number (SSN) or an assigned nine-digit number was used. Since 2002, DPS only assigns a ten-digit identifier which is randomly generated format. An example is A#########.

Document Appearance
The current license cards and ID cards, in circulation since 09/2003, are in a digitized format. The regular license has blue background, DL in large type in lower right. The ID Card is in red.

- **Security Characteristics** — The document has optical variable ink images and is multicolored with ultra violet images. There is a ghosted image of the photo, overlapping seal on photo, gradient color pattern and barcode with unique numerical information. Licenses issued to sex offenders are indicated in three places.
- **Position of Photo** — Regular license has picture on the right side, underage drivers and the ID Card has picture on left side. Small version of photo is also in middle.
- **Minor Age Driver Locator** — Card is vertical, picture on left side.
- **CDL Indicator** — Yellow background, large type CDL in lower right corner.
- **Sex Offender** — The driver license or ID card is clearly labeled with the words "sex offender" in the color red, in three distinct places.
- **Non-US Citizen** — The DL or ID is clearly labeled "Temporary."

Older Document
- **Security Characteristics** — License is laminated. State symbol overlaps licensing information. Camera number and location number runs along side of photo.
- **Position of Photo** — Top right.
- **Minor Age Driver Locator** — "Under 21 Until (date)" appears above name, left side, with date of 21st birthday in light red block.
- **CDL Indicator** — Gold area across top with notation "CDL" to the left of photo.

Issue and Renewal
Issuance Requirements
Anyone applying for an original driver license or identification card or anyone who has allowed a driver license or identification card to expire must show proof of legally being in the U.S. Documents accepted as proof will include a U.S. state-issued birth certificate, certificate of born abroad, U.S. issued passport, certificate of naturalization or a valid immigration document issued by the U.S. Customs and Immigration Service (USCIS). Sex offenders are required to renew the license or ID card annually.

Age Requirements

A Graduated Driver Licensing is in place for drivers under the age of 18. The minimum age for a regular license is 16. A learner permit is issued at 15 1/2 to students through an approved driver education school or parental certification of required training. More privileges are granted as the driver becomes more experienced. To hold an intermediate license, one must have had the learner permit for a minimum of 6 months and have no traffic violations. For a regular license, one must have had the intermediate license for 6 months and have no traffic violations. The Graduated Driver License law was strengthened in 2009 to restrict teens' driving time to the hours of 5am to 10pm, with exceptions for driving to work, school, church or related activities, or if a licensed driver is seated next to the teenager.

Renewal

Four years from date of issue on originals, renewals expire four years from previous expiration. Driver keeps same number when renewing or changes number, as long as the SSN is not used as the number. Renewal is not available online. Class D licenses can be renewed by mail, reusing the photo and signature on file with DPS. Also, see Issuance Requirements above.

Elderly-Related Restrictions

None indicated.

Residency

Non-resident's home-state license honored; must secure Oklahoma license upon establishing residency.

License Classes

Commercial Classifications

Class A	Any combination of motor vehicles with a GCWR of 26,001 pounds or more, providing the vehicle being towed has a GVWR of 10,000 pounds or more, with applicable endorsements.
Class B	Trucks or buses with GVWR of 26,001 pounds or more, or any such vehicle towing a vehicle weighing less than 10,000 pounds GVWR.
Class C	Trucks or buses weighing less than 26,001 pounds GVWR, or any such vehicle towing a vehicle less than 10,000 pounds GVWR. This class applies to vehicles which are placarded to transport hazardous materials or designed to carry sixteen or more passengers (including the driver).

Non-Commercial Classifications

Class D	All other vehicles will be Class D and will include cars, pickups, all recreational vehicles, fire trucks, and certain farm vehicles.
ID	Identification Card

HAZMAT Endorsement Procedure

The state is in compliance with the Patriot Act. All applicants applying for a new or renewal or transfer HAZMAT Endorsement (HME) must first obtain the application from https://hazprints.tsa.dhs.gov/Public/ or by calling 877-429-7746. The driver must also be fingerprinted. EMSI is the state-designated entity to process fingerprints. There are six locations in the state that perform this service. Visit the web page listed above to find the address locations. The cost of the fingerprint process is $89.25. The fingerprints and application information is sent to the Federal Transportation Security Administration (TSA). TSA performs the background checks and notifies the DMV whether the application is approved or denied. When completed and approved, the HME is valid until the license expires (on a four year cycle). For more information, visit www.dps.state.ok.us/news/2005/050207.htm.

Safety and Enforcement Facts

Insurance and Financial Responsibility

Oklahoma has compulsory liability insurance. Financial responsibility limit minimums are $25,000/50,000/25,000. The state does not have a no-fault insurance provision. Proof is required upon registration or renewal, after a reportable accident or certain violations. A Liability Insurance Security Verification form is used.

Alcohol and Chemical Testing

It is unlawful and punishable for any person to drive/operate or be in actual physical control of a motor vehicle who has a blood or breath alcohol concentration of .08 percent or above and .04% if operating a CMV. For an individual under the age of 21, any measurable amount is illegal. Oklahoma has an implied consent violation provision; .08 percent or more or refusal to submit to test(s) results in loss of driving privilege.

Accident Reporting

Collisions involving death, personal injury, or damage in excess of $300.00 must be reported if a settlement is not reached within six months. If requested by the Department of Public Safety, a report must be filed within ten days. The report must be completed on required forms with accompanying doctor's statement of personal injury, and repair estimate dated and signed by an authorized representative of a garage or body shop, and/or itemized estimate by property owner for property damage. The report should be sent to: Financial Responsibility Division, Department of Public Safety, PO Box 11415, Oklahoma City 73136-0415.

Suspensions and Revocations

Note: The Oklahoma DPS is in compliance with the provisions of the Motor Carrier Safety Improvement Act (MCSIA). See the Appendix for more information about these mandatory CDL disqualification sanctions.

Driving While License Suspended or Revoked .... Unexpired suspension is extended for three or four months.
Dropping Out of School While Under 18 ...... Indefinite suspension but minimum 2 months.

Point Accumulation of Ten Points Within 5 year Period:
- First Suspension .... One month.
- Second Suspension .... Three months.
- Third Suspension .... Six months.
- Fourth or Subsequent Suspensions .... Twelve months.

The following incur a one-month suspension on the first conviction, a six-month suspension on the second conviction, and a twelve-month suspension on the third or subsequent conviction:
- Attempting to Elude a Police Officer
- DWI
- DUI
- DUI or DWI if Under 21

Note: At the court's discretion, anyone under 18 can have their licensed suspended from 6 months to 2 years for any crime involving alcohol or a controlled dangerous substance.

The following incur a two-month suspension on the first conviction and a six-month suspension on the second conviction:
- Display or Possession of a Driver's License Bearing Altered Information
- Giving False Information When Applying for a License
- Lending a Operator's or Chauffeur's License to any Other Person
- Presenting a License that is not Your Own for the Purpose of Committing Fraud
- To Make, Print, or Otherwise Produce False Oklahoma Driver's Licenses
- To Display or Knowingly Possess a Counterfeit License
- To Display or Possess a License Having a Forged Signature or Picture of a Person Other Than Licensee

The Following Offenses Result in a Six-Month to Three-Year Revocation:
- Any drug conviction
- Any felony in which a motor vehicle is used
- Failure to pay for gasoline
- Failure to register vehicle
- Failure to stop and render aid if involved in a collision resulting in serious injury or death
- Manslaughter or negligent homicide resulting from operating a motor vehicle
- Perjury or making a false statement under oath to obtain a license or for any other legal matter related to the ownership or operation of a motor vehicle

Reinstatement Requirements

FR Suspension $100.00 fee; comply with requirements. Add-on a fee of $50.00 if failure to surrender driver license and registration tag within 30 days of suspension date. An additional $200.00 trauma care fee is assessed for certain violations.

DI Revocation $300.00 fee; expiration of revocation period.

Point System Overview

Points range from one to four. Accumulation of ten points within five years can result in a suspension. Two points are deducted for each twelve-month period in which there are no convictions of any pointable traffic violations or completion of a Defense Driving/Driver Improvement Course

License Plate Facts

Registration Renewal

All vehicles, boats and outboard motors in excess of ten horsepower are registered annually. There is no exclusion made for vehicles, boats, or outboard motors not in use. Renewal is available online at www.tax.ok.gov.

New Residents
New residents must register within thirty days of establishing residency.

Inspections and Emissions Testing
Oklahoma no longer requires an annual safety inspection for vehicles. There is no statewide emissions testing program.

Plate Descriptions

Typical Plate Patterns — Throughout 2009, Oklahoma will be reissuing most of their current plates. The present plate patterns will be valid along with some new patterns, Current valid passenger plates are LL-NNNN,LLL-NNN or NNN-LLL. New issue plates will begin with NNN-LLL. Current commercial truck plates are LNNN-NNN or LNN-NNN or NNN-NNN. The current letters used are "T", "C", "X", and "Y". The letter "Y" is being utilized in the reissue of commercial truck plates.

County Codes — Oklahoma does not use an issuing system that indicates on the plate pattern the county of plate issuance. However, month decals do have a county identifier indicating the county in which the decal was purchased.

Plates and Stickers in Force — One plate, two decals (MO) (YR).

Plate Remains with Car when Sold? — The vast majority of plates remain with the sold vehicle. However, for an additional fee the vehicle owner may retain the plate if the vehicle is sold.

Overview of Record Access

About Driving Records
Records Management Division, Attn: MVR DESK, PO Box 11415, Oklahoma City 73136-0415, 405-425-2262, fax is 405-425-2046. The current fee is $10.00, $13.00 if certified, $12.50 if electronic. The state does not charge for "no record found" reports when the record is requested over-the-counter, unless the requester asks for a printed report. There is a charge for a "no record found" report when the request is mailed to the state. The driver's license number, name, date of birth are needed when ordering. Note that requests for records can not be made by telephone or email; records *cannot* be faxed or emailed.

Request Methods – Mail, Walk-in, Online.

What You Should Know – Violations for speeding one to ten mph over the limit will not be included on the driving record unless the violation was committed while a CMV or the operator was the holder of a CDL at the time of the violation. Electronic access is available for qualified, approved users through www.ok.gov.

About Collision Reports
Copies of collision reports are available from the Records Management Division, P.O. Box 11415, Oklahoma City 73136-0415, 405-425-2192, for a fee of $7.00 uncertified or $10.00 if certified. Collision reports remain confidential for a period of 60 days after the report is filed with the DPS. Those qualified to obtain reports include permissible users per DPPA plus the media (newspapers, radio, and television broadcasters).

About Vehicle Records
Oklahoma Tax Commission, Motor Vehicle Division, 2501 Lincoln Boulevard, Attention: Research, Oklahoma City 73194, 405-521-3221, Liens 405-521-3344. Although telephone numbers are given please be aware that under NO circumstances will vehicle information be given over the telephone. To obtain vehicle information, the requester MUST complete the "Vehicle Information Request Form 769" and include the appropriate fees. Information is only released to statutorily qualified requestors. The fee for a computer screen printout of current ownership/lienholder information is $1.00. A computer generated title history (only 1992 or newer models) is $5.00. A microfilm title history is $7.50, and $10.00 if certified. A copy of a lien release is $7.50, if certified then $10.00.

Request Methods – Mail, Walk-in, Bulk.

What You Should Know – All requests must include either the OK title number, tag number, or VIN. Vehicle records are not researched by the owner's name. The Oklahoma Tax Commission holds lien records for vehicles, boats, and outboard motors. Lien records go back to July 1, 1979 for vehicles, and July 1, 1990 for boats. Inactive vehicle, boat and outboard motor records without active liens are removed from the computer record after three (3) years. However, most information is still available via microfilm and microfiche.

About Watercraft Records
Every boat used for transportation on the water of the state and every outboard motor in excess of ten (10) horsepower must be titled. Records are maintained by the agency described above, record access fees are the same. Record access is generally limited to law enforcement, government agencies, and requests related to boating safety.

Oregon

Administration	Important Telephone and Web Contacts

Tom McClellan
Administrator
Driver and Motor Vehicle Services
1905 Lana Avenue NE
Salem 97314
503-945-5000
 	
www.oregon.gov/ODOT/DMV/
	Driver Licensing..503-945-5000
	Financial Responsibility/SR.............................503-945-5400
	Commercial Driver License...............................503-945-5400
	IRV (Interactive)..503-945-5312
	Vehicle Information..503-945-5000
	State Department of Insurance.........................503-947-7980
	State Police...503-378-3720
	Contacts and Emails
	   www.oregon.gov/ODOT/DMV/contact_us.shtml
	Oregon Revised Statutes www.leg.state.or.us/ors/
	Oregon Administrative Rules
	   http://arcweb.sos.state.or.us/banners/rules.htm
	Oregon Motor Carrier Laws and Rules
	   www.oregon.gov/ODOT/MCT/LAWS.shtml

Driver License Facts

License Format
All newly issued numbers are seven digits; the older format is one to nine numbers. License numbers are computer-generated in numeric order. Numbers are eventually recycled after they meet certain specific criteria.

Document Appearance
Oregon has provided digital driver licenses and identification cards since November of 2003.

Current Document
- **Security Features** — Tamper-resistant laminate repeats "Oregon" across top; it varies in color depending on the viewing angle and glows under ultraviolet light. Has small "ghost image" of card holder's photo. There is overlapping type and graphics, including an image of the Capitol. The State of Oregon seal overlaps the card holder's photo. Bar-coded information is on the back of the card, and the card contains a digitized signature.
- **Minor Age Drivers** — Cards held by minors will bear age notices for alcohol and tobacco vendors. The notices, printed in a red border around the bearer's photo, state "Under 18 until ..." and "Under 21 until ...." Under 18 also has "Provisional License" printed in white inside blue header bar. Also, minors' photos are on the right side of the card instead of on the left.
- **CDL Indicator** — Looks the same as the regular license, except says "Commercial Driver License" in red header bar
- **Class C** — Standard Class C says "Driver License" in white print within blue header bar.
- **ID Card** — Has green header bar with "Identification Card" printed in white. Card says "Not A License to Drive."

Previous Documents
The documents described below are being replaced by the new format, which should be completed by 03/01/2012.
- **Appearance** — Photographic, credit card style with overlay on the front only.
- **Security Features** — Overlay with repetitive pattern of "OREGON" and gold state seals.
- **Position of Photo** — Upper left.
- **Minor Age Drivers** — All drivers under 18 years of age receive a license stating "PROVISIONAL DRIVER LIC" OR "PROVISIONAL LICENSE." Also "MINOR UNTIL (DATE)" appears on the right side of the license and is printed in red.
- **CDL Indicator** — Classification code and heading across top with "COMMERCIAL DRIVER LICENSE" printed in red.

Issue and Renewal

In 2007, the DMV stopped issuing plastic driver licenses, driver permits, and identification cards over-the-counter from field offices and moved to a centralized issuance based solution. A paper interim driver license, driver permit, or identification card is provided to the applicant in the field office, then later, after processing and verification has been completed, a plastic or permanent card is mailed from a separate, centralized location. Also since July 1, 2008, the Oregon DMV has been using "facial recognition" software, a new tool in the prevention of fraud and identity theft. The procedure is designed to prevent someone from obtaining a driver license or ID card under a false name or under multiple names

Age Requirements

The minimum age is 16. In 2000, Oregon instituted a graduated driver license for drivers under the age of 18. A Student Permit is issued at age 14 under special conditions. An Instruction Permit is issued at 15 and is required prior to issuance of a license, unless applicant is 18 years of age or older. Graduated licensing laws restrict the age and number of passengers that a driver under the age of 18 may have in a vehicle as well as the night time hours when the teenager may drive. Oregonians under 18 years of age who apply for their first driving privileges need to show proof of school attendance, completion of school, or exemption from attendance before DMV will issue a permit or a driver license. Proof of attendance or completion would include a Statement of Enrollment Form (available through the local school district or ESD), a diploma, or a GED certificate. If a person is home schooled or exempt from school attendance, he or she needs to obtain the form through the school district or ESD.

Renewal

Licenses are issued for eight years and expire on the person's birthdate. Renewal is not available online, but change of address is. Before the DMV will renew a driver license, an applicant must provide proof of legal presence, full legal name, identity, date of birth, and SSN, if not previously verified. The applicant must also submit proof of current residence address if the address has changed since the previous issuance date. An applicant who needs time to obtain the required proof of legal presence or proof of SSN or to take care of an issue with the SS Administration may be issued a 90-Day Oregon Temporary Driver License/ID Permit.

Elderly-Related Restrictions

None, other than a vision test required for renewals over age 50.

Residency

Non-resident's home-state license honored; Oregon license must be secured upon establishing residency.

License Classes

Commercial Classifications

- CDL-A Any vehicle or combination of vehicles with the proper endorsement.
- CDL-B Any single vehicle with the proper endorsements. May tow a trailer up to 10,000 pounds GVWR. If the trailer has a GVWR of more than 10,000 pounds, the gross weight of the combination (towing vehicle and trailer) must be less than 26,001 pounds.
- CDL-C Any single vehicle with proper endorsements which does not weigh more than 26,000 pounds and carries sixteen or more passengers or hazardous materials.
- PCDL CDL instruction permit.

Non-Commercial Classifications

- C Any single vehicle with proper endorsements weighing less than 26,000 pounds. Includes mopeds, vehicles designed to carry fewer than 16 passengers including driver, a motor home for personal use and any fire or emergency vehicle. May tow another vehicle with a loaded weight of 10,000 pounds or less. May also tow another vehicle over 10,000 pounds if the combined weight of the towing vehicle and trailer is not more than 26,000 pounds.
- C (Restricted) May only operate mopeds.
- PC Class C non-commercial instruction permit.
- MPM Motorcycle instruction permit.
- SP Special student driver permit. Issued to drivers as young as 14 in very limited circumstances.
- EP Emergency driver permit. Issued to drivers as young as 14 in very limited circumstances.

Note: Hardship and Probationary Permits are available for certain situations.

HAZMAT Endorsement Procedure

The state is in compliance with the Patriot Act. All applicants applying for a new or renewal or transfer HAZMAT Endorsement (HME) must first obtain the application from https://hazprints.tsa.dhs.gov/Public/ or by calling 877-429-7746. The driver must also be fingerprinted. EMSI is the state-designated entity to process fingerprints. There are three locations in the state that perform this service. Visit the web page listed above to find the address locations. The cost of the fingerprint process is $89.25. The fingerprints and application information is sent to the Federal Transportation Security Administration (TSA). TSA performs the background checks and notifies the DMV whether the application is approved or denied. When completed and approved, the HME is valid for five years. For more information, visit http://egov.oregon.gov/ODOT/MCT/news/CDLRULES.shtml.

Safety and Enforcement Facts

Insurance and Financial Responsibility

Oregon has mandatory liability insurance. Financial responsibility minimum limits are $25,000/50,000/10,000. There is a mandatory one-year license suspension for an uninsured driver involved in an accident. The state does not have no-fault insurance. With some exceptions, all motor vehicles registered in the state are required to meet the financial responsibility laws. Proof must be shown at time of drive test, renewal, when an accident occurs or upon a random sampling. SR-22 forms are used.

Alcohol and Chemical Testing

Oregon's illegal intoxication level is .08 percent. Breath, blood, and urine testing are authorized. Under Oregon's implied-consent law, drivers' licenses are suspended for failure or refusal of a test. Blood alcohol content levels for administrative suspensions are: Under twenty-one years of age - any amount; commercial vehicle offenses - .04 percent and above; all other operators - .08 percent and above.

Accident Reporting

An Oregon Traffic Accident and Insurance Report must be filed with DMV within 72 hours when:
- Damage to the vehicle you were driving is over $1,500
- Damage to any vehicle is over $1,500 and any vehicle is towed from the scene as a result of damages from this accident
- Injury or death resulted from this accident
- Damages to any one person's property other than a vehicle involved in this accident are over $1,500
- You are the owner of the vehicle involved in a reportable accident and the driver fails to report the accident.

This written report must be filed with the DMV, Reporting & Insurance Verification, 1905 Lana Avenue NE, Salem 97314, or local law enforcement. To download an accident report form, go to www.odot.state.or.us/forms/dmv/32.pdf. The Motor Carrier Crash Report is a part of this form and is required to be completed if there is a loss of life, bodily injury treated away from the accident scene, or if any vehicle was towed from the scene. The full report is sent to DMV, Reporting & Insurance Verification, 1905 Lana Ave NE, Salem, OR 97314, or to local law enforcement.

Suspensions and Revocations

The state is in compliance with the federally mandated disqualifications on CDLs, see the Appendix for details.

Any of the Following Offenses May Result in a **Suspension**—
- Attempting to Elude a Police Officer
- Altering Any License or Permit
- Criminal Action of Financial Responsibility
- Exceeding the Speed Limit While Driving 100 MPH or More (In any vehicle, but holding a CML)
- Exceeding the Speed Limit by 30 MPH or More When the Court imposes a Suspension (in any vehicle, but holding a CDL)
- Failure to Appear in Court
- Failure to File an Accident Report as Required by the Law
- Failure to File Financial Responsibility When Required
- Failure to Give Required or Correct Information in the Application
- Failure to Obtain Required Medical Clearance
- Failure to Pay a Fine or Obey a Court Order
- Failure to Pay Child Support
- Failure to Perform Duties When Involved in an Accident Resulting in Property Damage
- Failure to Settle Judgment
- Failure to Take Or Pass Exam Upon Request of the Division
- Knowingly Allowing the Use or Display of (or Permitting Display of) a Fictitious or Altered License or Permit
- Making a Fraudulent Application
- Manufacturing, Possession or Delivery of Controlled Substance
- Permitting Misuse of a License or Permit
- Reckless Driving
- Reckless Endangerment, Criminal Mischief Resulting from the Operation of a Motor Vehicle
- Refusing or Failing a Breath, Blood or Urine Test
- School Enrollment/Expulsion
- Tobacco Offense by Minor
- Too Many Traffic Violations

Any of the Following May Result in License **Cancellation**—
- Failure to Give Required or Correct Information in the Application

- Person Not Entitled to License or Permit
- Error or Defect Found on the License
- At Request of Parent/Guardian/Employer Who Signed Driver's Application
- Operation of a Motor Vehicle for any Purpose other than one approved under an Emergency Student Driver Permit

Any of the Following May Result in License **Revocation**—
- Murder, Manslaughter, Criminally-Negligent Homicide, or Assault Resulting from the Operation of Motor Vehicle
- Perjury or Making a False Affidavit to the Division
- Third or Subsequent conviction of DUI
- Felony Convictions Involving the Use of a Motor Vehicle
- Failure to Perform Duties to an Injured Person When Involved in an Accident
- Habitual Offender (see below)

Any of the Following May Result in Court-Ordered **Registration Suspension**—
- Conviction of Driving While License Suspended or Revoked
- Second or Subsequent Conviction of Driving While Under the Influence of Intoxicants

Habitual Offender Program
DMV will revoke driving privileges for five years for habitual offender if convicted of 20 or more traffic violations within five years, or if convicted of three or more of the following offenses within a five year period:
- Any degree of murder, manslaughter, criminally negligent homicide, assault, recklessly endangering another person, menacing or criminal mischief resulting from the operation of a motor vehicle.
- Driving while under the influence of intoxicants.
- Driving while your driving privileges are suspended or revoked.
- Reckless driving.
- Failure to perform the duties of a driver after a collision.
- Fleeing or attempting to elude a police officer.

More About Teen Drivers
For drivers under 18 who get: a) two convictions, b) two preventable accidents, or c) one of each, DMV will restrict driving privileges for 90 days to drive only for work purposes with no passengers except a parent, stepparent or guardian. For a third conviction or accident, DMV will suspend the teen's driving privileges for 6 months even if he or she turns 18 years of age during the suspension period. Each subsequent driver improvement violation or preventable accident will suspend driving privileges or right to apply for driving privileges for 6 months, regardless of a previous or current Driver Improvement Program suspension(s).

Reinstatement Requirements
Suspension $75.00 fee; time lapse, determined by reason; proof of financial responsibility (in many cases).
Revocation $75.00 fee; proof of future financial responsibility (in most cases); time lapse, determined by reason; complete licensing test and original fee.

Point System Overview
Oregon does not use a point system.

License Plate Facts

Registration Renewal
Registration is renewed on a bi-annual basis. Renewal may be done online as long as vehicle does not require a DEQ test or registration has been expired more than 75 days. Go to https://www.oregondmv.com/online/index.htm. Renewal for CMVs is at www.oregon.gov/ODOT/MCT/TOL.shtml.

New Residents
Non-residents must register vehicles upon establishing residency.

Inspections and Emissions Testing
There is no statewide provisions for safety inspections or emission testing of vehicles. However, two areas require bi-annual emission testing: Portland Metro(if vehicle is 1975 or newer) and Medford (if vehicle less than 21 years old).

Plate Descriptions
Typical Plate Pattern — Passenger plates are 3 alpha & 3 numbers, or 3 numbers & 3 alpha, or 2 alpha & 5 numbers, or 6 personalized characters. Heavy trucks (over 8,000 pounds) start with "T" then 6 digits. Commercial vehicles all have alpha prefix followed by numerical characters.

County Codes	The state does not employ a county coding system on the plates.
Plates and Stickers in Force	Two plates, two decals (MO) (YR) on both plates.
Plates Remain with Car when Sold?	Yes.

Overview of Record Access

About Driving Records
DMV Records Services, 1905 Lana Avenue NE, Salem 97314, 503-945-5254, fax 503-945-5425. The fee is $1.50 for a three-year non-employment record, $1.50 for a "open ended" non-employment record (available only to insurer or to subject), $2.00 for a three-year employment driving record, and $3.00 for a certified court print that includes major convictions for 10 years, minor convictions and accidents for 5 years for all driving. Fees are different for records accessed online. The fees for sanitized versions of these records are the same. A driver license information report is available for $1.50 per record. This report lists the driver's name, address, date of birth, license number, issue and expiration dates, original business date, restrictions, status, and—if applicable—the ID card expiration date. Other reports include: suspension package for $11.50; application history for $17.50; and insurance information for $10.00. Add $1.00 to certify any document not already certified. The state's charge for a "no record found" for most reports is $1.50.

Request Methods – Mail, Walk-in, Telephone, Fax, Online, Bulk.

What You Should Know – Suspensions are shown three or five years after reinstatement; closed suspensions do not show on three-year records. The fee for online records is $.250 per record, but there is a $2,500 set-up fee. For more information, contact the Records Policy Unit at 503-945-8906 or 503-945-8905.

Special Access Programs Available – IVR (the DMV's Interactive Voice Response System) is an automated record inquiry system available only to established Record Inquiry Account Holders. For questions about Record Inquiry Accounts, call 503-945-7950 or email to ODOTDMVRecordsPol@ODOT.state.or.us. The Automated Reporting Service (ARS) Program allows users who have a Record Inquiry Account to submit a name list and DMV will automatically produce a printed driving record whenever a conviction, accident or suspension is posted to the record. There is always a $3.00 fee whenever a record is produced. The maintenance of adding or deleting drivers can be done free of charge via Oregon's online DMV service. But if adding or deleting names is done by the DMV, there is a $2.00 fee per name. For more information about ARS, call 503-945-5427

About Crash Reports
Copies of police crash reports filed with DMV can be obtained from the DMV Accidents Reporting Unit, 1905 Lana Avenue NE, Salem 97314, 503-945-5098. Copies of reports can be requested by Record Inquiry Account Holders or by non-account holders by using the Request for Information Form 7122. The report will be provided without personal information unless the requestor qualifies under Oregon's Privacy Law ORS 802.175-802.191. The fee is $8.50 and turnaround time is usually 5 days plus mail time. It can take up to 3 months for reports to be filed with the DMV.

About Vehicle Records
Record Services Unit, 1905 Lana Avenue NE, Salem 97314, 503-945-5254. Personal information is not released unless the requester qualifies as a permissible user by completing a Request for Information Form or establishing a Record Inquiry Account. Account holders must first complete a Record Inquiry Account Application and pay the $70 fee. The current fee for vehicle record checks by mail or over-the-counter is $4.00, record information by phone only (IVR) is $2.50. Other reports include: vehicle title history, $22.50; previous owner, $14.00; insurance information, $10.00; and odometer history, $25.00 ($2.00 for current, $3.50 for previous). Add $1.00 to certify any document not already certified. A fee of $2.50 is charged for most no record found items. Call 503-945-7950 for Record Inquiry Account questions.

Request Methods – Mail, Walk-in, Telephone, Bulk.

Special Access Programs Available – The automated system called "IVR" (DMV's Interactive Voice Response Service) is open twenty-four hours. For an in-depth description of IVR see the driving record section. To set-up an account or more information, please call 503-945-7950..

About Watercraft Records
Oregon State Marine Board, 435 Commercial St NE #400, Salem 97301, 503-378-8587 fax 503-378-4597 www.boatoregon.com. Titles and registrations are issued on all motorized boats and on sailboats over 12 ft. Title records are available from 1997. Registration records on are microfiche from 1978 to 1998, and on computer from 1999 forward. Lien information is shown on the title record. There is no fee to do a registration or lien record search unless lists are presented, copies are $.25 per page if more than 5 pages. Single records can be requested by mail, phone, fax, in person, and email. Mail turnaround time is 7 to 10 days. Bulk mail lists may be purchased on paper or electronic format. There is an opt-out provision in effect regarding mail list purchases. Extremely large boats that move along the OR-WA-CA border for 60 days or more are registered with the US Coast Guard. Call 800-799-8362 for more information.

Pennsylvania

Administration	Important Telephone and Web Contacts

Janet Dolan, Director
Bureau of Driver Licensing
Department of Transportation
Riverfront Office Center, 4th Floor
1101 South Front Street
Harrisburg 17104
 	
www.dmv.state.pa.us
	Driver, Vehicle, & Financial Responsibility
	.... 717-391-6190, In-state only 800-932-4600
	Commercial Driver License.........................717-783-3653
	State Department of Insurance 717-787-2317
	State Police..717-783-5599
	Email contact list at:
	   www.dot4.state.pa.us/contact_us/index.shtml
	Vehicle Code - Title 75:
	   https://www.dot4.state.pa.us/vehicle_code/index.shtml

Driver License Facts

License Format
Eight numbers. Pennsylvania reports that there is no code in the sequential arrangement that determines the digits making the license number.

Document Appearance
The current version of the driver license has been in circulation since 07/31/2001, the current Temporary License/ID Card since 10/2007. The "PA" in the Keystone appears in all licenses and ID Cards effective 02/2008.

Security Characteristics	Features include a holographic overlay that displays the "Keystone" in the foreground and county names in the background. The cards have a thick security coating or hologram, an area to denote organ donors, and different colored bands to indicate product type. Regular licenses have a blue colored band appearing on left side, ID cards have a yellow band, under 18 drivers have a green band. There is a red banner on all restricted license documents. In the lower right corner of the license document is a visible box that indicates the type of license.
Position of Photo	On the left side, inside the colored band.
Minor Age Driver Locator	For driver under 21, cards are produced in a vertical format. Above the picture, the date the individual turns 18 is highlighted in yellow and the date they turn 21 is highlighted in red. Drivers under 21 have a blue band, drivers under 18 have a green band.
Occupational	The wording inside the red banner on the left side indicates Limited License. The Keystone in lower right corner indicates Occupational License.
Probationary	The wording inside the red banner on the left side indicates Limited License. The Keystone in lower right corner indicates Probationary License.
Ignition Interlock	The wording inside the red banner on the left side indicates Limited License. The Keystone in lower right corner indicates Ignition Interlock License.
CDL Indicator	"COMMERCIAL DRIVERS LICENSE" appears within blue band on left.

Note: Since October 2007, Pennsylvania has issued a *Temporary License/ID Card* to new applicants. This card looks like the other products except the banner is gray, the word "Temporary" is printed in red across the license and the expiration date is outlined in red. In addition, the overlay on the front is changed to include "PA" in the Keystone. The temporary product is valid for 15 days and provides PennDOT time to ensure the individual's photograph does not match another photograph in the database under a different driver name(s).

Issue and Renewal
Age Requirements
The minimum age is sixteen; eighteen for CDL. Below is information on various permits.

Learner's Permit	Required; sixteen; mandatory six months on learner permit before eligible to take skills test; certification of 50 hours behind-the-wheel skill building prior to skills test; must have parent/guardian consent and be accompanied by a licensed driver, twenty-one or older,

	licensed in the same class; driving permitted only between 5AM to 11PM.
Junior License	Sixteen and six months; must have passed all skills requirements of leaner's permit
Unrestricted License	Possible at seventeen and six months with; crash and conviction free record for twelve months; completion of approved driver's education course.

Note: Occupational Limited Licenses can be issued under certain circumstances, except to drivers convicted of homicide by vehicle and other serious traffic offenses in Chapter 37 Subchapter B, as well as all Subchapter C, convictions relating to accidents and accident reports.

Renewal
Licenses expire one day after the licensee's birthdate on fourth year; drivers over age sixty-five have the option of two-year renewals. Driver keeps same number when renewing. Renewal and address changes are available online, except for CDL drivers. Go to www.dot4.state.pa.us/centers/OnlineServicesCenter.shtml. Military personnel who have an expired license do not have to renew as long as they are active duty. In addition, if an out-of-state driver's license has been expired for more than six months, it cannot be transferred for a PA driver's license. The driver must apply for a PA Learner's Permit and complete all applicable knowledge and skills tests in order to obtain the driver's license.

Elderly-Related Restrictions
Individuals age 65 or older have the option of renewing their license every two years, instead of standard four years.

Residency
A license holder must secure Pennsylvania license within sixty days of establishing residency; a non-resident's home-state license is honored on a reciprocal basis.

License Classes
Commercial Classifications
Class A	Minimum age 18, required to operate any combination of vehicles with a GVW rating of 26,001 pounds or more, provided the vehicle being towed is in excess of 10,000 pounds; also includes Classes B and C.
Class B	Minimum age 18, required to operate any single vehicle with GVW rating of 26,001 pounds or more; also includes Class C.
Class C	Minimum age 18, required to operate any single vehicle with a GVW rating of not more than 26,000 pounds that is designed to transport 16 or more passengers, including the driver; or is a school bus designed to carry 11 passengers or more, including driver; or is used to transport hazardous materials.

Non-Commercial Classifications
Class A	Minimum age 18, required to operate any combination of vehicles with a gross weight rating of 26,001 pounds or more, where the vehicle(s) being towed is/are in excess of 10,000 pounds. Example: Recreational Vehicle, when the towing vehicle is rated at 11,000 pounds and the vehicle towed is rated at 15,500 pounds (total combination weight of 26,500 pounds).
Class B	Minimum age 18, required to operate any single vehicle rated in excess of 26,000 pounds. Example: Motor homes rated at 26,001 pounds or more.
Class C	Issued to persons 16 years of age or older to operate any vehicles, except those requiring a Class M qualification, and who do not meet the definitions of Class A or Class B. Any firefighter or member of a rescue or emergency squad who is the holder of a Class C driver's license and who has a certificate of authorization from a fire chief or head of the rescue or emergency squad will be authorized to operate any fire or emergency vehicle registered to that fire department, rescue or emergency squad or municipality. The holder of a Class C driver's license is also authorized to drive a motorized pedalcycle (a motor-driven cycle) or a three-wheeled motorcycle equipped with an enclosed cab, but not a motorcycle.
Class M	Issued to those persons 16 years of age or older to operate a motorcycle or motor-driven cycle. If a person is qualified to operate only a motorcycle or motor-driven cycle, he/she will be issued a Class M driver's license. If motorcycle is less than 50 CCs, an "8" restriction will appear on the driver's license and the license holder is prohibited from operating a motorcycle 50 CCs or larger.

Other License Types
- Occupational Limited License (OLL) for non-commercial classes. An OLL authorizes one to drive a designated motor vehicle, under certain conditions, when it is necessary for the driver's occupation, work, trade, medical treatment or study.
- Probationary Licenses for Class C only. Both limited licenses need an authorization letter that contains specific information pertaining to the operator, such as; vehicle information, operating hours, and destination. Both products must be carried together at all times.

- An Ignition Interlock License is issued to those individuals restricted to only driving vehicles with an ignition interlock device.

HAZMAT Endorsement Procedure
The state is in compliance with the Patriot Act. Customer submits a HAZMAT application, passes the HAZMAT knowledge test at a PennDOT Driver License Center, provides documentation at the PennDOT Driver License Center to prove U.S. citizenship or appropriate immigration status. At the same time, the customer will complete a Federal "Application for Security Threat Assessment" (Form DL-288) and pay $60 in Federal fees in the form of a check made payable to PennDOT. A set of fingerprints is required. After fingerprinting, PennDOT forwards customer information to TSA and Federal criminal history background check begins. To find the 81 fingerprint locations and detailed information about the program visit www.dmv.state.pa.us/commercial_licensing/hazmat.shtml. When completed and approved, the HME is valid for four years.

Safety and Enforcement Facts

Insurance and Financial Responsibility
Pennsylvania has a compulsory liability insurance law in effect with minimum limits for responsibility at $15,000/30,000/5,000. The state has no-fault insurance provisions. The state requires proof of insurance or financial responsibility at registration or renewal and after an accident or certain violations. The SR-22 form is not used. A person or company desiring to qualify as a self-insurer must file a proposal of self-insurance with PennDOT for approval.

Alcohol and Chemical Testing
The illegal intoxication level is 0.08 percent and above, .04 for CDL drivers except school bus drivers which is .02, and .02 for drivers under 21. There is a three-tier measurement system that dictates the penalties (.08 to .099%, .10 to .159%, and .16% and higher). Breath, blood, or urine testing are authorized. There is an implied-consent law, but not a provision for an administrative suspension per se. Operating a horse or bicycle under the influence is also considered illegal.

Accident Reporting
The police should be contacted immediately when there is an accident involving death, personal injury, or when a vehicle must be towed from the scene of the accident—regardless of the dollar amount of damage. If the police cannot be contacted, an "Operator's Report" must be filed within five days. Reports should be filed with Bureau of Highway Safety and Traffic Engineering, PO Box 2047, Harrisburg 17105-2047. Commercial carriers with operating authority of the Public Utilities Commission must file a report (with that agency) on any accident resulting in death, injury, or property damage in excess of $100.00. Fatal accidents must be reported within twenty-four hours; accidents involving injury should also be reported within twenty-four hours; and written reports should be filed for all accidents within thirty days. Drivers of motor carrier vehicles, buses, school buses or vehicles transporting hazardous materials must submit to testing for alcohol and controlled substances, if involved in a reportable accident. The cost is borne by the driver's employer.

Suspensions and Revocations
Note on CDL: The state is in compliance with the provisions of the Motor Carrier Safety Improvement Act (MCSIA). See the Appendix for more information about these mandatory CDL disqualification sanctions. Also, a Fact Sheet on CDL Sanctions is found at www.dmv.state.pa.us/pdotforms/fact_sheets/fs-pub7216.pdf.

DUI Convictions (Fines and jail sentences also imposed, which increase based on level and number of previous offenses.)

    .08 to .099% BAC - 2nd offense or 3rd offense .... Twelve-month suspension
    .10 to .159% BAC
        1st or 2nd offense .... Twelve-month suspension.
        3rd or 4th offense .... Eighteen-month suspension.
    .16% or higher BAC
        1st offense .... Twelve-month suspension.
        2nd or greater offense.. Eighteen-month suspension.
    DUI Commercial Driver, 2nd conviction... Lifetime disqualification.
    DUI ARD (Accelerated Rehabilitation Program)..................................... Maximum ninety days suspension.
Careless Driving Causing Serious Bodily Injury .... Three-month suspension.
Careless Driving Causing Unintentional Death .... Six-month suspension.
Child Support or Domestic Relations Issues.. Indefinite.
Conviction of Thirty-one mph Over Limit.. Fifteen-day suspension.
Drivers under age of eighteen
    Accumulation of Six or More Points... Ninety-day suspension.

High Speed Conviction (26 or more over posted limit)	Ninety-day suspension.
Second occurrence of either above	One hundred twenty-day suspension.
Driving Without Insurance	Three-month suspension.
Failure to Attend Departmental Hearings	Sixty-day suspension.
Failure to Comply With Crossing Gate or barrier	Thirty-day suspension.
Failure to Stop for School Bus With Flashing Red Lights	Sixty-day suspension.
Habitual Offender	Five-year revocation.
Operating a Vehicle Without Insurance or Financial Responsibility	Three-month suspension.
Point Accumulation of Six Points	
Second Time at Six Points (Departmental Hearing)	Fifteen-day suspension.
Failure to Attend Departmental Hearing	Sixty-day suspension.
Third Time at Six Points (Departmental Hearing)	Thirty-day suspension.
Failure to Attend Departmental Hearing	Indefinite suspension.
Point Accumulation of Eleven or More Points	
First Suspension	Five days per point.
Second Suspension	Ten days per point.
Third Suspension	Fifteen days per point.
Subsequent Suspensions	One-year suspension.
Possession, sale, or delivery of controlled substance regardless if motor vehicle involved:	
First Offense	Six-month suspension.
Second Offense	One-year suspension.
Third or Subsequent Offense	Two-year suspension.
Work Zone (active) Speeding if involved in accident or if 11 MPH or more over	Fifteen-day suspension.

Note About Points: Three points are removed from a driving record for every 12 consecutive months a person drives (from the date of the last violation) without a violation which results in points, license suspension or revocation.

Reinstatement Requirements
Suspension $25.00 to $100.00 fee; proof of financial responsibility.
Revocation $25.00 to $100.00 fee; proof of financial responsibility; must reapply for driving privilege by applying for learner's permit under some circumstances.

Point System Overview
Points range from 2 to 5. When an accumulation of 6 points occurs for the first time, the driver will receive written notice to take a special point examination. If the record reduces below 6 points and then reaches 6 or more points a second or subsequent time, suspensions, and more testing will occur. Accumulation of 11 or more points in one year will result in a suspension. Points recorded against any person shall be removed at the rate of 3 points for each 12 consecutive months (using the violation date) in which such person has not committed any violation which results in the assignment of points or in suspension or revocation. Three (3) points are removed from a driving record for every 12 consecutive months without a violation with points or action.

License Plate Facts

Registration Renewal
Renewal is annual, may be performed online including renewal for trailers, but insurance information is required.

New Residents
Non-residents must register vehicles at expiration of time granted by home-state reciprocity agreement or within twenty days of entry into Pennsylvania establishing residency.

Inspections and Emissions Testing
Pennsylvania has an annual vehicle safety inspection provision, but no statewide emission testing program. Four regional areas require annual emission testing: Pittsburgh area (Allegheny, Beaver, Washington, and Westmoreland counties); South Central (Berks, Cumberland, Dauphin, Lancaster, Lehigh, Northampton, and York counties); Philadelphia area (Bucks, Chester, Delaware, and Montgomery counties); and the Northern region (Blair, Cambria, Centre, Erie, Lackawanna, Luzerne, Lycoming, and Mercer counties). Thus, vehicles registered in 42 counties are not required to pass an emissions inspection.

Plate Descriptions
Typical Plate Pattern   Passenger plates are 3 alpha-4 numeric, or 6 numeric, or 1 alpha-5 numeric, or 3 alpha-3 numeric. Trucks and truck trailers are 2 alpha-5 numeric.

Pennsylvania — The 2010 U.S. Motor Vehicle Reference Book

County Codes — There is not a coding sequence which depicts county of issuance.
Plates and Stickers in Force — One plate, one decal (MO & YR).
Plate Remains with Car when Sold? — No, plate remains with seller..

Overview of Record Access

About Driving Records
Driver Record Services, Department of Transportation, PO Box 68695, Harrisburg 17106-8695, 717-391-6190. The in-state toll-free number for questions is 800-932-4600. A $5.00 fee is charged for each of four different record types: basic information; a three-year driving record; a ten-year record on a commercial driver; or a copy of a document from microfilm. Add $5.00 for a complete, certified record that contains all violations. Also, a Letter of Clearance may be requested for $5.00. Use DL-130, forms are downloadable from www.dmv.state.pa.us/forms/driversLicenseForms.shtml. Pennsylvania charges for "no record found" reports.

Request Methods – Mail, Walk-in, Online.

What You Should Know – Online access is available to approved requesters - usually businesses who obtain driver histories for the purpose of employment or insurance. Visit the Department's web site (www.dmv.state.pa.us) and click on the Online Business Services tab for more information.

Special Access Programs Available – PA licensed drivers may purchase their own driving record online at www.dmv.state.pa.us/centers/OnlineServicesCenter.shtml.

About Accident Reports
Copies of accident reports within last five years can be obtained from the State Police Headquarters, Crash Reports Unit, 1800 Elmerton Avenue, Harrisburg 17110, 717-783-5516, fax is 717-705-6368. However, only those involved or attorney or insurer may request a copy, per Section 3751(b) of the Vehicle Code. Reports are $8.00; prepayment is required. Requesters must include drivers' names, the date, and the incident number. It takes an average of 15 days before new records are ready for inquiry. Turnaround time on mail requests is usually 3 weeks. Reports can be returned by email, if so requested

About Vehicle Records
Vehicle Record Services, Department of Transportation, 1101 South Front St, PO Box 68691, Harrisburg 17106-8691, 717-391-6190, in-state 800-932-4600. Records are kept for all vehicles and unattached mobile homes. For a fee of $5.00 per report, the following is available: Title History, Odometer, Basic Record, Encumbrance, and Insurance Record (a copy of the title/renewal transaction is provided). There is an additional $5.00 for certification. Note that encumbrance or lien information is not considered public information and is only available per DPPA guidelines.

Request Methods – Mail, Walk-in, Bulk (limited).

What You Should Know – Requests must be submitted using Form DL-135 downloadable from the web at www.dmv.state.pa.us/forms/driversLicenseForms.shtml.

About Watercraft Records
PA Fish and Boat Commission, PO Box 68900, Harrisburg, 17106-8900, 717-705-7940, fax is 717-705-7931, www.fish.state.pa.us. Any boat powered by a gasoline, diesel or electric motor, including sailboats with auxiliary power must be registered. Boats must be titled if with inboard motor or outboard motor and 14 ft or longer and has a manufacture year of 1997 or newer. The agency follows the FCRA regarding the release of boat registration and ownership information. Liens are filed here for $5.00 per lien. As of 1998, this agency issues certificates of title. Search requests must be in writing and require signature of requester, reason for request, as much information about the boat or owner as possible. It can take as along as one month before new records are ready for inquiry. The Request Boat Title or Security Interest Information form is found at www.fish.state.pa.us/images/pages/forms/pfbc_t9.pdf. There is a $5.00 fee for either current ownership information or lien information. A title history report is $5.00 for each owner shown on the record chain. Credit cards are accepted.

Rhode Island

Administration	Important Telephone and Web Contacts
Sara R. Strachan Administrator, Motor Vehicles 100 Main Street, Pawtucket 02860 Operator Control The John O. Pastore Complex Harrington Hall - Lower Level 30 Howard Avenue - Bldg. 58 Cranston, RI 02920 www.dmv.ri.gov/	Operator Control ....401-462-0800 Main Number ....401-462-4368 Financial Responsibility ....401-462-5747 Titles...401-462-5774 Plates ....401-462-5801 State Department of Insurance ....401-222-2223 State Police..401-444-1000 There is no general email available for questions. RI Statutes: www.rilin.state.ri.us/

Driver License Facts

License Format
Seven numbers. The first two numbers represent the year of issuance, the third digit represents the location where was license issued, and the last four digits are sequential numbers. A "V" and six numbers indicate a disabled veteran.

Document Appearance
The document is a plastic laminate over a photocard.

Security Characteristics	A picture of the state appears in solid blue; security features are embossed in laminate.
Position of Photo	Top right for regular license; smaller ghost image is next to picture.
Provisional License	Yellow map of state on top. License is vertical, picture on bottom left with ghost image to the right. Above the photo states the day the driver will be 21.
Under 21 License	Blue map of state on top. License is vertical, picture on bottom left with ghost image to the right. Above the photo states the date the driver will be 21.
CDL Indicator	"CDL" appears on the license; also, the classification indicates a CDL.

Issue and Renewal

Age Requirements
The minimum age is 16 years and 6 months for a provisional. A Limited Instruction Permit is available for those between the ages of 16 - 18 who have completed a 33-hour driver education course certified by the Rhode Island Department of Education. An Instruction Permit is available for those 18 or older who have never held a driver's license in Rhode Island. If the license has expired over three (3) years, driver must apply for an Instruction Permit. This does not entail taking any driver education course, bus driver must pass written exam and road test given by the DMV.

Renewal
Renewal is on the birth month of fifth year except for drivers over 70 (see below). Driver keeps same number when renewing. License renewal can only be done in person and is not available online or by mail. A license held by a member of the U.S. Armed Forces is valid until 30 days after termination of service with Special Operator's License Form.

Elderly-Related Restrictions
Drivers who reach the age of 71 during a renewal cycle must renew their license in four years, drivers who reach the age of 72 must renew in three years, drivers 73 or older must renew every two years.

Residency
Non-resident's license honored on a reciprocal basis; Rhode Island license must be secured within thirty days of establishing residency.

License Classes

Commercial Classifications

Class A	Any combination of vehicles with a GVWR of more than 26,000 pounds—provided the GVWR of the vehicle(s) being towed is in excess of 10,000 pounds.

Class B	Any single vehicle with a GVWR of more than 26,000 pounds, or any such vehicle towing a vehicle not in excess of 10,000 pounds GVWR.
Class C	Any single vehicle with a GVWR of 26,000 pounds or less. This group applies to vehicles which are placarded for hazardous materials or designed to transport fifteen or more people (excluding the operator); school buses must have a special permit.

Non-Commercial Classifications

Class 0	Regular operator (Note: Can have "R" Restriction for Chauffeur)
Class 1	Jitney, taxi, bus.

HAZMAT Endorsement Procedure

The state is in compliance with the Patriot Act. All applicants applying for a new or renewal or transfer HAZMAT Endorsement (HME) must first obtain the application from https://hazprints.tsa.dhs.gov/Public/ or by calling 877-429-7746. The driver must also be fingerprinted. EMSI is the state-designated entity to process fingerprints. There is location in the state that perform this service, at 1006 Reservoir Avenue - 2nd floor, Cranston, RI 02920. The cost of the fingerprint process is $89.25. The fingerprints and application information is sent to the Federal Transportation Security Administration (TSA). TSA performs the background checks and notifies the DMV whether the application is approved or denied. When completed and approved, the HME is valid for five years. For more information, visit www.dmv.ri.gov/licenses/hazmat.php.

Safety and Enforcement Facts

Insurance and Financial Responsibility

Minimum liability limits are $25,000/50,000/25,000. The state has a compulsory insurance provision, but does not have no-fault insurance provision. Proof is required after insurance violations. SR-22 filing may be required.

Alcohol and Chemical Testing

The illegal intoxication level is .08 percent and above, .04 for CDL. The fines and suspensions will vary (see Section 31-27-2) as the BAC percentage increases to .10 and .15 percent. The same levels apply to under 21 aged drivers, but penalties are increased. Urine, blood, and breath testing are authorized. The state has an implied-consent law, but not a provision for an administrative per se suspension. Operating a bicycle under the influence is also considered illegal.

Accident Reporting

The operator of any motor vehicle involved in an accident in RI resulting in injuries and/or property damage in excess of $1,000.00, is required to report this accident in writing, within 21 days, to the Division of Motor Vehicles, Office of Safety Responsibility, 100 Main Street, Pawtucket, RI. If the operator is physically incapable of making out the report, it should be made by the owner within 21 days of having learned of the accident. For more information, call 401-462-5710. There is an accident report form available at www.dmv.ri.gov/forms/allforms.php.

Suspensions and Revocations

With regard to suspensions, there are many diverse reasons for which an individual may lose his/her license and registration. Some reasons are mandatory and many are at the discretion of the judge. *The MVR Access and Decoder Digest* lists the mandatory suspensions and revocations with corresponding codes.

MCSIA Compliance

Rhode Island is in compliance with the provisions of the Motor Carrier Safety Improvement Act (MCSIA). See the Appendix for a list of these mandatory CDL disqualification sanctions.

Reinstatement Requirements

To have a license reinstated, the driver must go to a DMV branch with the reinstatement notice, one identity document such as a birth certificate or passport, Social Security card, and proof of current address.

Suspension	$151.50 reinstatement fee.
Revocation	$151.50 reinstatement fee; proof of insurance.
Reinstatement if DUI or Refusal Related	$351.50.
Reinstatement for Suspended Registration (license plates)	$251.50.

Point System Overview

Rhode Island does not have a point system.

License Plate Facts

Registration Renewal

Renewal is available either online at www.dmv.ri.gov/onlineservices/ or by mail. You cannot renew in person, but one may renew at AAA (if a member) or use a dropbox at a DMV office. Renewal is annual. The DMV cannot process a renewal that has outstanding property taxes owed. If a person owes tax to a city or town, the person must first pay the tax and then have the tax assessor's office stamp the renewal form "Registration Approved.".

New Residents
Non-residents must register vehicles within thirty days of establishing residency; non-resident must also register vehicle, if owner uses it in connection with an established place of business in Rhode Island, otherwise non-resident's registration honored on reciprocal basis.

Inspections and Emissions Testing
Every car and light truck weighing 8,500 pounds or less must be safety and emission inspected every two years. All new motor vehicles have two years or 24,000 miles, whichever comes first, to obtain an inspection sticker. Trailers, semi-trailers, livestock trailers, motorcycles, and all other vehicles over 8,500 lbs must be inspected once a year. Vehicles registered as antiques (over 25 years old) or as being electric are exempt from the emissions inspection, but not the safety inspection. All trailers, semi-trailers with a GVW over 1,000 lbs., livestock trailers, and all motorcycles must be inspected before June 30 of each year.

Plate Descriptions
Typical Plate Pattern   Passenger plates have six numbers or can have a pattern of 2 letters, 3 numbers, but also all numeric or 1-2 alpha followed by 1-3 numbers. Commercial vehicle, light truck and combination plates are all numeric, either 5 or 6 numbers.
County Codes   There are no codes or indications to the county of issuance.
Plates and Stickers in Force   Two plates, one decal (MO & YR) on each plate.
Plates Remain with Car when Sold?   No, plates remain with seller.

Overview of Record Access

About Driving Records
Operator Control, John O.Pastore Complex, Harrington Hall - Lower Level, 30 Howard Avenue, Bldg. #58, Cranston, RI 02920 401-462-0800. The fee for a driving record is $17.50 by mail or in person, $19.50 if online. The state charges for "no record found" reports.
Request Methods – Mail, Walk-in, Online, Bulk (non-commercial purpose)
What You Should Know – Driving records are available in two manners from the DMV web portal. Anyone may request a masked record online at https://www.ri.gov/DMV/mvr/citizen/ for the $19.50 fee paid with a credit card, the record will be mailed. This three-year record does not contain the driver's address or SSN. For more information about becoming a subscriber for commercial full data records visit www.ri.gov/subscriber or call 401-832-8099, ext 260, or email rihelp@nicusa.com.

About Accident Reports
Copies of accident reports may be obtained directly from the Rhode Island State Police, Record Division, 311 Danielson Pike, North Scituate 02857, 401-444-1143, www.risp.dps.ri.gov/. Requesters are asked to submit drivers' names and date and location of the incident. There is a $10.00 charge per report.

About Vehicle Records
Registry of Motor Vehicles, 100 Main Street, Pawtucket 02860, 401-462-4368 or 401-462-5774. Requests are carefully screened for purpose. Records are not made available for commercial use, nor released over the phone.
Request Methods – Mail, Walk-in, Bulk (non-commercial purpose)
What You Should Know – The fee for VIN, ownership registration, name searches, and plate information is $11.50 per search. The fee for a lien search and/or title information is $51.50. These fees include a $1.50 surcharge imposed per record on all record requests. Title information can be obtained in person, registration information must be returned by mailed.

About Watercraft Records
Department of Environmental Management, Office of Boat Registration, 235 Promenade Rm 360, Providence 02908, 401-222-6647, fax (titles) 401-462-5783. All boats over 14 ft must be titled and registered. Lien information will show on a title record. All requests must be in writing and on their form. The agency will accept fax requests on their request form. Call or write for the form, it is not found on the web. The agency follows the mandates of the DPPA. There is no fee to do a simple name, file or registration search; otherwise the search is at least $15.00 per hour. Generally the turnaround time is within 1 to 2 weeks. For casual requesters, this agency will not release the name and address of a lien holder, but will indicate whether a lien does exist.

South Carolina

Administration	Important Telephone and Web Contacts
Marcia Adams Executive Director Department of Motor Vehicles PO Box 1498 Blythewood 29016 803-896-5599 www.scdmvonline.com	Driver Licensing.................................803-896-5000 SR-22 & Financial Responsibility..........803-896-5000 Commercial Driver License..................803-896-2673 Registration & Title Information............803-896-5000 Highway Patrol...................................803-896-7920 State Department of Insurance............803-737-6160 Email Help help@scdmvonline.com SC Code of Laws www.scstatehouse.net/code/statmast.htm

Driver License Facts

License Format
The South Carolina driver's license number consists of eleven numbers computer-generated on a sequential basis.

Document Appearance
The state issues a digitized license document with photo.
  Security Characteristics   Stiff lamination with a magnetic strip is on the top of the back. The state seal is in center of license. The document includes a hologram with state seal and state emblem.
  Position of Photo   Lower Right.
  Minor Age Driver Locator This is indicated across the top of the license.
  CDL Indicator   A CDL driver is designated by "CDL" on the license by a dark aqua green stripe with "COMMERCIAL DRIVER'S LICENSE" on the license itself, and shows class of license.

Issue and Renewal
Age Requirements
The minimum age is 16 for regular operator's permit. Beginner's Permits are issued in four classes according to the type of vehicle. You must be 14 years of age or older to drive a moped, Class G; 15 years of age or older to drive a passenger vehicle, Class D; motorcycle, Class M; and 18 years of age or older to drive a non-commercial, Class E or F vehicle. Beginner's Permit holders may drive from 6am to midnight. They must be accompanied by a licensed driver in the front seat who is 21 years of age or older, with at least one year of driving experience. A Conditional License is available to fifteen year olds, and a Special Restricted license is available to sixteen year olds. To drive a commercial vehicle Class A, B or C, you must be 18 years old to drive within the state of South Carolina and 21 years old to drive interstate.

Renewal
Both five and ten-year licenses are processed. Ten-year licenses are issued in branch offices to U.S. citizens who are under the age of 65. Five-year licenses are issued online and by mail to eligible applicants under the age of 65. Vision examinations are required every five years for all age applicants. Licenses expire on the applicant's birthday in the expiring year. Applicants may apply online at https://www.scdmvonline.com/DMVpublic/ or by mailing to the address listed above. ID cards can also be renewed online.

Elderly-Related Restrictions
Persons who are 65 years of age or older may only be issued a five-year license.

Residency
Non-resident's home-state license honored for ninety days; South Carolina license must be obtained upon establishing residency (except students and military personnel and their dependents). CDL holders must apply to a CDL license within 30 days.

License Classes
Commercial Classifications
  Class A   Any combination of vehicles with a GVWR of 26,001 or more pounds provided the unit being towed is in

		excess of 10,000 GVWR (except motorcycles).
	Class B	Any single vehicle with GVWR of 26,001 or more pounds, or any such vehicle towing a vehicle not in excess of 10,000 pounds (except motorcycles).
	Class C	Any single vehicle less than 26,001 pounds. GVWR placarded for hazardous materials or designed to transport sixteen or more persons, including driver (except motorcycles)..

Non-Commercial Classifications

- Class D — All vehicles not exceeding 26,000 pounds GVW (except motorcycles) that do no meet the definitions of Classes A, B and C.
- Class E — Single unit vehicles, including class D, exceeding 26,000 pounds GVW that do not meet the definition of Classes A, B & C (except motorcycles).
- Class F — All vehicle combinations (including Class D and E) exceeding 26,000 pounds GVW that do not meet the definition of Classes A, B & C (except motorcycles).
- Class M — Motorcycles.
- Class G — Moped.

HAZMAT Endorsement Procedure

All applicants applying for a new or renewal or transfer HAZMAT Endorsement (HME) must first obtain the application from www.scdmvonline.com/DLcdlHME.aspx. The driver must also be fingerprinted. There are ten locations in the state that perform this service. Visit the web page listed above to find the address locations. The cost of the entire process, including fingerprints is $83.00. The fingerprints and application information is sent to the Federal Transportation Security Administration (TSA). TSA performs the background checks and notifies the DMV whether the application is approved or denied. When completed and approved, the HME is valid for five years.

Safety and Enforcement Facts

Insurance and Financial Responsibility

Minimum financial responsibility limits are $25,000/50,000/25,000. Current South Carolina law requires when a driver's license is issued or renewed or if involved in an accident, drivers must certify on the driver's license application (DL 447) that they are insured by an automobile liability policy. Owners are required to provide proof that the vehicle being operated is insured. If a driver is stopped by a law enforcement officer and unable to provide proof that the vehicle being operating is insured, the driver may be issued a citation and be subject to a fine or imprisonment. South Carolina requires drivers to carry no-fault insurance. The state uses SR-22 forms. South Carolina law requires that insurance companies notify the department when a liability insurance policy is cancelled.

Alcohol and Chemical Testing

South Carolina's level at which a person may be inferred to be intoxicated is .08 BAC percent and above; .02 BAC or greater if under 21, and .04 BAC or greater in a CMV. There is an implied consent violation if under 21. There is also a separate violation if BAC is .15 or greater. Levels of BAC between .04 and .10 can be used with other evidence for a conviction.

Accident Reporting

Accidents resulting in death, injury, or property damage in excess of $1,000.00 must be reported immediately to the nearest law enforcement agency. At the time of an accident, South Carolina Law requires that the investigating officer issue a Notice of Requirement (Form FR-10) to verify that liability insurance was in effect. When the investigating officer issues the form, the owner is responsible for providing proof (via insurance company) that the vehicle involved in the accident was insured. Failure to provide insurance verification to the department within fifteen (15) days from the date of the accident may result in suspension of the owner's driver's license and/or registration privileges. The verification of liability insurance should be forwarded to the Department of Motor Vehicles, Financial Responsibility Office, PO Box 1498, Blythewood 29016-0050.

Suspensions and Revocations

South Carolina is in compliance with the provisions of the Motor Carrier Safety Improvement Act (MCSIA). See the Appendix for more information about these mandatory CDL disqualification sanctions.

The Following Violations Will Result in Driving Privileges Being Revoked—
- Conviction of Careless or Reckless Driving Resulting in Death
- Conviction of a Felony in Which a Vehicle Was Used
- Failure to Stop and Give Aid When Involved in an Accident Resulting in Death or Personal Injury
- Giving False Information Pertaining to Financial Responsibility or Vehicle Registration
- Mental or Physical Incompetence to Drive

The Following Violations Will Result in Driving Privileges Being Suspended—
Driving Under the Influence
    First Conviction .... Six-month suspension.
    Second Conviction .... One-year suspension.
    Third Conviction .... Two-year suspension.
    Fourth and Subsequent .... License revoked.
Felony DUI Conviction .... License revoked 3 years plus time served.
BAC of .02 or greater while under the age of 21 .... Three-month suspension.
Refusal to Submit to a Chemical Test, 21 and older .... Ninety-day suspension.
Refusal to Submit to a Chemical Test, under the age of 21 .... Six-month suspension.
Previous offenses of;
   Implied Consent, DUI, Felony DUI, BAC of .15 or greater within past 10 years One hundred eighty days suspension.
   Implied Consent under 21 with BAC of .02 or greater .... One year suspension.
   Implied Consent, DUI, Felony DUI, BAC of .15 or
      greater within the past 5 years .... One year suspension.
   BAC of .15 or greater .... Thirty-day suspension.
Previous offenses of Implied Consent under 21 with BAC of .15 or greater;
   Implied Consent, DUI, Felony DUI, BAC of .02 or greater within the past 10 years .. Sixty-day suspension.
   Implied Consent, DUI, Felony DUI, BAC of .02 or greater within the past 5 years .... Six-month suspension.
Second Conviction of Reckless Driving in Five Years .... Three-month suspension.
Each Subsequent Conviction in the Five-Year Period .... additional 3-month suspension.
Conviction for Hauling Illegal Whiskey .... Suspension.
Failure to Pay Traffic Ticket .... Suspension.
Failure to Satisfy Judgment Rendered When Involved in an Accident .... Suspension.
Habitual Offender .... Five-year suspension.
Point Accumulation of Twelve Points .... Suspension.
Note: Under SC law, a driver gets half of accumulated points removed each year. Also, a driver can take a class and have 4 points removed, but only once every three years.
   Taking Part in a Race on Any Public Road, Street, or Highway .. One-year suspension of license and registration.
   Assisting in a Race .... Three-month suspension of license and registration.

Any of the Following Will Result in Driving Privileges Being Canceled—
- If Driver is a Minor and Parent, Guardian, or Whomever Signed for Driver Withdraws his or her Signature from the License Application.
- Giving False Information on the Application.
- Driving While License Suspended, Revoked, or Canceled.

Since January 1, 2009, an **Ignition Interlock restriction** is required for persons who are convicted of a second or subsequent offense for the following violations:
   1) driving under the influence of alcohol or drugs,
   2) driving with an unlawful alcohol concentration, or
   3) causing great bodily injury or death while driving under the influence of alcohol or drugs.

Reinstatement Requirements

   Suspension .... $100.00 fee for each suspension; proof of insurance (SR-22); re-examination—varies depending on reason for suspension.
   Revocation .... Proof of financial responsibility; re-examination—varies depending on reason for revocation and failure to provide financial responsibility liability statement (first time issuance of driver license)..
   Vehicle Reinstatement ... When notified by department (liability insurance cancellation), the vehicle owner must reinstate insurance on the vehicle(s) or surrender license plates and registration to the department as soon as possible. Owner will be charged $5.00 per day, not to exceed $200.00, for a vehicle not insured, beginning on the date of the cancellation. If suspended, owner will be required to pay a $200.00 reinstatement fee.

Point System Overview

Points range from 2 to 6. Accumulation of 12 or more points can result in a suspension. Half of the accumulated points can be removed each year. A driver may take a driving class to have 4 points removed, but the driver is limited to taking the class once every 3 years.

License Plate Facts

Registration Renewal
Renewal is annual. In South Carolina, payment of personal property taxes is required before a license plate can be renewed. Citizens can pay both the property taxes and renewal fees at the county treasurer's office. If taxes are paid, renewal can be done online at https://www.scdmvonline.com/DMVpublic. These counties provide the ability to pay both taxes and registration fees online; Beaufort, Berkeley, Charleston, Chester, Darlington, Dorchester, Greenville, Lexington, Pickens, Richland, Spartanburg, and York.

New Residents
Registration must be obtained within 45 days of establishing residency.

Inspections and Emissions Testing
There are no provisions for statewide emission testing or annual safety inspections.

Plate Descriptions
Typical Plate Pattern ....Passengers and trucks not more than 7,000 lbs empty weight or 9,000 GVW are LLLNNN (in 1999, the pattern changed to NNNLLL). Light trucks are PS or P followed by 5 or 6 numbers. Commercial vehicles are PS or P followed by 5 or 6 numbers; or P7 (IRP).
County Code ....The county of issuance is not indicated on the plate.
Plates and Stickers in Force ....One plate, two decals (MO) (YR).
Plate Remains with Car when Sold? . No, it remains with seller.

Overview of Record Access

About Driving Records
Driver Records Mail-In Unit, PO Box 1498, Blythewood 29016-0028, 803-896-5000. The fee is $6.00 for manual processing and $7.25 for electronic access.

Request Methods – Mail, Walk-in, Online (commercial and public).

What You Should Know – South Carolina gives a second summary on CDL driver records. This summary separates all driver moving violations occurring while under a commercial status, including out-of-state violations. These second summaries show on all the access modes listed previously

Special Access Programs Available – Commercial records are available from the portal https://app.sc.gov/dmv/. One may obtain either a free summary of a driving record or purchase a three or ten-year record for $6.00 at https://www.scdmvonline.com/DMVpublic/.

About Vehicle Records
Registration (or Titles) Section, PO Box 1498, Blythewood   29016-0024, 803-896-5000, fax: 803-896-6682, www.scdmvonline.com. The state maintains the registration, title, and lien records for vehicles and mobile homes. The state will not release name and address information, but will confirm validity of name and address if provided by requester. The current fee for all VIN, registration, and lien checks is $6.00, add $20.00 for expedited service (see below).

Request Methods – Mail, Walk-in, Fax, Bulk.

What You Should Know – The title history contains odometer reading information, as known. Both title and registration records are held for 3 years on computer. Title records are held on microfiche since 1984.

Special Access Programs Available – Fax searching is only available to pre-approved, ongoing requesters. A deposit is required.

About Watercraft Records
Department of Natural Resources, Registration & Titles, PO Box 167, Columbia 29202, 803-734-3857, www.dnr.sc.gov/boating/index.html. All motorized boats must be titled and registered. All boat motors must be titled. There is a distinction between a boat title and a motor title. All outboard motors with five HP or greater are required to be titled. All sailboats must be titled. All sailboats over 14 foot must be titled and registered. A title search request will show any liens. The search fee is $10.00 per record. Thus, a search of boats w/no motor is $10.00 and a search of a boat and an outboard motor is $20.00. State law prohibits the release for records for commercial purposes. The Department suggests submitting VIN, hull # with description, but can run a name search if requested. SSNs are not released. Turnaround time is generally 7 to 10 days, but can take up to 3 weeks. The agency will sell the database in bulk to qualified entities. Records are maintained on microfilm or on a document imaging system and are retained for 75 years.

South Dakota

Administration	Important Telephone and Web Contacts

Tom Dravland, Secretary
Department of Public Safety
605-773-3178
 	
Cynthia Gerber, Director
Office of Driver Licensing
Department of Public Safety
118 W Capitol, Pierre 57501
605-773-6883
 	
Debra Hillmer, Director
Motor Vehicle Division, Revenue Department
445 E Capitol, Pierre 57501-3100
605-773-3541
 	
http://dps.sd.gov/licensing/driver_licensing/default.aspx
(Driver)
www.state.sd.us/drr2/motorvehicle/index.htm (Veh.)
	Driver Licensing..................................605-773-6883
	Financial Responsibility/SR-22 605-773-6883
	Commercial Driver License....................605-773-6883
	Accident Reports 605-773-3868
	Motor Carrier Services 605-773-4578
	Title and Registration Information 605-773-3541
	State Department of Insurance.................605-773-3563
	Highway Patrol......................................605-773-3105
	
	To Find Contact List for DL Matters:
	  http://dps.sd.gov/contact.aspx
	General Email for Vehicles: motorv@state.sd.us
	SD Codified Laws:
	  http://legis.state.sd.us/statutes/index.aspx
	Motor Vehicle Statutes - Title 10 and 32:
	www.state.sd.us/drr2/laws/motor_v/motorv_statutes.htm

Driver License Facts

License Format
The current DL is an eight digit computer-generated sequential number. Until July 2006, Social Security Numbers were used at the DL number. Prior to December 4, 1989, license numbers had six digits. Military and old suspended/revoked drivers may still have older licenses.

Document Appearance
The state began issuing a new driver license and ID Card in December 2009. The previous driver license document originally was issued in May 2000. Both documents are reviewed below.

Current Document

Security Characteristics	A ghost image of the driver's photo is in the lower right; 1 and 2-dimensional barcodes on rear; Mt Rushmore shows in the background. The laminate has various designs and includes the words "The Mount Rushmore State."
Position of Photo	Left.
Minor Age Drivers	The card is in a vertical format. A red colored header is used for driver license and ID Cards for ages 16 to 21. A green header is used for drivers under 18 driving on a restricted license. (Regular drivers have blue headers.) Date indicates when driver turns 21.
CDL Indicator	"COMMERCIAL DRIVER LICENSE" is printed in gold.

Older Document

Security Characteristics	A ghost image of the driver's photo is in the lower left corner; a 2-dimensional barcode on rear; the words "South Dakota" written all over the face of the document.
Position of Photo	Upper right.
Minor Age Driver Locator	A red colored header is used for drivers 16 to 21. A green header is used for drivers under 18 driving on a restricted license. (Regular drivers have blue headers.) A gray header is used for ID cards. Date indicates when driver turns 21.
CDL Indicator	"COMMERCIAL DRIVER LICENSE" is printed in gold header.

Issue and Renewal
Age Requirements
Effective 01/01/99, South Dakota implemented a Graduated Licensing System.

Minimum Age	Sixteen for an operator license; fourteen for Instruction Permit.
Instruction Permit	Fourteen; valid from 6AM to 10PM when accompanied by licensed driver who is at least 18 years of age and who has at least one year of driving experience. From 10PM to 6AM, permittee must be accompanied by a parent or legal guardian.
Restricted Minor's Permit	Must be at least 14 years of age and pass the vision, knowledge, and driving test, complete the requirements of the Instruction Permit, and have not been convicted of a traffic violation during the prior six months. An individual up to age 18 years of age may hold a Restricted Minor's Permit. This permit is valid from 6AM to 10PM; if accompanied by parent/guardian, valid from 10PM to 6AM.

Renewal
Birth month of fifth year. Driver keeps the same number when renewing, unless number is SSN. All SSNs are being converted to the computer-generated eight digit number. Active military licenses do not expire.

Elderly-Related Restrictions
None reported.

Residency
Non-residents must secure a license within ninety days of establishing residency. CDL holders must secure a license within thirty days of establishing residency.

License Classes
Commercial Classifications

Class A	Any combination of vehicles with a GCWR of 26,001 or more pounds—provided the GVWR of the vehicle(s) being towed is in excess of 10,000 pounds.
Class B	Any single vehicle with a GVWR of 26,001 or more pounds, or any such vehicle towing a vehicle not in excess of 10,000 pounds GVWR.
Class C	Any single vehicle less than 26,001 pounds GVWR, or any such vehicle towing a vehicle not in excess of 10,000 pounds GVWR. Applies only to vehicles placarded for hazardous materials or designed to transport sixteen or more passengers (including driver).

Note: Class A3, B3, C3 are commercial driver license classes with motorcycle.

Non-Commercial Classifications
1. Car/Light Truck/Moped
2. Class 1 and Motorcycle
3. Motorcycle Only

Note on Restricted Driver Licenses
Under certain circumstances, drivers whose license are under suspension or revocation may be issued a restricted (paper document) driver license enabling them to drive under certain restrictions imposed by the Department. These restrictions will be noted on the driver license document.

HAZMAT Endorsement Procedure
The state is in compliance with the Patriot Act. All applicants applying for a new or renewal or transfer HAZMAT Endorsement (HME) must first obtain the application from https://hazprints.tsa.dhs.gov/Public/ or by calling 877-429-7746. The driver must also be fingerprinted. IBT is the state-designated entity to process fingerprints. There are two state locations and fourteen sheriff offices in the state that perform this service. Visit the web page to find the address locations. The cost of the fingerprint process is $89.25. The fingerprints and application information is sent to the Federal Transportation Security Administration (TSA). TSA performs the background checks and notifies the DMV whether the application is approved or denied. When completed and approved, the HME is valid for five years. For more information, visit http://dps.sd.gov/licensing/driver_licensing/hazardous_materials_endorsement.aspx.

Safety and Enforcement Facts

Insurance and Financial Responsibility
Minimum limits are $25,000/50,000/25,000. South Dakota does not have no-fault insurance. Proof of financial responsibility is required for all residents and must be carried in the vehicle and presented at the request of law enforcement. SR-22 is required following conviction with no insurance, for unsatisfied judgments involving accidents, conviction of DWI, vehicular homicide, or conviction of a second offense for a reckless driving within a one-year period.

Alcohol and Chemical Testing
South Dakota's illegal intoxication level is BAC .08 percent and above; .04 BAC if driving a CMV; and .02 BAC if under age 21. Urine, blood, and breath testing are authorized.

Accident Reporting
Accidents involving death, injury, $1,000.00 property damage to any one person, or in excess of $2,000.00 combined property damage must be reported to the nearest law enforcement agency. There are no special state reporting requirements for CDL.

Suspensions and Revocations
The South Dakota DPS is in compliance with the provisions of the Motor Carrier Safety Improvement Act (MCSIA). See the Appendix for more information about these mandatory CDL disqualification sanctions.

Point Accumulation *(Fifteen points in twelve months or twenty-two points in twenty-four months)*

First Offense	Sixty-day suspension.
Second Offense	Six-month suspension.
Third or Subsequent Offense	One-year suspension.

Minor's Conviction of Class 1 Misdemeanor or Felony
    Suspended until 16th birthday or as directed by the courts.

Restricted Minor License *Traffic Violation Conviction or License Restriction Conviction*

First Offense	Thirty-day suspension.
Second Offense	Revocation until sixteenth birthday or ninety days, whichever is longer.

Driving While Intoxicated

First Conviction	Thirty-day revocation.
Second Conviction Within Ten Year Period	One-year revocation.
Third Conviction Within Ten Year Period	One-year revocation from sentence date or release from incarceration, whichever is longer.
*Refusal to Submit to Chemical Test	One-year revocation.

The Following Violations Will Also Result in Revocation or Suspension of Driving Privileges

- Alcohol Possession (not in a Motor Vehicle) by a Minor Under 21
- Conviction for False Information on Application
- Conviction for Possession of Suspended, Revoked or Altered Driver License
- Court Ordered Suspension or Revocation
- Under 18 years of age, Violation of License Restriction
- Driving While Under the Influence
- Driving While License is Revoked or Suspended
- Eluding Law Enforcement
- Failure to Maintain Proof of Insurance
- Failure to Pay Child Support
- Failure to Pay a Fine
- Failure to Satisfy a Judgment as a Result of an Accident
- Point Accumulation
- Possession/Consumption of Alcohol in a Motor Vehicle (Driver only)
- Possession/Consumption of Drugs in a Motor Vehicle
- Providing Alcoholic Beverages to Person Under 21
- *Refusal to Submit to a Chemical Test (.02 BAC only)
- Two Convictions for Reckless Driving Within Twelve Months
- Under 16 Years of Age, Conviction of Any Traffic Offense
- Vehicular Homicide

Notes 1) * = Implied Consent repealed except for .02 BAC, under age 21 arrests.
    2) Restricted licenses for work purposes are available on some suspensions and revocations.

Reinstatement Requirements
Suspension $50.00 fee; eye exam and written test required if license is expired more than 30 days.
Revocation $50.00 to $200.00 fee; eye exam; knowledge test; financial responsibility required after DWI, no insurance, vehicular homicide, judgment, or 2nd offense of reckless driving in one-year period.
Note: There are specific and varying reinstatement fees for certain, specific revocations

Point System Overview
Points range from 2 to 10 points. When multiple pointable violations occur, points are assessed on in-state and out-of-state convictions to determine if license should be suspended. Any operator who accumulates 15 points in any 12 consecutive months, or 22 points in 24 consecutive months is subject to possible suspension.

License Plate Facts

Registration Renewal
All motor vehicles, motorcycles, and trailers owned by South Dakota residents and operated on public highways must be registered with the County Treasurer of the applicant's residence. All snowmobiles used on public and private lands and

any frozen public waters within territorial limits of South Dakota must be licensed. Registration renewals are determined on a staggered registration renewal system based on the first letter in the last name. The chart is available at the web page www.state.sd.us/drr2/motorvehicle/index.htm. Renewal is available online at www.sdcars.org, exceptions are boats, snowmobiles, or if address change is necessary.

New Residents
New residents must register vehicles within ninety days, on reciprocal basis.

Inspections and Emissions Testing
South Dakota requires neither a vehicle safety inspection nor an emissions test..

Plate Descriptions

Typical Plate Pattern — Current plates issued have 6 characters, except personalized which may contain 7. Non-commercial vehicle plates are 1 or 2 numeric characters followed by 1, 2 or 3 alpha and 1, 2, 3 or 4 numeric. Example: 36A000 or 1A0000. Commercial vehicle plates are alpha and 4 or 5 numeric. Example: Z0000 or Z00000.

County Codes — The first 1 or 2 numeric characters designate the county of issuance. There are 66 (1-65 + 67) codes, but they are not in alphabetical order. To obtain this code list, we suggest calling the DMV.

Plates and Stickers in Force — Two plates, one decal (MO & YR) on both plates.

Plates Remain with Car when Sold? Since 07/01/2008, typical passenger and commercial plates no longer transfer with the vehicle and stay with the person. Organizational plates remain with the owner. Seller must provide purchaser with a seller's permit that is used by the new purchaser until plates can be obtained. A seller's permit can be obtained online as www.sdcars.org. Seller must also report the sale on a private transaction within 15 days of the sale. A report of sale form is used if the form is not on the title. The form is available on the web at www.state.sd.us/drr2/motorvehicle/forms.htm.

Overview of Record Access

About Driving Records
Driver License Program, 118 West Capital, Pierre 57501, 605-773-6883. The current fee is $5.00, the last fee increase was in 2009. The state does charge for "no record found" reports.

Request Methods — Mail, Walk-in, Telephone, Online.

What You Should Know — For online access, the system is open for pre-approved requesters 24 hours a day. There is a minimum of 250 requests daily. Call the number above.

About Accident Reports
Copies of officer-completed reports are available from the Department of Public Safety, Accident Records, 118 W Capitol Avenue, Pierre 57501, 605-773-4156. The fee is $4.00 per report. Records are available for ten years to present, five years on paper. The SSN is not released. New records are available for inquiry after one week, but can take 20 days. Full name, the date and location of the accident is required. Turnaround time is five to fifteen days

About Vehicle Records
Division of Motor Vehicles, Information Section, 445 E. Capitol, Pierre 57501-3185, 605-773-3541. Information is available on the following types of vehicles: cars, trucks, boats, snowmobiles, motorcycles, trailers, and motor-homes. The DMV took over the registration process for boats in 1992. The current fee for a computer printout of VIN, registration, ownership or a lien check is $2.00 per record. The fee is $5.00 for a complete title history from microfilm. Original paper documents are maintained for 18 months, but all records are maintained permanently on film. The record request DPPA Form can be downloaded from the web.

Request Methods — Mail, Walk-in.

What You Should Know — The titling and registering of motor vehicles is done through the local county treasurers offices. All snowmobiles used on public and private lands and any frozen public waters within territorial limits of South Dakota must be licensed.

About Watercraft Records
All boats over 12 feet in length and all motor boats regardless of length must be titled and registered; however, canoes, inflatable vessels, kayaks, sailboards and seaplanes are exempt from titling. Liens and registration records are available for boats 12 foot or longer and motorized boats. Liens on smaller boats are filed at the office of the Secretary of State. The fee is $2.00 for a title or registration check and $5.00 for a complete title history. Requesters must use the state's DPPA Form described above. The SSN is not released. Previous owner's address information is extremely limited.

Tennessee

Administration

Kenneth Birdwell, Director
  Financial Responsibility Division
Michael Hogan, Director
  Driver Services Division
Department of Safety, Nashville 37249-2000
615-251-5253

Linda Kelly
Taxpayer & Vehicles Services
Department of Revenue
44 Vantage Way, Ste 160
Nashville 37243-8050
615-741-3101

www.tennessee.gov/safety/ (Driver)
http://state.tn.us/revenue/vehicle/index.htm (Vehicle)

Important Telephone and Web Contacts

Driver Licensing & CDL 615-253-5221
SR-22 & Financial Responsibility 615-741-3954
Suspension/Revocation/Records.............. 866-903-7357
Vehicle Information .... 615-741-3101 or 888-971-3171
State Department of Insurance................. 615-741-2241
Highway Patrol.. 615-251-5175

General Email - Driver   safety@state.tn.us
General Email - Vehicle   revenue@state.tn.us

Rules and Regulations - Driver
    www.tennessee.gov/safety/laws.htm

Driver License Facts

License Format
Nine numbers (as of 2000), seven or eight numbers (pre-2000). Tennessee indicates the last digit is a check-digit based upon a confidential algorithmic formula. The older format was phased out as renewal licenses are issued, although military personnel may still have the old format. Those who still hold a valid license with only eight digits will have a leading zero (0) at the beginning of their current eight-digit number.

Document Appearance
The current document has been issued since 2003. The text below describes both old and new. Any Tennessee driver license issued to a minor has the word "INTERMEDIATE" as part of the license title.

Current Document

Appearance	Digitized photo and signature, laminated PVC card stock.
Security Characteristics	Ghost image of photo in lower right corner for over 18, lower left corner for under 18. Gold reflective "Tennessee - The Volunteer State" and state seal in top laminate.
Position of Photo	Top left corner for over 18, top right corner for under 18. For the ID only, the photo is in lower right corner and the document is in a vertical format.
Under 18 Age Driver	Photo on right with yellow header bar indicating "Intermediate" Restricted or Unrestricted Driver License.
Under 21 Age Driver	Photo on left with red bar running down left side of photo indicating "Under 21 Until xx-xx-xxxx."
CDL Indicator	"Commercial Driver License" on green header bar above the driver license number. Also, Tennessee state outline over lapping the ghost image with the letters "CDL" inside.

Old Document

Appearance	Digitized photo and signature, PVC card type, laminated.
Security Characteristics	A small ghost image of the photo was over data area. Reflective gold "Tennessee" and the state seal form a security pattern on front laminate; microdot signature line.
Position of Photo	Top left corner.
Minor Age Driver	Red portrait border, red header, "UNDER 21" to the left of the license number; twenty-first birthday in red in the data area.
CDL Indicator	"Commercial Driver License" on header above driver license. May be abbreviated as

"CDL" for temporary or seasonal CDLs, CDLs with CDL permit, or non-CDL's with CDL permit.

Issue and Renewal
Age Requirements
The minimum age for a D Class license is eighteen. Under eighteen falls under the Intermediate Class D. A Learner's Permit is granted at fifteen; must hold until sixteenth birthday; must be accompanied by a twenty-one or older who holds valid license. Those with an Intermediate Restricted License must have held a permit for 180 days and can only have one other passenger in the vehicle unless: 1) one or more of the passengers is age 21 or older and has a valid, unrestricted license; 2) the passengers are brothers and sisters, step-brothers or step-sisters, adopted or fostered children residing in the same house as the driver and going to and from school AND the intermediate license holder has in their possession written permission from their parent or guardian to transport their siblings.

Those with an Intermediate License are prohibited from driving between the hours of 11pm and 6am unless they are: 1) accompanied by a parent or guardian; 2) accompanied by a licensed driver 21 or older who has been designated by the parent or guardian and this designation is in writing and be in the possession of the teen driver; 3) driving to or from a specifically identified school sponsored activity or event and have in their possession written permission from a parent or guardian to do this; 4) driving to or from work and have in their possession written permission from a parent or guardian identifying the place of employment and authorizing the driver to go to and from work; 5) driving to or from hunting or fishing between 4am and 6am and have in their possession a valid hunting or fishing license. A Hardship License is granted at age fourteen or fifteen for those who have a legitimate need.

Renewal
Licenses are renewed on a five-year cycle (birth date), but may be first issued for 3-7 years. Driver keeps same number when renewing. Drivers are granted the option of renewing their non-commercial license by mail or Internet (www.tennessee.gov/safety/) every-other cycle and will receive a new license produced with the current digitized image on file and new expiration date. Military personnel stationed outside Tennessee are granted a "Code30" which does not expire until they are discharged or re-assigned to TN. Renewal by mail then is only necessary for those who did not establish their military status beforehand. Once the person has been honorably discharged or separated from such services or has been reassigned to a duty station within the state, he or she must renew his/her license within sixty (60) days following the date of separation on the DD-214 Form.

The Temporary Driver License (XD) or Identification (XID) will have the same expiration date as the holders authorized stay in the U.S. The could range from 2 days up to a maximum of 5 years.

Elderly-Related Restrictions
None indicated.

Residency
A non-resident must secure Tennessee license within thirty days of establishing residency and must provide examiner with 2 documents confirming Tennessee residence address. If a new resident brings a valid out-of-state driver license (or a certified driving record from that state showing the license has not expired), only the vision test is required, unless otherwise deemed necessary by the Examiner. However, if the license has expired over six months, all tests are required. New residents from other countries are required to take full tests: vision, knowledge and road tests.

License Classes
Commercial Classifications
Class A	Combination vehicles 26,001 pounds or larger GCWR, with trailers over 10,000 pounds.
Class B	Trucks/buses 26,001 pounds or larger GVWR and trailers equal to or less than 10,000 pounds.
Class C	Trucks/buses equal to or less than 26,000 pounds, requiring special endorsements H, X, P, or S.

Non-Commercial Classifications
Class D	Vehicles equal to or less than 26,000 pounds. No special endorsements required.
Class ID	Identification only.
Class M	Motorcycles and motor-driven cycles.
Class H	Hardship limited and restricted use Class D or M (age fourteen to sixteen). Valid only for daylight hours and for travel to authorized locations as specified in the approval letter.
Class P	Learner permit for class indicated.
Class TD	No longer issued. Previously, a Certificate for Driving (CFD) was available to persons who do not qualify for a Tennessee driver license, but this document was replaced by the TDL Class. As of October 1, 2007 the CFD is no longer issued to new applicants. Those holding an expired or expiring certificate will not be able to have it renewed and must apply for the new Temporary Driver License (Class XD) if they qualify.

Class XD   Effective October, 1 2007, the Tennessee Department of Safety began issuing a Temporary Driver License (TDL) to foreign nationals residing in Tennessee whose legal, temporary presence has been authorized by the federal government for an authorized stay at time of application. The new TDL documents are available only for non-CDL class licenses. The TDL Class is indicated by an "X" preceding the letter of the class (i.e. XD, XM, XPD, etc.). Only the "For Hire (F)" endorsement may be obtained on a TDL.

Class XID   A Temporary Identification License. For applicants who can provide federal proof of legal, temporary presence but do not drive. Requires minimum authorized stay of one year at time of application.

Note1:   On driving records, License Classes can show as a combination of the classification letters above. For example "Class BMP" is a Class B License with a Class M Permit and "Class DMPB" is a Class D License with Motorcycle and Class B Permit.

Note2:   Below are older classes; they do not exist after expiration of July 1993 issue, except for non-expiring military licenses.

Class OP   Operator
Class SC   Special Chauffeur
Class CH   Chauffeur
Class HS   Hardship.

HAZMAT Endorsement Procedure

The state is in compliance with the Patriot Act. All applicants applying for a new or renewal or transfer HAZMAT Endorsement (HME) must pass a vision and hazardous materials knowledge test, and complete the HME Application at a Department of Safety (DOS) Driver License Station. Testing and application must be completed before fingerprinting. Applicants for an HME must register to be fingerprinted by calling Tennessee Applicant Processing Services (TAPS) toll-free at 1-877-862-2425 or online at https://www.cogentid.com/tn/index_tn.htm. The cost of the fingerprint process by the state vendor, the background check and TSA Threat Assessment is $82.00. The fingerprints and background check are process by the TN Bureau of Investigation and forwarded to the Federal Transportation Security Administration (TSA). TSA notifies the DMV whether the application is approved or denied. For more information visit www.tennessee.gov/safety/driverlicense/hazmat.htm.

Safety and Enforcement Facts

Insurance and Financial Responsibility

Tennessee does not have compulsory liability insurance, but does require financial responsibility. The minimum limits (effective 01/01/2009) are $25,000/50,000/15,000. At the time a driver is charged with any moving violation or involved in a motor vehicle accident, the officer will request evidence of financial responsibility. Such evidence may include proof of liability insurance, self-insured certificate, certificate that bond has been posted with the Commissioner in the amount of $60,000, or if vehicle is regulated by ICC. If such evidence is not provided, the driver will be issued a citation. If convicted, driver is subject to a fine of not more than $100 and the driver's privileges are suspended. SR-22 forms are used when proof of financial responsibility for the future is required. The state has mandatory no-fault insurance if coverage is offered by the insurance company; otherwise, it is not mandatory.

Alcohol and Chemical Testing

Tennessee does not have a per se law, but rather a "presumptive" law. At .08 percent and above BAC, drivers are presumed to be driving while intoxicated; .04% if the driver has a CDL. If a person has one or more convictions of DUI, the presumptive BAC content level is .08%. For persons age 16 to 21, a BAC level of .02% creates a presumption the person is impaired. For persons age 21 or older, a BAC level of .08% creates a presumption the person is impaired. Urine, blood, and breath testing are authorized. If the court determines that test was refused, driving privileges are suspended for twelve months. Operating a horse or bicycle under the influence is also considered illegal.

Accident Reporting

Accidents resulting in death, personal injury, or damage in excess of $400.00 to any one person's property must be reported immediately to any law enforcement agency. A report must be filed within twenty days with the Financial Responsibility Section, Compliance and Reinstatement, Department of Safety, PO Box 945, Nashville 37202, 615-741-3954. Report forms are available from the Department or use www.tennessee.gov/safety/forms/owneroperator.pdf. There are no special reporting requirements for commercial drivers.

Suspensions and Revocations

The Tennessee Department of Safety is in compliance with the provisions of the Motor Carrier Safety Improvement Act (MCSIA). See The Appendix for more information about these **mandatory CDL disqualification** sanctions.

Letter of Proposed Suspension

The accumulation of twelve or more points in twelve months triggers a **Letter of Proposed Suspension**. This letter may serve as a request for a hearing, if the licensee checks the appropriate box and returns the letter to the Driver Improvement Section within twenty days. If a hearing is not requested within twenty days, the license is automatically suspended.

Drivers less than eighteen years of age that accumulate six or more points on their driving record within any twelve-month period are sent a notice of proposed suspension from the Department of Safety and are placed in the Driver Improvement Program. The driver will be required to attend an administrative hearing, with their parent or guardian present, to discuss the points assigned to their driving record. Certain actions could be imposed based on the outcome of the hearing and the number of points accumulated on the driver's record.

Alcohol-Related Withdrawals:

Implied Consent	Twelve months.
Implied Consent Involving Accident with Injury	Twenty-four months.
Implied Consent Involving Accident with Death	Five years.
Driving While Impaired 2nd offense	Two years, restricted license not available (repealed 07/03).

Driving Under the Influence, .08 BAC

1st time	One year.
2nd time	Two years, restricted license available (Ignition Interlock required after one year).
3rd time	Three to ten years, restricted license not available.
4th and subsequent time	Five years, restricted license not available.

Other Violations Which May Result in Revocation or Suspension

- Aggravated Vehicular Homicide (while driving intoxicated)
- Allowing Unlawful Use of License
- Altering Driver's License
- Conviction of Failure to Provide Evidence of Financial Responsibility
- Drag Racing
- Driving Under the Influence
- Failure to Pay Fine and/or Appear in Court for Moving Violation
- Failure to Resolve, Discharge, or Satisfy a Court Judgment Involving an Accident
- Failure to Stop and Give Aid
- Felony Involving Use of a Motor Vehicle
- Frequent Convictions of Traffic Law Violations
- Habitual Offender
- Leaving the Scene of a Personal Injury Accident
- Mental or Physical Difficulties
- Most Aggravated Drunk Driver (.20 or more BAC)
- Perjury, or Giving False Information Pertaining to Use or Ownership of a Vehicle
- Two Convictions of Reckless Driving in Twelve Months
- Violation of Restriction Codes

Reinstatement Requirements

Requirements vary with the specific violations. The agency provides an overview at www.tennessee.gov/safety/financialresponsibility.htm but there is not specific list of with fees and requirements. Upon request, the individual is advised by letter of requirement for reinstatement

Point System Overview

Points range from 1 to 8. Accumulation of 12 points in a 12-month period can result in a suspension. An excellent description of the points system and the Driver Improvement program is found at www.tennessee.gov/safety/PointSystem.pdf.

License Plate Facts

Registration Renewal

Registration is annual. Renewal is unavailable online on a statewide system, but some counties offer online renewal.

New Residents

Non-residents employed in Tennessee must register vehicles after thirty days; new residents must register immediately.

Inspections and Emissions Testing

Tennessee has no statewide provisions for vehicle annual safety inspections. Residents of Davidson, Hamilton, Rutherford, Sumner, Williamson and Wilson counties located in the middle of Tennessee, and residents of Memphis (Shelby County within city limits) must have their vehicles pass an emissions inspection prior to registration or registration renewal. This inspection is not required for vehicles of model year 1974 and older in the middle Tennessee counties. However, in Memphis an inspection is required for vehicles of all model years.

Plate Descriptions

Typical Plate Pattern	Passenger and light truck plates are made up with 3 numbers and 3 alphas. Commercial vehicle plates are 1 alpha and 5 or 6 numbers.
County Code	The county of issuance appears on one of the stickers on the plate.
Plates and Stickers in Force	Usually 1 plate, 2 or 3 decals (MO) (YR) (County). There can be up to 5 decals if a wheel tax is applicable.
Plates Remain with Car when Sold?	No, it remains with the seller.

Overview of Record Access

About Driving Records

Dept of Public Safety, Financial Responsibility Section, MVR Request, PO Box 945, Nashville 37202, 615-741-3954 or 866-903-7357. The fee for a three-year record is $5.00, $7.00 if obtained online. Tennessee charges for "no record found" reports.

Request Methods – Mail, Walk-in, Online, Online Status, Bulk.

What You Should Know – For non-CDL drivers, all convictions are listed on the driver's record for three years, if license is valid; for seven years, if not valid. CDL drivers have at least ten years of activity shown on the record

Special Access Programs Available – Tennessee offers commercial online record service via the e-government services website at www.tennesseeanytime.org/imvr or www.tennesseeanytime.org/tndlr/. The program is called the Interactive Moving Violation Record application (IMVR). Users must complete a Network Registration Agreement and be authorized per DPPA. Subscribers may purchase a driving record for $7.00 or verify status information on a Tennessee driver license for $1.25 per search.

About Accident Reports

Copies of accident reports are available from the investigating agency or by mail from the Records Unit, Financial Responsibility Section, Department of Safety, PO Box 945, Nashville 37202. The driver's name, date of accident, and location (county) must be included with the request. A form is available at www.tennessee.gov/safety/forms/recorddppa.pdf. The fee is $4.00 per report.

About Vehicle Records

Taxpayer & Vehicle Services, 44 Vantage Way Suite #160, Nashville 37243-8050, 615-741-3101 or 888-871-3171. The current fee for general inquiries, such as name and plate searches, is $1.00; a photocopy of the current title record the fee is $5.00; a certified computer printout of a vehicle record is $1.50 per record, and for an advanced search (including complete title history) the fee is $15.00. Records are maintained for twelve years. Trailers used for the transportation of boats are exempt from both title and registration.

Request Methods – Mail, Walk-in, Online.

What You Should Know – Online access is available from the same subscription-based program mentioned above for driving records.

About Watercraft Records

Wildlife Resources Agency, Boating Division, PO Box 40747, Nashville 37204, 615-781-6585 www.state.tn.us/twra. All motorized boats and all sailboats must be registered; there are no titles. It takes 30 days before new records are ready for inquiry. A TN ID#, hull#, name, or SSN is needed to perform a search. Requests may be processed by phone or mail. There is no fee to do 1 or 2 searches. Turnaround time is normally 2-3 days. One may request records via email to darren.rider@state.tn.us. Lien information is not available here and must be secured from the office of the Secretary of State.

Texas

Administration

Michael Kelley, Assistant Director,
Driver License Division
Texas Department of Transportation
PO Box 4087, Austin 78773-0001
512-424-2600   www.txdps.state.tx.us

Victor Vandergriff, Chariman
Texas Department of Motor Vehicles
Vehicle Title and Registration Division
4000 Jackson Ave., Austin, TX 78731
888-368-4689   www.dmv.tx.gov

Per state legislation, on November 1, 2009 the Texas Department of Motor Vehicles (TxDMV) became a new state agency. Four former divisions in the Texas Department of Transportation moved into this new agency. The four divisions are: Vehicle Title and Registration (VTR), Motor Carrier (MCD), Motor Vehicle (MVD), and Auto Burglary and Theft Prevention Authority (ABTPA).

Important Telephone and Web Contact

Driver Licensing..512-424-2600
Driver Records Bureau....................................512-424-2032
Automated Conviction Reporting (ACR)........512-424-2031
SR-22 and Financial Responsibility...............512-424-2600
Commercial Driver License............................512-424-2010
Driver Improvement & Compliance Bureau
          512-424-7120; Fax 512-424-2501
Title and Registration Information.................512-465-7611
Texas Department of Insurance......................512-463-6169
Dept. of Public Safety (Highway Patrol).........512-424-2000

General Email for Driver License:
   customerservicedl@txdps.state.tx.us
Email Contacts for Vehicles:
   www.dmv.tx.gov/wheretogo/contact_us.htm

Title 7 Transportation Code:
   http://tlo2.tlc.state.tx.us/statutes/tn.toc.htm
Texas Statues:
   www.legis.state.tx.us/

Driver License Facts

License Format
Eight numbers, beginning with 0, 2, or 3. License numbers are sequential and computer-generated.

Document Appearance
A redesigned driver license document and identification card with new and enhanced security features were put into production on April 15, 2009. The current driver licenses and ID cards are still valid and will be phased out as they expire.
An abbreviated description of the new documents is shown below.

New Documents
License has digital photo with state capitol in light blue on right side on a beige background, with TEXAS at the top left side in blues

Security Characteristics   At this time, the agency has deferred from describing the security features.
Position of Photo   Photo is located on the left side.
Minor Age Driver Locator   This driver license is presented vertically and reads "Under 21 DL" on the top in red and "under 21 until MM/DD/YYYY" next to the photo
CDL Indicator   License reads 'CDL' in brown on top.

Older Documents
License has digital photo with state capitol featured on a beige background, with TEXAS at the top in *red* and DEPARTMENT OF PUBLIC SAFETY in *blue* below. A color bar is displayed in the header behind TEXAS.

Security Characteristics   Security laminate has TEXAS printed in metallic ink across the entire face of the card, TEXAS will glow green under ultraviolet light. There is a bar code, magnetic strip and endorsement/restriction codes printed on back.
Position of Photo   Photo is located on the right side; the DPS audit number appears along the side of the photo and the director's signature falls halfway on the beige background on the top of the photo.
Minor Age Driver Locator   Vertical format license with forward facing photo at bottom right. For ages 18-21,

"under 21 driver license" is printed in *red* across the top; if CDL, "under 21 commercial DL" is brown. Also, "under 21 until (MMDDYY)" appears in red on first detail line of license. For ages 16-18, "provisional driver license" is printed in *purple* across the top.

CDL Indicator COMMERCIAL DRIVER LICENSE appears in brown in the header line. "CDL" appears in text next to the eight-digit license number.

Issue and Renewal
Age Requirements
The minimum age for a Regular License is 18; 16 with completion of approved driver education course. Texas adopted a graduated license program. An Instruction Permit can be issued at 15; must be accompanied by licensed driver age 21 or over. The restriction "B" will not be removed until an individual reaches the age of 16, has held an Instruction Permit at least 6 months and completes Phase I of Driver's Ed., or has applied for a MRDL (Minor's Restricted Driver License), or has turned 18 years of age and has passed a driving test. If over the age of 18, driver may remove the "B" restriction once the road test is passed.

A Provisional License may be issued at 16: must have held an Instruction Permit or MRDL at least 6 months and complete Phase I of Driver's Ed. during first 6 months of the graduated driver license program. During Phase II, the minor is restricted to for one year to:
1) No more than one non-family member passenger under 21.
2) No driving after 10pm or before 5am unless driving is necessary for employment, school or school related activity or medical emergency. If an individual is accompanied by a licensed operator age 21 or over in the front seat, he./she is not limited to hours of operation or passengers.
3) No operating vehicle when using a wireless communication device, including cell phones.

The Two-Year Instruction Permit Program allows an Instruction Permit to be issued to a person, under the age of 18 with an expiration date of next birthday plus one year.

A Hardship License can be issued at 15, under necessary conditions.

Renewal
Since 01/01/02, all renewals are issued for 6 years. Driver keeps same number when renewing. Renewal and address changes are available online or at 866-357-3639. Military personnel may renew their expired TX licenses by mail. Upon renewal, military personnel may be assigned a new driver license number. Although licenses carried by military personnel are legally valid, they may be purged if not renewed within two years of expiration. All drivers who renew in person, regardless of age, must take and pass a vision exam.

Elderly-Related Restrictions
Effective September 1, 2007, state law requires drivers age 79 or older to visit a driver license office in person. and prohibits renewing a driver license by alternative means such as by mail or through online services. Additionally, drivers age 85 or older receive a two-year renewal instead of the standard 6-year renewal.

Residency
New residents must secure Texas license 90 days after entry into the state.

License Classes
Commercial Classifications
The holder of a valid commercial driver license may drive all vehicles in the class in which he/she is licensed and all lesser classes of vehicles (except for motorcycles and mopeds). Persons operating motorcycles which carry hazardous materials requiring a placard must hold a Class M license in conjunction with a Class A, B, or C - CDL license.

Class A   Any combination of vehicles with a GCWR of 26,001 pounds or more, providing the GVWR of the vehicle or vehicles being towed exceeds 10,000 pounds.

Class B   Any single vehicle with a GVWR of 26,001 pounds or more, any one of those vehicles towing a vehicle that does not exceed 10,000 pounds GVWR and any vehicle designed to transport twenty-four passengers or more (including the driver).

Class C   Any single vehicle or combination that is not a Class A or B if either vehicle is:
    a. Designed to transport sixteen to twenty-three passengers, (including the driver); or
    b. Used in the transportation of hazardous materials that require the vehicle to be placarded under 49 C.F.R. Part 172, Subpart F.

Non-Commercial Classifications
The holder of a valid non-CDL may drive all vehicles in the class in which he/she is licensed and all lesser classes of vehicles except for motorcycles and mopeds. A driver may not operate a CMV with a non-CDL license unless they are specifically exempt from the CDL Act.

Class A	Any vehicle or combination of vehicles with a GCWR of 26,001 pounds or more, provided the GVWR of the vehicle(s) being towed is in excess of 10,000 pounds.
Class B	A single vehicle with a GVWR of 26,000 pounds or more, and any such vehicle towing either a vehicle with a GVWR that does not exceed 10,000 pounds or a farm trailer with a GVWR that does not exceed 20,000 pounds; or a bus with a seating capacity of twenty-four passengers or more (including the driver).
Class C	A single vehicle or combination of vehicles that is not a Class A or B vehicle and a single vehicle with a GVWR of less than 26,001 pounds towing a trailer that does not exceed 10,000 pounds GVWR, or farm trailer with a GVWR that does not exceed 20,000 pounds.
Class M	Motorcycle or moped.

HAZMAT Endorsement Procedure

The state is in compliance with the USA Patriot Act. Effective January 31, 2005 states were required to implement fingerprinting and background check requirements for new HME applicants. The effective date for procedures related to processing renewal and transfer applicants was delayed until May 31, 2005. As of that date, all applicants applying for a new, renewal or transfer of the HAZMAT Endorsement (HME) must first complete an HME threat assessment application from DPS. The applicant will be provided a packet entitled "FAST" Fingerprinting Applicant Services of Texas, which includes fingerprint information to be taken to an L-1 Identity Solutions (formerly Identix) location in order to initiate the required background check. The process includes the collection of an individual's fingerprints and verification of citizenship. Visit the website www.ibtfingerprint.com/ for site locations or call 1-888-467-2080 to schedule an appointment and pay for the transaction ($68.25 plus $9.95 processing fee). The fingerprints and application information are sent to the Transportation Security Administration (TSA). TSA performs the background checks and notifies the Department whether the applicant is approved or denied. An automatic 90-day extension will be given to current HME holders while the background is being processed. Once DPS receives approval notification from TSA, the HME is valid for 5 years. If denied, DPS will notify the applicant in writing on how to appeal the denial through TSA. For more information visit www.txdps.state.tx.us/administration/driver_licensing_control/hme.htm.

Safety and Enforcement Facts

Insurance and Financial Responsibility

The state has compulsory liability insurance, but does not have a no-fault insurance provision. Minimum financial responsibility limits are $25,000/$50,000/$25,000. The limits increased effective 04/01/2007. Another increase, scheduled for 01/01/2011, will require limits of $30,000/$60/000/$25,000. Proof of insurance is required upon request by a law enforcement officer at the time of vehicle registration or original driver license issuance, upon vehicle inspection, and upon a reportable crash. A second conviction for operating a vehicle without liability insurance results in automatic suspension.

Alcohol and Chemical Testing

Texas' illegal intoxication level is .08 percent for 21 years and older for Class C licensees. The level is .04 for CDL drivers and any detectable amount for persons under 21 years of age. Blood and breath testing are authorized; urine testing is authorized only for CDLs. Texas has an implied-consent law provision.

Crash Reporting

Crashes involving death, injury, or property damage in excess of $1,000 or more to one person's property must be reported immediately to the local authorities. If the crash is not investigated by the police, a written report (Form CRB-2, Driver's Crash Report) must be filed by the involved drivers within ten days with the Department of Transportation, Crash Records Bureau, PO Box 149349, Austin 78714. Download crash report forms at www.dot.state.tx.us.

Suspensions and Revocations

Texas is in compliance with the provisions of the Motor Carrier Safety Improvement Act (MCSIA). See the Appendix for more information about the mandatory CDL disqualification sanctions.

The Following can Trigger an Automatic Suspension or Revocation as Indicated—

Subsequent conviction of no liability insurance .... Indefinite.
   A $100 Reinstatement fee and SR-22 must be filed and maintained with the Department for two years from conviction date.
Child Support (No Reinstatement Fee) .... Indefinite.
Drug Conviction .... 180-day suspension.
Failure to Maintain Financial Responsibility (SR-22) as required for subsequent conviction for no insurance
.... Indefinite.
Fraudulent Use of License .... 90 days to one year (determined by the court).
Liability Judgment Rendered as Result of Automobile Crash ...... Indefinite.

Using Motor Vehicle to Transport, Conceal or Harbor an Alien .. Lifetime Disqualification.
DWI First Offense .... 90-day to one-year suspension, determined by the court.
DWI Second Offense .... 180-day to two-year suspension, determined by the court.
DWI Third or Subsequent Offense .... 180-day to two-year suspension, determined by the court.

Notes:
1) DWI offenses have tougher punishments if a minor is found in the car. First-time offenders are automatically suspended and repeat offenders are subject to an extended suspension period.
2) If the DWI is probated, the subject may be required to complete a DWI Education Program within to the 181 days of the conviction. Failure to do so may result in a revocation of driving privileges. Upon a subsequent conviction, the Department will impose a twelve-month suspension.

Motor Fuel Theft - Subsequent Conviction .... 180-day suspension.

Note: ALR refers to the Administrative License Revocation law that provides for suspension due to .08 or higher BAC or refusal of driver to comply with officer's request for such a test.

ALR - Failure First Offense .... 90-day suspension.
       Subsequent Offense .... One-year suspension.
       With prior alcohol-related conviction .... One-year suspension.
ALR - Refusal First Offense .... 180-day suspension.
       Subsequent Offense .... Two-year suspension.
       With prior alcohol-related conviction .... Two-year suspension.
Drivers under 21 years of age ....
    DWI 1st Offense (includes when operating a watercraft) .... One-year suspension.
    DWI 2nd Offense .... 18-month suspension.
    ALR Failure 1st Offense .... 60-day suspension.
    ALR Failure 2nd Offense .... 120-day suspension.
    ALR Failure w/ Prior Alcohol Related Conviction .... 180-day suspension.
    ALR Refusal First Offense .... 180-day suspension.
    ALR Refusal Subsequent Offense .... Two-year suspension.
    ALR Refusal With prior alcohol-related conviction .... Two-year suspension.
    ALR 1st Offense/Any Detectable Amount .... 60-day suspension.
    ALR 2nd Offense/Any Detectable Amount .... 120-day suspension.
    ALR Subsequent Offense/Any Detectable Amount .... 180-day suspension.

Public intoxication, Alcohol Beverage Code Offenses (minor in possession, attempt to purchase, purchase of alcohol, consumption of alcohol, misrepresentation of age) - No reinstatement fee

    1st Offense .... 30-day suspension.
    2nd Offense .... 60-day suspension.
    3rd Offense .... 180-day suspension.
    Fail to Complete Minor Education Program . One month to 12 months (determined by the court).
    Juvenile under 17 years of age:
        Drug and DWI .... 365 days or until 19th birthday.
        Truancy .... Not to exceed 12 months.

Note: A driver issued a speeding ticket and found guilty of driving at a speed of 95 miles per hour or higher is prohibited from taking a driving safety class to dismiss the ticket.

Suspension or revocation of driving privileges is automatic unless an administrative hearing is requested. The suspension period is 90 days or, in certain circumstances, an indefinite revocation is imposed.

An Administrative Hearing may be requested within 20 days from the date notice is received. The outcome can be suspension of the license for up to one year, probation up to two years, revocation of the license for an indefinite period, probation, or dismissal of the hearing. A hearing may be held for any of the following reasons.

- Commission of Offense in Another State, which would be grounds for Suspension/Revocation in TX
- Driving While License Invalid
- Determined Medically Incapable by the Medical Advisory Board (results in revocation)
- Failure to Take or to Pass an Examination Required by the Department (results in revocation)
- Failure to Provide Medical Records Required by the Medical Advisory Board (results in revocation)
- Responsible as a Driver for Serious Personal Injury or Property Damage
- Habitually Reckless or Negligent
- Habitual Violator (defined as 4 moving violations in 12 months or 7 moving violations in 24 months)
- Incapability of Safe Driving (results in revocation)
- Minor, Failure to Appear for a Traffic or Non-Traffic related offense (results in revocation)

- Non-Compliance With the Terms of the Non-Resident Violator Compact (results in revocation)
- Provisional License Holder, Convicted on Two or More Moving Violations Within a 12-Month Period
- Restriction Violations

Driver Responsibility Program (DRP) and Point System

Points are issued as part of a Driver Responsibility Program (DRP). Below is a description of the major components of the DRP. Traffic offenses resulting in points are designated by 37 TAC 15.89

Conviction Based Surcharges

Drivers who receive a conviction for an offense listed below pay an annual surcharge for a period of three (3) years from date of conviction. No points are assessed for these offenses. Once the conviction is reported to DPS the following surcharges are assessed:

Driving While Intoxicated, Intoxication Assault, and Intoxication Manslaughter

First time offense	$1,000
Second or subsequent offense	$1,500
DWI 0.16 or greater	$2,000
Failure to Maintain Financial Responsibility	$250
Driving While License Invalid	$250
No Driver License	$100

The surcharges are cumulative; therefore, an initial conviction for DWI will be assessed $1000 annually, and a subsequent DWI conviction within the same three-year period will be assessed an additional $1500 annually.

Point Assessment

Points are assessed to moving violations classified as Class C misdemeanors and remain on the driver record for a period of three years from conviction date. Points are as follows:
- Two points for a moving violation conviction in Texas or that of another state.
- Three points for a moving violation conviction in Texas or another state that resulted in a crash.

Points will not be assigned for speeding less than 10% over the speed limit or seat belt convictions. DPS assesses a surcharge when the driver accumulates a total of six (6) points or more on their driver record during a three-year period. The driver must pay a $100 surcharge for the first six points and $25 for each additional point.

Annual Assessment

The surcharge assessment will be reviewed annually. If driver record continues to reflect six or more points during the prior three-year period, the surcharge will be assessed. Therefore, drivers may be required to pay for **one or more years if six or more points continue to accumulate on the driver record**. Point surcharges are cumulative and may vary with each annual assessment if convictions are added or removed from the driver record. An offense committed prior to September 1, 2003 will not apply to the assessment of surcharges. Failure to pay surcharges results in an indefinite suspension.

Deferred Adjudication - Defensive Driving Course

No points will be assessed or surcharges applied if the conviction is deferred, or a DDC course is taken. Only non-CDL drivers may be granted deferred adjudication, and/or take a defensive driving course (DDC) for any points-based citation and No-DL citations. No-Insurance and DWLI offense are eligible for deferred adjudication. DWI, Intoxication Assault, and Intoxication Manslaughter are NOT eligible for deferral.

Reinstatement Requirements

Suspension	$100 fee; SR-22, if mandatory or no insurance suspension.
Revocation	$100 fee.
ALR (blood/breath test refusal)	$125 fee.

The renewal/issuance of a Texas license will be denied until the reinstatement fee is paid.

License Plate Facts

Registration Renewal

Renewal is set on a 12, 24 or 36 month basis and can be done in person or by mail. *Renewal is online via the web page* - go to www.dmv.tx.us. Counties have the ability to enforce a program to block registration to those who have not paid traffic court fines. However, only a few counties instituted this program (El Paso and Dallas to name two).

New Residents

New residents must register vehicles within thirty days of establishing residency or accepting employment.

Inspections and Emissions Testing

All Texas registered vehicles are required to receive an annual inspection. This program is administered by the Texas

Department of Public Safety (DPS). Visit www.txdps.state.tx.us/vi/ for details on criteria and locations.

Some vehicles are required to have an emissions test in addition to the safety inspection if registered in these designated counties: Brazoria, Fort Bend, Galveston, Harris, Montgomery, Collin, Dallas, Denton, Ellis, Johnson, Kaufman, Parker, Rockwall, Tarrant, Travis, Williamson and El Paso counties. Diesel powered vehicles and motorcycles are exempt from the emissions standards, but are still required to have the annual safety inspection.

Plate Descriptions

Typical Plate Pattern	Passenger plates are NNNLLL, LLLNNN, LLLNNL or LNNLLL. All trucks, either commercial or non-commercial rated, are NNNLL, NNLLLN, LLNNNN or NLLLNN.
County Codes	Texas has no coding on license plates signifying the county of issuance.
Plates and Stickers in Force	Two plates, one windshield decal. Vehicles with no windshield (trailers, motorcycles, etc.) have one plate with one decal showing MO/YR of expiration.
Plates Remain with Car when Sold?	Yes, except for certain special category license plates or if by request. Individuals have the option of transferring their license plates (passenger vehicle or light truck only) from a vehicle they sell or transfer to another vehicle titled in their name. When an individual sells their vehicle to another individual (private party) they have the option of removing the license plates when they sell the vehicle and using them on another vehicle they own. When an individual sells/trades a vehicle to a license dealer, the dealer must remove the license plates and return them to the individual. The individual can then decide to transfer the license plates to a newly purchased vehicle, a vehicle they already own, or dispose of the license plates. If plates remain with the vehicle then using the vehicle transfer notification let's the state know the vehicle has been sold.

Overview of Record Access

About Driving Records

Department of Public Safety, Driver Records Section, PO Box 149246, Austin 78752, 512-424-2600. See summary of fees below. Note the DPS sells a license status (see fees below). Also, a certified copy of an original license or ID card application for $1.00. Also, a certified abstract (more extensive) with a summarization of crashes and convictions is available for $20.00, Form DR-36 is required for this report. The state does charge for "no record found" reports.

Driving Record Types and Fees

The following types of records can be requested through this application:

- Status Record (Type 1): name, date of birth (DOB), license status, and latest address. ($4.00, $4.50 if online)
- 3-year History Record (Type 2): name, DOB, license status, list of crashes and violations in record within past 3-year period. ($6.00, $6.50 if online)
- Certified 3-year History Record (Type 2A): certified version of Type 2. This record is not acceptable for Defensive Driving Course (DDC). ($10.00, $12.00 if online)
- List of all Crashes and Violations in Record (Type 3): name, DOB, license status, list of all crashes and violations in record. ($7.00, $7.50 if online). **Only furnished to the license holder.**
- Certified List of All Crashes and Violations in Record (Type 3A): certified version of Type 3. This record is acceptable for Defensive Driving Course (DDC). ($10.00, $12.00 if online) **Only furnished to the license holder.**
- Certified Abstract of Driving Record ("AOR"): Certified text abstract of complete driving record of a license holder. ($20.00, $22.00 if online)

There is no record offered that shows just CDL violations

Request Methods – Mail, Online, Bulk.

Special Access Programs Available – Eligible Texas Driver License holders may purchase their own driving record online at www.texasonline.state.tx.us/NASApp/txdps/TXDPSLicenseeManager. The record cannot be viewed; a printed copy is returned by mail.

About Crash Reports

The fees are $6.00 per record, $8.00 if certified. Either the CR-3 (copy of the peace officer's crash report) or CR-2 (copy of driver's crash report) can be ordered. The request forms are found at www.txdot.gov/drivers_vehicles/crash_records/reports.htm. Records are available for 10 years to present, first available 10 days after the event. Information needed must include two of the following: the date, specific location including city and county, and full name of one party involved. Normal turnaround time is 15 to 20 days, but can take as long as 4 weeks. Written requests should be mailed to: Texas DOT, Crash Records, PO Box 149349, Austin 78714. Phone 512-486-5780, fax 512-486-5794.

About Vehicle Records
Vehicle Title and Registration Division, Texas Dept of Motor Vehicles, Austin 78779-0001, 512-465-7611, fax: 512-302-2162. The current fee for VIN and plate checks is $2.30, $3.30 if certified. A title history is $5.75, if certified then $6.75. The SSN is not released. There are no "name checks" available. To obtain a title history on a motor vehicle or RV, completion of Request Form VTR-275 is required.. Records remain in the active files until the record has no activity for 18 months. After 30 months of inactivity records are archived. Title history information is available either on microfilm or digital imaging for 16 years.

Request Methods – Mail, Walk-in, Online, Bulk.

What You Should Know – Per state legislation, on November 1, 2009 the Texas Department of Motor Vehicles (TxDMV) became a new state agency. Four former divisions in the Texas Department of Transportation moved into this new agency. The four divisions are: Vehicle Title and Registration (VTR), Motor Carrier (MCD), Motor Vehicle (MVD), and Auto Burglary and Theft Prevention Authority (ABTPA).

Special Access Programs Available – Texas recently started a new vehicle insurance verification system called TexasSure. This program has a database that holds vehicle registration information (such as the VIN, owner name and address, and make, model and year) and insurance policy information (such as address, insured drivers, insurance company name and policy effective dates). Only authorized users, which includes insurance agents and insurance companies as well as government officials, have access to the database.

About Watercraft Records
Parks and Wildlife Department (TPWD), 4200 Smith School Rd, Austin 78744, 512-389-4828, in-state at 800-268-2755, www.tpwd.state.tx.us/fishboat/boat/owner. Boats, boat motors and personal watercraft are titled and registered with the Texas Parks and Wildlife Department: all motorized boats must be registered and titled; all sail boats 14 ft and over must be registered and titled. There are two type of records commonly requested: for current data including lien holders there is no fee, a complete ownership history is $11.00. Use of Form PWD 763 is strongly advised. The form, downloadable from web, requires the signature of the requester who must attest that the use of the data is for legal purposes. The signature of the subject is not required. Record checks can be processed by any TPWD Law Enforcement Field Office or at a participating County Tax Assessor-Collector office, as well as the office listed above. If the form is not used, the name and/or registration number is required and request must contain the following phrase in the request: "The information obtained will be used for a lawful purpose." Turnaround time is 2 days, can be longer in the summer months. Online access to current owner/lienholder names, addresses, and vessel or outboard motor description is provided as long the user provides a valid TX number or serial number. Visit https://apps.tpwd.state.tx.us/tora/jump.jsf.

Utah

Administration

Nannette Rolfe, Director
Driver License Division
PO Box 144501
Salt Lake City 84114-4501
801-965-4437; 888-353-4224

Brad Simpson, Director
Motor Vehicle Division
Tax Commission
801-297-7500

http://publicsafety.utah.gov/dld/ (Driver)
www.dmv.utah.gov/ (Vehicle)

Important Telephone and Web Contacts

Driver Licensing..801-965-4437
Problem Driver Pointer Hotline..................801-965-3872
SR-22...801-965-4437
Financial Responsibility 801-965-4393
Commercial Driver License........................801-288-5350
Vehicle Information.....................................801-297-7780
State Department of Insurance 801-538-3805
Highway Patrol..801-965-4518

Email Contacts:
   http://publicsafety.utah.gov/dld/contact.html
Utah Statutes:
   www.le.state.ut.us/documents/code_const.htm

Driver License Facts

License Format
Can be four to ten numbers, but currently only nine digit numbers are being issued. Sometime in the future ten digit numbers will be utilized. Utah reports there is no code or sequential arrangement that determines the characters making the license number.

Document Appearance
The state has four versions of driver license and ID cards. The newest cards began issuance in November 2006, replacing the format released in August 2001. Cards issued prior to August 2001 will not be completely phased out until 2011. All three versions are described below. Note that the Division also issues a Driving Privilege Card (DPC) to individuals who do not meet the requirements to obtain a DL or ID. The Card has a one-year expiration. The DPC changed its format and color as of September 1, 2009.

Current Document
Effective January 1, 2010, the Utah Driver License Division began issuing a **new card type**; limited-term license, limited-term CDL and limited-term identification card. The new limited-term card will be issued to an individual who is not a U.S Citizen, National, or Permanent Resident Alien but have documentation showing they are in the country legally. This certificate will be valid for their approved length of stay in the country or five years, whichever is shorter or one year if no ending date exists. The division has also changed the look of the Temporary Permit (paper document) for all driving certificates and ID cards.

Since the release of the new cards coincides with the printing of this book, please refer to samples of the new document types found at the Division's site at www.publicsafety.utah.gov/dld/documents/LawEnforcementupdate1-2010.pdf.

Document Issued from 11/2006 to 01/2010
Security Characteristics	All cards have laser perforation spelling the letters "DLD." Overlapping data can be seen over the image and a smaller "ghost" as well. An optical variable device appears on the card surface, forming an outline of the state with the letters "DPS" inset. A tamper-proof barcode is on the back.
Position of Photo	Left side, middle. There is also a smaller "ghost image" photo appearing to the right.
Minor Age Driver Locator	Card is vertical. The Under 21 designator is over the "ghost" in red; under 19 is in blue. The DOB shown in red.
CDL Indicator	Commercial Driver printed on card.

Older Document Issued from 08/2001 to 11/2006
Security Characteristics	A two dimensional barcode on the back is tamper proof and contains the bearer's demographic information found on the front. There is a one-dimensional barcode on the

Position of Photo	Right side, there is also a smaller "ghost image" photo appearing on the left side.
Minor Age Driver Locator	"Under 21 Until MM-DD-YY" appears in red. "Under 19 Until MM-DD-YY" appears in blue. After 07/01/03, the card is vertical with the picture in the bottom left corner. Prior to that the card is horizontal.
CDL Indicator	License class appears in the upper right corner.

Oldest Document Issued Prior to 08/2001

Security Characteristics	Laminated card with Utah Seal, color code over DOB, Utah embossing through laminate, color bar shows type of license.
Position of Photo	Right side.
Minor Age Driver Locator	Top left, Minor (under 21) or Adult (over 21).
CDL Indicator	CDL purple color bar at top and classification in code data area.

Issue and Renewal
On January 1, 2010, the requirements to obtain a Utah driving certificate and/or ID card changed. The Utah Driver License Division will issue a "regular" driver license, CDL, or ID card to applicants who are U.S. citizens; legal permanent residents, or nationals; the Division will issue a "limited-term" driver license, CDL, or ID card to applicant who provide proof of legal/lawful presence; the Division will issue a Driving Privilege card to applicants who do not qualify for a regular or limited-term certificate.

Age Requirements
To apply for a first time Utah license one must be at least 16 years old, have held a Utah Learner Permit for 6 months if under 18 years old, furnish proof of a prior driver license or proof of driver education training, proof of resident address, proof of legal presence (if applicable), and present 2 forms of positive identification. Since August 1, 2006 an applicant who is at least 15 years of age may apply for a Learner Permit. This driver must be accompanied by parent, legal guardian, or adult spouse, in front seat.

Renewal
Birth day of fifth year and can be renewed within 6 months of expiration date. Driver keeps same number when renewing. With the new issuance laws in effect, renewal must be in-person. Online renewal is not available at this time. If a CDL driver moves or changes names at a time other than renewal, the driver is required to apply for a duplicate license within 30 days of the change. A military personnel license does not expire until 90 days after discharge.

Elderly-Related Restrictions
None are reported.

Residency
Non-residents must secure Utah license upon accepting other than temporary employment or establishing residency; home-state license (as a visitor) honored up to six months.

License Classes
Commercial Classifications

Class	Age	Description
Class A	21	Over 26,000 pounds combination vehicle and over 10,000 pounds towed unit
	18-21	Intrastate Only Restriction
Class B	21	Over 26,000 pounds single or combination vehicle, under 10,001 pounds towed unit.
	18-21	Intrastate Only Restriction
Class C		Under 26,001 pounds, if used to transport:
	21	1. Sixteen or more occupants;
	21	2. Placarded amounts of hazardous material
	21	Under 10,001 pounds towed unit "S" endorsement available
Class D	16+	Under 26,001 pounds, no passenger or hazmat endorsement

A CDL Class C is required if these vehicles are used to haul hazardous materials or when carrying sixteen or more occupants.

Non-Commercial Classifications
Class D   16+ .... Regular operator

*Note: For motorcycles, as of July 1, 2008, all class M licenses were repealed and replaced with endorsements. A regular operator license (Class D) or CDL (Class A, B, or C) must be obtained before a motorcycle endorsement (M) may be added to the license. All motorcycle riders are restricted to riding a motorcycle based on the cc size of the motorcycle upon which the rider is tested with 3 restrictions used. If an operator is tested on a motorcycle 650 cc or greater no restriction will be placed on the license and the operator will be permitted to ride any size motorcycle.

HAZMAT Endorsement Procedure
The state is in compliance with the Patriot Act. All applicants applying for a new or renewal or transfer HAZMAT Endorsement (HME) must first obtain the application from https://hazprints.tsa.dhs.gov/Public/ or by calling 877-429-7746. The driver must also be fingerprinted. EMSI and COMNETIX are the state-designated entity to process fingerprints. There are two locations in the state that perform this service. Visit the web page listed above to find the address locations. The cost of the fingerprint process is $89.25. The fingerprints and application information is sent to the Federal Transportation Security Administration (TSA). TSA performs the background checks and notifies the DMV whether the application is approved or denied. When completed and approved, the HME is valid for five years.

Safety and Enforcement Facts

Insurance and Financial Responsibility
Utah has compulsory and no-fault insurance laws. Minimum liability limits are $25,000/65,000/15,000. Proof must be shown at the request of a police officer, after a reportable accident, and after certain violations. SR-22 forms are used.

Alcohol and Chemical Testing
Utah's illegal intoxication level is .08 % and above for adults, .04 for drivers of CMVs, and a zero tolerance level if the driver is under 21. Breath, blood, oral fluids, and urine testing are authorized; the type of testing used is determined by the arresting officer. Utah has both an implied-consent violation and a provision for an administrative suspension.

Accident Reporting
Accidents involving death, injury, or damage $1,000 or more must be reported to the local authorities. Reports are filed by the investigative agency.

Suspensions and Revocations
The state is in compliance with the federally mandated disqualifications on CDLs. See the Appendix for details. On July 1, 2009, the legislation changed the suspension periods for a number of DUI offenses committed on or after that date, as shown below.

Controlled Substance/Metabolite (Arrest)
    First Offense .... 120-day Suspension.
    Second or Subsequent Offense .... Two-year Suspension.
Controlled Substance or Paraphernalia .... Six-month Suspension.
Discharging (or Allowing) Firearm or Explosive Device or Chemical from Vehicle ... One to five-year Revocation.
DUI If Over 21
    First Offense .... 120-day Suspension.
    Second or Subsequent Offenses .... Two-year Revocation.
Eluding a Police Officer .... One-year Revocation.
False Application .... Three-month to one-year Suspension.
Habitually-Negligent Driver .... One-year Suspension.
Leaving Scene of Accident Involving Personal Injury or Death .... One-year Revocation.
Manslaughter or Negligent Homicide .... One-year Revocation.
Per Se (DUI Arrest)
    First Offense .... 120-day Suspension.
    Second Offense .... Two-year Suspension.
Operating (or allowing) motor vehicle Without Insurance or FR .... Indefinite Suspension.
Point Accumulation .... One-month to one-year Denial or Suspension.
Reckless Driving, Second Offense in One Year .... One-year Revocation.
Refusal to Submit to Chemical Test
    First Offense .... Eighteen-month Revocation.
    Second or Subsequent Offense .... Thirty six-month Revocation.
Speed Contest or Exhibition on Highway
    First Offense .... Sixty-day Suspension.
    Second or Subsequent Offense .... Ninety-day Suspension.
Unlawful Use of a Driver's License .... Three-moth to one-year Suspension.
Use of a Motor Vehicle to Commit a Felony .... One-year Revocation.

Other Sanctions of Note

Drivers may be designated "Alcohol Restricted." This means they must not drive with any alcohol in their system. Under this designation, the electronic driver history record is updated to show the Alcohol Restricted Driver status, and the driver is notified by mail of the restriction. Law enforcement has access to the Alcohol Restricted Driver status and will issue a citation when they make contact with a driver who has alcohol in their system and is Alcohol Restricted. If a driver is convicted for a violation of the Alcohol Restricted Driver law, their driving privilege will be revoked for a period of one year from the conviction date.

- When individuals have been convicted of a DUI or Alcohol Related Reckless Driving second or subsequent, or they have been revoked for refusal to submit to a chemical test after being arrested for driving under the influence, they are restricted to driving a vehicle that has an Ignition Interlock Device installed for a period of 3 years from the date of conviction or effective date of the revocation.
- A Felony DUI carries a 6-year Ignition Interlock Device restriction, and Automobile Homicide carries a 10-year Ignition Interlock Device restriction.
- If a restricted individual operates a vehicle without an Ignition Interlock Device installed, the vehicle may be impounded. In addition, the driver may be cited for violating the "IRD" law. A conviction for violating the IRD law will result in an additional 3-year Ignition Interlock Device restriction from the date of conviction.
- Although effective July 2009, Utah no longer issues a "no alcohol conditional license," some of these licenses are still in effect and this license is described herein. A "no alcohol conditional license" dictates one must not drive with any alcohol in their system. The constraint period is in effect for two years from the issue date of the conditional licenses for a first "qualifying conviction," and ten (10) years from the issue date of the conditional license for a second or subsequent "qualifying conviction." The "no alcohol" conditional license information is encoded on the new driver license certificate. Insurance companies and employers will not have access to this information, but it will be available to law enforcement, courts and other legitimate requesters.

Reinstatement Requirements

Suspension .... $30.00 fee ($65.00 if alcohol or drug-related); SR-22 for three years for financial responsibility actions; $170.00 administrative fee for alcohol/drug actions.
Revocation .... $30.00 fee ($65.00 if alcohol or drug-related); must apply for new license; $170.00 administrative fee for alcohol/drug actions.
Denial .... $30.00 fee ($65.00 if alcohol or drug-related)
CDL Disqualification .... $30.00 fee ($65.00 if alcohol or drug-related); $170.00 administrative fee for alcohol/drug actions.

Point System Overview

Points range from 35 to 88. Under the state point system, if a driver has no moving violation convictions for one full year, one-half of the points on the record will be removed. If the driver has two successive years with no convictions, all points on the record will be removed. Individual conviction points are automatically removed from the record three years after the date of violation. Fifty points may be removed from the driving record after completion of a Driver Improvement Course recommended by the Department. This deduction is only allowed once every three years.

License Plate Facts

Registration Renewal
Renewal, which is annual, may be done online at www.utah.gov/registration/. The program, called Renewal Express, is available to people receive a mailed renewal notice which contains a designated PIN. To renew, the address and name submitted must match the current registration data on file.

New Residents
For vehicle registration purposes, a resident is anyone who engages in a trade, profession, occupation or gainful employment in Utah for more than sixty days.

Inspections and Emissions Testing
Vehicles with model years less than 8 years old are required to a safety inspection once every 2 years. Older vehicles must pass safety inspections every year. All vehicles registered in Davis, Salt Lake, Utah and Weber counties with model years less than six years old are required to have an emission test once every two years. Vehicles in this category that have even-numbered model years must have an emission test in even-numbered years, and vehicles that have odd-numbered model years must have an emission test in odd-numbered years. Vehicles with model years six years old and older (to 1967) must have an emission test every year. Emission certificates are not required for vehicles with model years 1967 or older. For more information visit http://dmv.utah.gov/registerinspections.html.

Plate Descriptions

Typical Plate Pattern	The standard issued passenger plates are LNN NLL; however, many operating vehicles still use either a LLL NNN or NNN LLL format. Commercial IRP plates LNNNNNN, with many operating vehicles still using 6 numbers with "APP" down the right side.
County Codes	No codes are in use now. Prior to 05/02 two alpha characters designating county of registration were displayed on left of validation block.
Plates and Stickers in Force	Two plates, two decals (MO) (YR) on rear plate.
Plates Remain with Car when Sold?	No, they remain with seller.

Overview of Record Access

About Driving Records

Driver License Division, 4501 South 2700 West, Salt Lake City 84118 (PO Box 144501, Zip 84114-4501), 801-965-4437. All state DMV offices are open Monday through Thursday, from 7 a.m. to 6 p.m. and are closed on Fridays. This includes telephone call-in centers, email assistance, and all field office. The current fee is $6.00, $9.00 if online. A certified record is $10.75 for the first 15 pages. The state charges for "no record found" reports. Address questions regarding MVRS to nmitchell@utah.gov.

Request Methods – Mail, Walk-in, Online.

What You Should Know – Motor vehicle information is available online on a subscription basis for approved users from Utah.gov at www.utah.gov/registration/

Special Access Programs Available – Through the online service provider Utah.gov, a notification program is offered that enables insurance companies and insurance support firms to track activity of submitted drivers. By statute, the program is not available to employers. The cost for the service is $.12 per driver and the driving record fee if issued. Eligible organizations may subscribe by visiting www.utah.gov/registration.

About Accident Reports

Copies of accident reports are protected and may only be obtained by a person involved in the accident, a person suffering loss or injury in the accident, an agent, parent or legal guardian of a person involved in the accident or suffering loss, government agencies using the report for official business, and private investigators. Members of the press or broadcast media are limited to the information they receive from reports. Reports may be obtained from the Driver License Division, PO Box 144501, Salt Lake City 84130, 801-965-4428. The fee is $5.00 per report. Requests must be in writing; use of Form DI-8 is recommended. Also, include the date of the incident. Turnaround time depends on staffing. It can take 2 weeks or more before new incidents are available.

About Vehicle Records

State Tax Commission, DMV, 210 North 1950 West, Salt Lake City 84134, 801-297-3507. All state DMV offices are open Monday through Thursday, from 7 am to 6 pm and are closed on Fridays. This includes telephone call-in centers, e-mail assistance, and all field offices. Records are available for past 15 years. The current fee for non-online VIN and registration information is $3.00, $4.00 if faxed, and $6.50 if the record must be searched on microfilm. A written request, stating the purpose, must be submitted with bulk requests. The procedures described are for obtaining ownership and lien records for watercraft, snowmobiles, and off-highway vehicles. Snowmobiles and off-highway vehicles must be titled if 1988 or newer. The state will not release medical records, SSNs, or insurance information..

Request Methods – Mail, Walk-in, Telephone, Fax, Online, Bulk.

Special Access Programs Available – Motor vehicle information is available by subscription to qualified requestors via the online "Title, Lien and Registration Information Service" (TLRIS) 24/7 Eligible organizations will find subscription details at http://utah.gov/registration/. Phone ordering and fax back results are available for approved requesters. There is an additional $1.00 to fax back.

About Watercraft Records

Records are managed by the State tax Commission, record request procedures are as outlined above. All boats manufactured in 1985 or newer must be titled. All boats except canoes must be registered. An excellent description on registering and titling watercraft is found at http://tax.utah.gov/forms/pubs/pub-09.pdf. SSNs, insurance information and medical information are not released.

Vermont

Administration	Important Telephone and Web Contacts

Robert Ide, Commissioner
Department of Motor Vehicles
120 State Street, Montpelier 05603-0001
802-828-2011
 	
http://dmv.vermont.gov
	Driver Licensing..802-828-2000
	SR-22, Financial Responsibility 802-828-2050
	Vehicle Information.......................................802-828-2000
	Commercial Driver License..........................802-828-0597
	State Department of Banking/Insurance 802-828-3301
	State Police..802-244-7345
	
	Submit general question via email to
	    CommissionersOffice@state.vt.us
	See Vermont DMV Laws at
	    http://dmv.vermont.gov/safety/laws/statutes
	See Vermont State Codes at
	    www.leg.state.vt.us/statutes/statutes2.htm

Driver License Facts

License Format
Eight digits; the last digit is a check-digit which may be numeric or alpha "A." Vermont reports there is no code or sequential arrangement which determines the characters making the license number, other than numeric order from the computer.

Document Appearance
In Vermont, a photo license is mandatory for all licenses issued after 07/01/2005. In 2009, Vermont began issuing enhanced driver's licenses, which allows holders to cross the United States-Canada border without a passport or other supporting documents. It denotes both identity and citizenship, per the Western Hemisphere Travel Initiative. Anyone applying will have to present extensive documentation to prove their identity and be interviewed by a motor vehicle employee. The license is mailed once the information has been verified. The enhanced drivers' licenses contain an electronic transponder, like those used in E-Z Pass toll-paying systems.

Current Document
The card is laminated and has a "credit card" appearance. There is a bar code with information such as the name, DOB, height and weight encoded. Normal Operator Licenses have a green header.

Security Characteristics	Ghost image of photo appears on right side, state seal in middle towards right.
Position of Photo	Upper left for regular operator, lower left for Under 21 operator.
Underage	PURPLE header bar, The dates are shown when the driver is both 21 and 18.
CDL Indicator	"COMMERCIAL DRIVER LICENSE" appears in a BLUE header bar.

Old Document
Photo card is laminated. There is a magnetic strip with the name, DOB, height and weight encoded.

Security Characteristics	Ghost image of photo appears on right side, state seal in middle towards right.
Position of Photo	Upper left for regular operator, lower left for Under 21 operator.
Minor Age Driver Locator	"JUNIOR OPERATOR" appears in a Yellow header bar.
Age 18-19-20	PURPLE header bar, "UNDER 21 UNTIL XX-XX-XXXX" appears in red letters.
CDL Indicator	"COMMERCIAL DRIVER LICENSE" appears in a BLUE header bar.

Issue and Renewal

Age Requirements
Individuals under eighteen are subject to the provisions of a Graduated Driver License Program. The first level is a Learner's Permit, the next level is the Junior Operator. The Senior Operator minimum age is eighteen; sixteen for a Junior Operator; fifteen for a two-year Learner's Permit and must be accompanied by licensed driver age twenty-five or over, or certified driver training instructor.

Renewal
Birth month and day of second or fourth year. Driver keeps same number when renewing. Renewal is available by mail and in person. Online renewal is not available, but drivers may change their addresses at https://secure.vermont.gov/dmv/express. Military personnel (stationed out-of-state) licenses are valid for 4 years after expiration and until 30 days after discharge.

Elderly-Related Restrictions
None indicated.

Residency
Non-resident's home-state license is honored on a reciprocal basis not to exceed thirty days. Vermont requires proof of residency to obtain licenses and ID cards.

License Classes
Commercial Classifications
- Class A — Combination vehicles with GCWR of 26,001 pounds or more—provided towed vehicle is 10,001 pounds or more.
- Class B — Single vehicles with GVWR of 26,001 pounds or more—provided towed vehicle is 10,000 pounds or less.
- Class C — Single vehicles with GVWR of 26,000 pounds or less which transport placarded hazardous materials or sixteen or more passengers (including the driver).

Non-Commercial Classifications
- Class D — All motor vehicles except motorcycles and school buses, includes licenses for minors.

Note: Vermont law does not provide for a "hardship license" or a "work license."

HAZMAT Endorsement Procedure
The state is in compliance with the Patriot Act. All applicants applying for a new or renewal or transfer HAZMAT Endorsement (HME) must first obtain the application from the DMV. The driver must also be fingerprinted. All fingerprinting is done by an authorized contractor with the Transportation Security Administration. Visit https://hazprints.tsa.dhs.gov/Public/ to find the locations in the state that perform this service. The cost of the security threat assessment is currently $89.25. The fingerprints and application information is sent to the Federal Transportation Security Administration (TSA). TSA performs the background checks and notifies the DMV whether the application is approved or denied. When completed and approved, the HME is valid for four years.

Safety and Enforcement Facts

Insurance and Financial Responsibility
Vermont has compulsory insurance. Minimum liability limits are $25,000/50,000/10,000. The state does not have a no-fault insurance provision law. Evidence of insurance is required after certain violations or an uninsured reportable accident and when the vehicle is inspected. SR-22 forms are used.

Alcohol and Chemical Testing
Vermont's illegal intoxication level is .08 percent and above; however, content of .05 to .08 percent can be used with other evidence for a conviction. Drivers under 21 have a legal limit of .02 percent, drivers of CMVs have a limit of .04 percent. Blood and breath testing are authorized. Vermont has both an implied-consent violation and a provision for an administrative suspension.

Accident Reporting
Accidents involving death, injury, or property damage in excess of $1,000.00 must be reported within seventy-two hours to the DMV, Agency of Transportation, 120 State Street, Montpelier VT 05603. Use form # TA-VA-04 to file a report of an accident. The form is found at www.aot.state.vt.us/dmv/documents/TA/VA/Tava004.pdf. There are no other special state reporting criteria for commercial drivers.

Suspensions and Revocations
The Vermont DMV is in compliance with the provisions of the Motor Carrier Safety Improvement Act (MCSIA). See the Appendix for more information about these mandatory CDL disqualification sanctions. Below is an overview of significant withdrawals.

Impersonating Another on an Application or Aiding an Applicant by False Representation .... Sixty-day suspension.
Refusal to Submit to Breath or Blood Alcohol Test -- Civil Violation ..... Six-month to life suspension.

Under the Influence of Alcohol or Drugs
  All Offenses, Blood Alcohol Content .08 Percent or More.................. Ninety-day to life suspension.
Points .... Ten or more points in two years will initiate suspension proceedings.
Habitual Offender (8 or more convictions with 6 or more points or major violations within 5 years) .... Two-year revocation.
Vermont law requires that anyone suspended for an alcohol-related offense must complete an alcohol treatment program.

Reinstatement Requirements
Suspension $71.00 fee; plus requirements specific to the suspension.
Revocation $71.00 fee; investigation (for DWI); plus requirements specific to the revocation.

Point System Overview
Points range from 2 to 10. There is an automatic suspension for accumulation of 10 points within 2 years.

License Plate Facts

Registration Renewal
Renewal is annual and is available online or by telephone. Go to https://secure.vermont.gov/dmv/express or call 866-259-5368. This service is available 24/7.

New Residents
Non-residents must register vehicles at expiration of time period granted by home-state reciprocity agreement, not to exceed six months; or within six months of accepting employment.

Inspections and Emissions Testing
All motor vehicles registered must be inspected once each year at state approved inspection stations. Any newly registered vehicle not currently inspected in this state must be inspected within 15 days from the date of registration. 1996 and newer gasoline powered vehicles, and 1997 and newer diesel powered vehicles having a gross vehicle rating of 8,500 pounds or less, must have an On-Board Diagnostics (OBDII) examination as part of their annual safety equipment inspection. The OBDII examination tests the emission control system of the vehicle..

Plate Descriptions
Typical Plate Pattern   Passenger and light truck plates, since 1990, are issued as 3 alpha - 3 numeric. Commercial vehicle plates are 2 numeric - 1 alpha - 2 numeric.
County Codes   Counties are not designated by code nor are they spelled out on the plate.
Plates and Stickers in Force   Two plates. Until July 1, 2009 two decals each with the MO & YR were issued, once decal per plate. Effective July 1, 2009 the state began to issue one decal only, which needs to be placed on the rear plate.
Plates Remain with Car when Sold?   No, they remain with seller.

Overview of Record Access

About Driving Records
Driver Improvement Information, 120 State Street, Montpelier 05603, 802-828-2050, fax is 802-828-2098. The cost of a three-year driving record by mail or walk-in is $11.00 for a three-year record or $16.00 for complete (all years) and certified record; the fee for an electronic three-year record is $15.00. The state charges for "no record found" reports.

Request Methods – Mail, Walk-in, Online, Bulk.
What You Should Know – Ongoing requesters must process a certain form depending on access mode. The standard agreement form is TA-VG-118. Occasional users with a permissible purpose must use form TA-VG 116.
Special Access Programs Available – Vermont.gov, manages the Vermont enterprise eGovernment Web Portal and provides the subscription online access to Vermont MVRs.

About Accident Reports
Copies of accident reports may only be obtained from at the 120 State Street location. The fax line to the Accident Report Section is 802-828-2098. The fee for a police report is $15.00, for an individual's accident report is $10.00, for insurance information of an accident is $6.00. The SSNs and individual's addresses are protected and are not released. Records are available for 4 years to present. Normal turnaround time is up to 15 days. If there is criminal action involved (DWI, fatality) it may take as long as three months after the accident to get a copy of the accident report

About Vehicle Records

Department of Motor Vehicles, Registration-License Information, 120 State St, Montpelier 05603-0001, 802-828-2000. The DMV maintains records on vehicles, motor homes, trailers, and boats. Lien record information is provided for all of these conveyances. The fee for listings of up to four current or expired registrations is $6.00. A certified copy of an original registration application is $6.00. A certified copy of a vehicle title search, title info, or lien info is $20.00. A certified copy of a vessel, snowmobile or ATV title search is $13.00. Vehicle and vessel records are available for fifteen years back to present. Statistical research is provided at $35.00 per hour.

Request Methods – Mail, Walk-in, Bulk.

What You Should Know – Potential lien-holders are provided a "yes or no" answer when asking about liens on a vehicle. If specific details (such as current lien-holder, etc.) is requested, a TA-VG-116 Form is required along with a title search fee. At a minimum, a VIN or registration plate number must be provided by the requester.

About Watercraft Records

As of July 1, 2007, Vermont titles vessels that are 15 years old or newer, based on calendar year, with a length of 16 feet or longer (including shuttlecraft). Exceptions include any vessel which is a canoe, kayak, or similar watercraft designed to be manually propelled or such a vessel equipped with a motor of 10 horsepower or less. Previously, all boats that operate with an attached motor had to be registered. One may operate in Vermont for a period of 90 consecutive days if the home state grants like privileges to Vermont boats or if the boat has a federally issued number. However, if the vessel is used in Vermont waters for 30 days or more one must obtain a vessel validation sticker. A title search with lien information is $13.00; a registration check is $6.00. TA-VG-116 Form is required.

Virginia

Administration	Important Telephone and Web Contacts
Demerst B. Smit, Commissioner Millicent N. Ford, Director, Driver Services Department of Motor Vehicles PO Box 27412, Richmond 23269 804-367-6602 www.dmvnow.com	Driver Licensing............................804-367-0538 SR-22, Financial Responsibility..................804-367-0538 Commercial Driver License........................804-367-0538 Vehicle Information....................................804-367-0538 Bureau of Insurance...................................804-371-9741 State Police...804-786-2567 General Email Contacts: www.dmvnow.com/webdoc/utilities/contact.asp Virginia Statutes: http://leg1.state.va.us/000/src.htm

Driver License Facts

License Format
All licenses issued since July 1, 2003 display a computer generated random number consisting of an alpha character followed by eight numbers. Social Security Numbers were once used as the driver license number, but now are nearly all phased out.

Document Appearance
Virginia rolled out a newly designed license and ID documents in July 2009. The new cards are made of laser engraved polycarbonate. It will take at least 8 years to phase-in these new cards. The existing style of digitized driver's licenses has been in production since April 1999. Both styles are reviewed below.

Format of Current Licenses Issued

Security Characteristics   Driver's licenses banners have blue lettering; ID card banners have green lettering; and children's ID card banners have gold lettering. Cards for individuals age 21 and over bear an image of the Virginia state capitol building; cards for individuals under 21 show images of the state flower - the dogwood. Polycarbonate card construction features include security printing on internal layers and a clear window secondary photo. Laser engraved personalization features include black printing burned into card body, grayscale photos burned into card body, and tactile raised engraving.

Position of Photo   All primary photographs are grayscale, full faced and are displayed on the left side of the cards. Secondary photographs are grayscale, full faced and displayed in a clear window, visible from the front and back of the cards.

Minor Age Driver Locator   Minors aged 15 to 21 have a vertical card; minors under 15 have a horizontal card. Licenses and ID cards for minors show the date that the individual turns 18 and 21.

CDL Indicator   Indicated by class. License reads "Commercial Drivers License" across the top.

Format of Licenses Issued Prior to Summer 2009

Security Characteristics   A blue band runs across the top portion of the license. The security laminate contains small outlines of the state and the word Virginia that changes color depending on the angle viewed. The word Virginia appears across the top of the license. Bar codes on the back of the license replicate information on the front, providing added security.

Position of Photo   All photographs are taken full faced and are displayed in the lower left corner (lower right corner on ID cards).

Minor Age Driver Locator   Minors aged 15 to 21 have a vertical card; minors under 15 have a horizontal card Licenses and ID cards for minors show the date that the individual turns 18 and 21 (printed in red next to photo.)

CDL Indicator   Indicated by class. License reads "Commercial Drivers License" across the top.

Issue and Renewal

Age Requirements
The minimum age is 18 for full license privileges. A Learner's Permit is issued at 15 years, 6 months—there are passenger and curfew restrictions. At age 16, 3 months and after holding the Learner's Permit for 9 months, a limited driver's license is issued. There are restrictions on passenger limits and curfew until the driver reaches the age of 18. Also, any teen under the age of 19 must complete a state-approved driver education program.

Renewal
As of July 1, 2008, driver's licenses issued are valid for 8 years instead of 5. However, the validity period for ID cards remains at 5 years. Other exceptions to the 8-year validity law include teens, registered sex offenders and those with limited duration driver's licenses issued to customers who are in the United States for a limited amount of time. Previously, all renewals expire on a year when the driver's age is divisible by 5 (i.e., 25, 30, 35, 40, etc.). Driver keeps same number when renewing. Renewals and address changes can be done online. A Military Extension is granted and valid for 3 years, including spouses and dependents; additional extensions may be granted. When renewing a driver's license at age 20, the driver is required to take the knowledge test if driving record reflects at least one demerit point conviction. If a demerit point conviction (including safety belt or child restraint violations) while driver is under age 20, driver is required to attend a driver-improvement clinic (web-based clinics may not be taken). Note the DMV does not issue driver's licenses and ID cards in DMV customer service centers. Customers receive new secure licenses and ID cards by mail.

Elderly-Related Restrictions
None indicated.

Residency
Individuals moving to VA have 60 days to obtain a VA driver's license, or 30 days if for a CDL. Non-resident's home-state driver's license honored for up to one year after expiration for the purpose of exchange for a VA license without testing requirement. Applicants must be a resident of Virginia in order to obtain any type of license or ID card.

License Classes

Class A	Any combination of vehicles with a GVWR or a gross combination weight rating of 26,001 pounds or more, providing the vehicle(s) being towed is in excess of 10,000 pounds. Holders of a Class A license may, with appropriate endorsements, also operate vehicles listed under Classes B and C.
Class B	Any vehicle with a GVWR of 26,001 pounds or more, or any such vehicle towing a vehicle *not* in excess of 10,000 pounds. Holders of a Class B license may, with appropriate endorsements, also operate vehicles listed under Class C.
Class C	Any vehicle that does not fit the definition of a Class A or Class B vehicle and is either designed to transport sixteen or more passengers (including the driver) or is used to transport hazardous materials.
Class M	Motorcycles - This class may be added to a driver's license or CDL or holder may be licensed to operate motorcycles only.

Note: There is no class code for a non-commercial license. The state refers to this document as the "Driver License."

HAZMAT Endorsement Procedure
The state is in compliance with the Patriot Act. All applicants applying for a new or renewal or transfer HAZMAT Endorsement (HME) must first obtain the application from the DMV or by visiting https://hazprints.tsa.dhs.gov/Public/.. The driver must also be fingerprinted. To complete a background records check application and be fingerprinted, the applicant must visit one of the fourteen DMV customer service centers equipped to process the application. The cost of the application and the fingerprint process is $83.00. The fingerprints and application information is sent to the Federal Transportation Security Administration (TSA). TSA performs the background checks and notifies the DMV whether the application is approved or denied. When completed and approved, the HME is valid for five years. For more information, visit www.dmv.virginia.gov/webdoc/citizen/drivers/hazmatreqs.asp.

Safety and Enforcement Facts

Insurance and Financial Responsibility
Virginia law requires a vehicle to have liability insurance or pay a $500 Uninsured Motor Vehicle (UMV) fee. This does not provide any insurance but allows one to drive an uninsured vehicle at one's own risk for a one-year period. There are a number of insurance monitoring programs including insurance company electronic automobile liability insurance reporting of new business and cancellations, suspected uninsured accidents, police accident reports, citizen information and law enforcement notification. It is unlawful to register or operate or permit the operation of an uninsured motor vehicle, subject to Virginia registration, without meeting one of the above requirements. Minimum liability limits for

financial responsibility are $25,000/50,000/20,000. Form SR 22 is used for this filing. However, persons required to provide proof of financial responsibility due to a driving under the influence related conviction must have an insurance policy with double the minimum limits ($50,000/$100,000/$40,000). Form FR-44 is used for this filing.

Virginia is not a no-fault insurance state. Proof of Financial responsibility is generally required for a three-year period. SR-22 forms are used for uninsured suspension orders; and longer periods for alcohol and drug-related suspension.

Alcohol and Chemical Testing

The illegal intoxication level is .08 % and above, .02% and above for drivers under 21, and .04% for CDL. Breath testing is authorized. Virginia has an implied-consent violation. A refusal to submit to a breath test or having a BAC of .08% or greater will result in an immediate 7-day administrative license suspension. Second offense of refusal and/or BAC of .08% or greater is 60 days or until trial; third offense is until trial. Anyone driving during a DUI suspension or DUI restricted license with a BAC of .02% or greater is subject to an additional one-year revocation. Also, driving on a DUI-related suspended or revoked license results in a 30-day impoundment of the vehicle being operated.

Accident Reporting

Accidents involving death, injury or total damage to an apparent extent of $1,000.00 or more must be reported by the investigating police/law enforcement officer to the DMV. The police must submit all necessary accident reports within 24 hours of completing an investigation. If a commercial driver is involved in an accident, a truck team may be sent to investigate, but the driver does not have to file any special reports.

Suspensions and Revocations

The Virginia DMV is in compliance with the provisions of the Motor Carrier Safety Improvement Act (MCSIA). See the Appendix for more information about these mandatory CDL disqualification sanctions.

Child Support ....Suspension initiated by Department of Social Services.
Driving While Intoxicated
    First Offense..One-year revocation or restricted driving privileges.
    Second Offense (within 5 years) ....Three-year revocation or one-year revocation and two years restricted driving privileges. Ignition interlock required.
    Second Offense (within 10 years) ....Three-year revocation or four-month revocation and two years and eight months restricted driving privileges. Ignition interlock required if court ordered.
    Third Offense ....Indefinite revocation. Eligible for restricted privileges after three years and for full restoration after five years. Ignition interlock required.
    Driving While Under the Influence ....Felony—six points.

Note: Drivers under 21 with BAC of .02 can be charged and the suspension is for one year. If an underage person merely possesses alcohol, there is a loss of the DL for six months.

Failure to Pay Fines-Motor Vehicle/Criminal Offenses Court suspension.
Making a Bomb Threat
    First Offense..One-year revocation or until age 17 (whichever is longer).
    Second Offense ....One-year revocation or until age 18 (whichever is longer).
    If Over 18 Years Old...One-year revocation, Class 5 Felony
Manslaughter (Voluntary or Involuntary) ....Indefinite revocation, eligible for restricted privileges in three years, six points. Full restoration after 5 years.
Providing Alcohol to Minor or Intoxicated Person ....One-year suspension.
Point Accumulation
    Eight Points in Twelve months or
        Twelve Points in Twenty-four Months.............Advisory letter.
    Twelve Points in Twelve Months or
        Eighteen Points in Twenty-four Months ....Driver improvement clinic; 6-month probation; 18-month control period.
    Eighteen Points in Twelve Months or
        Twenty-four Points in Twenty-four Months.......90-day suspension (rapid violator) and DI clinic; 6-month probation; 18-month control period.
Taking a Driver's License Test for Another Person or Appearing as Another
        Person to Renew Their License ....One-year revocation.
Under 18 Safety Belt/Child Restraint Violation
    1st Conviction ....Clinic and passenger restriction until 18.
    2nd Conviction...Ninety-day suspension*.

3rd Conviction...One-year revocation or until 18, whichever last.

* = May petition the Juvenile and Domestic Relations Court for restricted privileges from home to place of employment only.

Reinstatement Requirements

Reinstatement fees for suspensions and revocations range from $45 to $160. Depending upon the suspension or revocation order, other applicable compliance item(s) may apply. Persons with DWI revocations must pay a $160 reinstatement fee and provide proof of insurance for three years from the revocation end date. In some cases, the requirements for completion of alcohol treatment/education program, and installation of an ignition interlock system may be required.

Point System Overview

Points range from 3 to 6. For drivers age 18 or older, accumulation of 18 points in a 12-month period can result in a suspension. Different requirements apply to drivers under age 18. Points are dropped after 2 years from the offense date. Virginia gives safe driving points. For every full calendar year a driver has no violations or suspensions, the driver earns one safe driving point. A driver may earn up to five safe points to offset demerit points. Also, attending a Driver Improvement program can delete points or allow one to earn safe driving points.

License Plate Facts

Registration Renewal

One may renew for one, two, or three years. Renewal can be done online or for one, two or three years by using DMV's automated phone service at 888-337-4782. The DMV charges extra fees if renewal is done at a Service Center or a Satellite Office.

New Residents

Every person residing in the state who owns a motor vehicle must register their vehicle within 30 days of purchase. Non-resident owners of passenger vehicles with current out-of-state (or country) may operate the vehicle for 6 months, then the vehicle must be registered in Virginia. There is an exception for a non-Virginia resident active duty military service member, activated reserve or national guard member, or mobilized reserve or national guard member living in Virginia and the sole owner of a vehicle that is titled and registered in another state - these people are not required to title or register their vehicle in Virginia.

Inspections and Emissions Testing

An annual safety inspection on all vehicles is required. Vehicles garaged in the counties of Arlington, Fairfax, Loudoun, Prince William, or Stafford, or the cities of Alexandria, Fairfax, Falls Church, Manassas or Manassas Park, must meet the emissions inspection requirement before registering the vehicle with the DMV. The emissions inspections are valid for two years. Motor vehicles exempted from emissions inspections include any gasoline powered passenger or property carrying vehicle with a model year that is more than 25 model years old before January 1 of the current calendar year and with a manufacturer's designated gross vehicle weight rating of more than 10,000.

Plate Descriptions

Virginia's standard issue license plate is blue and white. This current design replaces the 400th anniversary of Virginia and the Jamestown settlement plate, which has been standard since 2002. The current plate design accommodates up to seven characters.

Typical Plate Pattern	Passenger and light truck plates are LL-NNN or LLL-NNN or LLL-NNNN. Commercial vehicle plates are L over L followed by 5 or 6 numbers, ranging from TA-TZ1001 to TA-TZ999,999.
County Codes	Counties are not designated on the license plate.
Plates and Stickers in Force	Two plates, two decals (MO) (YR) both plates.
Plates Remain with Car when Sold?	No, they remain with seller.

Overview of Record Access

About Driving Records

Department of Motor Vehicles, Customer Records Work Center, PO Box 27412, Richmond 23269, 804-367-0538, fax is 804-367-0390. The release of records is restrictive, as mentioned above. The current fee is $7.00 for online record requests and $8.00 for manual ordered records, add $5.00 for certification. When a subject orders own record for insurance companies it is a 5-year history; if for employment purposes, the subject will receive a 7-year history; if not specify a reason, subject will receive an 11-year history. The last fee increase was May 2002 and no increases are planned in the near future. Records are maintained for 10 years. The state charges for "no record found" reports. Online record access is provided by Virginia Interactive, a state entity that serves as Virginia's Internet Services Network Manager.

Request Methods – Mail, Walk-in, Fax, Online.

What You Should Know – Insurance records display only the last five years of the record; employment records display the last seven years of the record; and unrestricted records display the last eleven years, unless a conviction resulting in suspension or revocation is still in force. Written requests must be submitted on Form CRD93 at www.dmvnow.com/webdoc/pdf/crd93.pdf.

Special Access Programs Available – The DMV provides a Voluntary Monitoring Program to monitor the driving records of individuals employed by participating public and private transportation companies and other organizations employing large numbers of drivers. Also A Mandatory Driving Record Monitoring Program is available since Virginia law requires the DMV to actively monitor the driving records of public school bus drivers, public and private school driver education instructors and commercial driving school instructors.

About Accident Reports

Copies of accident (crash) reports are available from the Department of Motor Vehicles, Attention: Customer Records, Rm 514, PO Box 27412, Richmond 23269-0001, 866-368-5463. Records are not considered open and are only released to persons involved in the crash or their representatives. A written request (including the driver, date and location of accident) must be submitted. The fee is $8.00 per report. Credit cards are accepted. Turnaround time is 5 days. It takes 25 to 30 days before new records are available for inquiry. Records are maintained for 40 months.

About Vehicle Records

Department of Motor Vehicles, Customer Records Work Center, PO Box 27412, Richmond 23269 804-367-0538, fax is 804-367-9705. The fee for vehicle ownership and registration information is $8.00 per record, add $5.00 for certification. Approved, on-going requesters must sign an agreement and are issued a "User ID." Normal turnaround time for mail-in requests is 7 to 10 working days. Lien information is available upon written request from lending institutions, collection agencies, and businesses. The current fee is $8.00 per request.

Request Methods – Mail, Walk-in, Online, Bulk.

What You Should Know – Online and bulk access of records is provided by Virginia Interactive, a state entity that serves as Virginia's Internet Service Network Manager. Go to www.virginiainteractive.org/cmsportal3/ and click on Premium Services. There is a $95.00 annual administrative fee. The search fee is $7.00 per vehicle record.

Special Access Programs Available – Prospective Purchaser Inquiry (PPI) produces a summary about a vehicle for $12.00. See https://www.dmv.virginia.gov/dmvnet/ppi/intro.asp.

About Watercraft Records

Game & Inland Fisheries Department, 4010 W. Broad Street, Richmond VA 23230-1104, 800-898-2628, 804-367-6135 www.dgif.virginia.gov. All motorized boats must be registered and titled. Non-motorized boats sailboats over 18 ft are titled. Liens are included on the record. The records are open to the public to the extent that information is released with either a title or hull #. Submit either the title or hull #. Name searches are not performed by this agency. Records are available from 1989 to present.

Online access is available thru the same agency that supplies driving and vehicle records. Record fees vary from $1.00 or less for batch inquiries.

ps 238   Washington   The 2010 U.S. Motor Vehicle Reference Book

Washington

Administration	Important Telephone and Web Contacts

Doron N. Maniece, Assistant Director
Driver Policy and Programs Division
Department of Licensing
PO Box 9030, Olympia 98507-9030
360-902-3850
 	
Mykel Gable, Assistant Director
Driver and Vehicle Services Division
Department of Licensing
PO Box 9020, Olympia 98507-3820
360-902-3820
 	
www.dol.wa.gov/
	SR-22 & Financial Responsibility 360-902-3900
	Commercial Driver License 360-902-3900
	Vehicle Information 360-902-3770
	Registration 360-902-3770
	Office of the Insurance Commissioner 800-562-6900
	State Police 360-753-6540
	
	Driver License Laws may be accessed from:
	www.dol.wa.gov/about/publicdisclosurelawsandrules.html
	
	General Email Help:
	    Drivers: drivers@dol.wa.gov
	    Vehicles: titles@dol.wa.gov

Driver License Facts

License Format
First five letters of last name, first initial, middle initial, three numbers, and two letters or numbers (i.e., WASHI G E 222 O3). Coding of the last five characters is not released due to security reasons; however, this code is widely known among commercial MVR vendors and insurance industry personnel.

Document Appearance
Enhanced Document (Issued Since December 2007)
The *enhanced* driver licenses, CDLs, and ID cards are similar overall to the documents issued since 2001, but have several important upgrades. There is an updated format with a ghost photo on the right side of the card, the U.S. flag overlapping the photo, and on the back a machine readable zone. The licenses have a salmon color header bar with fish and evergreen trees; for ID cards the header bar is light green in color.

Prior to enhancement, the current digitized license began statewide distribution on July 1, 2001. It will take a number of years before all the older license documents are phased out. The information below describes the old and new license cards as some older cards may still be in use by military personnel.

Document 2001 to December 2007
Security Characteristics	These licenses are created using a digital imaging process. An optically variable ink coats the inside of the front laminate. The ink changes color with changes in the angle of viewing under normal light. Ultraviolet sensitive inks used in printing the card are visible under normal light but fluoresce under any "black light." If the laminate is tampered with, the word VOID displays across the document. The front of every card features a view of Mt. Rainier, larger and bolder printing, and a digital portrait of the individual. Printed on the back are the individual's endorsements and restrictions along with barcodes containing machine-readable information matching the printed information on the card's face.
Position of Photo	Right 1/3 of document.
Minor Age Driver Locator	The Intermediate License features a vertical orientation and includes the words "Intermediate License." Minors are indicated by "Age 21 on mm/dd/yy" or "Age 18 on mm/dd/yy" in a vertical orientation.
CDL Indicator	Shown in endorsement field below license number and expiration, and above yellow highlight bar.

Document prior to 2001
Security Characteristics	The older documents are plastic laminate over Polaroid photo stock. Gold

	"WASHINGTON" in two columns on laminate, separated by gold Washington state seal. Department logo overlaps.
Position of Photo	Right 1/3 of document.
Minor Age Driver Locator	"NOT 21 UNTIL ..." appears in yellow highlight bar.
CDL Indicator	Shown in endorsement field below license number and expiration, and above yellow highlight bar.

Issue and Renewal
Age Requirements
The minimum age for a regular license is 18; 16 with completion of approved driver education course. Since July 1, 2001, the DOL has issued a Intermediate Driver License to all drivers under age 18. The Intermediate License has the following restrictions: For the first 6 months after issuance, the holder of the license may not have any passengers in the car under the age of 20, except for members of the holder's immediate family. After the first 6 months, the holder may not have more than 3 passengers in the car under the age of 20, except for members of the holder's immediate family. The holder of an Intermediate Driver's License may not operate a vehicle between the hours of 1 a.m. and 5 a.m. except when the holder is accompanied by a parent, guardian, or a licensed driver who is at least 25 years of age.

Renewal
The license expires after 5 years. Driver keeps same number when renewing, unless a name change. Online renewal is available at https://fortress.wa.gov/dol/olr/. Licenses can be renewed or extended by mail for individuals who are out of the state when the license expires. Military personnel and their dependents can have a military designated expiration date on the license, which expires 90 days after discharge. A military driver license issued to a reservist who has been called to active duty, or the spouse or dependent child of the reservist, remains in effect only while the person remains on active duty.

Elderly-Related Restrictions
None indicated.

Residency
Non-resident's home-state license honored; must secure Washington license within thirty days of establishing residency.

License Classes
Commercial Classifications
Class A Any vehicle or combination of vehicles (except motorcycles). Class A required for combination vehicles only when both the GCVWR exceeds 26,001 pounds, and the GVWR of towed vehicle(s) exceeds 10,000 pounds.

Class B Any vehicle except Class A, combination vehicles and motorcycles. All single vehicles with a weight rating (GVWR) of more than 26,001 pounds.

Class C Vehicles rated less than 26,001 pounds, provided they are designed to carry 16 or more passengers and/or hazard materials requiring placards.

Note: Additional vehicles included in the CDL program:
- Vehicles designed to transport 16 or more persons (including driver)
- Public school buses, regardless of size. Private and parochial school buses are covered if and when they carry 16 or more persons (including driver)
- Any size vehicles carrying hazardous materials which require vehicle to be placarded.

Non-Commercial Classifications
The "Basic License," while not considered a class, is valid for any vehicle with GVWR or GCVWR of 26,000 pounds or less (except motorcycles).

The "ORL - Occupational/Restricted Driver License" is used for the following reasons:
- Employment
- Undergoing continuing healthcare or providing continuing care to another person who is dependent on you
- Enrolled in an educational institution and pursuing a course of study leading to a diploma, degree or other certification
- Court-ordered community service
- Work First, apprenticeship, or on-the-job training
- Attending substance abuse treatment, or 12-step meetings (unless transit service is available)
- The Ignition Interlock License (IIL), used for DUI/alcohol related suspensions. Requires installation of device, no driving restrictions.

HAZMAT Endorsement Procedure
The state is in compliance with the Patriot Act. All applicants applying for a new or renewal or transfer HAZMAT

Endorsement (HME) must first obtain the application from https://hazprints.tsa.dhs.gov/Public/ or by calling 877-429-7746. The driver must also be fingerprinted. EMSI is the state-designated entity to process fingerprints. There are four locations in the state that perform this service. Visit the web page listed above to find the address locations. The cost of the application and fingerprint process is $89.25. The fingerprints and application information is sent to the Federal Transportation Security Administration (TSA). TSA performs the background checks and notifies the DMV whether the application is approved or denied. When completed and approved, the HME is valid for five years. Visit www.dol.wa.gov/driverslicense/cdlhazmat.html for more information.

Safety and Enforcement Facts

Insurance and Financial Responsibility

Insurance is compulsory; motorists are required to carry proof of insurance or financial responsibility. Washington does not have a no-fault insurance provision. Minimum limits are $25,000/50,000/10,000. This law applies to out-of-state drivers with similar proof-of-insurance laws. There is a $250.00 fine for non-compliance. Proof is required upon reinstatement of a suspension or revocation, accident involvement, and before a drive test is administered. SR-22 forms are used. Operators of vehicles registered as antique vehicles, collector vehicles older than 30 years, state or publicly owned vehicles, motorcycles, motor-driven cycles, mopeds, or vehicles registered with the Washington Utilities and Transportation Commission as common or contract carriers are exempt from mandatory insurance requirements. Persons or companies with 26 vehicles or more may qualify for self-insurance.

Alcohol and Chemical Testing

Washington's illegal intoxication level for adults is .08 percent, .04% for CDL drivers, and .02 per cent for drivers under 21. Blood and breath testing is authorized. Washington has an implied-consent violation and an administrative per se law. Based on breathalyzer reading level and number of arrests, subject may be suspended, revoked or disqualified. A probationary license is required when a person enters into a deferred prosecution or is convicted of a DUI or Physical Control. Operating a vessel or bicycle under the influence is also considered illegal.

Collision Reporting

Collisions involving death, injury, or property damage in excess of $700.00 (that are not investigated by law enforcement) must be reported immediately to the nearest law enforcement agency having jurisdiction over the collision. Within four days the original report must be filed with the Washington State Patrol, Records Section, PO Box 42628, Olympia 98504. There are no special state reporting requirements for commercial drivers.

Suspensions and Revocations

The Washington Department of Licensing is in compliance with the provisions of the Motor Carrier Safety Improvement Act (MCSIA). See the Appendix for more information about the new mandatory CDL disqualification sanctions.

Administrative Per Se
- First Incident - Adult .... Ninety-day suspension.
- Second/Subsequent Incident - Adult .... Two-year revocation.
- First Incident - Minor .... Ninety-day suspension.
- Second/Subsequent Incident - Minor .... Revocation for 1 year or until age 21, whichever is longer.

Aiding or Abetting an Applicant in Falsifying an Application. Thirty to 364-day suspension.

Alcohol & Possession of Firearms Offenses - Minors, Thirteen to Seventeen
- First Offense .... One-year, or until age seventeen, whichever is longer.
- Second or Subsequent Offense .... Two-years, or until age eighteen, whichever is longer.

Cancellation of Fraudulent Driver License .... Five-year cancellation.
Child Support Enforcement (fail to meet obligations) .... Suspension until obligation met.
Display Another's License .... Thirty to 364-day suspension.
Display or Possess a Counterfeit or Altered License .... Thirty to 364-day suspension.

Driver Awareness Program
- Continuing Offenses .... Thirty to 364-day suspension.
- Habitual Traffic Offender .... Revoked until reinstated.

Driving Under the Influence (penalty depends on BAC)
- First Conviction in Seven Years .... Ninety-day suspension or one-year revocation.
- Second Conviction in Seven Years .... Two-year or 900 days revocation.
- Third Conviction in Seven Years .... Three-year or four-year revocation.

Driving While Suspended/Revoked .... Additional one-year suspension/revocation.
Driving While Revoked - HTO .... Additional one-year revocation.

Drug Offenses - Minors, Thirteen through Twenty

First Offense	One-year, or until age seventeen, whichever is longer.
Second or Subsequent Offenses	Two-years, or until age eighteen, whichever is longer.
Eluding a Police Officer	One-year revocation.
Failure to Appear or Respond to Traffic Citation or Infraction	Suspended until adjudicated.
Failure to Pay Judgment Resulting From Collision	Suspension until judgment satisfied.
Failure to Submit Alcohol Report or Report Indicates Non-Satisfactory/Incomplete Treatment	Variable length suspension
Felony in Which a Vehicle is Used	One-year revocation.
Fraudulent Application	Thirty to 364-day suspension.
Hit-and-Run (attended vehicle, injury, or fatality)	One-year revocation.
Intermediate (Minor) License Holder convicted of:	
2nd traffic violation or violation of license restriction	Six months suspension or until age 18, whichever first.
3rd traffic violation or violation of license restriction	Suspension until age 18.
Leaving Children Unattended in Vehicle	
First Conviction	No action.
Second Conviction	One-year revocation.
Leaving Scene of Fatality Accident	One-year revocation, Class B Felony.
Loaning a Driver's License	Thirty to 364-day suspension.
Manufacturing Counterfeit License	Thirty to 364-day suspension.
Motor Fuel Theft	Up to six months (court determination).
Perjury or Making a False Affidavit Under Any Law Relating to the Operation of a Motor Vehicle	One-year revocation.
Physical Control	Same as DUI.
Racing	Same as Reckless Driving.
Reckless Driving	
First Conviction in Two Years	Thirty-day suspension.
Second Conviction in Two Years	Thirty-day suspension.
Third Conviction in Two Years	One-year revocation.
Reckless Endangerment - Construction Zone	Sixty-day suspension.
Refuse Breath/Blood Test - Based on Court Conviction	
First Incident	Two-year revocation.
Second Incident	Three-year revocation.
Third/Subsequent Incident	Four-year revocation.
Refuse Breath/Blood Test - Based on DUI Arrest	
First Incident - Adult	One-year revocation.
Second/Subsequent Incident - Adult	Two-year revocation.
First Incident - Minor	One-year revocation.
Second/Subsequent Incident - Minor	Revocation for 2 years or until age 21, whichever longer.
Unauthorized Person Signing for a Minor	Thirty to 364-day suspension.
Unlawful Application for Driver License	Thirty to 364-day suspension.
Vehicular Homicide	Two-year revocation.
Vehicular Assault	One-year revocation.
Violation of Court Probation	Thirty- or Extended Thirty-day Suspension.
Violation of License Restrictions	120-day suspension.

Vehicle Collision with Lack of Financial Responsibility
If driver/owner insurance information not provided and there is a reasonable possibility of judgment being entered against the driver owner, the license is suspended up to three years or until one of the following is met:
- Enter into payment agreement with adverse party for damages
- Provide proof of insurance in force at time of collision
- Pay claim and provide signed release by adverse party
- Deposit security, amount based on damages/injuries
- Provide civil court decision showing no liability for damages
- Submit an affidavit of non-suit (3 years from date of collision)

Ignition Interlock. Those required to use Ignition Interlock device (IIL) include deferred prosecution for an alcohol-related incident 2 years and DUI or Physical Control conviction 1 year for the first offense, 5 years for a second offense, and 10 years for subsequent offenses.

Reinstatement Requirements

Suspension	$75.00 to $150.00 fee; SR-22 may be required.
Revocation	$75.00 to $150.00 fee; SR-22 may be required; reexamination (written and driving); apply for new license.
If DUI Related	The reissue fee is $150. In addition, evaluation from a state-approved facility for alcohol/drugs and satisfactory progress in any required treatment must be completed. Actions on DUI related convictions and Deferred Prosecution includes issuance of probationary license.
If DUI Conviction	Proof of installation of an ignition interlock device (IID) is required
If CDL Positive Test	Evaluation from a substance abuse professional (SAP) is required
If Medical	A current Medical/Visual Certification and/or re-exam may be required
If Child Support	Compliance with DSHS rules and agreements

Point System Overview

Washington does not have a point system. However, four moving violations within 12 months or five within 24 months will bring about a conditional status or suspension.

License Plate Facts

Registration Renewal
Registration renewals are required annually. Renewal options for vehicles and vessels are available online at www.dol.wa.gov, or in person at any County Auditor or vehicle licensing subagent office statewide. RCW 46.16 defines what vehicles are required to be registered in Washington.

New Residents
Non-residents must register vehicles within thirty days of establishing residency. Annual renewal is required for all vehicles operated on highways, unless exempted.

Inspections and Emissions Testing
Washington does not require an annual vehicle safety inspection, but does require a VIN inspection if a discrepancy is noted for an incoming out-of-state vehicle or a destroyed vehicle that was rebuilt. There is no provision for a statewide emission test program; however, certain regions in Spokane, King, Pierce, Snohomish, and Clark Counties have instituted such an inspection. Call 800-272-3780 to determine the specific ZIP Codes that are in the emission areas.

Plate Descriptions
The state issues replacement license plates every seven years.

Typical Plate Pattern	Passenger plates are NNNLLL or LLLNNNN. Commercial and light truck plates are LNNNNNL. The alpha designation PR designates a prorated vehicle.
County Codes	Current plates have no codes nor is the county spelled out on plate.
Plates and Stickers in Force	Two plates, one decal with (MO) (YR) on rear plate only.
Plates Remain with Car when Sold?	Yes, unless special/personalized. However, standard issue plates may be transferred to a replacement vehicle for a fee.

Overview of Record Access

About Driving Records
Driver Services Division, Driver Record Section, PO Box 9048, Olympia 98507-9048, 360-902-3913. The driving record fee is $10.00. To request an address of an individual who has a Washington driver license, identification card, or permit number use form DR-500-002. The fee is $2.00 for each address up to ten and $.15 for each additional. Detailed information on access to records, required forms and when releases are necessary can be found at the website www.dol.wa.gov.

Request Methods – Mail, Walk-in, FTP Batch, Online Status, Bulk.

What You Should Know – There are **eight different types of driving records** that can be ordered. Listed below is each record type with typical requesters.
1. Complete record: the driver, justice agencies, attorneys
2. 3-year noncommercial insurance abstract: the driver, insurance industry
3. 3-year commercial insurance abstract: the driver, insurance industry
4. 3-year life insurance abstract: the driver, insurance industry
5. Employment record: the driver, current employer, prospective employer (to determine if driver can be hired as a CDL driver)

6. Volunteer vanpool record: the driver, employees of agents of a transit authority
7. Volunteer for organization record: the driver, volunteer organizations
8. School bus driver record: the driver, school districts

Special Access Programs Available – The Department operates a monitoring system for insurance companies to review the driving records of existing policyholders for changes to the driving record. The program is only available to entities with an account (as described above) that access 2,000 or more records per month. Service bureaus (MVR vendors) can provide the service for the insurance companies.

FTP retrieval is offered for high volume requesters, minimum of 2,000 requests per month. Requesters must be approved and sign a contract. Call Data Sales Management at 360-902-3851

Online access is available for drivers to obtain their own driving records at https://fortress.wa.gov/dol/dolprod/dsdiadr/.. Use of a credit card is required. The driver's SSN must be on file. Requesters can then view and print a PDF copy of the record.

About Collision Reports

Records are stored for 6 years plus the present year at the *Washington State Patrol, Collision Reports, PO Box 42628, Olympia 98504-2628, 360-570-5200 (fax is 5220)*. Records are provided to only entitled parties who have "proper interest." It is suggested to use their form when requesting a report. Records are $5.00 each.

One may also request a copy of the collision report from WSDOT using their Request for Copy of Collision Report form. The request form provides detailed instructions and information about the request process. There is a non-refundable $5.00 fee for each copy requested. The form is available on the WSDOT website, or by calling 360-570-2355. For reports filled out by drivers, contact the Department of Licensing, 360-902-3900. The fee is $1.00 per copy to authorized requesters.

About Vehicle Records

Department of Licensing, Public Disclosure Unit, PO Box 2957, Olympia 98507-2957, 360-359-4001, fax is 360-570-7088. Washington will not perform a name search. This department maintains the database for registrations, titles, and liens for vehicles, mobile homes, and vessels. Records are available for six years plus the current year. Generally new records are placed in the system within one day. If copies of documents are required, be aware it takes 2-3 weeks for new records to be available for search. The fee for microfilm or microfiche searches is $.75 per page. Fee for a photo copy or printout is $.15 each.

Request Methods – Mail, Walk-in, Telephone, Fax, Online, Bulk.

What You Should Know – The DOL works with the Department of Social and Health Services Division of Child Support (DCS) to enforce child support and collect delinquent payments. If someone owes child support, the DCS will place a lien on the person's vehicle or vessel through the DOL.

Special Access Programs Available – A commercial Internet online search is available for pre-approved accounts to access a system known as IVIPS (Internet Vehicle/Vessel Information Processing System). With an account, you can obtain lien holder name(s). Without an account, a requester can only find out if there is a lien holder on the title. There is a one-time deposit of $25 and a charge of $.04 per inquiry. Contact the Public Disclosure Section at 360-902-3760 or Records Section at 360-359-4001 for more information.

About Watercraft Records

All vessels with propulsion machinery are required to be titled or registered. This requirement also includes sailboats 16 feet and over without any propulsion machinery. The Department keeps records for 7 years. Access and fee requirements are the same as for vehicles. You must title and register a boat in Washington State within 60 days of moving to Washington with your boat, or within 15 days of buying the boat if living in Washington and bought the boat in another state.

West Virginia

Administration	Important Telephone and Web Contacts
Joseph E. Miller, Commissioner Division of Motor Vehicles 5707 MacCorkle Ave SE, Ste 200 PO Box 17300 Charleston 25317 304-558-2723 www.transportation.wv.gov/DMV	Driver Licenses, CDL..................................304-558-2350 Point System...304-558-0238 Revocation or Suspension Due to DUI............304-558-3913 Compulsory Motor Vehicle Insurance.............304-558-4444 Ignition Interlock...304-558-1672 Titles, Registration, or Plates........................304-558-3900 State Department of Insurance ....304-558-3386 West Virginia State Police..............................304-746-2100 Code of State Rules - Title Series 91 www.sos.wv.gov/Pages/default.aspx State Statutes www.legis.state.wv.us/WVCODE/Code.cfm

Driver License Facts

License Format
A seven digit alpha/numeric series, with no correlation to type of license issued, is used as follows—

0000001 - 0999999.	C000001 - C999999	S000001 - S999999
1X00001 - 1X99999	D000001 - D999999	XX00001 - XX99999
A000001 - A999999	E000001 - E999999	
B000001 - B999999	F000001 - F999999	

Document Appearance
Security Characteristics   License is a digital/PVC card, overlay with WV outline in bold (hologram).
Position of Photo   Top left.
Minor Age Driver Locator   Vertical format, picture in left corner.
All licenses for driver 15-17 are RED, if 18-21 are BLUE.
CDL Indicator   "COMMERCIAL DRIVER LICENSE" is printed across the top of the license.

Issue and Renewal
Age Requirements
A Graduated Driver's License Program was instituted 01/2001 with three levels or licensing steps, as related below. An Instruction Permit minimum age is 15, valid until 18th birthday with a 30-day extension. An Intermediate License minimum age is 16; minimum 6 months infraction-free driving at Instruction Permit level. A Full License is the level three and is valid until age 21. One must have a minimum of 12 months infraction-free driving at Intermediate Level. A Class E minimum age is twenty-one; which is the adult license.

Renewal
WVDMV issues driver licenses with expiration of up to 5 years. Renewal is not available online at this time. Vision screening is required. Driver keeps the same number when renewing, after age eighteen, for life. Licenses of military personnel out-of-state do not expire, but must be renewed within 6 months after discharge. Any driver whose license has been expired for more than six months will be required to retest.

Elderly-Related Restrictions
None are reported.

Residency
Non-resident's home-state license is honored on a reciprocal basis for up to 30 days.

License Classes
Commercial Classifications
Class A   Any combination of vehicles with a GCWR of 26,001 or more pounds, providing the GVWR of the vehicle(s) being towed is in excess of 10,000 pounds.

Class B Any single vehicle with a GVWR of 26,001 pounds or more, or any such vehicle towing a vehicle not in excess of 10,000 pounds GVWR.

Class C Any single vehicle or combination of vehicles less than 26,001 pounds GVWR, or any such vehicle towing a vehicle not in excess of 10,000 GVWR. This group applies to vehicles which are placarded for hazardous materials or designed to carry sixteen passengers or more (including the driver)..

Non-Commercial Classifications

Class D Commercial vehicles; non-CDL classes (e.g., taxi cabs, delivery vans, etc.).
Class E Operator's license; operation of a vehicle for personal use.
Class F Motorcycle license only. The holder of this license class may not possess any other type of license. West Virginia began issuing "Motorcycle Only" licenses as of July 1, 1992.
Class G Bioptic licensed drivers.

License Types

1. Level 1 Instruction Permit
2. Level 2 License
3. Level 3 License
5. Operator Instruction Permit
6. Operator
7. Operator/Motorcycle Endorsement
8. Operator/Motorcycle Endorsement/CDL
9. Operator/CDL
10. Motorcycle Instruction Permit
11. Motorcycle Only License
12. CDL Instruction Permit
13. Level 2 License/Motorcycle Endorsement

Note: Motor Vehicle Truck registration Classes 'K' and 'E' were eliminated. At renewal, these vehicles are issued Class 'B' registration plates. Trailer registration Class 'L' will be eliminated and replaced with Class 'C' registration plates, however Class 'L' registrations will be renewed as usual.

HAZMAT Endorsement Procedure

The state is in compliance with the Patriot Act. All applicants applying for a new or renewal or transfer HAZMAT Endorsement (HME) must first obtain the application from https://hazprints.tsa.dhs.gov/Public/ or by calling 877-429-7746. The driver must also be fingerprinted. EMSI is the state-designated entity to process fingerprints. There are three locations in the state that perform this service. Visit the web page listed above to find the address locations. The cost of the application and fingerprint process is $89.25. The fingerprints and application information is sent to the Federal Transportation Security Administration (TSA). TSA performs the background checks and notifies the DMV whether the application is approved or denied. When completed and approved, the HME is valid for five years.

Safety and Enforcement Facts

Insurance and Financial Responsibility

Liability insurance is compulsory; minimum liability limits are $20,000/40,000/10,000. West Virginia does not have no-fault insurance. Proof is required at registration or renewal, vehicle inspection and after an accident or certain violations. Vehicle registrations are randomly sampled for validity. SR-22 forms are not used by the state. Any violation of the compulsory insurance law will result in the suspension of the driver license and revocation of the license plate. Failure to satisfy a civil judgment resulting from an accident requires an indefinite suspension until restitution is made.

Alcohol and Chemical Testing

West Virginia's illegal intoxication level is .08 percent and above, .05 percent and above for administrative drivers license suspension, .04 percent for drivers of CMVs, and .02 percent for drivers under 21. Blood tests can be requested or obtained with a search warrant. Breath tests are the designated secondary chemical tests. West Virginia has an implied-consent violation provision, an administrative suspension provision, and any measurable alcohol provision for drivers under the age of 21 with BAC of .02 to .08.

Accident Reporting

Accidents involving death, injury, or damage in excess of $500 must be reported immediately to the nearest police department. There are no special reporting criteria for commercial drivers.

Suspensions and Revocations

Mandatory Suspension will occur with accumulation of 12 or more points within a 2-year period as follows:

12-13 Points	Thirty Days.
14-15 Points	Forty-five Days.
16-17 Points	Sixty Days.
18-19 Points	Ninety Days.
20+ Points	License is Suspended until Accumulated Points are Reduced to 11 or Less.

Mandatory Revocation (six months to one year) For Conviction of any of the Following:
- Manslaughter or Negligent Homicide
- Felony Involving a Motor Vehicle
- Leaving the Scene of an Accident Resulting in Death or Personal Injury
- Court Ordered Judgments.
- Three Reckless Driving Convictions in Twenty-four Months
- Drag Racing
- Driving While License Suspended/Revoked

DUI Revocations
First Offense	Varies, 15 day minimum suspension.
Second Offense	Will include one-year suspension.
Third Offense	Will include one-year suspension of driving privileges.

No Proof of Insurance
For failure to show proof of insurance during a notice for verification of coverage the driving privilege will be suspended for 30 days. If a law enforcement officer or insurance company reports a driver is operating a vehicle without insurance, the license will be suspended for 30 days. A second offense will result in a 90-day suspension. There is no provision in the Motor Vehicle code for a driving permit during a suspended period.

CDL Suspensions, Revocations, and Disqualifications

West Virginia is in compliance with the provisions of the Motor Carrier Safety Improvement Act (MCSIA), see the Appendix. Below is an overview of many CDL sanctions.

Any one of the following will disqualify a WV Commercial Driver's License holder:
- Causing fatality thru negligent operation of a CMV
- Controlled substance DUI
- Driving a CMV while suspended, revoked, or disqualified
- Driving Under the Influence (DUI), blood alcohol content (BAC) .04 or above
- Drug felony while operating a commercial motor vehicle
- FMSCA Notice that driver poses an imminent hazard
- Leaving the scene of an accident
- Violation of an out-of-service order
- Railroad crossing violation committed in a CMV
- Refusal to submit to a BAC test

A 60-day suspension will be assessed against any person who operates a commercial vehicle:
- Without a valid CDL
- Without proper license endorsements
- While serving a disqualification

DMV disqualifies CDL holders who are convicted of two or more of these offenses within a 3-year period:
- Reckless driving
- Improper lane changes
- Following too closely
- Speeding 15 MPH or more above limit
- Any violation of traffic law in connection with a fatal accident
- Driving a CMV without obtaining a CDL
- Driving a CMV without a CDL in possession
- Driving a CMV without proper license class or endorsements

Reinstatement Requirements

If alcohol or drug related, completion of Safety & Treatment Program is required. Repeat offenders must participate in the WV Alcohol Test & Lock program. All suspension and revocation fees are $50.00 with the exception to Compulsory Insurance files which are: revocation of license plate is a $100.00 reinstatement fee; secure order to State Police for license plate is a $50.00 penalty fee.

Point System Overview

Points range from 2 to 8. If a driver accumulates twelve or more points, there is a mandatory suspension. The DMV may deduct 3 points from the licenses of drivers who complete an approve Defensive Driving Course. Licensees are not eligible who have taken the course within the last two years. Points are automatically removed from the record two years after the conviction date.

License Plate Facts

Registration Renewal

Renewal is annual. At this time renewal is not available online.

New Residents
Non-residents must register vehicles if stay exceeds 30 days. New residents must title the vehicle in West Virginia within 30 days of establishing residency.

Inspections and Emissions Testing
West Virginia requires a routine safety inspection every twelve (12) months for all vehicles. Inspections are performed at any official inspection station licensed by the State Police. A sticker is placed on the inside of the windshield. New residents have 10 days from the date they title a vehicle to have a West Virginia inspection. West Virginia has reciprocity with Louisiana, Mississippi, Missouri, New Hampshire, New York, Oklahoma, Texas, Utah, and Wyoming. Therefore, out of state inspection stickers from these states are valid in West Virginia until expiration. Any vehicle purchased or otherwise acquired within West Virginia not having a valid inspection sticker must be inspected within ten days. There is no provision for vehicle emission testing.

Plate Descriptions
Typical Plate Pattern .... Passenger and light truck plates are 1 numeric, 1 alpha, 4 numeric. Commercial plates are, generally, a "B" followed by 1 to 5 numbers.
County Codes .... Counties are not designated by codes or printed on the plates.
Plates and Stickers in Force .... One plate, one decal (yr).
Plate Remains with Car when Sold? ..... No, it remains with seller.

Overview of Record Access

About Driving Records
Compulsory Insurance Section, Driving Records, 5707 MacCorkle Ave SE, Ste 200 Charleston 25317, 304-558-4444. For mail or walk-in requests, the fee is $5.00 for a certified or non-certified record if a DL# is provided and $6.00 for a certified or non-certified if the DL# is NOT provided. The fee is $8.00 for a record obtained electronically. If a driver's license number is not provided, submit the SSN and/or date of birth with an additional $1.00 fee. All fees are non-refundable. The Message Forwarding Service fee is $5.00. The state charges for "no record found" reports. All requests for a driving record on an employee or client must have a completed DMV-101-PS-2 form.

Request Methods – Mail, Walk-in, Online, Status Check, Bulk.

What You Should Know – West Virginia does not report accidents or speeding on interstate if less than eleven MPH over the limit (for non-CDL only, this conviction will show on a CDL).

Special Access Programs Available – West Virginia offers a free Driver's License Status Check at www.transportation.wv.gov/dmv/Pages/dlverify.aspx. West Virginia Interactive is the portal service manager for online access to WV driving records. All requesters must complete three agreement documents necessary for account approval. For more information, call WVI at 304-414-0265. If no consent or permissible use is presented, records are not released. However, the state permits the requester to use the Message Forwarding Service that enables the state to forward a request to the license holder to approve the record request. This is an additional $5.00.

About Accident Reports
West Virginia's State Police Records Section sells copies of accident reports that they have investigated. Send $20.00 per request and a written letter explaining the purpose and requester's involvement (family member, lawyer, participant, etc.) to: Superintendent of Department of Public Safety, 725 Jefferson Road, South Charleston 25309-1698, 304-746-2128.

Vehicle Records
Division of Motor Vehicles, Vehicle Records - Box 17150, 5707 MacCorkle Ave SE, Ste 200, Charleston 25311, 304-558-0282. The DMV maintains records for vehicles, boats, and unattached mobile homes. The fee for a VIN, plate and registration checks is $1.00; $5.00 per vehicle for lien information with registration; $5.00 per title copy; $10.00 for certified title copy; $25.00 per vehicle for a complete title history (which includes lien data), and $5.00 Message Forwarding fee (see above). Title copies are available from the early 1960's.

Request Methods – Mail, Walk-in, Bulk.

What You Should Know – Requests are available by mail or over-the-counter with state issued photo ID. The fee must accompany the request along with the reason for the request.

Watercraft Records
All boats with a motor or a sail must be titled and registered. Registration records are available from 1975. The same vehicle records access requirements and fees apply as described above.

Wisconsin

Administration

Taqwanya Smith, Director
Bureau Driver Services
Division of Motor Vehicles
PO Box 7983, Madison 5370-7983
608-266-9890

Anna Biermeier, Director
Bureau of Vehicle Services
Division of Motor Vehicles
PO Box 7949, Madison 53707
608-267-5121

www.dot.wisconsin.gov

Important Telephone and Web Contacts

Driver Licensing..608-266-2353
SR-22 & Financial Responsibility......................608-266-2261
Commercial Driver License 608-264-7049
Accident Records 608-266-8753
Vehicle Record Information...............................608-266-3666
Vehicle Registration Research & Information.....608-266-1466
State Department of Insurance 608-266-3585
State Police..608-266-3212

General Email for DL   driverrecords.dmv@dot.wi.gov
Motor Vehicle Laws at:
  www.dot.wisconsin.gov/drivers/lawbook.htm
Transportation Laws at:
  www.dot.wisconsin.gov/library/research/law/index.htm

Driver License Facts

License Format

One letter followed by thirteen numbers. The coding of driver license numbers is as follows: License Number "A5364683945805"

A	=	First letter of last name
536	=	Coded from last name
468	=	Coded from first name and middle initial
39	=	Birth year
458	=	Coded month and day of birth, sex
05	=	Tie-breaker, check-digit

Document Appearance

As of September 20, 2005 Wisconsin began issuing a new style driver license and ID card. Old licenses are laminated; new ones are digitized.

Security Characteristics Cards are covered with a special security overlay to prevent tampering and alterations. The hologram design pre-printed into the overlay includes the word WISCONSIN and the coat of arms. Capturing new digital images enables DMV to compare customer images on file with the new ones to reduce the potential for identify theft. Also, vital information such as the license number, date of birth and name are in an increased font size, making the new card easier to read. The new driver license has a pink hue and the ID card has a green hue. The image background is light blue. Images that were captured before September 20, 2005 have a gray background. License types are color coded by using different colored fonts for the words DRIVER LICENSE and the type of license; occupational (black); commercial (green); regular (blue); probationary (red).

Position of Photo Upper left.

Minor Driver Locator Card is printed in a vertical format. "Turns 21 on (date)" appears under the photo in white lettering on a red background. "Turns 18 on (date)" appears under "Turns 21..." and is printed with black letters on a yellow background. The date of birth is printed in red.

CDL Indicator Red (if under 21) or green (if over 21) letters on upper left - label "Commercial."

Legal Presence Indicator "Temporary" will appear in blue on lower right corner if subject is not U.S. citizen or permanent resident.

Old Document

Security Characteristics	The laminated has the state seal and state outline super-imposed beneath text description. Digitized license has security overlay with holographic design that includes state Coat of Arms and the word WISCONSIN. Magnetic strip on back is encoded.
Position of Photo	Laminated is bottom left; digitized is upper left.
Minor Driver Locator	Laminated, in red background "Under 21 Until (date)" or "Under 18 Until (date)" below picture on license. Digitized is gray background with red box around the photo and WISCONSIN license/product type is in red print. "Under 21 Till (date)" appears at the top of the photo in red print.
CDL Indicator	Laminated is red letters on right side of laminate - label "Commercial Driver License." Digitized is red (if under 21) or green (if over 21) letters on upper left - label "Commercial."

Issue and Renewal
Age Requirements
With the Graduated Driver Licensing Program, the Instruction Permit minimum age is 15 1/2; one must pass the knowledge test, be enrolled in Driver Education, have an adult sponsor and pass the vision screening. Also, one must hold an Instruction Permit for at least 6 months, and cannot have been convicted of any moving traffic violations for the 6 months prior to applying for Probationary License, and pass a skills test. For a Probationary License and if under 18, one must complete Driver Education, have an adult sponsor, and accumulate 30 hours of supervised driving experience.

An Occupational License is a **restricted** driver license. Driving is limited to and from work or church or other places indicated on the license for only specific times of the day. Operation for recreation or pleasure is not allowed for an Occupational License. Total driving time must be no more than 12 hours for any one day and no more than 60 hours for the entire week. Those eligible to obtain an occupational license include drivers whose operating privilege was revoked or suspended under the following circumstances: under the general provision statute; a drug conviction under S.961.50 (except juveniles); nonpayment of child support under S.767.303; and a Habitual Traffic Offender (HTO) under Ch. 351. No commercial operators are permitted to use an occupational license.

Renewal
Licenses expire in the birth month of the eighth year. Renewal is not available online. Driver keeps same number when renewing, unless there is a name, DOB, or gender change.

Military personnel stationed out-of-state are not required to renew, but an out-of-state renewal is recommended. The renewal requires a vision test from another state DMV or authorized visual examiner. For more information, write to Qualifications & Issuance Section, PO Box 7995, Madison WI 53707-7995 or call 608-264-7049..

Elderly-Related Restrictions
None indicated.

Residency
Drivers with a CDL are required to apply for a Wisconsin driver license within 30 days. Other drivers new to Wisconsin are required to apply for a Wisconsin driver license within 60 days of establishing residency. The home state license of a non-resident age 16 or over is on a reciprocal basis.

License Classes
Commercial Classifications

Class A	Any combination of commercial motor vehicles weighing over 26,000 pounds. In addition, the towed unit must weigh more than 10,000 pounds.
Class B	A single commercial motor vehicle weighing over 26,000 pounds. In addition, any towed trailers must weigh less than 10,000 pounds.
Class C	Any vehicles that do not meet the definitions of Classes A and B. In addition, these vehicles must carry sixteen or more passengers (including the driver) or transport hazardous materials. *Please note: You cannot drive this class of vehicle without the endorsement for passengers or hazardous materials.*

Non-Commercial Classifications

Class D	Non-commercial vehicles other than motorcycles; includes regular passenger cars, light trucks, and mopeds.
Class M	Motorcycles.

Other License Types

REGI	Class D Instruction Permit
PROB	Probationary (points double on second and subsequent violations)
SPRR	Special Restricted License.
JUVP	Juvenile Restricted License

CYCI	Cycle Instruction Permit
JUVI	Juvenile Instruction Permit
MPDI	Moped/Motor Bicycle Instruction Permit

HAZMAT Endorsement Procedure

The state is in compliance with the Patriot Act. All applicants applying for an original or renewal or transfer of the HAZMAT Endorsement (HME) must first obtain the application from the DMV and pay a $34.00 fee. The driver must also be fingerprinted. PearsonVue has been selected as the vendor to collect fingerprints. Fingerprinting services are provided in various locations around the state, fees involved. The fingerprints and application information are sent to the Federal Transportation Security Administration (TSA). TSA performs the background checks and notifies the DMV whether the application is approved or denied. When completed and approved, the HME is valid for four years. Visit www.dot.wisconsin.gov/drivers/drivers/apply/types/hazmat.htm for more information.

Safety and Enforcement Facts

Insurance and Financial Responsibility

Wisconsin has a mandatory liability insurance requirement beginning 06/01/2010; however, the current Safety Responsibility Law remains. Minimum insurance liability limits are $30,000/100,000/15,000. Proof of insurance is required after certain suspensions and revocations. SR-22 forms are used.

Alcohol and Chemical Testing

Wisconsin's illegal intoxication level is .08 percent and above for first, second and third offenses, and .02 percent and above for fourth and subsequent offenses. The intoxication level for persons driving a CMV is .04 percent and the level for persons under the age of 21 is .00 percent. Urine, blood, and breath testing are authorized. Wisconsin has both an implied-consent violation and a provision for an administrative suspension.

Accident Reporting

Accidents involving death, injury, or property damage of $1,000.00 or more to one person's property, or over $200.00 damages to government property other than vehicles must be reported immediately to the nearest law enforcement authority. If the police do not file a copy of the accident investigation with the Department of Transportation, the motorists involved must file. Reports should be sent to: Department of Transportation, Qualifications and Issuance, PO Box 7919, Madison 53707-7919. There are no special filing requirements for commercial drivers.

Suspensions and Revocations

The Wisconsin DMV is in compliance with the provisions of the Motor Carrier Safety Improvement Act (MCSIA). See the Appendix for more information about these mandatory CDL disqualification sanctions.

Regular License - Point Accumulation During Twelve-Month Period and Length of Suspension
    Twelve to Sixteen Points..Two months.
    Seventeen to Twenty-two Points..............................Four months.
    Twenty-three to Thirty Points ....Six months.
    Thirty-one or More Points...One year.
Probationary License Point Accumulation
    Twelve to Thirty Point Accum. ....Six months.
    Thirty-one or More Points   One year.
Refusal to Submit to Chemical Test
    First Offense..One-year revocation.
    Second Offense ....Two-year revocation.
    Third or Subsequent Offense...................................Three-year revocation.
Administrative Suspension (Violation of Alcohol
Content) Based on Arrest ....Six-month suspension.
Operating While Intoxicated
    First Offense..Six- to nine-month revocation.
    Second Offense ....Twelve- to eighteen-month revocation.
    Third or Subsequent Offense...................................Two- to three-year revocation.

Wisconsin takes action on any out-of-state convictions for which Wisconsin statutes require a **mandatory suspension or revocation** of the operating privilege. Those convictions include:

- Operating while under the influence or with a prohibited alcohol concentration
- Attempting to elude an officer
- Failure to stop and render aid after an accident resulting in:

- Death of another
- Great bodily harm to another
- Personal injury to another
- Serious property damage (if specified by the court)
- Injury by negligent operation of a motor vehicle while under the influence
- Great bodily harm resulting from the operation of a motor vehicle while under the influence
- Homicide resulting from the operation of a motor vehicle while under the influence
- Perjury or making a false affidavit or statement to the department
- Reckless driving
- Vehicle used in the commission of a felony

Reinstatement Requirements

Suspension $60.00 fee; proof of financial responsibility required if suspension was due to violation of safety responsibility or damage judgment laws; re-examination may be required. An additional $50 reinstatement fee is required for all damage judgments and for safety responsibility suspensions if vehicle registration were also suspended.

Revocation $60.00 fee; proof of financial responsibility may be required for revocations (EXCEPT for a first offense of operating while intoxicated or non-compliance with court-ordered alcohol assessments or driver safety plans); re-examination may be required

Point System Overview

Points range from 2 to 6. Accumulation of 12 points in a 12-month period can result in a suspension. For individuals holding probationary licenses, points are doubled on second and subsequent offenses. Within a 12-month period, upon the completion of a Wisconsin approved Traffic Safety Course, one can request a 3-point reduction of point total. One can also request a 3-point reduction upon completion of a motorcycle rider course for violations and convictions incurred while operating a motorcycle. Courses can be taken often; however, there is only one point reduction every 3 years.
At the Transportation Chapter 101 (www.legis.state.wi.us/rsb/code/trans/trans101.pdf) is a complete list of points and assessments at.

License Plate Facts

Registration Renewal
Renewal is annual. Non-CDL vehicles can renew online if operator received an RRN number and the correct address is on file. Renewals may be done by touch-tone phone by calling 800-236-7368. The address has to be correct and current in order to use online renewal.

New Residents
When becoming a Wisconsin resident, one must obtain Wisconsin registration (license plates) for a vehicle within two days of moving here. To legally operate a vehicle one must display Wisconsin license plates within 2 business days of establishing residency.

Inspections and Emissions Testing
Wisconsin has no mandatory safety inspection requirement. Vehicles are required to have an emissions inspection every other year at the time of license plate renewal, beginning in the third year following the vehicle's model year. Vehicles under this requirement include cars and trucks with a manufacturer's gross vehicle weight rating under 8,501 pounds that are customarily kept in the Wisconsin counties of: Kenosha, Milwaukee, Ozaukee, Racine, Sheboygan, Washington, and Waukesha. Exceptions are vehicles produced prior to the 1996 model year and motorcycles. Vehicles are tested every second year at the time of renewal of license plates, beginning in the third year following the vehicle's model year. Additionally, vehicles more than 5 model years old are required to be tested at the time of change of ownership. Effective January 1, 2010, the inspection requirements include model year 2007 and newer vehicles that are powered by diesel fuel; and/or have a GVWR between 8,501 pounds and 14,000 pounds. Motorcycles and dedicated farm vehicles are exempt from inspection.

Plate Descriptions

Typical Plate Pattern   Since July 2000, Wisconsin issues auto plates in a NNN-LLL pattern. Previously, passenger plates were LLL-NNN. Previously, light truck plates were two letters set vertically followed by five numbers, now they are five or six numbers, or a combination of letters and numbers. Commercial vehicle plates are two letters set vertically followed by four numbers. The sticker on the plate indicates the weight class for both light trucks and commercial vehicles.

Wisconsin

County Code — The state indicates there is no code sequence designating the county of issuance.
Plates and Stickers in Force — Two plates, two decals (MO) (YR) on the rear plate.
Plates Remain with Car when Sold? — No, they remain with seller.

Overview of Record Access

About Driving Records

Division of Motor Vehicles, Driver Records, PO Box 7995, Madison 53707-7995, 608-266-2353. Email questions to driverrecords.dmv@dot.wi.gov. The fee is $7.00 per written record request, add $5.00 for certification, and $5.00 for an electronic record request. The state charges for "no record found" reports. The driver's full name, sex, date of birth, or license number is needed when ordering. Casual requesters must submit Request Form MV2896.

Request Methods – Mail, Telephone, Online, Online Status, Email, Bulk.

What You Should Know – Counter service is not offered for driving record requests, this includes all Field Offices. For more information or how to register for online access, call 608-266-0928 or email to pars@dot.wi.gov.

Special Access Programs Available – Check the status of a driver license free at www.dot.wisconsin.gov/drivers/online.htm or call 608-264-7133. The SSN is needed. Employers of commercial motor vehicle drivers may enroll in the Employer Notification Program operated by PARS. The program is not available to employers of non-commercial drivers. For more information or to register, call 608-266-0928 or email pars@dot.wi.gov.

About Accident Reports

Copies of accident reports can be obtained from the investigating law enforcement agency or from the Accident Records Unit of the Division of Motor Vehicles, 608-266-8753. The fee for mailed copies of reports is $6.00 per report, prepayment is required if ordering more than one report. Records are available on average 2 weeks after receipt of the accident report and for 4 years to present. Requests should be sent to the Wisconsin Department of Transportation, Qualifications and Issuance, Traffic Records Unit, PO Box 7919, Madison 53707-7919, 608-266-8753. Information involving juvenile citations is not released.

About Vehicle Records

Department of Transportation, Vehicle Records Section, PO Box 7911, Madison 53707-7911, 608-266-3666 or 266-1466. Email questions to vehiclequestions.dmv@dot.state.wi.us. The DOT maintains the database for vehicle titles, registrations, and liens. Boat and ATV information is with the Department of Natural Resources. Records are stored five years to present. It takes seven days before new records are available for inquiry. Effective July 2000, the titling of mobile homes was moved to the Department of Commerce. Note that in-person counter service for record access was discontinued.

Request Methods – Mail, Online, Bulk.

What You Should Know – The fee for VIN, lien and registration checks is $5.00 per record plus $.25 per photocopy. An additional $5.00 is charged for certification. Counter service is not offered.

Special Access Programs Available – Wisconsin offers a free license plate check and a free title inquiry at www.dot.wisconsin.gov/drivers/online.htm.

About Watercraft Records

Department of Natural Resources, 101 S. Webster, Madison 53703 608-266-2621, 888-936-7463, fax: 608-261-4380, www.dnr.wi.gov. All motorized or sail boats 16 ft and over must be titled and registered. All motorized or sail boats under 16 ft must be registered. Lien information appears on the title record. Record information can be requested by the owner name or boat registration information number. There is no fee if under 10 records. 10 records or more is considered a bulk records request and fees follow the Electronic Records Instructions, which can place fees as high as $200. Credit cards are accepted. Turnaround time is 10 days. One can request information over the telephone, or by fax at 608-264-6130. The office is open 7AM-10PM seven days a week.

Wyoming

Administration	Important Telephone and Web Contacts
John Cox, Director Department of Transportation 307-777-4484 Tom Loftin, Support Services Div. Admin. 307-777-4484 Don Edington, Driver Services Program Manager 307-777-4802 Deborah Lopez, Motor Vehicle Srvs Manager 307-777-4851 5300 Bishop Boulevard Cheyenne, WY 82009-3340 www.dot.state.wy.us/wydot/	Driver Licensing..307-777-4810 Vehicle License/Title.................. 307-777-4851 or 4709 Financial Responsibility/SR-22 ....307-777-4800 Commercial Driver License.........................307-777-4810 Vehicle Information..................... 307-777-4709 or 4825 State Department of Insurance ....307-777-7401 Highway Patrol..307-777-4301 Wyoming Statutes Title 31 – Motor Vehicles: http://legisweb.state.wy.us/statutes/compress/title31.doc Email Contact List at www.dot.state.wy.us/ContactWYDOT/

Driver License Facts

License Format
The driver's license is nine numbers (six numbers, hyphen, three numbers; i.e., 101565-142). Numbers are computer-generated with a "check digit." An ID Card is composed of two numbers, hyphen, then seven numbers.

Document Appearance
License is a tamper proof laminate.

Security Characteristics Signature of director appears vertically overlaying photographs. The driver license has a photo of the Devil's Tower, the ID Card has a photo of the Grand Teton mountain range.

Position of Photo Right side, except minor driver (see below).

Minor Age Driver Locator Photo on left side with red script above photo stating the expiration date and "Age 21 in (year)."

CDL Indicator "Commercial Driver License" in dark green header on top left..

Issue and Renewal
Age Requirements
To obtain a WY license with full driving privileges a person must be at least 17 years of age; unless the person is 16 ½ years of age, has held a graduated driver's license for at least 6 months, and completed/passed an approved driver's education course. To obtain a commercial license for interstate driving, a person must be at least 21 years of age. A commercial license can be issued to a person under the age of 21, however, they will be restricted to driving in Wyoming only (intrastate). To obtain a learner's permit, a person must be at least 15 years of age. To obtain a restricted license a person must be between the ages of 14 and 16 years of age. A person applying for the restricted class C license must first apply and receive a restricted instruction permit.

Renewal
Birth date of fourth year. Driver keeps same number when renewing. Renewal is not available online, but licenses can be extended by mail. Military personnel stationed out-of-state are required to renew every four years, unless restriction has been issued stating "Expiration waived when accompanied by active military duty Identification Card."

Elderly-Related Restrictions
None indicated.

Residency
Home-state licenses of non-residents (if over sixteen years of age) are honored. One must apply for a Wyoming driver license within one year from the time residency is established, providing license currently held is NOT issued by one of

the following states: Georgia, Massachusetts, Michigan, Tennessee or Wisconsin. These states are not part of the Driver's License Compact. If a license is held from one of these states, the driver must apply for a Wyoming license when residency is established. Those holding a CDL must transfer their driver license within 30 days.

License Classes
Commercial Classifications
A   Any combination of vehicles with a GCWR of 26,001 pounds or more—provided the GVWR of the vehicle or vehicles being towed is in excess of 10,000 pounds, including all vehicles under Class C (except motorcycles).

B   Any single vehicle with a GVWR of 26,001 or more pounds, or any such vehicle towing a vehicle which does not have a GVWR in excess of 10,000 pounds, including all vehicles under Class C (except motorcycles).

C   Any single vehicle or combination of vehicles that does not meet the definition of a Class A or B, but that either is designed to transport sixteen (16) or more passengers including driver or is placarded for transportation of hazardous materials.

Note: Wyoming also offers a CDP (Commercial Driving Permit) which entitles a driver to operate a commercial vehicle only when accompanied by a person who possesses a commercial drivers license for the vehicle being operated.

Non-Commercial Classifications
A   Same as above (issued to farmers/ranchers, firefighters, military).

B   Same as above (issued to farmers/ranchers, firefighters, military).

C   For cars and pickups. Any single vehicle or combination of vehicles (except motorcycles) with a GVWR less than 26,001 pounds, or any such vehicle towing a vehicle which does not have a GVWR in excess of 10,000 pounds.

I   Instruction Permit for drivers who have applied for a Class C License or a restricted Class C License.

I2   An intermediate permit for drivers aged 16-17, to operate a motor vehicle with restrictions as to time of day and restricts the number of non-family passengers.

M   Motorcycles or all terrain vehicle; may be added to license valid for other Classes, or may be issued as only class, if the applicant is not licensed for other classification.

RC   Restricted Class C - authorizes the holder, aged 14-16 years, to operate a motor vehicle (Class C type) between the hours of 5 a.m. and 8 p.m. within a 50 mile radius of domicile.

HAZMAT Endorsement Procedure
The state is in compliance with the Patriot Act. All applicants applying for a new or renewal or transfer HAZMAT Endorsement (HME) must first obtain the application from https://hazprints.tsa.dhs.gov/Public/ or by calling 877-429-7746. The driver must also be fingerprinted. EMSI is the state-designated entity to process fingerprints. There are three locations in the state that perform this service. Visit the web page listed above to find the address locations. The cost of the fingerprint process is $89.25 and is subject to change. The fingerprints and application information is sent to the Federal Transportation Security Administration (TSA). TSA performs the background checks and notifies the DMV whether the application is approved or denied. When completed and approved, the HME is valid for four years.

Safety and Enforcement Facts

Insurance and Financial Responsibility
Minimum responsibility limits are $25,000/50,000/20,000. No owner may operate a motor vehicle without liability insurance. Wyoming does not have a no-fault insurance provision. Proof is required after conviction of an offense that carries mandatory suspension/revocation (DUI, reckless, etc.), uninsured accident suspension and compulsory insurance violation. SR-22 forms are used.

Alcohol and Chemical Testing
Wyoming's illegal intoxication level is .08 percent and above, .02 percent and above for youthful offenders, and .04 percent and above for CDL drivers. Urine, blood, and breath testing are authorized. Wyoming has provisions for an implied-consent violation and administrative suspension. Operating a horse, bicycle, or boat under the influence is also considered illegal.

Accident Reporting
For involvement in an accident in which there is an injury or property damage to an apparent extent of $1,000, all drivers must file an Operator's or Owner's Traffic Accident Report. This is regardless who is at fault. The Wyoming Insurance Certificate (SR21) at the bottom of the accident report must be completed, even if insurance information was given to the investigating officer at the accident scene. Accident reports should be sent to the Department of Transportation, Accident Records Section, 5300 Bishop Blvd, Cheyenne 82009-3340.

Suspensions and Revocations

The Wyoming DMV is in compliance with the provisions of the Motor Carrier Safety Improvement Act (MCSIA). See the Appendix for more information about these mandatory CDL disqualification sanctions.

The difference between a suspension and a revocation is that after a suspension is completed one can get the old driver's license back if it is still valid. A revocation cancels the driver's license, and the driver must go through an investigation to be re-licensed once the revocation is over. The offenses that will cause a revocation are: 1) 3rd or subsequent DWUI; 2) leaving the scene of an injury accident; 3) homicide by vehicle; 4) felony that is a direct result of the manner of driving; 5) third or subsequent reckless driving conviction.

Below is a list of typical suspensions and revocations.

Offense	Penalty
Admin Per Se (over .08%)	Ninety-day suspension.
Admin Per Se Youthful offenders (.02 up to .08%)	
First Offense	Ninety-day suspension.
Second Offense	Six-month suspension.
Third or Subsequent Offense	Six-month revocation.
Any Four Moving Violations in Twelve-Month Period	Ninety-day suspension.
DWUI	
First Conviction in Five Years	Ninety-day suspension.
Second Conviction in Five Years	One-year suspension.
Third or Subsequent Conviction in Five Years	Mandatory three-year revocation.
Fourth or Subsequent Conviction in Five Years, Felony	Mandatory three-year revocation.
First Citation (moving violation) on Restricted License	Ninety-day suspension.
Each Consecutive Violation on Restricted License	Additional one-year suspension.
Leaving Scene of an Injury Accident	One-year revocation.
Felony Which is a Direct Result of Manner of Driving	One-year revocation.
Refusal of Chemical Test First Conviction	Six-month suspension.
Second Conviction or Existing DWUI on Record	Eighteen-month suspension.
Homicide by Vehicle	One-year revocation.
No Liability Insurance	Indefinite suspension.
Reckless Driving	
First Conviction in Five Years	Ninety-day suspension.
Second Conviction in Five Years	Six-month suspension.
Third or Subsequent Conviction in Five Years	One-year revocation.
Second Refusal of Chemical Test or Prior DUI	Eighteen-month suspension.
Transporting Liquor to a Minor	One-year suspension.
Youthful Driver with Alcohol	
First Conviction	Ninety-day suspension.
Second Conviction or Subsequent Conviction within Two Years	Six-month suspension.

Other Suspensions

  Multiple Moving Violations - Driver allowed up to 3 moving violations within a 12-month period. On the 4th moving violation, driving privilege will be suspended for 90 days. Each additional moving violation received within a 12- month period of last 3 moving violations, will cause an additional 90-day suspension. If driver has a restricted class (RC) license, driving privilege will be suspended for 90 days for 1st moving violation conviction, and 1 year for 2nd moving violation.

  Non Resident Violator Compact - Suspension remains until requirements for reinstatement are met.

  Uninsured Accident - Suspension remains until requirements for reinstatement are met.

  Ignition Interlock - An Ignition Interlock Law relating to drivers suspended for DUI related offenses became effective July 1, 2006. In 2009, additional legislation created mandatory use of Ignition Interlock for certain time periods regarding alcohol-related offenses. Any person who has been convicted with a BAC of .15% or greater or for 2nd or subsequent conviction of a DUI or a refusal must have a vehicle equipped with the Ignition Interlock. An extensive list of the time periods is found at the home page. There is restricted driver's license (IIR) available to eligible drivers.

Reinstatement Requirements

  Suspension $50.00 Reinstatement fee; any applicable fines; proof of financial responsibility.

  Revocation $50.00 Reinstatement fee; conditions placed on license; proof of insurance for three years; alcohol evaluation if required; investigation conducted by the Division.

Note: Suspension for nonpayment of child support is a $5.00 fee.

Point System Overview
Wyoming does not employ a point system.

License Plate Facts

Registration Renewal
Renewal is annual. At this time renewal is not available online.

New Residents
New residents must register vehicles upon accepting employment or establishing residency.

Inspections and Emissions Testing
Wyoming has no provisions for emission testing or safety inspection for gasoline and diesel motored vehicles.

Plate Descriptions

Typical Plate Pattern	Passenger plates are normally county prefix followed by Bucking Horse, then either 1 to 5 numbers or 1 or more numbers and alpha characters at end. Commercial vehicle are the same pattern as passenger plate with "Commercial" at top.
County Codes	The numbers 1 to 23 preceding the Bucking Horse image designate the county of issuance. The county codes for these 23 numbers are as follows: 1-Natrona; 2-Laramie; 3-Sheridan; 4-Sweetwater; 5-Albany; 6-Carbon; 7-Goshen; 8-Platte; 9-Big Horn; 10-Fremont; 11-Park; 12-Lincoln; 13-Converse; 14-Niobrara; 15-Hot Springs; 16-Johnson; 17-Campbell; 18-Crook; 19-Uinta; 20-Washakie; 21-Weston; 22-Teton; and 23-Sublette.
	Specialty plates (firefighter, EMT, etc.) do not have a county prefix. The symbol (firefighter, etc.) is printed in place of the county prefix.
	Apportioned and transperter plates do not have the county prefix and are number "A1-A99999" and "T1-T99999" respectively.
Plates and Stickers in Force	Two plates, one decal (MO & YR) on each plate.
Plates Remain with Car when Sold?	No, they remain with seller

Overview of Record Access

About Driving Records
WY Department of Transportation, Driver Services, 5300 Bishop Boulevard, Cheyenne 82009-3340, 307-777-4800 or 4810. The current fee is $3.00 for electronic requests and $5.00 for mail-in or walk-in requests. The record can be ordered as a three to five-year record (for insurance purposes-see below), or as a ten-year record (for commercial employers). Both records are available for commercial drivers. Add $2.50 fee if a credit card is used. The last fee increase was in November of 1990 and no increases are planned for the near term. The state charges for "no record found" reports.

Request Methods – Mail, Walk-in, Fax, Online, Bulk.

What You Should Know – All convictions are listed on the driving record except non-CDL drivers who speeding 5 or less MPH over the limit on highways with a 55 or greater posted limit.

Special Access Programs Available – Wyoming supports FTP and RJE access of driving record requests for approved vendors and permissible users. Call Marianne Zivkovich, Driver Services at 307-777-4830. Fax requests are accepted. A credit card can be used, but an additional $2.50 service fee is charged per record.

Obtaining Accident Reports
Copies of accident reports can be obtained by writing to the Department of Transportation, Accident Records Section, 5300 Bishop Blvd, Cheyenne WY 82009, 307-777-4450. The date of the accident, location (county), driver's name and DOB should be included with the request, along with $5.00 per request for a certified record or $3.00 for a non-certified record. Records are available for the past 10 years. Normal turnaround time is 2 to 3 days. Limited information is released by phone for no fee, no copies are sent until payment received. If photos, a CD, or a video is ordered, the fee is $25.00.

About Vehicle Records
Department of Transportation, Motor Vehicle Services, Licensing and Titling Section, 5300 Bishop Blvd, Cheyenne 82009-3340, 307-777-4825 or 777-4710. As of 01/01/2010, watercraft title records are also available form this agency. In Wyoming, regular county license plates and vehicle registrations are issued by the local county treasurers' offices in the county seat of the county of residence. Wyoming titles and lien filings are processed by the local county clerks' offices in the county seat of the county of residence. The DOT maintains the record database for vehicles and vessel titles, but not vessel registrations (see below). Records are searchable for 40 years for title records and up to 8 years for registration records; however a complete title or registration history is not available. The current fee for VIN and registration checks is $5.00. Records may be requested via a credit card for an additional $2.95 fee.

Request Methods – Mail, Walk-in, Fax, Bulk.

What You Should Know – Lien records on vehicles and watercraft are not available from the DOT and must be obtained from the 23 Wyoming County Clerk Offices.

Special Access Programs Available – Approved, ongoing requesters may order records via fax, a credit card may be used for payment.

About Watercraft Records
Watercraft Title Records
Effective 01/01/2010 titles must be issued for watercraft, light trailers (weighing 1,000 pounds), and snowmobiles. Records are managed by the same agency that manages vehicle titles. All existing watercraft, light trailers and snowmobiles are "grandfathered in" meaning that they do not need to have a title unless desired by the owner. Technically, as the law is written, all watercraft must be titled including canoes and rubber boats. However, since the Wyoming Game and Fish only issues registrations to motorized watercraft and a boat must be registered to be titled, only motorized watercraft will be able to be titled. As described above, titles will be issued at the local county agency, but the central database of record will be kept by the Department of Transportation. It will take up to 3 days for the title information to be forwarded on and placed on the centralized computer. Liens will not be found on the centralized computer and must be searched at the county level or state level if filed as a UCC.

Watercraft Registration Records
Wyoming Game and Fish Department, Watercraft Section, 5400 Bishop Blvd, Cheyenne 82006, 307-777-4575, fax 307-777-4610. All motorized boats must be registered. Simple name search requests are honored. There is no fee to do a registration record search by fax or phone, but the agency prefers that long lists be mailed. They can search by name, hull # or registration #. Lists are available. All requests must be in writing and submitted to the Director's office. Fees are based on agency time involved. Call for further details. Records are indexed on computer for 2 years plus present years, and archived on paper for 3 years prior to those on computer. Turnaround time is 2 to 3 days. Liens are recorded at the county level.

Appendix

The Appendix has four Sections:
1. A glossary of important organizations, programs, and laws that are closely involved with driver and vehicle records. **This section is presented in alphabetical order**.
2. Tables of Federally Mandated CDL Disqualifications
3. Federal Mandated Data Retention for Commercial Drivers
4. Table of State Driver License Format and Driving Record Fees

1. Glossary of Key Organizations, Programs, and Laws

American Association of Motor Vehicle Administrators (AAMVA)

The American Association of Motor Vehicle Administrators (AAMVA) is a nonprofit organization that develops and coordinates model programs in the administration motor vehicle matters, law enforcement and highway safety. Founded in 1933, AAMVA members are administrators and public service executives who are responsible for motor vehicle administration, driver licensing issues, and the enforcement of state and national laws that govern the safe use of vehicles in the United States and Canada. Members also include corporate partners and representatives from other associations.

AAMVA plays an important role in helping the states implement the changes demanded by Congressional legislation that affect the motor vehicle industry. Examples include The Driver's Privacy Protection Act (DPPA), the Commercial Motor Vehicle Safety Act of 1986 (CMVSA), the Motor Carrier Safety Improvement Act of 1999 (MCSIA), and the REAL ID Act. The programs and agreements profiled later in this section are administered to a large degree by AAMVA. AAMVA can be reached at 4310 Wilson Blvd #400, Arlington, VA 22203, 703-522-4200, www.aamva.org.

Commercial Driver License Information System (CDLIS)

The Commercial Motor Vehicle Safety Act of 1986 (CMVSA) established a Commercial Driver License Information System (CDLIS) to serve as a clearinghouse of information related to all US commercial drivers.

CDLIS helps states to determine if a license applicant holds a commercial license (and history) elsewhere. CDLIS is actually an index or pointer file – not a complete database with historical records. There is a central site that holds basic identification information about each licensed commercial driver. This data includes the name, DOB, SSN, state driver license number, and AKA information, and the current State of Record (SOR).

When a state receives an application to issue a CDL, a request is made to the CDLS central site to compare this data to the existing index. If a match occurs, CDLIS then points the requester to the state that holds the driving history. This state of record (SOR) then relays this information to the state of inquiry (SOI) in a matter of seconds.

Commercial Motor Vehicle Safety Act of 1986 (CMVSA)

Another significant piece of Federal legislation affecting motor vehicle records is The Commercial Motor Vehicle Safety Act of 1986 (CMVSA). The primary purposes of the Act were to improve highway safety by regulating Commercial Motor Vehicles (CMVs) and regulate the issuance of Commercial Driver Licenses (CDLs). CMVSA retained the states' right to issue a CDL, but established minimum national standards for licensing CDL drivers. Since April 1, 1992, drivers have been required to have a CDL in order to drive a commercial motor vehicle.

Important highlights of the CMVSA include—

- Definitions of commercial license classes, license endorsements, and license restrictions.
- CDL knowledge and skills testing requirements, including the Hazardous Materials (HAZMAT) Endorsement.
- Defining the components that must appear on the actual CDL document (the driver's license).
- The establishment of the Commercial Driver License Information System (CDLIS).
- A standardized disqualification conviction table and BAC standards.

In addition, important provisions of the CMVSA affecting motor vehicle records are—

- If a CDL holder is disqualified from operating a CMV, the driver cannot be issued a "conditional" or "hardship" CDL, but may continue to drive non-commercial vehicles.
- CDL drivers must report any driving conviction within 30 days (except parking violations) to their employer regardless of the nature of the violation.
- Employers must be notified if a driver's license is suspended, revoked, or canceled. The notification must be made by the end of the next business day following receipt of the notice of the suspension, revocation, cancellation, or disqualification.
- Employers cannot hire a driver who has more than one license or whose license is suspended, revoked or canceled, or is disqualified from driving.

CMVSA set minimum standards; the states can implement additional guidelines.

Driver License Compact (DLC)

The DLC, developed in 1961, gives states the means for the reporting of convictions for major moving violations to a driver's home state and requiring the surrender of all other states' driver licenses before the issuance of a new license. Thus, the major objective is to promote the one driver license and one record concept. Member states voluntarily contribute information concerning driver license suspensions and revocations to the NDR. Then the NDR will, in turn, transmit data, upon request, to other states. 46 U.S. jurisdictions are members of the DLC. Non-members are Georgia, Massachusetts, Michigan, Tennessee, and Wisconsin. Nom-members may still comply with the procedures.

Driver License Agreement (DLA)

At present, the DLC and NRVC Compacts are being revised and combined into a new Driver License Agreement (DLA). In an effort to truly establish a one driver one record license system, the new DLA will be a more efficient and effective agreement for the jurisdictions to share and transmit driver and conviction information.

Driver's Privacy Protection Act (DPPA)

The Driver's Privacy Protection Act (DPPA), signed into law by President Clinton in 1994, protects the personal privacy of persons licensed to drive. It prohibits disclosures of certain information maintained by the states.

DPPA prohibits disclosure of personal information from state driver history, vehicle registration and title files, except for 14 specific Permissible Uses. The Act also defines Personal Information and Highly Restricted Personal Information. In general, the Permissible Use list permits ongoing, legitimate businesses and individuals to obtain full record data on their promise to follow compliance procedures. While the DPPA implemented a minimum set of standards, states' privacy rules can be and often are more restrictive.

A key concept is that the DPPA does *not* limit who can or cannot access motor vehicle records. Instead it *does* dictate or limit who can access records containing personal information. A state may choose to sell driving records without personal information to a requester with a non-permissible use, or a state may not release any information to a casual requester unless the subject's signed release is presented as consent.

A 2000 amendment (Public Law 106-60, also known as the FY 2000 DOT Appropriations Act) to DPPA modified Section 350 of the DPPA. The amendment replaced the "opt-out" provision with and an "opt-in" policy, and defined sensitive personal information.

A copy of the Act is found at www.mvrdecoder.com.

Electronic Lien and Title (ELT)

Electronic Lien and Title (ELT) is the paperless means that lien holders and state motor vehicle agencies use to exchange motor vehicle lien and title information. AAMVA developed the standards for exchanging motor vehicle information which ELT uses to simplify lien information exchanges between participating lien holders and motor vehicle agencies. Instead of printing a title and forwarding it to the lien holder, the state sends an electronic lien message. The lien holder stores the message electronically instead of filing the paper title. If there is an error, the lien holder will be able to notify the motor vehicle agency immediately. When the lien is satisfied, the lien holder sends a message to the state to release the lien. The state prints the title and sends it to the vehicle owner.

International Registration Plan (IRP)

The International Registration Plan (IRP) is a registration reciprocity agreement for licensing fees for commercial motor vehicles among U.S. states and provinces of Canada. The IRP, an organized entity belonging to AAMVA, acts as an agreement among the license-issuing jurisdictions. The IRP provides for payment of license fees on the basis of fleet miles operated in various jurisdictions. The Plan authorizes proportional registration of commercial vehicles and for the recognition of such registrations in the participating jurisdictions. A carrier registers in a single "base jurisdiction." Fees for the vehicles are then calculated for each IRP jurisdiction according to the jurisdiction's unique fee requirements, then apportioned based on the percentage of total miles declared in that jurisdiction. For each vehicle, a carrier receives one license plate and one cab card listing each jurisdiction where the vehicle is registered. All IRP members are bound to recognize these documents as authorization for vehicles to operate in the jurisdictions specified. The base jurisdiction is responsible for collecting and distributing the fees.

For more information about IRP visit www.irponline.org/

Motor Carrier Safety Improvement Act of 1999 (MCSIA)

The Motor Carrier Safety Improvement Act of 1999 (MCSIA) established additional provisions to CMVSA. MCSIA amended the Code of Federal Regulations 49 CFR § 383.51 by: establishing the Federal Motor Carrier Safety Administration (www.fmcsa.dot.gov); providing additional standards for maintaining and checking conviction records of commercial drivers; and providing enhanced penalties for traffic convictions by commercial drivers.

The new provisions mandated by MCSIA forced the states to pass new laws or set administrative rules in order to comply with the MCSIA deadline of 2006. MCSIA also significantly modified and strengthened the licensing and sanctioning requirements for truck and bus drivers required to hold a CDL. Below is a summary of these significant provisions that affected license issuance and motor vehicle record keeping.

1. New Major Disqualifying Offenses When Operating Any Vehicle
2. New Major Disqualifying Offense When Operating A CMV and Specific Disqualifying Periods
3. Any CDL Holder Using Any Motor Vehicle in the Commission of a Felony Involving Manufacturing, Distributing or Dispensing a Controlled Substance Will Be Disqualified for Life.
4. New Disqualifying Offenses If NOT Driving a CMV
5. New Serious Offenses (added to the list of serious traffic offenses)
6. Disqualification for Being an Imminent Hazard
7. Ten Year Driving History and State Reciprocity
8. School Bus Endorsement Required with CDL for School Bus Drivers.
9. Prohibiting the Masking of Certain Convictions

The specific offenses and periods of time for the disqualifications are show in the tables starting on page on pages 265.

National Motor Vehicle Title Information System (NMVTIS)

The Anti Car Theft Act of 1992 (Public Law 102-519, H.R. 4542) established a model for the National Motor Vehicle Title Information System (NMVTIS). The NMVTIS is designed to grant availability of information to the states, law enforcement, prospective purchasers, and insurance carriers in order to reliably verify information on a vehicle prior to issuing a new title. NMVTIS is a DOJ program and DOJ is fully responsible for NMVTIS policy and operations. The American Association of Motor Vehicle Administrators (AAMVA) has acted as the third-party operator since inception and operates the system today.

NMVTIS inhibits title fraud and auto theft by making it harder for thieves to title stolen vehicles. Law enforcement officials get information on any particular vehicle or title and are provided access to junkyard and salvage yard information, helping them identify illegal activities. The consumer has access to the latest odometer reading and any current or former title brands related to the value and condition of a particular vehicle. This allows consumers to make more informed decisions on whether to purchase a vehicle and at what price. Businesses, who are prospective purchasers (e.g., dealers or auctions), and insurance carriers also are allowed access to title history, odometer, and brand data.

As of January 1, 2010, all states are required to participate. The NMVTIS web page reports that 76% of DMV data is in NMVTIS system.

In 2009 NMVTIS made news with the announcement that consumers can now search the NMVTIS database to find vehicle condition and history information. To search, go to www.nmvtis.gov/index.htm and select an approved provider.

National Driver Register (NDR)

The National Driver Register (NDR) is a national repository for information on problem drivers that functions under the control of the National Highway Traffic Safety Administration, an agency of the U.S. Department of Transportation.

One purpose of the NDR is to prevent the issuance of a driver's license to drivers whose licenses have been withdrawn or denied. State motor vehicle agencies provide NDR with names of individuals who have lost their driving privilege or who have been convicted of a serious traffic offense. When a person applies for a driver's license, a state will first checks to see if the name is on the NDR file. This is to determine if the applicant has revocations, suspensions, denials or cancellations in other states. This system is called the Problem Driver Pointer System (PDPS), which is reviewed on a later page.

Access to the NDR is not limited to state motor vehicle agencies. There are nine named groups who can obtain information, including non-government entities. For example, an individual may request a NDR file check per the provisions of the U.S. Privacy Act.

The National Driver Register can be reached at USDOT/NHTSA West Bldg, NVS-422, 1200 New Jersey Avenue, SE Washington, DC 20590, 202-366-4800 or 888-851-0436.

The exact page URL for the NDR is quite lengthy and buried. We suggest to visit www.nhtsa.dot.gov and use the search mechanism to find web material about NDR.

Non-Resident Violator Compact (NRVC)

The NRVC enables a participating jurisdiction (state) to inform another when a driver is cited out-of-state and has not complied with the terms of the citation. If the terms of the citation are not met (failure to pay traffic ticket, etc.), then the home state of the violator can then suspend the licensee. Thus, the out-of-state citations affected include not only major violations, but also moving traffic violations that do not necessarily carry an automatic suspension or revocation.

The exchange of information governed by this Compact applies to citations for traffic offenses issued to all drivers. NRVC should not be confused with the exchange that occurs in the CDLIS (Commercial Drivers License Information System). 45 U.S. jurisdictions are members. Non-members are Alaska, California, Michigan, Montana, Oregon, and Wisconsin. Some of the non-member states will participate in the exchange of information for specific circumstances.

Problem Driver Pointer System (PDPS)

The Problem Driver Pointer System (PDPS) is used to search the National Driver Register index. Based on the search of identification data on problem drivers, the PDPS "points" to the state of record(s) (SOR) where an individual's driver status and history information is stored. Based on the information received from the SOR(s), the issuing state will decide if the applicant is eligible to receive a new or renew his driver license.

Under PDPS, states report within 31 days to the NDR any individual—

- Who is denied a motor vehicle driver's license for cause;
- Whose motor vehicle driver's license is canceled, revoked, or suspended for cause;
- Who is convicted of the following motor vehicle related or comparable offenses:
    1. Operation of a motor vehicle under the influence of, or impaired by, alcohol or a controlled substance;
    2. A traffic violation arising in connection with a fatal traffic crash, reckless driving, or racing on the highways;
    3. Failure to render aid or provide identification when involved in a crash which results in a fatality or personal injury;
    4. Perjury or the knowingly making of a false affidavit or statement to officials in connection with activities governed by a law or regulation relating to the operation of a motor vehicle.

Although states may submit an inquiry on any license applicant, they are required to query the PDPS each first-time, above minimum age driver license applicant before issuing a license to the applicant. States are required to submit inquires on behalf of entities authorized to access the NDR.

REAL ID Act of 2005

The REAL ID Act of 2005, signed by President George W. Bush as part of Public Law No: 109-13, is meant to improve the security state-issued driver licenses and identification cards. The Act prohibits the federal government from accepting state-issued driver's licenses or identification cards for any federal purpose (e.g. accessing federal facilities, boarding federally regulated commercial aircraft, etc.) unless the state-issued document meets standards developed by the Department of Homeland Security (DHS). The Act calls for non-compliant licenses and IDs to be clearly identified as such. A copy of the Act can be found at http://thomas.loc.gov.

Although the Real ID Act does not directly affect motor vehicle record keeping or record access, it will play a critical role in how state motor vehicle agencies will license drivers. The Act established new national standards for state-issued driver licenses and non-driver identification cards. Provisions include what data must be included on the card and what documentation must be presented before a card can be issued. For example, before a card can be issued, the applicant must provide the following:

- A photo ID or a non-photo ID that includes full legal name and birthdate.
- Documentation of birthdate.
- Documentation of legal status and Social Security number
- Documentation showing name and principal residence address.

Portions of the Real ID Act were originally scheduled to take effect on May 11, 2008, but the deadline was extended to May 2011 for certain qualifying states. An example of the documentation that is a state has determined is permissible is a document recently posted by the Nevada Department of Motor Vehicles at www.dmvnv.com/pdfforms/dmv004.pdffoundat.

A great many organizations and a number of states are strongly opposed to the Act. One reason is cost. The amount of money the states must spend to implement the REAL ID Act goes well beyond what Congress has appropriated to assist the states. Another reason is privacy. Many groups feel that the act is, in effect, creating a National ID that will lead to even more ID theft, as opposed to thwarting ID theft. A great deal of interesting reading can be found on the web about the Real ID Act.

2. Tables of Federally Mandated CDL Disqualifications

Per the Code of Federal Regulations 49.CFR §383.5, jurisdictions are required to impose a disqualification on CDL drivers who have been convicted of certain offenses. The following summary of these rules are categorized as follows—

- Serious Offenses
- Major Offenses
- Imminent Hazard Disqualification
- Railroad-Highway Grade Crossing Offenses
- Violating of Out-of-Service Orders

Each table indicates the specific offenses and the disqualifications.

Major Offenses and Disqualifications Table

Keep in mind that some of the offenses apply to any driver operating a CMV, some to a CDL holder operating any motor vehicle, and some specific to a CDL holder operating a CMV.

Major Offenses	Disqualifications
1. Driving a motor vehicle while under the influence of alcohol as prescribed by state law 2. Driving a motor vehicle while under the influence of a controlled substance) 3. Driving a commercial motor vehicle while the person's blood alcohol concentration is 0.04% or more 4. After operating a motor vehicle, refusing to take an alcohol or drug test as required by a State or jurisdiction under its implied consent laws or regulations as defined in § 383.72 5. Leaving the scene of an accident (driving a motor vehicle) 6. A felony involving the use of a motor vehicle, other than "use of a motor vehicle in the commission of a felony involving manufacturing, distributing, or dispensing a controlled substance" 7. Driving a commercial motor vehicle when as a result of prior violations committed operating a CMV, the driver's CDL is revoked, suspended, or canceled, or the driver is disqualified from operating a CMV 8. Causing a fatality through the negligent operation of a commercial motor vehicle, including but not limited to the crimes of motor vehicle manslaughter, homicide by motor vehicle, and negligent homicide	**For 1st Major Offense:** • 1 year Disqualification - if the vehicle <u>was not</u> transporting hazardous materials required to be placarded • 3 years Disqualification - if the vehicle was transporting hazardous materials required to be placarded **2nd and separate incident of any major offense:** • Lifetime disqualification, but eligible for 10 year reinstatement **Incident after reinstatement** • Lifetime disqualification, not eligible for reinstatement
Use of a motor vehicle in the commission of a felony involving manufacturing, distributing, or dispensing a controlled substance	**For 1st Conviction** • Lifetime disqualification, not eligible for 10 year reinstatement

Serious Offenses and Disqualifications Table

Serious Offenses	Disqualifications
1. Speeds excessively, involving any speed of 15 mph or more above the posted speed limit 2. Drives recklessly, as defined by State or local law or regulation, including but not limited to offenses of driving a motor vehicle in willful or wanton disregard for the safety of persons or property 3. Makes improper or erratic traffic lane changes 4. Follows the vehicle ahead too closely 5. Violates State or local law relating to motor vehicle traffic control arising in connection with a fatal accident 6. Driving a CMV without obtaining a CDL 7. Driving a CMV without a current CDL in the driver's possession 8. Driving a CMV without the proper class of CDL and/or endorsements for the specific vehicle group being operated or for the passengers or type of cargo being transported	**For 1st Conviction:** • No disqualification **2nd and separate incident of any offense in this table, during a 3 year period:** • 60 days disqualification **3rd or subsequent conviction of any incident of any offense in this table, during a 3 year period:** • 120 days disqualification

Violating Out-of-Service Orders and Disqualifications Table

Violating Out of Service Orders	Disqualifications
If the driver with an out of service order operates a commercial motor vehicle and is transporting hazardous materials required to be placarded, and/or transporting 16 or more passengers, including the driver.	**For 1st Conviction:** • 180 days to 2 year disqualification **2nd and separate incident of any offense in this table, during a 10-year period:** • 3 to 5 year disqualification) **3rd or subsequent conviction of a separate incident of any offense in this table, during a 10-year period:** • 3 to 5 year disqualification
If the driver with an out of service order operates a commercial motor vehicle and is not transporting items listed in the row above.	**For 1st Conviction:** • 90 days to 1 year disqualification, goes to 180 days minimum in September 2010 **2nd and separate incident of any offense in this table, during a 10-year period:** • 1 to 5 year disqualification, goes to 2 years minimum in September 2010 **3rd or subsequent conviction of a separate incident of any offense in this table, during a 10-year period:** • 3 to 5 year disqualification (W52)

Railroad-Highway Grade Crossing Offenses Table

These offenses receive their own classification.

Railroad-Highway Grade Crossing Offenses	Disqualifications
If the driver operates a commercial motor vehicle in violation of a federal, state or local law and: 1. The driver is not required to always stop, but fails to slow down and check that tracks are clear of an approaching train 2. The driver is not required to always stop, but fails to stop before reaching the crossing, if the tracks are not clear 3. The driver is always required to stop, but fails to stop before driving onto the crossing 4. The driver fails to have sufficient space to drive completely through the crossing without stopping 5. The driver fails to obey a traffic control device or the directions of an enforcement official at the crossing 6. The driver fails to negotiate a crossing because of insufficient under-carriage clearance	**For 1st Conviction**: • No less than 60 days **For 2nd Conviction of any offense in this table in a separate incident within a 3-year period**: • No less than 120 days CMV disqualification **3rd or subsequent conviction of any offense in this table in a separate incident within a 3-year period**: • No less than 1 year CMV disqualification

Imminent Hazard Disqualification

FMCSA 49 CFR §382.52 defines that a driver is considered to be an Imminent Hazard if:

"...the existence of a condition that presents a substantial likelihood that death, serious illness, severe personal injury, or a substantial endangerment to health, property, or the environment may occur before the completion date of a formal proceeding begun to lessen the risk of that death, illness, injury or endangerment."

Description: Allowing the driver to continue to operation a commercial vehicle would create an imminent hazard

Disqualification: Up to One Year

3. Federal Mandated Data Retention for Commercial Drivers

Record keeping for the records of commercial drivers or drivers who are operating a commercial vehicle is much different than record keeping for non-commercial drivers.

According to federal regulation 49 CFR §383.51 state motor vehicle agencies must follow minimum standards that spell out how long certain convictions and withdrawals must be maintained and the reporting requirements for the Commercial Driver License Information System (CDLIS). These minimum retention periods apply to convictions and withdrawals incurred by a driver operating a CMV, and by CDL holders operating any motor vehicle. State jurisdictions may longer choose retention periods; in fact some states have never purged their database. Both the CMVSA and MCSIA (reviewed in Appendix 2) played a significant role in defining the regulations within 49 CFR §383.51.

A key factor is that the records of convictions and withdrawals must be kept by the state where the most recent license was issued. Thus, when a driver moves from one state to another, the driver's new state of record (SOR) will receive and maintain any records sent from the previous state. It is important that the SOR maintain the retention period for two reasons: 1) if the conviction data determines the length of a disqualification; 2) if accumulated convictions over time could lead to a disqualification.

The categories below indicate the minimum time a conviction or withdrawal must be retained from the conviction date for CDL or CMV-related convictions. Lists of the specific convictions that are considered **Major** or **Serious** are presented earlier in this section

The categories below indicate the minimum time a conviction or withdrawal must be retained from the conviction date for CDL or CMV-related convictions.

Date Retention Table

Major Convictions	55 Years

- An exception to this rule applies to a second conviction for the "Use of a commercial motor vehicle in the commission of a felony involving manufacturing, distributing, or dispensing a controlled substance." This conviction must be kept on the record for life.

Serious Convictions	4 Years
Railroad Grade Crossing Convictions	4 Years
Out-of-Service Convictions	15 Years
All Other Convictions	3 Year minimum
Withdrawal Actions	The length of time conviction is kept as specified in the tables above.

Lists of the specific convictions that are considered **Major** or **Serious** are presented earlier in the Appendix.

4. Table of State Driver License Format and Driving Record Fees

Three Important Facts...

1. Additional fees are often charged for an online subscription accounts. These sign-up and/or annual fees usually range from $35 to $100 per year, but they can be higher. For example, in California there can be a one-time fee of $10,000.
2. Several states charge different fees if a licensee is obtaining his or her own driving record.
3. Per federal law, the SSN has been phased out as a driver license number. However, some states may still have a few of the older documents in circulation, as indicated.

State	License Format	Electronic Fee	Mail-in Fee	Walk-in Fee
Alabama	7#'s	7.00	5.75	5.75
Alaska	7#'s	10.00 (some vendors sell for 5.00)	10.00	10.00
Arizona	1 Let+8#'s or SSN	4.25 - 39 month 6.25 - 5 year	3.00 - 39 month 5.00 - 5 year	3.00 - 39 month 5.00 - 5 year
Arkansas	9#'s or SSN	8.50 - 3 year 11.50 - CDL	7.00 - 3 year 10.00 - CDL	7.00 - 3 year 10.00 - CDL
California	1 Let + 7#'s	2.00	5.00	N/A
Colorado	9#'s	2.00	2.20 / 2.70 cert	2.20 / 2.70 cert
Connecticut	9#'s	15.00	20.00	20.00
Delaware	1-7#'s	15.00	15.00	15.00
District of Columbia	7#'s or SSN	13.00	7.00 - 3 year 13.00 - 10 year	7.00 - 3 year 13.00 -10 year
Florida	1 Let + 12#'s	8.00 - 3 year 10.00 - 7 year	8.00 - 3 year 10.00 -7 year or cert	8.00 - 3 year 10.00 -7 year or cert
Georgia	9#'s or SSN	6.00 - 3 year 8.00 - 7 year	6.00 - 3 year 8.00 - 7 year	6.00 - 3 year 8.00 - 7 year
Hawaii	H + 8# or SSN or 9#'s	10.00	7.00	7.00
Idaho	2 Let + 6 #s + 1 Let	9.00	7.00	7.00
Illinois	1 Let + 11#'s	12.00	12.00	12.00
Indiana	10#'s	7.50	4.00/8.00 cert	4.00/8.00 cert
Iowa	9 digits (new) or SSN or 3#-2Let-4#	8.50	5.50	5.50
Kansas	"K" + 8#'s or SSN	6.00 batch 6.50 interactive	10.00	10.00
Kentucky	1 Let + 8#s	5.00	3.00	3.00
Louisiana	00 + 7#'s	6.00	15.00	15.00
Maine	7#'s or 7#'s + *	7.00 - 3 year 12.00 - 12 year	5.00 - 3 year 10.00 - 10 year	5.00 - 3 year 10 - 10 year
Maryland	1 Let + 12#'s	9.00	9.00/12.00 cert	9.00/12.00 cert

State	License Format	Electronic Fee	Mail-in Fee	Walk-in Fee
Massachusetts	1 Let (usually S) + 8#'s	6.00 (RMV)	20.00	20.00
Michigan	1 Let + 12#'s	7.00	7.00/8.00 cert	N/A
Minnesota	1 Let + 12#s	5.00	9.50/10.50 cert plus $1.00 per printed page	9.50/10.50 cert
Mississippi	9 #'s or SSN	11.00	11.00	11.00
Missouri	1 Let + 5-9#'s or 9#s or SSN	No set fee per record. bulk purchase only	5.88	5.88 cert
Montana	13#s or 9 digits or SSN	7.25	4.00/10.00 cert	4.00/10.00 cert
Nebraska	1 Let + 3 to 8#'s	3.00	3.00	3.00
Nevada	10#s	7.00	7.00	7.00
New Hampshire	2#'s +3 Let +5#'s	12.00	15.00	15.00
New Jersey	1 Let + 14#'s	12.00	15.00	15.00
New Mexico	9#'s	4.95	No charge	No charge
New York	9#'s	7.00	10.00	10.00
North Carolina	1 TO 12#'s	8.00	8.00/11.00 cert	8.00/11.00 cert
North Dakota	3 let + 6#'s or 9#'s or SSN	3.00 interactive	3.00	3.00
Ohio	2 let + 6#'s	5.00	8.50	8.50
Oklahoma	One alpha+9#'s or SSN	12.50	10.00/13.00 cert	10.00/13.00 cert
Oregon	Usually 7#'s can be 1-9#'s	2.00	1.50 3 year non-empl 2.00 3 year empl 3.00 court	Only at field offices, fee may vary.
Pennsylvania	8#'s	5.00	5.00/10.00 cert	5.00/10.00/cert
Rhode Island	7#'s or "V" + 6#'s	19.50	17.50	17.50
South Carolina	11#'s	7.25	6.00	6.00
South Dakota	SSN or 8#'s or some old 6#'s	5.00	5.00	5.00
Tennessee	9#'s or 7-8 #'s	7.00	5.00	5.00
Texas	8#'s	6.50	6.00/10.00 cert	n/a
Utah	9#'s, can be 4-10#'s	9.00	6.00/10.75 cert	6.00/10.75 cert
Vermont	8#'s or 7#'s + "A"	15.00	11.00 3-year 16.00 complete	11.00 3-year 16.00 complete
Virginia	1 Let + 8#'s or SSN	7.00	8.00/13.00 cert	8.00/13.00 cert
Washington	5Let + 3# + 2Let or 2#	10.00	10.00	10.00
West Virginia	7 digits (1-2 let +5-6#'s)	8.00	5.00	5.00
Wisconsin	1 Let + 13#'s	5.00	7.00/12.00 cert	N/A
Wyoming	9#'s	3.00 (FTP or RJE)	5.00	5.00

Send Me A Copy!

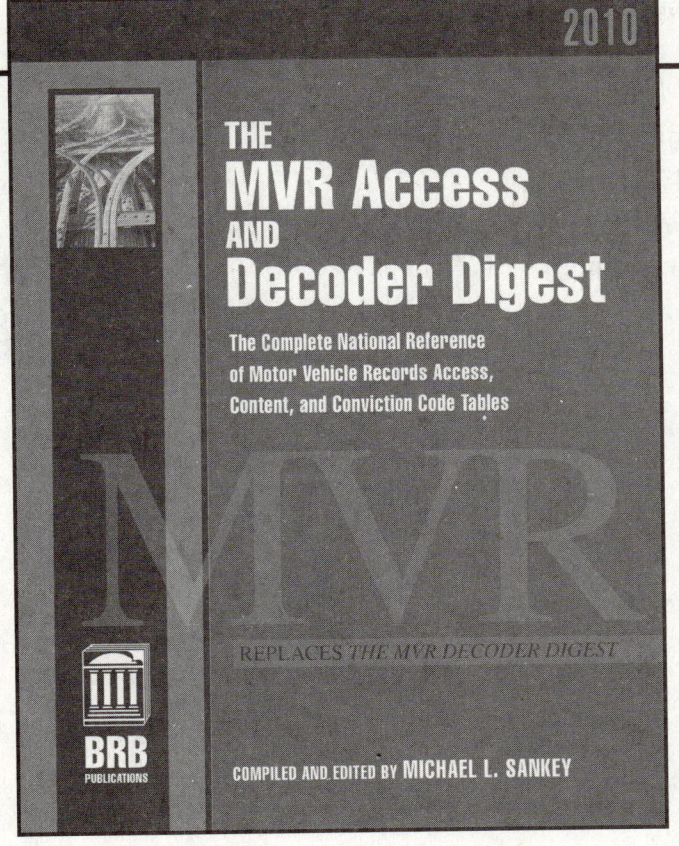

The Companion to *The U.S. Motor Vehicle Reference Book*

I want a copy of *The MVR Access and Decoder Digest*.
❏ Here's my check for $31.95 + $4.25 S&H   ❏ Order by Credit Card

NAME _____

ADDRESS _____

COMPANY _____ PHONE _____

CITY _____ STATE _____ ZIP _____

❏ VISA ❏ MC ❏ AMEX ❏ DISC   CREDIT CARD # _____

EXPIRES _____   SIGNATURE _____

Fill out and mail to: BRB Publications, Inc. • PO Box 27869 • Tempe, AZ 85285-7869
To order this or other BRB publications or for a free catalog call **1-800-929-3811**
Order Online: **www.mvrdecoder.com**

Prefer to View The Books Online?

THE Comprehensive Online Reference for Professionals Using Driver History and Motor Vehicle Records

MVR

The entire contents from both books, *The MVR Access and Decoder Digest* and *The U.S. Motor Vehicle Reference Book*

Available online at:
www.mvrdecoder.com

BRB PUBLICATIONS